AMERICAN WOMEN

in the

NINETIES

Today's Critical Issues

Edited with an Introduction by

SHERRI MATTEO

NORTHEASTERN UNIVERSITY PRESS

Boston

Library of Congress Cataloging-in-Publication Data

American women in the nineties : today's critical issues / edited with
an introduction by Sherri Matteo.
p.   cm.
Includes bibliographical references and index.
ISBN 1-55553-150-4 (alk paper)—ISBN 1-55553-151-2 (pbk.)
1. Women—United States—Social conditions.   2. Women—Health and
hygiene—United States.   I. Matteo, Sherri Marie, 1951–
HQ1421.A48   1993
305.4′0973—dc20   92-46574

Designed by Books By Design, Inc.
Composed in Palatino by DEKR Corporation, Woburn, Massachusetts.
Printed and bound by Edwards Brothers, Inc., Ann Arbor, Michigan.
The paper is Glatfelter Offset, an acid-free sheet

MANUFACTURED IN THE UNITED STATES OF AMERICA
97   96   95   94   93   5   4   3   2   1

❖ ❖ ❖

CONTENTS

❖

❖ ❖ ❖

ACKNOWLEDGMENTS

This book would not have been possible without the enthusiasm, support, and guidance of a number of individuals. First, I would like to thank William Frohlich, Director of Northeastern University Press, not only for suggesting the idea for this volume but also for his continued patience and expert assistance with every phase of this project. Next, I would like to express my gratitude to all of the contributors. To ensure that this book would be published in the early 1990s, we had to cut our publication schedule to a hair-raising nine-month time frame. It is to our essayists' credit, and their dedication and commitment to women's issues, that, after the initial shock of being asked to do the impossible, they rearranged their lives and work schedules and met our deadline.

I am further indebted to Michelle Pearl, Lorraine Macchello, Monisha Pasupathi, and Kim Yang for the superb editorial assistance they provided. Equally deserving of credit are Sally Schroeder, Dee Gustavson, and Gini Gould of the Institute for Research on Women and Gender of Stanford University for their patience with me throughout the preparation of this volume. Dan Morrow provided encouragement and enthusiasm. Finally, I thank Iris F. Litt, Director of the Institute, for her support and belief in the importance of this work.

Grateful acknowledgment to reprint is made to the following:

"The Political Woman," by Ruth B. Mandel, reprinted, with changes, from *The American Woman 1988–89: A Status Report*, ed. Sara E. Rix (New York: W.W. Norton & Co., 1988), 78–122, by permission of the author and the publisher. Copyright 1988 by W.W. Norton & Co.

"Some Political Implications of the Stanford Studies of Homeless Families," by Sanford M. Dornbusch, reprinted, with changes, from *The Stanford Studies of Homeless Families, Children and Youth* (Stanford, Calif.: The Stanford Center for the Study of Families, Children and Youth, 1991), by permission of the author and the publisher. Copyright 1991 by The Stanford Center for the Study of Families, Children and Youth.

"Gender Dilemmas in Sexual Harassment: Policies and Procedures," by Stephanie Riger, reprinted, with changes, from *American Psychologist* 46(5) (1991): 497–505, by permission of the author and the publisher. Copyright 1991 by the American Psychological Association. Adapted by permission.

"Gender Equality and Employment Policy," by Deborah L. Rhode, reprinted, with changes, from *The American Woman 1990–91: A Status Report*, ed. Sara E. Rix (New York: W.W. Norton & Co., 1990), 170–200, by permission of the author and the publisher. Copyright 1990 by W.W. Norton & Co.

"Girls, Gender, and Schools: Excerpts from *The AAUW Report: How Schools Shortchange Girls*," by Susan McGee Bailey, Lynn Burbridge, Patricia Campbell, Barbara Jackson, Fern Marx, and Peggy McIntosh, reprinted, with changes, from *The AAUW Report: How Schools Shortchange Girls* (Washington, D.C.: American Association of University Women, 1992), by permission of the publisher and the authors. Copyright 1992 by the American Association of University Women Educational Foundation.

INTRODUCTION

American[1] women have had much to ponder during the early 1990s. Some of the news has been good. For example, the National Institutes of Health has committed itself to improving the quality and quantity of research on women's health issues; the Family and Medical Leave Act was passed by the House and Senate (though vetoed by former President Bush); the number of women holding House and Senate seats reached an all-time high of 6 percent; and unprecedented numbers of women have entered educational, political, and professional arenas.

Most of the news, however, has left us reeling and aware of profound gender differences in the quality of women's lives. We have witnessed the Gulf War and its behind-the-scenes effect on women and children; the quintessential patriarchal procedures of the Thomas-Hill hearings; federally imposed gag rules on abortion counseling along with the continued resistance to providing contraceptive and safe-sex information to anyone who needs it; events that threatened the 1973 *Roe v. Wade* ruling; soaring numbers of women reporting sexual and other violent assaults and harassment; a glass ceiling that seems to have become an adobe ceiling;[2] and the beginnings of a pervasive, more general backlash, as documented by author Susan Faludi, among others, against what progress women have made.

More often than not, each major step forward has been accompanied by a political tug-of-war that either prevents women from immediately progressing further or drags them back a few feet. Potential breakthroughs in establishing greater equality for women are compromised by the need to constantly monitor, and sometimes reengage in battles to protect, previously won rights.[3] In spite of this, or perhaps because of it, women in the United States have become more aware and more unified in their efforts to improve the quality of life for themselves and their families.

Several factors have contributed to the privileging of women's issues in the United States. Increased media coverage, greater numbers of women in politics and special-interest movements, and the commitment by certain funding agencies and scholars to providing necessary research and data on the status of women have all served to focus attention on these issues. However, the single most important factor to the advancement of women's concerns has been the success of the feminist movement in opening our eyes to inequalities of gender, race, and class. While there are many *feminisms*, stemming from different philosophical and theoretical underpinnings, all are united in wanting a better quality of life for women everywhere.

The feminist approach to research evidenced in this volume includes a variety of methods and techniques used in the study of gender issues. Although the contributors would no doubt agree that the essence of feminist research is to do research *for* and *with* women, and not simply *on* them, their individual perspectives reflect a diversity that we feel provides a representative sample of the types of research currently being conducted about American women. Thus, we have not asked the contributors to conform to a particular type of feminist analysis or theoretical orientation; rather, we have asked them to give us a state-of-the-art report of what is known about women in their respective areas.

To a large extent, this involves assimilating the existing data about women in order to highlight the gaps in our knowledge. Descriptive analysis is often the first step in determining whether there are gender (or race, or class) inequalities about an issue. It can also be used to assess the validity of commonly held notions or stereotypes that typically exist and flourish in the absence of real data. More important, the resulting information can guide the design of future research projects and be of use to those involved in educational outreach programs and policy-setting efforts.

To this end, we have assembled a collection of essays by leading academicians on the most critical issues facing women in the United States in the 1990s, with an eye toward delineating the policy recommendations that would best address these issues. Our central challenge was to choose among the numerous critical issues facing women, knowing that the number we would have to exclude far exceeded the precious few that would make their way into this volume. We sought a collection that would present an overview of those issues receiving consistent national attention, but not lead readers to assume that if an issue did not appear it was not considered *critical* by scholars. At the same time, we wanted to keep the book accessible, in terms of both length and cost.

We have chosen to focus on issues that not only are central to current research but have an obvious and immediate policy component as well. We asked our contributors to integrate the most recent scholarly research with information (if available) on race, ethnicity, and social class and to discuss the policy implications of such work. One of our most valuable lessons (and perhaps our greatest frustration) was to see how little of the available data on women were broken down by race and ethnicity. Statistics on health, education, and employment, for example, are typically presented for males and females or by income level (socioeconomic status), but not always by racial or ethnic groups. When statistics did include race, they were often only on blacks and whites, or would use a homogeneous term such as *Hispanic* without revealing the specific population under study.

Despite this difficulty, we chose to integrate information on minority women throughout the book, rather than having one chapter specifically addressed to minority issues. We did this primarily because we did not feel that one chapter would be sufficient to consider the full range of critical issues facing each U.S. group. To attempt to address the diverse needs of minority women in a single chapter would surely result in inadequate treatment at best, and marginalization at worst.

The chapters in this book represent, and in most cases overlap across, five recurring themes in research on the status of American women today: the importance of women in politics and to political thinking, the health of women, employment policies and practices, economic issues, and education.

Our specific topics—foreign policy, political representation, employment, education, aging, health, AIDS, poverty, abortion, pornography, and sexual harassment—form only a partial list of the issues that American women today can no longer afford to ignore. Each of these areas has had and will continue to have an inescapable impact on most women throughout their lives. Yet, as Kathleen Jones points out in the opening chapter, Toward a Woman-Friendly New World

Order, if we continue to accept traditional gender roles, we aid and abet the system that has so successfully kept women from having power over their own lives.

It is time for us to consider the impact women are capable of having on how and for whom this system works. To help us do so, Jones takes us on a journey beyond our borders and local concerns to consider how women have fared in other countries, often as a direct result of U.S. foreign policy. As we fight for our place and our voice in our country's domestic policies concerning women, we often overlook international politics or foreign-policy issues as a women's issue. Jones suggests that this is due to our tendency to see these areas as male preserves. Even women who are involved in these policy areas feel pressured to play the game in male terms, down to the language used to describe policy decisions. Jones argues that we must develop "a perspective that considers the *geography of gender*" so that we as women may see ourselves as a "formidable political force" to make women visible throughout the world.

Jones takes us smoothly through numerous examples, helping us to see not only the connections between national defense and global development but also how these connections affect women. She then explores how we might rethink the concept of citizenship from one of boundary building to one of interdependence. The basis of this interdependence lies in our ability—our responsibility—to become citizens who are "world travelers"; that is, citizens of our country who stress "our connection with and responsibility toward others, without having to turn those 'others' into 'us.'" Jones ends with a sobering and chilling narrative of her own experiences with the quest to develop such a concept of citizenship. It is a testament to the difference one woman can make in the effort to bring greater visibility and caring to women's concerns throughout the world.

The difference women can make is a theme carried through the chapter on women and public office. Ruth Mandel, in The Political Woman, traces American women's increased involvement in public office from the early 1970s, a change that Mandel sees as due to the formation of the National Women's Political Caucus in 1971.

That the presence of women in public office has had an impact on the representation of women's issues and the growing acceptance of women politicians cannot be doubted. As Mandel notes, in 1983, 80 percent of the public said they would vote for a qualified female presidential candidate if one were nominated by their party. While the overall numbers of women in public office have grown slowly (only 2 percent of senators and 6 percent of representatives are women, for example), the number of women presenting themselves as candidates for Congress and getting their major-party nomination is increasing.

In addition to discussing the numbers of women in public office and the likely profile of the political woman, Mandel describes the obstacles and advantages (often one and the same) that women face when seeking and occupying political office as well as the support networks and groups that have developed from the large women's political community. She ends with a chronology of the most important milestones for women in politics.

While the percentage of female officeholders will have to change substantially before women's concerns are brought easily and regularly to legislative agendas, there is little doubt that the latter will follow from the former. Such a shift in the numbers should help end the categorization of women as a *single issue* at the same time that it recognizes the impact of policies on women that have not been traditionally associated with them.

This tendency can most clearly be seen in the areas of aging, health, and poverty. In the next chapter, Women of a Certain Age, Laura Carstensen and Monisha Pasupathi point out that Medicare, social security, national health insurance, and nursing-home placement have not been seen by the media as women's issues; rather, they have been seen as relating to the general concerns of our aging population.

As Carstensen and Pasupathi make clear, aging is seen as "the great equalizer"—everyone ages, regardless of sex, ethnicity, or social class. However, even though over 12 percent of our population is elderly (and some estimates are that by the year 2040 the percentage will increase to 23), little attention is paid to the fact that most of the elderly are women. These women are more likely than men of the same age to be poor, living alone, or in nursing homes, or caring for other elderly individuals.

The fictitious example of Helen and Paul, a typical white middle-class couple, nicely illustrates how the above statistics combine with a lifetime of more subtle gender inequalities to lead to an impoverished existence for Helen's final years. Helen and Paul, like "Mary" in Diana Pearce's chapter, have done everything "right." They are educated, married with children, employed, and yet we see how fragile their existence is in the face of inadequate health care and social-support systems.

These are not the individuals we expect to find in poverty; they are not extreme cases. Because we have conceptualized poverty as something that happens to someone else (to minorities, the uneducated, or those who have made the wrong choices), it has been easy for us to ignore that poverty cuts across racial and ethnic lines and affects *all* women. But, as Carstensen and Pasupathi recommend, women *must* plan for their futures—by knowing about retirement benefits, health-insurance policies, and social-support services—especially since most women will end up living alone and many will live in poverty.

Diana Pearce's chapter, Something Old, Something New: Women's Poverty in the 1990s, introduces us to the reality of women's poverty through the story of someone who has become poor despite being a somewhat privileged member of America's middle class and doing what many women do (pursue an education, marry, have children, and divorce). Pearce explores the demographic changes that have contributed to women's poverty, women's disadvantaged position in the labor force, and the special burden children represent, emotionally as well as economically. Pearce discusses two areas of public policy that are most critical to the halting and reversal of the feminization of poverty. The first concerns restructuring employment options, opportunities, and salaries to help alleviate women's poverty. The second focuses on women's need for adequate and affordable housing. Her recommendations underscore the seemingly obvious but often overlooked point that "addressing women's poverty is about addressing the structural inequalities faced by women . . . and for women of color, the racism . . . that perpetuates poverty for all people of color."

Health care emerges as one of the most important components of the overall quality of life for women in a number of chapters. Diana Dutton, in Poorer and Sicker: Legacies of the 1980s, Lessons for the 1990s, explores the extent to which the poor and people of color have actually lost ground on many health measures. She shows us that those on each step of the economic ladder tend to have better health than those on the steps below them on just about every measure of illness typically studied. However, she also points out that, while our economic status directly influences our health status, this relationship is neither fixed nor inevitable.

Dutton's most striking data are those showing that in the decade before Reagan took office, the "health gap" between rich and poor had been steadily decreasing owing to programs such as Medicaid and Medicare. During the Reagan years, many programs were cut or eliminated and by the end of the 1980s the gap had widened once more.

Some of the lessons Dutton says we have learned from the 1970s and 1980s are that, first, trickle-down economics doesn't work; in fact, by the end of the 1980s more people were at the bottom than during the 1970s. Second, conventional medical care is not sufficient to meet the needs of the poor; however, models such as the Community Health Centers, begun in the late 1960s, offered clinic services as well as services ranging from sanitation and housing to transportation and education. One of the more impressive statistics from the model used in Mississippi is that the infant death rate dropped 40 percent during the first four years of this program. Finally, health-care services must be matched to the needs of those they serve rather than to their ability to pay.

Dutton provides a useful discussion of the five key questions women should ask about the health-care proposals currently under discussion by politicians: (1) Will universal coverage be guaranteed? (2) Will financial and structural barriers to care be eliminated? (3) Will services covered be comprehensive and include disease prevention? (4) Will the financing system include some equitable means of controlling health-care costs? and (5) Will administrative complexity and waste be minimized?

While specific health-care reforms are important—indeed, critical—to the improved health of women and children, Dutton closes her chapter with a discussion of the equally important role the general economic situation plays. We must work to support economic policies that would narrow the inequalities in income level and provide women and their families with a better standard of living across the board at the same time that we scrutinize various health-care plans put forward by our politicians.

The success of any health-care reform or plan to improve the quality of services for women will depend, in part, upon the medical community's ability to identify the specific needs of women. In Health Issues for Women in the 1990s, Iris Litt demonstrates that although women have been viewed as the healthier sex because of their longer life span, there are several factors that negatively influence the quality of women's health. Illnesses that are specific to women as well as those they share with men are often made worse by the lack of research on women's health and the tendency of medical professionals to diagnose certain diseases (such as heart disease) in women at later and more severe stages than in men, and to favor more aggressive treatments for men.

Additional barriers to improving women's health include inadequate access to, and the availability and affordability of, care. Women (and their children) are also less likely to have adequate health insurance than are men. Age, sex, ethnicity, and socioeconomic and employment status all affect the quality and quantity of women's health care. Legal, political, and religious issues further limit the range of health-care choices and options available to women. In addition, these factors shape the content and extent of research and testing on women's health problems and products. As Litt points out, although women's health problems constitute more than two-thirds of health-care costs in the United States, only 13 percent of our medical research addresses those problems.

Among Litt's recommendations are the need for policymakers to have a greater awareness of and sensitivity to concerns about access to, and availability and affordability of, health care. Like Carstensen and Pasupathi, she calls for some form of national health insurance that would include preventive measures such as mammograms and contraceptive products.

The major issues covered thus far—poverty, health care, health insurance, affordable housing, and employment opportunities—re-emerge in Sanford Dornbusch's description of the Stanford studies of homeless families. The majority of homeless families are headed by women who are likely to be younger, less well educated, and less likely to have necessary job skills than homeless men. In these studies, Hispanics of Mexican descent and African Americans accounted for more of the homeless families than other ethnic or racial groups. In addition to the factors just mentioned, homeless families encountered additional problems, such as language barriers, in gaining access to social-support systems and medical services.

While the major strategies for getting people out of homelessness include access to affordable housing and adequate social support, Dornbusch lists several initiatives for a revitalized welfare system that would increase available resources to homeless and at-risk families. These include help for the working poor, long-term assistance for those unable to work, training for those who are inadequately prepared to compete in the workplace, training in English for those who are not fluent, child-care services and payments, and greater sensitivity to the needs of parents and their children.

We move next to considering two of the most politically charged health issues facing women today: AIDS and the psychological impact of abortion. In Women and AIDS, O'Leary, Jemmott, Suarez-Al-Adam, AlRoy, and Fernandez discuss the prevalence of AIDS (acquired immunodeficiency syndrome) among women, particularly in the black and Latina populations of the East Coast. Early diagnosis and treatment of AIDS has been problematic because of the asymptomatic nature of the illness: It can take years for the full-blown disease to manifest itself. Women are often diagnosed later than men, in part because AIDS has been primarily associated with the gay male community and because women's symptoms tend to be reproductive-system disorders that historically have not been associated with AIDS.

The authors also address the special concerns of mothers and children with AIDS, preventive measures that can and should be taken by women, and, finally, the media's influence on describing women with AIDS in sexual and racially stereotyped ways. They stress the need for more research along with the need for greater clinical attention to the medical aspects of AIDS in women. They advocate innovative educational and prevention strategies as well as enlightened public discussion, free of demeaning and debilitating sexual and racial stereotypes.

Nancy Adler and Jeanne Tschann bring a psychological perspective to the issue of abortion in The Abortion Debate: Psychological Issues for Adult Women and Adolescents. Although there are conflicting religious, political, and cultural arguments about abortion, these authors address two important charges made by pro-life groups: that abortion leads to psychopathology and that adolescent women are incapable of making well-informed decisions about abortion because of their age and stage of cognitive development.

The latter argument is especially critical in view of the recent Supreme Court ruling in *Planned Parenthood v. Casey*, in which the Court upheld three of the four restrictions placed on women and adolescents seeking abortion in Pennsylvania. While the Court did uphold *Roe v. Wade*, which says that women have a fundamental right of access to abortion, its current ruling, together with its 1989 decision in *Webster v. Reproductive Health Services*, poses serious obstacles to adolescents and poor women seeking abortions.

By affirming that doctors must present information designed to change the woman's decision to have an abortion, that women must wait 24 hours after receiving this information before going ahead with the abortion, and that adolescents must obtain the permission of one parent or a judge, the Court has essentially endorsed state-imposed restrictions on this most private decision. While the Court argued that these restrictions do not place an undue burden on women seeking abortions, the relevance of that argument for poor women and adolescent women must be questioned. For both, the imposition of a waiting period, particularly in areas where extensive travel may be necessary to reach a clinic, may indeed be an undue burden that women of means are less likely to experience. For the adolescent, the waiting period is essentially made longer if she needs to obtain court approval.

The ruling concerning adolescents stems from adults' uncertainty that adolescents are capable of making informed decisions about abortion or that they will be abnormally traumatized by the experience. Adler and Tschann's review of the psychological literature shows quite clearly that for the vast majority of adult women and adolescents who have had abortions, the procedure is not an abnormally stressful or traumatic experience. In fact, adolescents who had abortions showed an increase in self-esteem and a decrease in anxiety over a two-year period when compared with adolescents who gave birth. The authors also review studies on the frequency of adolescent abortion and whether a parental consent mandate is in the best interest of these girls. They conclude that adolescents are as capable as adult women of making careful and considered choices about abortion. They further argue that, while parental support of the adolescent's decision is optimal, it is the adolescent herself who is best able to make this decision, especially if she has access to information and guidance that can best be obtained through health-care counseling.

Adler and Tschann recommend that we think carefully about the more negative aspects, especially for adolescents, of carrying a pregnancy to term. When women have the right to choose, there are fewer negative consequences both physically and mentally. They also stress the need for more research on adolescent decision making, particularly across ethnic groups who are underrepresented in the literature. Finally, they call for more resources to be directed toward the prevention of unwanted pregnancies.

Aside from the issue of reproductive rights, few issues have shaken the American public with the immediacy and power of recognition as that of sexual harassment. In light of the Thomas-Hill hearings, sexual harassment has taken center stage as one of the most pervasive, if least well understood, social problems facing women—particularly working women—today. In Gender Dilemmas in Sexual Harassment: Policies and Procedures, Stephanie Riger describes the extent and frequency of sexual harassment and explores the gender bias inherent in both the definition of harassment and the grievance procedures that currently exist. Women and men define sexual harassment differently and are governed by different concerns when deciding whether to report complaints. While Riger takes the educational environment (universities and colleges) as the central context for her discussion, her analysis can readily be extended to any work setting in the United States that is vulnerable to sexual, social, and political inequalities that reflect the imbalance of power between women and men in our society.

Riger calls for well-publicized policies that use an inclusive definition of harassment, have informal dispute resolution options, include advocacy for the victim, and allow multiple offenders to be identified. She underscores the importance of continued education about how sexual harassment is defined from the woman's perspective.

Addressing the more widely debated though equally politicized topic of pornography, Madeleine Kahn argues that pornography has become a critical issue for women both because of concerns about whether women are willing participants in or victims of pornography and because of the fine line between the legal protection of women and the violation of first-amendment rights. Further complicating this issue are the various and conflicting feminist perspectives that pit the antipornography movement against the anticensorship group. Kahn elucidates this debate by first presenting the traditional arguments about pornography and then comparing them to the feminist's concerns. Finally, she presents a new framework that would end the divisiveness among women on this issue. Her model is one of working from within the system and using the tools already available to us, such as education, the improvement of job conditions and protection against abuse for sex-industry workers, and the election of more women to public office to unify women's voices and make women's issues central to our concerns.

The last two chapters explore employment and education in greater detail. Deborah Rhode addresses the legal response to the structural inequalities underlying gender equality and employment policy. She argues that most of the responses have been reflected in the law's formal treatment of the sexes, leaving the disparity in status between women and men unchanged: Occupations remain segregated by sex, with women occupying lower-status and lower-paying jobs; their promotional opportunities lag behind those of men; couples still give preference to the man's career while the woman continues to assume the greater share of domestic duties; and women's jobs continue to be valued less and do not offer adequate provisions for family leave, child care, or flexible schedules.

Rhode's analysis shows that theories and models of labor-force participation and the traditional legal focus on gender differences rather than gender disadvantages have had little effect on changing cultural and individual stereotypes that gird the structural obstacles to gender equality in the workplace. While affirmative action and pay-equity strategies have been employed as two methods of addressing some of these issues, they are not enough, Rhode posits, to change and correct the more subtle, unconscious forms of discrimination directed against working women. A more comprehensive set of strategies is necessary to close the gender gap in employment opportunities and policies.

The final chapter, Girls, Gender, and Schools: Excerpts from *The AAUW Report: How Schools Shortchange Girls*, explores how girls have remained absent from our national agenda on education. Despite the passage of Title IX 20 years ago and the Bush administration's plan for improving education in America by the year 2000, little attention has been paid to the different experiences of girls and boys within the educational system.

The authors discuss the available data on differences due to gender, race, and class on achievement scores, courses taken, career plans, and dropout rates. They find, for example, that from the age of three, girls and boys differ in their educational preparedness and classroom needs. At the younger ages, these differences involve language and motor skills; as students age, differences emerge in reading, math, and science. In the early years, the gaps between the sexes are often small; however, by high school, boys have an observable advantage in math and science achievement that is carried over to greater career opportunities in those areas.

Finally, the authors discuss how the formal curriculum and the classroom environment place girls at a disadvantage. From the books used in classrooms to the different treatment received from teachers and peers, girls are taught that women do not matter as much as men, that they are less powerful at best, and invisible at worst. As the authors point out, even in books that do mention the contributions of women to their fields, the examples are of the most famous women, ignoring the ongoing contributions of women as members of the society.

Within the classroom, boys continue to receive more attention, more instructional time, and, indeed, more hugs for good performance than girls. There are similar differences in the treatment of racial and ethnic groups as well. Moreover, incidents of sexual harassment by peers is increasing. It is clear that girls are learning more than the intended subject matter of the K–12 curriculum. They are learning about power and powerlessness and the politics of gender.

As with all the issues included in this volume, the political importance of sex and gender,[4] as well as race, ethnicity, and class, in the struggle to improve the quality of women's lives cannot be under-estimated. When the feminist movement resurfaced in the 1960s, the reverberating cry was "The personal is political." This slogan helped us see clearly that the private, hidden, and often overlooked concerns of women needed to become politicized before action could be taken. What we have learned since then is that the political is most definitely personal, and not necessarily in ways that benefit women.

The add-women-and-stir approach, used by many to assuage the demands of reform-minded feminists, focused on changing the numbers rather than redressing the inherent inequalities in our socie-tal and political structures. As the contributors make clear in each of their chapters, the inequalities are still there. We have certainly made progress and through that progress have become more knowledgeable about and more determined to eradicate the obstacles that keep women powerless.

American women in the 1990s must meet the challenge set out by the contributors to this book; that is, we must become *involved* in bringing about political and personal change that will guarantee a decent standard of living for all women. We must become and stay informed of the issues; broaden our perspectives beyond our psycho-logical and geographical borders; question that which we do not un-derstand or with which we do not agree; and act, in whatever way we can, to ensure that the policies and laws meant to serve the people serve women equally.

We believe that the issues included in this volume, while not all-inclusive of the critical issues facing women today, will set the stage for our thinking and foster an ongoing dialogue about the wider domain of women's concerns. It is our hope and intent that this book will be read not only by students, academicians, and policymakers but by women and men everywhere who wish to be informed and challenged in their thinking about some of the most important issues facing American women today. We further hope the volume will be a useful guide in evaluating the political stances and platforms of those state and local, as well as national, individuals who would represent us politically. If we do this together, we will see for ourselves the difference that women can make.

Notes

1. Our choice to use the word *American* to refer to women currently residing in the United States may raise some questions among feminist scholars who feel that the term should apply equally to our Canadian and South

American neighbors. In making our decision, we consulted with scholars and colleagues from both places as to the commonly accepted usage of this word outside the United States. The general feeling is that residents of Canada would identify themselves as Canadians or French-Canadians rather than Americans and that residents of South America generally reserve the term *American* (or *Americano*) to refer to residents of North America. It is our understanding that, depending upon whether the speaker is from within or outside South America, the term *Latino Americano* or *Americano* may be used. We further understand that within South America there is a greater tendency to use terms associated with each country (for example, Brazilian) when speaking about the specific population.

2. I wish to thank Cecilia Burciaga, Associate Dean of Multicultural Development and Support at Stanford University, for coining this wonderful phrase.

3. We use these words—*tug-of-war, battles,* and *won*—consciously and intentionally to draw attention to the fact that women's concerns are negotiated through a judicial and political system that overwhelmingly underrepresents them at the same time that it describes them through the use of male-identified language. Some feminists, such as Marilyn French, have argued that the current treatment of women throughout the world can be seen as a war on women (see M. French, *The War Against Women* [New York: Summit Books, 1992]).

4. In general, the word *sex* has been used to denote biological female- and maleness, whereas the word *gender* denotes that which is associated with cultural definitions of femininity and masculinity.

TOWARD A WOMAN-FRIENDLY NEW WORLD ORDER

Kathleen B. Jones

In Euripides's *The Trojan Women*, Talthybius, a messenger from the conquering Greeks, brings words to Andromache, one of the women of defeated Troy, that her son, Astyanax, is to be hurled to his death from the towers of the city, since the Greeks have ordered that no son of a hero of the Trojans should survive. Talthybius advises Andromache to cooperate with this order, and to mourn quietly, since passivity is the state to which woman is born. "Listen to me! Your city is gone, your husband. You are in our power. How can one woman hope to struggle against the arms of Greece?"

Talthybius's words echo across the centuries of Western civilization to the present day: "How can one woman hope to struggle against the arms of Greece?" The tumultuous transformations in world politics since 1990—from the fall of the Berlin Wall to the devastation of Iraq during and after Operation Desert Storm—have left women's lives in most of the world untouched or worsened. Press reports indicate that the forces of nationalism and ethnic rivalry in Eastern Europe and among the Commonwealth of Independent States (11 of the former republics of the Soviet Union) are on the increase, leading to the massacre of civilian populations (many of whom are women and young children); growing economic instability, which is increasing the number of working hours, both inside and outside the home, that women labor just to ensure their families' survival; and the spread of traditionalist attitudes about the family and women's *natural* domestic roles. In Poland and other Eastern European countries, the Church has moved into the vacuum created by the collapse of state-controlled societies. The result has been renewed attacks on women's reproductive rights.

In June 1991, American officials and representatives of international relief agencies estimated that more than 5 million people from more than 30 countries had been temporarily or permanently displaced by the Gulf War.[1] The United Nations (UN) estimates that women and children make up approximately 70 percent to 80 percent of the world's 14 million refugees.[2] It is likely that this pattern prevails for those who have been displaced by the Gulf War. Within Iraq, international health workers have reported scandalous rates of malnutrition and disease, the aftermath not only of the U.S. bombing raids but also of the continued effects of the U.S. blockade of Iraq. Saddam Hussein has been little affected personally or politically by the U.S. embargo, but there are millions of women and men who suffer the effects of George Bush's hard-line strategy. MADRE, a U.S.-based international women's association, led a women's truck convoy with medical and other supplies into Iraq from Jordan on January 16, 1992, hoping to help the more than 900,000 children under the age of five suffering from disease and malnutrition in Iraq; 50,000 children have died already from the effects of the embargo.[3] As a further, particularly ironic commentary on the U.S.-led liberation of Kuwait, *Ms.* reported that the restored autocracy in Kuwait was continuing its ban on women's suffrage.[4]

Now, perhaps more than ever, conditions such as these make it imperative that we ponder again not how *one* woman, but how women as a formidable political force, can work together and work across our ethnic, racial, and class differences to construct a world more representative of women's diverse interests and needs. We need to consider the relationship between American foreign policy and the quality of lives of women in the United States and beyond if we want to build a new world order friendly to women.

We need to assess the impact of American foreign policy in real terms. Does it live up to its stated norms? Does it contribute to democracy, equitable and ecological development, and the construction of a world where the gap between the rich and the poor diminishes? There is another significant reason for an informed analysis of the Bush administration's foreign policy. What little remains of Bush's popularity, steadily declining since the end of the Gulf War, has to do with lingering beliefs that Bush is strong on foreign policy. In this chapter, I will offer some insights into what this alleged strength has done for women throughout the world during the late 1980s and early 1990s.

INTERNATIONAL POLITICS AND THE GENDER SYSTEM

There are several reasons why it takes more than the usual effort to think about the impact of foreign policy on women's lives. First, more than any other political arena, international politics and foreign policy have been defined as male preserves. Only 6 (3.8 percent) of the 159 UN member states were headed by women at the end of 1990.[5] The number of member states had risen to 175 by March 1992, but no more women had been added to the roster as government heads. Only 16 women have been either presidents or prime ministers of governments in the entire twentieth century. In neither ministerial posts responsible for helping formulate policy nor in the diplomatic corps that carries out the day-to-day policies of a government on foreign soil are women well represented. For example, in the United States, women hold 21.2 percent of the foreign-service positions, but only 5 percent of these are senior officer positions; none of these women in foreign-service positions was a woman of color. Only 56 of the 400 people who staff the Pentagon's Under Secretary for Policy posts are women. At the international level, women occupy a tiny minority of senior positions in organizations like the World Bank or the United Nations.[6] Since foreign policy is made by heads of state in consultation with key senior advisors, the overwhelming majority of whom are men, it seems natural to think of it as a field in which women have little interest or little stake.

Second, even among women who have made it to critical policy-making positions, the pressure to conform to the existing rules of the game in order to protect career mobility remains strong. These rules tend to promote business as usual, not the search for creative alternatives to conflict-laden global politics. As in domestic politics, women in the international political policymaking arena, who constitute such a tiny minority, try to underplay the extent to which they represent women's interests.

Third, the language of foreign policy contributes to our thinking about it in ways that conceptualize it as planning strategies that affect relations between nations, understood as abstract entities, like colored shapes on a "Risk" game board, instead of determining the quality of life of flesh-and-blood human beings in remote regions of the globe. Whenever the impact of foreign policy is discussed, euphemisms such as "national security," "economic interest," "global stability," "balance of power," "balance of payments," and "balance of trade" are used to structure and direct the discussion, leading to the illusion that foreign policy has minimal impact on anyone's daily life, female or male. Yet behind these phrases are average citizens whose lives are influenced intimately and deeply by governmental decisions about what regimes to recognize and support, what countries to arm or to aid and under what conditions, and what developmental strategies to pursue.

The combination of these factors makes the question of which foreign policies best meet women's needs all the more difficult to determine. As Kate Young has argued, in the context of her discussion of the impact of development strategies on women's lives, "The question of how to meet women's needs raises a prior question: that of the need for a clear-cut framework by which to identify, assess, and prioritize needs."[7] Both the relative lack of access of women to foreign policymaking arenas as well as the discourse of foreign policy itself contribute to the lack of a general theory of gender differentiation that would connect the structuring of international power and privilege with the sexual division of labor. Yet, as Jane L. Parpart and Kathleen Staudt have argued, "Gender is at the heart of state origins, access to the state, and state resource allocation. States are shaped by gender struggle; they carry distinctive gender ideologies through time which guide resource-allocation decisions in ways that mold material realities."[8]

For example, leaders of the developing countries have called upon U.S. policymakers to join the European Community's commitment to hold emissions of gases that warm the atmosphere to their 1990 levels and to contribute aid to Third World countries to enable them to develop in environmentally sustainable ways. As of 1992, the United States has refused to make such a commitment, and has agreed to contribute only a minimal amount ($75 million, or .0002542 percent of the proposed U.S. military budget of $295 billion dollars for fiscal year [FY] 1993) to a global fund for environmentally sound development. Third World countries are already shouldering the costs of earth-damaging developmental strategies that the industrialized nations have used for years, in the form of increased health risks from environmental threats, compounded by lack of adequate sanitation and health care, depletion of natural resources by energy-hungry industrialized powers—the United States, with 6 percent of the world's population, consumes more than 50 percent of the world's natural resources—and poorer wages and working conditions. Yet, within these countries, women bear a large part of this burden, not only in increased health risks but also in higher rates of poverty and illiteracy. Thus, the persistence of patterns of gender inequality are implicated in discussions of questions of environmental stability and ecological balance.

To assess alternative foreign policies we must have a sense of global politics from a perspective that considers the *geography of gender.* This means examining where women and men are socially located in the world, and how basic ideas about masculinity and femininity structure the shape of international politics. As Cynthia Enloe has written, this means looking carefully at how foreign-policy makers have "tried to hide and deny their reliance on women as feminized workers, as respectable and loyal wives, as 'civilizing influence,' as sex objects, as obedient daughters, as unpaid farmers, as coffee-serving campaigners, as consumers and tourists."[9] If we understand better how the global system of inequality depends on all women and men continuing to act in predictable ways *as* women and men, accepting established ideas about what is proper for women and men to do, then it will be possible for us to consider how we each contribute to sustaining the present order. Even if we are not policymakers, our behavior as consumers, tourists, wives, soldiers, workers, investors, and media watchers contributes to sustaining a particular world order. If we explore these interconnections, we may want to design strategies for changing ways of defining and resolving global conflicts and tensions, and learn to judge political candidates by the extent to which they subscribe to these alternative designs.

Thinking about alternative designs for foreign policy may mean not always limiting demands for change to what will work within the parameters of the existing gender system and its "rules of the game." It may mean that fully bringing women into the organizational arena ought to shake up the values of that arena and not simply frame women's demands for recognition of the relevance of their knowledge to "demands within existing definitions and existing institutions."[10]

CROSSING BORDERS: RETHINKING CITIZENSHIP IN AN INTERDEPENDENT WORLD

Most Americans are dissatisfied with the state of the U.S. economy. A 1992 *New York Times* poll found that 82 percent of those surveyed thought that the U.S. economy was either "fairly bad" or "very bad." At the same time, most Americans did not feel that any candidates who ran for office in 1992 understood what everyday life is like for people like them.[11] In this context of dissatisfaction and alienation it becomes difficult to focus political concern or political dialogue beyond the borders of one's own group, beyond the borders of one's own nation. The problems at home seem overwhelming enough. The potential for U.S. voters to be persuaded that a policy of isolationism is in their personal and economic interests is high. Witness the appeal of Patrick Buchanan's "border wall" that would seal off U.S. borders to "illegal" immigration and restrict Mexican imports: an appeal that plays on racist sentiments that fly in the face of the fact that American companies benefit from terrorized illegals since they can pay them less for frequently unsafe and unrewarding jobs that U.S. citizens refuse.

The attraction of isolationism as a solution to domestic problems compounds the difficulty of urging citizens to look seriously at the consequences of U.S. foreign policy on others' lives. Yet, I remain convinced of the importance of this task if we are to find creative solutions to the global problems of homelessness, poverty, malnutrition, illiteracy, disease, ecological destruction, and racial hatred that have a disproportionately negative impact on the lives of the world's women. Part of this task requires that we forge a new definition of citizenship: Rather than thinking of ourselves as members of rival nation-states, we should engage in a practice of citizenship as civic-minded world protection. In the words of the Secretary of Tourism and Environmental Protection of Senegal, Jacques Boudin, it is the developed world that is being looked to "to curb its national egoism and save planet earth."[12]

Particular strategies for achieving national security reinforce certain notions of citizenship over others. The dominant model of citizenship that we inherited from the cold war era represents citizens as armed subjects of warring, hostile states, intent on securing rigid boundaries between the native and the foreign, between us and them. Citizenship becomes a practice of obligation to state policies that reinforce our distance from *them* and the distinctiveness, the exceptionalism, of *us*. "The images the concept of boundary invites," Jennifer Nedelsky has written, "focus the mind on barriers, rules, and separateness. . . . [B]oundary imagery teaches . . . that security lies in walls. . . . Boundaries structure relationships, but they do not help us to understand or evaluate those structures, and often the structures are undesirable."[13]

The boundaries that constitute modern citizenship in nation-states are, as I have argued elsewhere, "contingent upon the ultimate subordination of the specific bonds of gender, race, and class—indeed all particularized identities—in favor of, most often, a *national identity and loyalty to the state* [emphasis added]. To become a citizen is to trade one's particular identity for an abstract, public self."[14] Here, I am concerned with the nature of boundaries constructed *between* the citizens of one nation-state and another, and how these boundaries act as limits on the articulation and practice of what I call *feminist citizenship.* I am interested in considering whether the logic of feminist criticisms of the concept of citizenship might provide an alternative to the understanding of citizenship as boundary building. A different idea of citizenship, one that defines it as an activity of world protection, seems necessary today because so many of the world's problems stretch beyond the parameters of one nation.

The implication of much feminist research has been that if women's discourses, practices, and rituals of *belonging to* were taken as paradigmatic, citizenship might be founded differently. This has meant that the rights enjoyed by and the demands placed on the feminist citizen have stretched beyond the question of individual political and social freedoms and ordinary political obligations to include, for instance, the right to be free from sexual harassment and the notion of care-taking responsibilities to others, even those who are not like us. Insofar as feminist theory breaks with liberal conceptualizations of citizenship, it has tended to put the emphasis more on civic-mindedness, and less on the possession of individual civil and political rights, as the hallmark of citizenship. Moreover, the concept of citizens' duties has been framed within global political parameters and extended, in some cases, to include the nonhuman world.

Feminist theory has suggested specific alternatives to the dominant model of political action by citizens that, implicitly, reject its nationalistic and antagonistic parameters. By arguing that the ways that nations have been constructed have often been at the expense of women and what women have represented, and by claiming that agonistic conflict is incompatible with many of the interests of care giving associated with "maternal practices," the logic of feminist discourse challenges the parameters of citizenship understood in nationalistic and agonistic terms. In place of nations, the world; in place of national security, world protection.[15]

MAKING CONNECTIONS: NATIONAL SECURITY AND GLOBAL DEVELOPMENT

The first step for U.S. citizens to contribute to the development of civic-minded world protection involves understanding the effect of U.S. foreign policies, or those of international organizations such as the International Monetary Fund (IMF) of the World Bank largely influenced by the United States, on the enormity and scope of both global and domestic problems. Beginning with the most obvious— U.S. national defense policy—might enable us to grasp basic connections. The United States has, since 1945, relied heavily on a defense-driven strategy of economic growth, coupled with tax breaks mostly for the wealthy, disinvesting in a civilian infrastructure and programs of public works, education, training, and health. The current structural problems with the American economy are, at least in large part, traceable to the failure of this strategy. Following the postwar boom of 1948–1966, the rate of growth of real gross national product (GNP) (controlling for inflation) has declined steadily. Moreover, the pace of real capital investment—investments in productive industry, instead of corporate buy-outs—has "declined by a quarter during the most recent business cycle [1979–1989]."[16] This decline reflects the immediate effects of the Reagan-Bush economic strategy of cuts to social services coupled with enormous tax breaks for the wealthy, and a doubling of the defense budget under the Reagan administration.

FY93 offered a unique opportunity for the Congress to consider revamping the military budget, with a rippling effect on redesigning domestic and foreign policy. With the collapse of the Soviet Union— the ideological threat that had fueled an immense defense industry for decades of the cold war—the possibility of an engaged debate about a "peace dividend" being redirected to shriveled domestic programs in health care, education, and community development seemed likely. The U.S. foreign policy of the containment of communism, understood as checking the Soviet system's ideological expansion around the globe, had resulted in the building of a massive military-industrial defense complex by the United States and the Soviet Union that has expended $3 trillion to $4 trillion since 1945 on the nuclear arsenal alone.[17]

The costs of this system of militarized security should be measured not only in actual dollars spent by the United States and its allies and enemies but in terms of a major commitment of world industrial production and use of vital natural and human resources for military requirements. Marilyn Waring has estimated that, on an annual basis, world military spending, the majority of which comes from the United States, has been "more than the total value of gross fixed capital formation in all of the developing countries combined and about the same as global public expenditure on education."[18] This means that military expenditures divert needed monies from the sorts of development projects that could prevent the outbreak of crises caused by disparities of wealth. For instance, instead of U.S. military aid to El Salvador at the rate of $1.6 million per day for the last decade, which helped sustain the government-led troops in a protracted civil war there that led to more than 70,000 mostly nonmilitary deaths—deaths that were the result of the actions of death squads supported by U.S. aid—monies could have been spent helping resettlement projects that have stressed cooperative farming endeavors, locally based public-health projects, and similar democratically controlled programs.[19] The year 1992 appeared to be the time to consider alternatives to a military-driven domestic and global development agenda. Such consideration depended upon reshaping definitions of what and whose activities contributed best to economic productivity if international monetary sources, such as the World Bank, were to assess women's contributions seriously.

With the Soviet system gone, justification of a proposed $295 billion expenditure on the military in the United States appeared to strain credibility. At least half the U.S. military budget had gone to defend Europe and Japan against the perceived Soviet threat. That threat has vanished. Yet, as Robert Borosage reported, the Joint Chiefs of Staff now argue that we need to continue to arm against a threat that is undefinable: "'The real threat we now face is the threat of the unknown, the uncertain.'" We need massive expenditures just in case "a crisis or war that no one predicted or expected" occurs.[20] This amounts to grounding the justification for sustained U.S. military buildup not in foreign policy but in fiction! In his 1992 State of the Union address, Bush announced a savings of $50 billion over the next five years in cut or frozen military programs, yet this "represents barely 3 percent of the $1.46 trillion the President plans to spend on the military in that time."[21]

American defense spending is now being driven more by domestic policy—the feared loss of jobs directly or indirectly dependent on defense in many localities—than by foreign-policy initiatives. Although a government accounting office study suggested that the United States could afford to cut its military budget in half over the next five years, with resulting savings of some $200 billion, members of Congress have been scrambling to keep bases open and military equipment production lines moving in their constituencies for fear that lost jobs in their areas will mean lost congressional races.[22] Also lost is the chance for a serious reassessment of our national interest that could transfer the support of 72 percent of the American population for military savings to domestic needs through creative public investment strategies designed to increase our long-term productivity and, at the same time, provide needed jobs.[23] Such a reassessment could explore the possibility that global development might not have to be at the expense of either national security or domestic employment.

If we were to follow the logic that the current shifts in global politics permit a reassessment of U.S. foreign policy, we might follow the lead of our now-ally Boris Yeltsin, who has drastically cut military procurement in Russia. The opportunity would then exist to convert those savings into needed job-training programs and community-development projects, necessary income safety nets for those displaced civilian and military workers previously dependent on defense, as well as economic aid to nations in distress. The U.S. Department of Labor has estimated that for every billion dollars spent on the military, 76,000 jobs are created; but for every billion dollars spent on education, 187,000 jobs are created, and, in health care, a billion dollars buys 139,000 jobs.

Beyond these numbers lies the fact that those who benefit *least* from military spending's spinoff into the civilian sector are those who need opportunities the most: poorer classes, especially women and men of color. The jobs in electronics, communications, high technology, shipbuilding, and aircraft building supported by military spending are overwhelmingly occupied by white males. Marion Anderson, director of Employment Research Associates in Michigan, has estimated that for every billion dollar increase in military spending, "9,500 jobs disappear for American women."[24]

Introducing such data into debates about national security changes the criteria by which security is measured. Militarily driven development, both at home and abroad, tends to favor disproportionately the enhancement of chances for some few men over those of most women in the world. At the same time, given its current design, it tends to promote traditional patterns of masculinity and femininity.

For instance, the consequences of U.S.–supported, military-driven development abroad are evident in the Philippines, long seen as an essential link in America's Pacific Rim security chain. By 1985, Cynthia Enloe has noted, "the U.S. military had become the second largest employer in the Philippines, hiring over 40,000 Filipinos" as full-time base workers, contracted laborers, domestics, and consessionaries. By 1987, that number had grown to 68,000, many of whom were women.[25] Yet Filipino women's activists have argued that the shifting tide of the Filipino economy, affected by the declining price of sugar on the world market and the concentration of land ownership into fewer hands, has driven record numbers of women into "mak[ing] a living by servicing the social and sexual needs of American military men. . . . There are more Filipino women workers working as prostitutes in the tourist industry than around U.S. bases," although it is the presence of the U.S. military that drives the prostitution industry in the Philippines.[26] By January 1987, 25 AIDS cases were reported in the Philippines; all were women who worked as bar girls around the major U.S. military bases.[27] Partly as a result of the politicizing of this issue by Filipino feminists and the efforts of Filipino nationalists to secure an alternative development strategy, the Filipino Congress voted against President Aquino's recommendation to extend the U.S. lease of the base at Subic Bay and demanded American withdrawal. As I have argued, changes in the structure of global politics support U.S. endeavors to rethink its security strategy—a strategy legitimated by a now nonexistent Soviet threat in the Pacific—and to consider the global security at stake in contributing to the Philippines' development in more even, equitable, and healthy ways. So far, the U.S. government has not responded positively to calls for more economic aid.

Perhaps what women need to do is to contribute to a transformation of the logic of national security by developing practices of civic-minded world protection within the arena of foreign policy. Whereas the concept of citizenship has depended upon drawing boundaries or borders between citizens and outsiders, leading to increasingly restrictive immigration policies, in one area of American foreign policy—trade policies—the effort, of late, has been to erase borders. Within this area we might contrast the Bush administration's strategy to open the borders of nations to free trade to those of different women's groups concerned with the impact of free trade on women's lives.

The Bush administration's efforts to secure agreement for including Mexico in the North American Free Trade Agreement (NAFTA) already established between the United States and Canada reflect the idea that removing virtually all barriers to trade between participating nations encourages the development of U.S. industry by enhancing opportunities for U.S. investment abroad, creating a nearly "$6 trillion market stretching from the Yukon to the Yucatan"[28] Yet the benefits are likely to fall disproportionately to wealthy industrialists, and the costs are expected to be borne disproportionately by poorer classes and countries. For instance, Jean Swanson has noted that since January 1989, when NAFTA was implemented between the United States and Canada, "315,000 jobs have been lost [in Canada]—many in manufacturing and food processing where there are proportionately more women employed." In addition, Canadian government subsidies of unemployment insurance have "been severely cut back because it is seen as an illegal subsidy to employers under the new Canadian Free Trade Agreement, since U.S. employers must pay themselves."[29]

Of course, certain U.S. workers, especially in the fish-processing industry, have benefited from the agreement because their wages are lower than those of the Canadian workers. Fish is trucked across the Canadian–U.S. border, enhancing the possibility of contamination, to be processed by American workers at lower cost. The result could be to pit vulnerable workers of each nation against one another, while industrialists continue to benefit through higher profit margins. In an effort to build an international solidarity movement resisting the free-trade agreement, and lessening the negative effects of fueling nationalistic labor rivalries, the Action Canada Network has built linkages with labor groups in the United States and Mexico to find creative alternatives that recognize how workers' interests "cross borders."[30]

The inclusion of Mexico in NAFTA, supported by the Bush administration and applauded by Mexican President Salinas, is viewed with alarm by others. Instead of creating "first world" jobs in Mexico, labor activists and feminists alike point to the likelihood that increasing foreign investment under NAFTA, as presently defined, will encourage U.S. companies "to set up production plants, pay low wages, contribute fewer taxes, and pollute the environment."[31] Because of the economy, Mexico is in a poor position to enforce tough environmental standards, standards that are seen as discouraging to foreign investment. Its environmental protection agency is underfunded and understaffed. Privately, Mexican authorities "acknowledge that the competitive pressures of free trade will encourage domestic companies to cut costs at the expense of sound environmental policies."[32] Evidence of this already occurring is widespread: noxious fumes, foul water, hazardous chemicals dumped in 55-gallon drums "purchased from used furniture stores" with English labels warning Mexican residents that "[t]his container will be hazardous when emptied."[33] In La Cienega, residents who have noticed the effects from *maquiladoras* (foreign-owned firms) in nearby Tijuana don't complain, except among themselves; they feel that pollution is what they must accept as part of "progress."[34]

Those who will suffer most are the vulnerable ones: the predominately female work force employed at shockingly low wages and unhealthy work conditions—some working for six days a week for $33 U.S. *a week*—in the more than 2,000 *maquiladoras* allowed in Mexico under special trade rules since 1965.[35] The number of such industries that move south to cut labor costs is expected to increase dramatically if NAFTA is ratified. Along with the increasing export of industry will come a net loss of predominately minority female jobs in the United States over a ten-year period of NAFTA, predicted at a figure of 550,000 jobs lost in textiles, garment making, food processing, electronics assembly, and other light manufacturing, as well as a net increase in the export of pollutants that foul Mexican water, air, and soil. More than 12 million gallons of raw sewage flow into the Tijuana River everyday because the city is ill-prepared for the increased sanitation needs caused by explosive rates of rural migration to the city by those looking for any work, no matter how dangerous.[36] Again, rather than pit national worker against national worker, labor activists and women's rights activists are calling for an inclusion of "uniform minimum standards for worker's rights and working conditions." They call for "begin[ning] to know each other better, break[ing] down the borders and barriers, and organiz[ing] ourselves to demand that NAFTA improve the situation of women."[37]

CIVIC-MINDED WORLD PROTECTION, RESPONSIBLE WORLD TRAVELING, AND GLOBAL POLITICS

Feminist commitment to a political defense of diversity and, at the same time, to structural transformation of a world political economy that systematically deprives most of the world's women and men of adequate food, clothing, and shelter suggests a desire both to repudiate xenophobic conceptions of citizenship and to situate citizenship as civic-minded world protection within a truly new world order founded on principles of justice and care.

Yet, nagging questions remain. Can world protection avoid the pitfalls of the national security state? Can world protection be non-nationalistic? Should feminist world protection be wedded to theories of citizenship? In a world where most women are not yet visible on the terrain of citizenship, whose interests govern the rejection of the nation-state as an appropriate territory for feminist citizens? What does the feminist critique of citizenship mean in a world where proliferating groups are reclaiming a part of previously federal states, as in Yugoslavia, or where record numbers of women are participating in national liberation struggles, such as that of the Intifada for the right of a Palestinian state to exist? What does the critique of citizenship as the politics of exclusion mean within the context of feminist theory's belated response to the challenge of feminists of color that feminist theory itself become more inclusive?

Contradictions abound. In a world secured through the hegemony of a supra-imperialist nation-state—the United States in Bush's new world order—feminist arguments about the need for equality for women and the need for women to escape the prison of second-class citizenship, are linked to urging U.S. women to take up arms, hunker down, and drop smart bombs on civilian targets in thousands of sorties that could (and did) leave behind five million refugees, mostly women and children.

Jean Bethke Elshtain argues that familial authority is at odds with the "governing presumptions of democratic authority." She continues, "[t]o establish an identity between public and private lives and purposes would weaken, not strengthen, democratic life overall."[38] Her argument resists the notion that we should collapse the private with the public; that we should attempt to structure our intimate life through the same principles that structure our public life. She refuses one version of the feminist project to construct family relations on the same individualist and voluntarist norms as democratic public life.

Here I have called attention to the opposite problem: What are the limits of the feminist critique of citizenship in a national-security state for reconfiguring citizenship? Can we sustain a practice of citizenship as political action in concert if we embark on this project from a feminist perspective that stresses the global parameters of the responsible citizen's obligations, increases the range and intensity of these obligations, and, at the same time, broadens the scope of citizens' rights? Will we need to move beyond the parameters of citizenship to reach this global solidarity? How far can we go in reconstructing social relations in terms of the ethic of care?

In this context, citizens need to become responsible world travelers. The following personal reflections are meant to provide the foundation for the articulation of a concept of citizenship that stresses our connection with and responsibility toward others, without having to turn those "others" into "us." I ask again, what difference can women make in the struggle against the perpetuation of the old world order masquerading as a new one? "'[W]orld'-travellers have the distinct experience of being different in different 'worlds' and ourselves in them."[39] I use the second person in the following narratives in order to invite you to world-travel with me.

You are at a picnic, high in the mountains of Isle de Réunion, a tiny, multicultural jewel of a place in the middle of the Indian Ocean. It was colonized by the French in the seventeenth century with slave labor imported from neighboring Madagascar and other parts of Africa (there was no indigenous population). Réunion is precisely that: the constant reunion of the peoples and cultures and languages of Asia, Africa, and Europe. This picnic is a cornucopia of unimaginable delight and sadness. There are giant cauldrons of steaming, spicy meats and vegetables, enormous coffers of rice, and champagne and rum. There is a sense of camaraderie, cooperation, and friendship among this political family of friends who work for social change in this small place where identities are so intermixed it seems ridiculous to think in terms of borders. But here, nevertheless, the issues of borders and boundaries will be debated as this bastard country—for that is how she has been represented in the French colonialist literature of a previous era, as the bastard child of a white French man and a woman of color—still attached to her mother France, became part of the European Community of 1992.[40]

You are thinking about borders and boundaries as you remember, at this feast, the little girl you met earlier that day, yards away from the apartment where you have been a comforted and protected guest. She and her brothers and sisters and nephews and mother live together in a tiny room, the noise and the heat competing for dominion. One of her sisters is already pregnant, at 16, with her second child. "It's one way to gain a little extra income for the family," a Réunionaise who has worked as a political organizer in the neighborhood tells you. The little girl, practicing her English, says to you, "I want to be a teacher, like you."

You think about the meeting you attended earlier in the week. Local elections for mayor of Le Port, a meeting of the *Parti Communist de la Réunion*, a party that stresses building roads, public-work projects, and improving transportation networks so that people like "Maria," who works as a maid in one of the French diplomat's estates on the island, won't have to wait hours for a bus to take her to and from work, worried about her children's dinner, and her children's safety. Maria, who is forbidden to eat leftovers from the feast she had prepared for the diplomat's friends, supports the Communists. "Of course," she says, and she will continue to do so despite the dissolution of the Soviet Union and the changes in Eastern Europe.

When you talked with the women of this island, women of so many different races and classes, about what issues they saw as most important to them today, without hesitation they said, "work and development."

So you have been made different by this traveling, and yet you returned home. You have a responsibility to remember and to witness:

"[S]anctuary is about crossing lines, about making connections rather than exclusions. If I choose to create my own safe place by closing my eyes and heart, then I will not be safe for long."[41] In your home, in feminist theory, people are rushing to put up fences to keep others out. There can be no safety, no sanctuary in a world of sovereign borders and boundaries. You have to create a new kind of home, a "new culture—*una cultura mestiza*—with [your] own lumber, [your] own bricks and mortar and [your] own feminist architecture."[42] It has to be strong and sturdy, which is why you need the bricks and mortar; it also has to be open to diversity, which is why you need the principles of feminist architecture.

Again you travel. This time, along with your Réunionaise friend, who is also a feminist scholar, you decide to go to El Salvador to extend your co-authored research project on women's political organizations—and to extend yourselves. About a week before you leave, you begin to have nightmares; your friend is troubled by premonitions of an unnameable fear. These are normal fears, you reassure each other. If one hadn't been worried about going to El Salvador, the other would have doubted her friend's ability to react quickly if the fears became reality. You never imagined the worst would occur.

In this state of mind—watchful, cautious, but not immobilized— the two of you and three companions are stopped by heavily armed government troops in a rural province early on a summer Sunday morning, allegedly for traveling without safe-conduct passes. You never make it to the meeting of the rural women's cooperative that had been organized by your companions—another U.S. woman and two Salvadorans.

With no charges brought against you, you are detained under the surveillance of Salvadoran forces of the Atlacatl brigade. Then they transfer you all into the custody of the infamous Treasury Police. Your Salvadoran companions weep. You refuse to relinquish your passports until your embassies are informed of your incarceration. All demands are ignored. "It will go worse for you if you refuse to cooperate," your captors intone. So you give up your passports, all your personal possessions, your liberty, and, you are certain, your life, to the parade of captors who interrogate you with more than 30 hours of pointless, yet terrifying, questions.

Huddled together in a barren cubicle, you try to make sense of the insanity you are witnessing. Would these men abuse you? Would you or the Salvadorans be tortured? How would you live, if you lived, with the knowledge of the risk that the two young Salvadorans had taken so that you could witness and recount to North Americans the horror of Salvadorans' daily lives? Would anyone listen? Did anyone know where you were?

All along, you have the nagging sense that Kafka's world was not a metaphor, but a prescient image of a world where resistance seems to be as unavailable as a breath of fresh air; and, all along, as long as you are thinking, and making jokes, and inventing games, you know you are not dead yet. You have an incredible sense of victory when you outwit your interrogator, who understands no English, by pretending you understand no Spanish and by sneaking verbal messages to your friend, who is translating only some of your words, in between the actual answers to questions. Yet this victory is laced with a sense of dread that it may be bootless if there is no more ability to be outside this world.

Men come to look at you. One accuses you of having been there before. "You are a subversive! We have pictures of you in demonstrations! Don't lie!" he shouts at you. For a few minutes you're uncertain—maybe he's right. Your release papers say *sospechosas de ser D/T* (suspected of being a delinquent terrorist).

Although you remain scarred by the journey to a place where truth is whatever the powerful declare it to be at the moment, this is a journey that the Salvadoran people make everyday. You visit the University of El Salvador after your release. A psychology professor tells you that she cannot conduct her research on the victims of torture because she has received repeated death threats and has been told to leave the country in 48 hours if she dares to continue her investigations.

One mural in the biological sciences building speaks volumes. It depicts a pregnant woman's body. The fetus inside is grasping a miniature rifle in its hand. The woman is shackled. The lock on the shackles is painted red, white, and blue, with the tiny initials "USA" barely visible.

Now back in the United States, you wonder how this experience that is yours, but doesn't belong to you, and which happened to you when you weren't looking, will work into efforts to build the democratic political space needed to discuss the shape of a world that is friendly to women.

World travelers have to become unencumbered, vulnerable selves. They have to be willing to risk thinking about justice within and beyond the borders. They have to be willing to risk engaging in a practice of citizenship that challenges national security with the logic of civic-minded world protection.

NOTES

1. *New York Times*, June 16, 1991, sec. 4, 3.

2. *The World's Women. 1970–1990: Trends and Statistics* (New York: U.N. Publications, 1991), 74.

3. *Ms.*, "Sisterhood Is Global: International News" (January/February 1992), 12.

4. Ibid., 20.

5. *The World's Women*, 31.

6. C. Enloe, *Bananas, Beaches, and Bases* (Berkeley: University of California Press, 1990), 117, 118, 120–122.

7. K. Young, *Women and Economic Development: Local, Regional, and National Planning Strategies* (Oxford, England: Berg Publishers, 1988), 1.

8. J. Parpart and K. Staudt, "Women and the State in Africa," in *Women and the State in Africa*, ed. Jane L. Parpart and Kathleen Staudt (Boulder, Colo.: Lynne Rienner, 1989), 6.

9. Enloe, 17.

10. N. Kardam, *Bringing Women In: Women's Issues in International Development Programs* (Boulder, Colo.: Lynne Rienner, 1991), 14.

11. R. Toner, "In Poll, Voters Are Unhappy with All the Choices," *New York Times*, March 3, 1992, A1.

12. Ibid., A3.

13. J. Nedelsky, "Law, Boundaries, and the Bounded Self," *Representations* 30(1990): 175.

14. K. B. Jones, "Citizenship in a Woman-Friendly Polity," *Signs* 15(4) (Summer 1990): 781–812.

15. See S. Ruddick, *Maternal Thinking Toward a Politics of Peace* (New York: Ballantine Books, 1989).

16. S. Bowles, D. M. Gordon, and T. Weisskopf, "An Economic Strategy for Progressives," *The Nation* (February 10, 1992): 163.

17. M. Waring, *If Women Counted: A New Feminist Economics* (New York: Harper and Row, 1988), 166.

18. Ibid., 167.

19. *Global Perspectives* (Minneapolis: Augsberg College, Winter 1992), 2.

20. R. Borosage, "Defensive About Defense Cuts," *The Nation* (March 9, 1992): 292.

21. Ibid., 292.

22. Ibid., 293.

23. Ibid.

24. B. Robinson, *Women, Taxes, and Federal Spending* (Philadelphia: Women's International League for Peace and Freedom, 1983), 15.

25. Enloe, 86.

26. Ibid., 86–87.

27. Ibid., 88.

28. *Los Angeles Times*, November 17, 1991, A18.

29. J. Swanson, "Canadian Women Say: 'Free Trade Isn't Free!'" *Equal Means: Women Organizing Economic Solutions* 1 (Winter 1991): 25.

30. Ibid., 26.

31. R. A. G. Alvinas, "Opening Borders to What?: Mexican Women and the Free Trade Agreement," *Equal Means: Women Organizing Economic Solutions* 1 (Winter 1991): 27.

32. *Los Angeles Times*, November 17, 1991, A18.

33. *Los Angeles Times*, November 19, 1991, A24.

34. Ibid.

35. Alvinas, 27; *Los Angeles Times*, November 19, 1991, A24.

36. *Los Angeles Times*, November 19, 1991, A24.

37. Swanson, 27.

38. J. B. Elshtain, "The Family and Civic Life," in *Power Trips and Other Journeys: Essays in Feminism as Civic Discourse*, ed. J. B. Elshtain (Madison: University of Wisconsin Press, 1990), 54, 55.

39. M. Logones, "Playfulness, 'World'-Traveling, and Loving Perception," in *Making Face, Making Soul—Haciendo Caras: Creative and Critical Perspectives by Women of Color*, ed. G. Anzaldúa (San Francisco: Aunt Lute Foundation Books, 1990), 396.

40. F. Verges, "Memories of Origin: Sexual Difference and Feminist Polity," *Issues in Reproductive and Genetic Engineering* 4(1) (1991): 3–15.

41. J. McDaniel, *Sanctuary: A Journey* (Ithaca, N.Y.: Firebrand Books, 1987), 69.

42. G. Anzaldúa, *Borderlands—La Frontera; The New Mestiza* (San Francisco: Spinsters/Aunt Lute, 1987), 22.

THE POLITICAL WOMAN

Ruth B. Mandel

The first wave of American feminism, surfacing in the mid-nineteenth century, gave rise to the suffrage movement and, after seven decades, the vote for women. The reemergence of American feminism almost 50 years after suffrage arose most directly from two sources: (1) the experience of sexism and the training in activism gained by women in the civil-rights, peace, and student movements of the 1960s, and (2) the thwarted expectations and experience of discrimination and powerlessness encountered by highly educated professional women.[1] This time feminism burst upon a communications- and media-wired America with great speed and force, its power due in no small part to a public receptiveness produced by several decades of significant change in patterns of education, labor-force participation, marriage, and fertility.[2] Not only did the burgeoning women's movement of the 1970s demand changes in law and reform in public policy to grant women equity in employment, education, credit, housing, and other areas but it also stimulated a fundamental and far-reaching reexamination of sex roles, gender identity, individual life-styles, family arrangements, and women's proper place in society. If contemporary feminism has not managed to produced a complete social revolution, it certainly can claim credit for changes in perceptions about the sexes as well as for shifts in Americans' social, economic, and political lives.

It is in this context that over 20 years of enormous change in women's patterns of political participation must be examined.

Beginning in the 1970s, American women have sought and entered both elective and appointive public office in unprecedented numbers. By word and deed, women signaled their intention to seek a place in the public world, to share responsibility and power with men in governing. Women were ready to leave the relative calm of private life and behind-the-scenes political activity for the rough contest for public power.

The most useful chronological signpost marking this turning point in women's political lives bears the date July 1971, when the National Women's Political Caucus (NWPC) was founded. Regardless of how much credit historians ultimately give NWPC for influencing women's political behavior, its very establishment was highly significant. NWPC was the first national membership organization to promote women's entry into politics at leadership levels. The political arm of the women's movement, it was created by feminist activists (many of whom belonged to the National Organization for Women [NOW] and had been active in electoral politics) who believed that to effect real and lasting progress on their agenda, women would have to seek political leadership in their own right, on behalf of their own issues. The time had come to focus women's attention on achieving political power for women.

In justifying as well as encouraging women's political advancement throughout the 1970s, several reasons were cited repeatedly by feminists and others sympathetic to the idea of full and equal political participation. First, there was the simple matter of equity: A representative democracy would not de facto exclude the majority of its population from leadership. Second, a pragmatic country could hardly afford to ignore the skills, intelligence, and energies of over half its citizens, especially in the domain of public service, where more talent was urgently needed. Third, women in politics would bring a different perspective, and perhaps different values and priorities (derived from varying combinations of biology, socialization, and gender-based experiences), to a broad range of public issues; moreover, they would advance a set of special concerns, or women's issues, that had not received attention from men. Also, by virtue of their presence in the public arena, women in politics would be role models, inspiring and influencing other women to follow their example. A balance of sexes in government might just carry the hope of more balance all around: more fairness and equity in society; more representativeness in experience, interests, and outlook; more willingness among more people to share responsibilities for the larger community.

American women had traditionally been active as volunteers in civic and social community efforts, and in electoral politics as political wives, party loyalists, and—since 1920—as voters; but women's involvement had not been regarded by political scientists or practitioners as political behavior, and women's political status had been understood as subordinate. While a few unusual women had sought and won elective office, the overwhelming majority of politically minded women had accepted their place as secondary and auxiliary to the real politicians and leaders—the men.[3] The vast majority of women interested in electoral politics had worked at party housekeeping tasks or had joined campaigns behind the scenes. They staffed campaign storefronts, performed the well-known licking and sticking duties, and organized candidates' evenings and fundraising parties. Virtually all of them worked on a volunteer basis for male party leaders and male candidates.

In the 1970s, some of these women with years of service and valuable experience in electoral politics, as well as in civic and community volunteer activities, responded to the feminist movement's call. Many of them began to apply their skills to building their own political careers, competing and risking themselves in public, dealing with public success or defeat, and, eventually—after some hesitation—even acknowledging ambition for power.[4]

The feminist announcement that the country needed women in positions of political power coincided with women's growing belief in their political efficacy and in their own potential as leaders.[5] Women granted themselves permission to climb over fences erected by culture and custom and to head toward the door marked "candidate," "elected official," "leader"—the door traditionally reserved for politically ambitious men. Underlying the move into new areas of political activity was a change in self-concept whereby women now envisioned themselves as seeking the number one spot, becoming the people in charge of the public good. After a centuries-old history of understanding the terms *woman* and *leader* as contradictory and the private and public domains as separated by gender as well as by function, women challenged these accepted dichotomies.

The change in women's self-concept went hand in hand with a shift in public attitudes. Surveys of public opinion demonstrated that the populace increasingly accepted women's political participation. Poll data revealed a gradual growth in approval even for the idea of women seeking the highest offices.[6] For example, the percentage of people who told Gallup pollsters that they would vote for a qualified woman for president if their party nominated her rose from 31 percent in 1937 to 80 percent in 1983.[7]

Those who sounded the call for women to enter politics and those who answered it believed there was some value to working within the U.S. two-party system. Whether partisan liberals or feminist activists in the mainstream of the women's movement, or both at once, they held a reformist view of American politics, confident that its institutions and practices were basically sound and worth preserving, and capable of responding constructively to pressures for timely change.

Many women entered the electoral fray in the 1970s. Some emerged from years of homemaking, from the League of Women Voters where they had learned the issues, or from local grassroots organizations and activism in various movements for social change.[8] Many had been active in their communities, working on problems ranging from getting potholes filled and streetlights installed to fighting for state income taxes. For some, the launching pad was issue politics—nuclear disarmament and freeze campaigns, school busing, or the Equal Rights Amendment (ERA). An increasing number of women moved into electoral politics from female-dominated fields such as nursing and social work that were organizing to have an impact on the political system.

Sometimes the connection between the feminist call to get involved and the decision to try was direct. Kathy Whitmire, mayor of Houston, Texas, from 1982 to 1992, remembers when she first thought of running. She "recalls coming back into town from a business trip one night and finding a copy of the newspaper her husband had marked for her—circled was a story about the coming meeting in Houston of the National Women's Political Caucus. It was the Caucus that gave her the idea she could run for office and the courage to try."[9]

The election years of 1972 and 1974 demonstrated the strong appeal of the call to political action. An early NWPC project called Women's Education for Delegate Selection (WEDS) informed women about party rules and procedures and encouraged them to become delegates to the 1972 presidential nominating conventions. That year, women comprised an unprecedented 40 percent of the Democratic delegates and 30 percent of the Republican delegates; whereas, in the previous two decades, women's representation as delegates to the two national party conventions had remained between 10 and 18 percent.[10] The year 1972 also saw a record number of women (32) running as major-party nominees for the U.S. House of Representatives (just two years later a new record of 44 was set). Congresswoman Shirley Chisholm of New York ran for the Democratic nomination for president in 1972. Although her candidacy was controversial among women and blacks who thought she could not win the nomination, many women worked enthusiastically on her grassroots, people's campaign.[11] Despite not being taken seriously, Chisholm remained in the race until the Democratic convention, where she won 151.95 delegate votes on the first ballot. Frances ("Sissy") Farenthold, a former Texas legislator, received the second-highest number of votes for the vice-presidential nomination at the 1972 Democratic national convention after her name was placed in nomination by feminist leader Gloria Steinem. While male party leaders never took Farenthold's nomination seriously, her vote count signaled that a new voice was emerging in national politics.[12]

Ann Armstrong delivered the keynote address at the 1972 Republican National Convention—the first woman ever to perform that function. In 1974, Mary Louse Smith of Iowa became the first woman to chair the Republican National Committee. Also in 1974, Ella Grasso was elected governor of Connecticut, the first woman ever to be elected a state governor in her own right.[13] Firsts for women in partisan and electoral politics dotted the 1970s and 1980s (see Milestones for Women in Politics, 1971–1991, at the end of this chapter). Because women had no significant representation in leadership anywhere in the political system, each new appointment, nomination, or victory was a breakthrough.

Some firsts remain to be achieved for women in the hierarchies of the political parties, campaign-staff positions, staff jobs in the offices of powerful government officials, media consulting, polling, and, of course, candidacy and officeholding for both elective and appointive positions. However, the atmosphere has changed dramatically in 20 years. No longer a matter of a society rethinking its concepts of *leader* and *woman*, the situation today is more a matter of keeping the list of firsts going and moving on to seconds, thirds, and parity. This is neither easy nor inevitable. Nevertheless, the challenge in the early 1990s is quite different from that faced in the early 1970s.

THE NEW POLITICAL WOMAN[14]

The turning point in American women's political participation occurred when a social movement's call to action encountered a condition of readiness among women; actually moving women into positions throughout the political system, however, loomed as a formidable challenge. Having accepted the challenge, how successful have women been? Who were the pioneers and from where did they come? What routes have they taken? What support systems have they used? What obstacles have they encountered? Have they found their sex to be an advantage?[15]

NUMBERS

Women's representation in federal, state, county, and municipal elective offices increased significantly between the mid-1970s and the early 1990s (Table 1). Until 1974, no woman had been elected a state governor in her own right; since then, eight have gained governorships: the late Ella Grasso, governor of Connecticut from 1975 to 1980 (she resigned because of illness halfway through her second term); Dixy Lee Ray, governor of Washington from 1977 to 1981; Martha Layne Collins, governor of Kentucky from 1984 to 1988; Madeleine Kunin,

TABLE 1

WOMEN AS A PERCENTAGE OF ELECTED OFFICEHOLDERS, SELECTED OFFICES, 1975–1992

OFFICEHOLDERS	1975	1977	1979	1981	1983	1985	1987	1989	1991	1992
Members of U.S. Congress	4	4	3	4	4	5	5	5	6	6
Statewide elective officials	10	8	11	11	13	14	15	14[4]	18	18
Members of state legislatures	8	9	10	12	13	15	16	17	18	18
Members of county governing boards[1]	3	4	5	6	8	8[2]	9	9	NA	NA
Mayors and members of municipal/township governing boards	4	8	10	10	NA	14[3]	NA	NA	NA	NA

[1]Three states (Connecticut, Rhode Island, and Vermont) do not have county governing boards and were not included in calculating this figure.
[2]Figure represents 1984.
[3]Data are incomplete for the following states: Illinois, Indiana, Kentucky, Missouri, Pennsylvania, and Wisconsin.
[4]Although there was an increase in the number of women serving between 1987 and 1989, the percentage decrease reflects a change in the base used to calculate these figures.
NA = not available.

SOURCE: © Center for the American Woman and Politics, Eagleton Institute of Politics, Rutgers University, 1993. Reprinted by permission of the Center for the American Woman and Politics.

governor of Vermont from 1985 to 1991; Kay Orr, governor of Nebraska (and the first Republican woman governor ever) from 1987 to 1991; Joan Finney (Kansas), Ann Richards (Texas), and Barbara Roberts (Oregon)—all elected in 1990 as governors of their states.

In 1970, no state had an incumbent female lieutenant governor, and only one state had ever elected a woman to that office.[16] By 1992, 22 women had been elected lieutenant governors; two of these (Collins and Kunin) went on to win their states' governorships.

Women's recent history in state legislatures is indicative of the overall national pattern of change for women in politics. State legislatures are important arenas for the politically ambitious. Although the size of constituencies, competition for seats, availability of staff support and offices, salary levels, length and frequency of legislative sessions, and distances to state capitals vary greatly across the country, in every state the legislature is often both a base for building a political career and a springboard to higher office. Women's share of seats in state legislatures has quadrupled since 1971; in early 1992, the 1,375 women state legislators represented 18.4 percent of the total (7,461) (Table 2). Every state counts at least four women in its house in 1992, and every state has at least one woman in its senate. Representation by minority women remains quite low; the 129 African-American women, 17 Asian/Pacific Islander women, 16 Hispanic women, and 5 Native-American women accounted for 12.2 percent of all female state lawmakers.

At local levels, too, women began the climb into elective office from a position of virtual invisibility, pushing their representation upward over the years to what are still small shares of the total. The proportion of women in elected county offices rose from 3 percent to 9 percent between 1975 and 1988; and, among municipal officials, from 4 percent to 14 percent between 1975 and 1985 (Table 1). As of January 1992, 145 cities with populations over 30,000 (about 16 percent of all such cities) had women mayors, according to the U.S. Conference of Mayors. In early 1992, women were also mayors of 19 of the 100 largest U.S. cities.

Significant progress notwithstanding, women occupy proportionately fewer positions throughout the hierarchy of electoral politics, and the rate of change has been quite slow. In numerical terms, at any rate, progress has been slowest at the federal level. A very high percentage of elections for the U.S. House and Senate involve incumbents, and incumbents have nearly always prevailed over challengers, regardless of gender. Competition is intense for nominations in races where there is reasonable chance for a newcomer to win—generally

TABLE 2

WOMEN IN STATE LEGISLATURES, 1971–1992

YEAR	TOTAL NUMBER OF WOMEN LEGISLATORS	WOMEN AS A PERCENTAGE OF ALL LEGISLATORS
1971	344	4.5
1973	424	5.6
1975	604	8.0
1977	688	9.1
1979	770	10.3
1981	908	12.1
1983	991	13.3
1985	1,103	14.8
1987	1,168	15.7
1989	1,270	17.0
1991	1,368	18.3
1992[1]	1,375	18.4

[1]The party breakdown for women serving in all state legislatures in 1992 is 826 Democrats (60 percent), 540 Republicans (39 percent), and 9 nonpartisans (1 percent).

SOURCE: © Center for the American Woman and Politics, Eagleton Institute of Politics, Rutgers University, 1993. Reprinted by permission of the Center for the American Woman and Politics.

this means one of the few open seats—and women simply do not acquire enough of these "good" nominations to swell the ranks of women on Capitol Hill. In 1992, of 100 U.S. senators, only two are women—no more than in 1960 (Table 3). Progress has been slightly better in the House, but, even there, women have only achieved 6 percent representation. While these numbers are discouraging for those interested in women and men sharing leadership, it is important to emphasize that in recent years the women entering the House and Senate are less likely than before to be widows inheriting their husbands' seats and more likely to be ambitious politicians pursuing office in their own right.

With so few women in Congress, the United States compares poorly with other countries, placing among the nations with the smallest proportions of women in national legislative bodies.[17] It should be said, however, that some modest headway is apparent in the rising numbers of women presenting themselves as candidates for Congress

TABLE 3

NUMBER OF WOMEN IN THE U.S. CONGRESS, 1917–1992

CONGRESS	DATES	WOMEN IN SENATE	WOMEN IN HOUSE	TOTAL WOMEN
65th	1917–19	0	1 (0D, 1R)	1 (0D, 1R)
66th	1919–21	0	0	0
67th	1921–23	1 (1D, 0R)	3 (0D, 3R)	4 (1D, 3R)
68th	1923–25	0	1 (0D, 1R)	1 (0D, 1R)
69th	1925–27	0	3 (1D, 2R)	3 (1D, 2R)
70th	1927–29	0	5 (2D, 3R)	5 (2D, 3R)
71st	1929–31	0	9 (5D, 4R)	9 (5D, 4R)
72nd	1931–33	1 (1D, 0R)	7 (5D, 2R)	8 (6D, 2R)
73rd	1933–35	1 (1D, 0R)	7 (4D, 3R)	8 (5D, 3R)
74th	1935–37	2 (2D, 0R)	6 (4D, 2R)	8 (6D, 2R)
75th	1937–39	3 (2D, 1R)	6 (5D, 1R)	9 (7D, 2R)
76th	1939–41	1 (1D, 0R)	8 (4D, 4R)	9 (5D, 4R)
77th	1941–43	1 (1D, 0R)	9 (4D, 5R)	10 (5D, 5R)
78th	1943–45	1 (1D, 0R)	8 (2D, 6R)	9 (3D, 6R)
79th	1945–47	0	11 (6D, 5R)	11 (6D, 5R)
80th	1947–49	1 (0D, 1R)	7 (3D, 4R)	8 (3D, 5R)
81st	1949–51	1 (0D, 1R)	9 (5D, 4R)	10 (5D, 5R)
82nd	1951–53	1 (0D, 1R)	10 (4D, 6R)	11 (4D, 7R)
83rd	1953–55	2 (0D, 2R)	12 (5D, 7R)[1]	14 (5D, 9R)[1]
84th	1955–57	1 (0D, 1R)	17 (10D, 7R)[1]	18 (10D, 8R)[1]
85th	1957–59	1 (0D, 1R)	15 (9D, 6R)	16 (9D, 7R)
86th	1959–61	2 (1D, 1R)	17 (9D, 8R)	19 (10D, 9R)
87th	1961–63	2 (1D, 1R)	18 (11D, 7R)	20 (12D, 8R)
88th	1963–65	2 (1D, 1R)	12 (6D, 6R)	14 (7D, 7R)
89th	1965–67	2 (1D, 1R)	11 (7D, 4R)	13 (8D, 5R)
90th	1967–69	1 (0D, 1R)	11 (6D, 5R)	12 (6D, 6R)
91st	1969–71	1 (0D, 1R)	10 (6D, 4R)	11 (6D, 5R)
92nd	1971–73	2 (1D, 1R)	13 (10D, 3R)	15 (11D, 4R)
93rd	1973–75	0	16 (14D, 2R)	16 (14D, 2R)
94th	1975–77	0	19 (14D, 5R)	19 (14D, 5R)
95th	1977–79	2 (2D, 0R)	18 (13D, 5R)	20 (15D, 5R)
96th	1979–81	1 (0D, 1R)	16 (11D, 5R)	17 (11D, 6R)
97th	1981–83	2 (0D, 2R)	21 (11D, 10R)	23 (11D, 12R)
98th	1983–85	2 (0D, 2R)	22 (13D, 9R)	24 (13D, 11R)
99th	1985–87	2 (0D, 2R)	23 (12D, 11R)	25 (12D, 13R)

TABLE 3

NUMBER OF WOMEN IN THE U.S. CONGRESS, 1917–1992, *continued*

CONGRESS	DATES	WOMEN IN SENATE	WOMEN IN HOUSE	TOTAL WOMEN
100th	1987–89	2 (1D, 1R)	23 (12D, 11R)	25 (13D, 12R)
101st	1989–91	2 (1D, 1R)	29 (16D, 13R)	31 (17D, 14R)
102nd	1991–93	2 (1D, 1R)	29 (20D, 9R)[2]	31 (21D, 10R)[2]

[1]Includes a nonvoting Republican delegate from prestatehood Hawaii.
[2]Includes a nonvoting Democratic delegate from Washington, D.C.

Note: Table shows maximum number of women elected or appointed to serve in that Congress at one time. Some filled out unexpired terms and some were never sworn in.

SOURCE: © Center for the American Woman and Politics, Eagleton Institute of Politics, Rutgers University, 1993. Reprinted by permission of the Center for the American Woman and Politics.

and getting major-party nominations (Table 4). Not only do women nominees for high office increase the visibility and plausibility of women as influential players in the political process, but the growing number of female nominees represents an expanding base of women entering politics and gaining experience at lower or less visible levels.

More time will be required to produce scores of victories by women with viable combinations of experience, ambition, readiness, political and financial support, and the luck of finding open seats or vulnerable incumbents at the right moment. In the meantime, as long as lists of female potential candidates lengthen and the numbers of actual female nominees continue to mount, the odds increase for making further significant gains at the ballot box, even for high-level offices.

By the early 1990s, then, the record shows enormous expansion in women's participation in a blink of the historical eye: women quadrupling their numbers in elective offices since the early 1970s; women moving to the center of the political stage. In 1972, Gloria Steinem's placing Sissy Farenthold's name in nomination for the vice presidency was understood to be a symbolic gesture. Only 12 years later, Geraldine Ferraro was the actual Democratic nominee for vice president.

On the other hand, there is still a very long road ahead if the goal is parity with men: In 1992, women still hold less than 20 percent of elected legislative or executive political positions at any level of the system (see Table 1).[18] Wherever one looks in electoral politics, one

TABLE 4

NUMBER OF MAJOR-PARTY FEMALE CANDIDATES FOR THE U.S.
CONGRESS, 1968–1990

YEAR	SENATE	HOUSE
1968	1 (1D, 0R)	19 (12D, 7R)
1970	1 (0D, 1R)	25 (15D, 10R)
1972	2 (0D, 2R)	32 (24D, 8R)
1974	3 (2D, 1R)	44 (30D, 14R)
1976	1 (1D, 0R)	54 (34D, 20R)
1978	2 (1D, 1R)	46 (27D, 19R)
1980	5 (2D, 3R)	52 (27D, 25R)
1982	3 (1D, 2R)	55 (27D, 28R)
1984	10 (6D, 4R)	65 (30D, 35R)
1986	6 (3D, 3R)	64 (30D, 34R)
1988	2 (0D, 2R)	59 (33D, 26R)
1990	8 (2D, 6R)	70 (40D, 30R)

SOURCE: Center for the American Woman and Politics, Eagleton Institute of Politics, Rutgers
University, 1990. Reprinted by permission of the Center for the American Woman and
Politics.

finds women advancing to leadership in a pattern perhaps most aptly labeled *incremental progress.*

PROFILE

As noted earlier in this chapter, many of the female candidates who came forward in the 1970s had experience in either the political system—generally working for male politicians—or in community projects and charitable causes, or both. The majority of these pioneer political women shared a number of demographic characteristics: They tended to be middle-aged, of middle-class socioeconomic status, relatively well educated, and with occupational experience in traditionally female fields. Elected women then, as now, were typically white, married, and the mothers of children over 12 years old.[19] Substantial proportions of women holding elective office in the 1980s were members of women's organizations; in proportions ranging from one-third of women local council members to over three-fourths of women state legislators, elected women belonged to at least one of the following national organizations: the American Association of University

Women, the Federation of Business and Professional Women's Clubs, the League of Women Voters, NOW, and NWPC. The higher her office, the more likely a woman official was to belong to such feminist groups as NOW and NWPC; for example, 58 percent of state senators and 46 percent of state representatives, but only 29 percent of county commissioners and 7 percent of local council members, were members of feminist groups in 1981.[20]

Black women constitute a very small proportion of America's elected officials,[21] yet they represent a distinctive, vanguard group of political women in several respects. Larger proportions of black elected women than of women officeholders overall acknowledge the important role played by various organizations (including civil-rights groups, church groups, community groups, and women's groups) in developing their political candidacies (Table 5). Indeed, elected black women are more likely than women officeholders overall to be members of women's organizations; moreover, they are substantially more likely to belong to feminist organizations. Black women more often than white women report that women's organizations encouraged them to run and supported their candidacies.

TABLE 5

THE ROLE OF WOMEN'S ORGANIZATIONS IN THE POLITICAL CAREERS OF BLACK WOMEN AND ALL WOMEN, 1981 (IN PERCENTAGES)

ROLE	STATE REPRESENTATIVES		COUNTY COMMISSIONERS		LOCAL COUNCIL MEMBERS	
	BLACK WOMEN	ALL WOMEN	BLACK WOMEN	ALL WOMEN	BLACK WOMEN	ALL WOMEN
Member of a major women's organization	84	77	63	58	47	37
Member of a feminist organization	68	46	47	29	30	7
Encouraged by a women's organization to run for office	59	27	32	24	18	15
Received campaign support from a women's organization	54	54	32	18	13	7

SOURCE: © Center for the American Woman and Politics, Eagleton Institute of Politics, Rutgers University, 1985. Reprinted by permission of the Center for the American Woman and Politics.

In the aggregate, women and men in elected office fit a similar demographic profile with respect to socioeconomic status, educational attainment, race, ethnicity, and median age. However, some differences by gender are apparent in background and experience. While the great majority of elected men and women are married and are parents, elected women are more likely than elected men to be widowed, separated, or divorced, and they are less likely to have young children at home. Furthermore, elected women are more likely than elected men to report that the age of their children was an important factor in their decision to run for office.[22] Among married officeholders, women are more likely than men to report strong spousal support for their political activities.[23] It seems to be more necessary for a successful woman politician to have her husband's encouragement for her political ambitions than it is for her male counterpart to have his wife's support.

Among elected officials at municipal, county, state, and federal levels overall, women are more likely than their male colleagues to have attended college, but less likely than men to hold law or other degrees.[24] A smaller proportion of elected women than elected men have paid jobs in addition to their elected offices. Not surprisingly, those women who are employed are concentrated in traditionally female occupations: the four most often cited by elected women in the early 1980s were secretarial/clerical, elementary/secondary teaching, nursing/health technical, and social work.[25]

Even though the growing number of women in politics is also more diverse than it used to be, elected women typically have more in common with each other than with elected men when it comes to political background. For example, among state legislators serving in 1981, women were less likely than their male counterparts to have had previous experience in elective office, but were more likely to have held appointed office. The women more often than the men had worked in someone else's political campaign before becoming candidates themselves (Table 6).

As to the routes they took to political office, women are more likely than their male colleagues to give an organization credit as an important factor in getting them to seek office. In addition to citing help and encouragement from women's organizations, political women often attribute inspiration or assistance with their political careers to female role models, mentors, and the campaigns of other female candidates for whom they worked.[26] There were notable differences, at least as of 1981, between female and male elected officials with respect to the organizations to which they belonged. Women

TABLE 6

PREVIOUS POLITICAL EXPERIENCE OF WOMEN AND MEN IN STATE
LEGISLATURES, 1981 (IN PERCENTAGES)

	STATE SENATORS		STATE REPRESENTATIVES	
EXPERIENCE	WOMEN	MEN	WOMEN	MEN
Held one or more previous elective offices	47	49	25	34
Held one or more appointive government positions	55	43	42	26
Worked in a campaign	84	72	82	74
Worked on the staff of an elected official	25	12	24	16

SOURCE: © Center for the American Woman and Politics, Eagleton Institute of Politics, Rutgers
University, 1984. Reprinted by permission of the Center for the American Woman and
Politics.

were less likely to belong to business groups and commercial associations. Few women elected officials belonged to veterans' organizations and none to fraternal organizations. Political women and men
have much in common, but a gender-segregated and stratified society
means that they have depended on different professional connections
and political bases of support.

SUPPORT SYSTEMS—A WOMEN'S POLITICAL COMMUNITY

The conviction among women candidates and women voters continues to be that considerations of the candidate's gender should come
after values, issues, and ideologies. Nonetheless, there also appears
to be a new sense of purpose about electing and appointing women
to positions of leadership, a growing belief that having women in
leadership positions is in itself important to other women.

Many women entering politics are connected to a women's political community that began to develop in the 1970s and continued to
grow during the 1980s. While still neither large nor wealthy, its very
existence and continued expansion are significant. In addition to the
encouragement and support political women receive from membership in various women's organizations, the efforts of independent, as
well as partisan, women's groups have produced recruitment and

training projects, contributions of money, technical assistance, and volunteer support for women's campaigns.[27]

Beginning in 1974, when the Women's Campaign Fund was founded in Washington, D.C., women have established political action committees (PACs) to raise and distribute campaign money for female candidates, and, in some cases, for male candidates who support a feminist agenda. As of the 1990 elections, there were 35 PACs or campaign funds that either gave money predominately to women candidates or have a predominately female donor base (not including state affiliates of national organizations or issue PACs). Among these were several affiliated with feminist organizations or women's professional associations, some affiliated with the major political parties, some independent, and some whose activities were limited to a particular state or locality. In 1990, a few of the women's PACs were able to raise and distribute over $100,000 each to various races. EMILY's List, a donor network that supports Democratic candidates, raised almost $1.5 million for women running in statewide and federal races in 1990. State and local groups distributed less, but the candidates they supported usually had smaller campaign budgets than those required for statewide or federal offices.[28] While not competitive with the combined size and wealth of older political networks on which male candidates have traditionally depended, the women's political community has made a difference for female candidates.

At all levels of government, female officeholders have also formed and joined a variety of organizations for elected and appointed women. By 1992, cross-jurisdictional statewide associations for elected women had been established in about a dozen states. The oldest of these associations is the California Elected Women's Association for Education and Research, formed in 1974. The Congresswomen's Caucus, established in 1977 for women only, became the Congressional Caucus for Women's Issues in 1981 and admitted congressmen to its membership, while retaining its primary goal of advocating a policy agenda of issues particularly important to women.[29] For high-level officeholders in the states, Women Executives in State Government was formed in 1985. Associations of women officials also formed within such existing national groups as the National Conference of State Legislatures (the Women's Network), the National Association of Counties (NACo) (Women Officials of NACo), the National Conference of Black Mayors (Black Women Mayors' Caucus), and the National League of Cities (Women in Municipal Government). Organizations of women officials are not large, and not all eligible women belong to them, but their very establishment is evidence of a felt need among women officials to convene for purposes of mutual support and advancement, and to promote public policy and political issues of special concern to them. The issues agendas for which they lobby are most likely to be about matters of rights, justice, and equity for women.

The various educational, funding, issue-advocacy, partisan, and professional networks of the women's political community have developed over only a few years. Modest in number and size, they nevertheless represent a recognition that women need other women in order to succeed in American politics.

OBSTACLES AND ADVANTAGES

The main assets a woman brings to politics are simultaneously some of her greatest liabilities. The fact that she has grown up and lived her life as a woman, played women's roles in her family and community, and functioned in women's networks means that she has some perspectives and is responsive to some constituencies less familiar to, and possibly neglected by, men. Difficulty arises because at the same time a woman feels a responsibility to represent those constituencies and perhaps champion new issues, she must also show that she is able to fit into the political system as it is presently structured. Although elected women may have a keen sense of being different from their male colleagues, most women believe they must prove themselves in the eyes of the men in power because it is men who still control politics and distribute the rewards that help to enhance women's influence and effectiveness.

In many ways, it is an advantage to be a newcomer. A newcomer can bring a fresh perspective to an old process, a new outlook to an ancient institution, and a set of concerns different from the familiar litany of policy issues. To some extent, this is what the public wants from political women: something different, an untainted approach, and new ideas for solving old problems. Unrealistic expectations about women's potential for bringing about ameliorative change may arise from stereotypes that have served in the past both to elevate and to limit women: the notion that women are more pure than men, more dutiful, less interested in self-promotion and personal gain, and more conscientious and hardworking. These are sometimes men's perceptions of women, but they have also been women's perceptions of themselves.

Often, the woman campaigning for office or the new official fresh from her swearing-in ceremony hears someone say, "The men have been in charge long enough, and they've made a fine mess of things.

Let's see what she can do!" Perhaps she can do better: She arrives in office with much of the energy, enthusiasm, and even idealism reserved for those who have not been jaded, worn down, or simply desensitized by years of routine frustrations.

Soon, however, the newcomer woman, alone or nearly so in a political institution, realizes how heavy is the weight of expectation with which she is saddled. As a newcomer, she must contend with inexperience, which can be a great liability in a tough, competitive political environment. As a newcomer woman in surroundings controlled by men, she feels isolated—even, sometimes, like a misfit.

As in any traditionally male-dominated line of work, high visibility is an aspect of newcomer status for women. It is at once an advantage for any ambitious person desiring to be noticed and a liability, in that one's mistakes are conspicuous. High visibility can make the newcomer an easy target for political attack. Being the first woman this or that virtually guarantees that when she does make a mistake, or even when her performance is merely unremarkable, the judgments made about her will be generalized to all women, one woman's ordinariness projected as all women's weakness. The pressure to perform perfectly is added to other burdens the new political woman shoulders above and beyond the duties of office.

Because women are such a small minority among elected officials, elected women are special. But this specialness is less often a blessing than a liability because it does not compensate for the disadvantages facing the outsider, who is perceived as lacking in knowledge and experience of the way things work, and thus perhaps not trusted; who is excluded—more by habit than by malice—when the inner circle gathers; who is treated as less serious, less potentially powerful, and less in need of being informed and consulted; who is ghettoized by stereotyped assumptions about what she knows, what she cares about, and how she will behave; and who is, in short, made less effective by her very specialness.

The political woman faces yet another mixed blessing not shared by her male colleagues. Especially if she is in Congress or other high-level office, a newly elected woman is likely to receive a flood of requests for her participation in programs and activities far beyond the legal boundaries of her constituency. She feels honored and needed because she is one among so few women on whom so many women call, but she is also overtaxed by the extra demands inherent in this special status.

Finally, conflicts between the demands of public life and private life—specifically, family life—still appear more likely to affect the political woman than the political man. This is particularly true in the case of women with young children, which may explain why so few elected women have children under age 12. The fact is that during the present period of societal transition, or perhaps for the indefinite future, a woman's obligations in the domestic sphere and her commitments to it (perhaps somewhat modified) usually continue when she enters public life. This situation makes for a double set of major responsibilities that often conflict with one another, resulting in strain and guilt. Whether she has a supportive husband, whether she has paid housekeeping help, and whether her children understand her ambitions, a woman whose life outside the home is a demanding political life is less likely than her male colleagues to see a week go by without a clash between her private and public worlds.

Individually or in combination, then, a number of factors—among them, inexperience and a history of powerlessness over institutions and resources created by and for men, the effect of stereotypes, the fact and effect of being in the minority, and the conflicts between public life and family roles and responsibilities—present a formidable force against which the new political woman contends.

Within the electoral system are at least three additional barriers: the power of incumbency, the high cost of political campaigns, and candidate recruitment patterns. As long as men hold the overwhelming majority of all elective offices—especially high-level offices—and remain in them, and as long as incumbency continues to confer such an overwhelming reelection advantage, women remain in the unenviable position of challengers and outsiders.[30]

Related to the power of incumbency is the power of money. As campaign costs continue to rise exponentially, no one can make a serious run for most political offices without spending enormous amounts of time fundraising. Incumbents, whether men or women, find the task easier because they begin with a base of support already in place and with the odds favoring their victory on election day. For newcomers with no established base, especially those who are challenging incumbents, raising money is an onerous burden.

Women are still less likely than men to be recruited as candidates by the political parties or elected officials, and are less likely, too, to be part of the business and community leadership networks that breed potential candidates and ease their way into the system. Not yet integrated into the inner circles of interlocking institutions and informal networks that serve as feeders for the electoral system, women still must consider independent methods and organizations for recruiting female candidates and supporting their campaigns. Unless a systematic grassroots effort is made to develop the women's political community further, and especially to enhance its ability to search out and recruit new candidates, women will most likely continue to enter elective office only in a trickle.

THE IMPACT OF WOMEN IN POLITICS

Do public politics, political processes, and government institutions change when women enter politics? Do women approach public leadership differently from men? Do they view issues differently? Do the agendas of political women differ from those of political men? How can differences best be measured? How do views about women as well as women's self-perceptions affect expectations and assessments of their impact? How are proportional representation and the notion of reaching a critical mass related to impact? These types of questions cannot be answered well until women fill many more leadership positions throughout the political system. Research from the Center for the American Woman and Politics (CAWP) and some informed observations offer food for thought and early evidence. Comprehensive answers await future inquiry after we see significant new progress in women's leadership status.

Early information about whether and how the post-1970s generation of political women is making its mark comes from surveys of female candidates and women and men holding office. In her study of women running for congressional, statewide, and state legislative offices in 1976, Susan Carroll found that "an overwhelming majority of women candidates, and of those elected, feel that they can do a better job of representing women's interests than their male counterparts."[31]

In surveying elected women and men at local, state, and federal levels in 1977 and again in 1981, CAWP found women's views to be more liberal and more feminist than men's on a number of public-policy issues.[32] (A feminist attitude here, as in CAWP's surveys, refers to a position on an issue taken by the women's rights movement and endorsed by national feminist organizations such as NOW and NWPC.) In the 1981 survey, officeholders were asked about their views on eight issues. A gender gap emerged on matters as diverse as whether the ERA should be ratified, whether the private sector could resolve our economic problems, and whether there should be a death penalty for murderers. Although the gap was smallest at the municipal level and largest at the state legislative level, women's attitudes differed from men's at all levels of office, within both political parties, and across the ideological spectrum. Republican women, for example, expressed more liberal and feminist views than Republican men, and women who called themselves conservative appeared to be somewhat more liberal about policy issues and more feminist about women's issues than men labeling themselves conservative. Differences were most pronounced in attitudes toward women's issues; for example, whether there should be a constitutional ban on abortion and whether the ERA should be ratified. Across all levels of office, black women were the most liberal.[33]

In the 15 states that did not ratify the ERA by the 1982 deadline, CAWP's survey of state legislators found a 40-point gender gap. Seventy-six percent of the women legislators in these states, compared to 36 percent of their male counterparts, agreed that the ERA should be ratified.

A 1988 CAWP survey of women and men serving in state legislatures provides evidence not only of a continuing gender gap in public-policy attitudes among elected officials but also of an identifiable difference between women's and men's actions as legislators.[34] Women legislators are having a distinctive impact by working to make the agendas of legislative institutions more responsive to women's demands for equal rights as articulated by the contemporary women's movement and more reflective of women's concerns stemming from their roles as caregivers in the family and in society more generally. For example, women legislators are more likely than their male colleagues to have legislative priorities that deal with health care, children's and family issues, or women's rights. Overall, the research shows that women are making a difference and that this difference is evident regardless of party, ideology, feminist identification, constituency ideology, seniority, age, or political insider status. The study also provided preliminary evidence that, in addition to reshaping the public-policy agenda, women officeholders are having an impact on the way that government operates. By bringing more citizens into the process, opting for government in public view rather than behind closed doors, and behaving more responsively to groups traditionally lacking access to the policy-making process, elected women are making their presence felt.[35]

Another piece of evidence suggesting that the new political woman brings something different to government and is having an impact on public policy emerges from agendas of the various caucuses and networks of women officials. At the federal level, the Congressional Caucus for Women's Issues has, since its founding, been concerned with the "rights, representation, and status of women." Over the years, this caucus has promoted such issues as the ERA, employment opportunities for women, women's health concerns, programs for displaced homemakers, assistance for women business owners, programs for victims of domestic violence, and dependent-care and parental-leave legislation.[36] Women in state legislatures have worked together across party lines on agendas of particular interest to them as women. Such alliances range from formal women's legislative caucuses to informal networks meeting on issues and legislation affecting the lives of women and children, including the ERA, child care, equity in pensions and insurance, rights of divorced women, pay equity, counseling services for displaced homemakers, rape law, marital law, and domestic violence.[37] A case in which women legislators worked together forcefully and successfully in West Virginia in 1987 resulted in getting the legislature to override the governor's veto of a bill providing medical-care assistance for poor pregnant women and poor children. The women lawmakers won this victory over powerful opposition by "first, threatening to filibuster both houses of the legislature throughout the remaining week of the session; second, getting a resolution passed through the House on a unanimous voice vote calling on the Senate to reconsider the bill; and third, staging a quickly called candlelight vigil outside the Capitol by various advocacy groups."[38]

Similar signs of a political women's consciousness can be seen in towns and counties with women elected officials—sometimes it is a county shelter for battered women, sometimes a park for children, or sometimes a local health-care program for elderly women living alone. In 1985, San Francisco, which had a woman mayor and several women supervisors, adopted an ordinance requiring developers building office space in central business areas to make provisions for on-site or nearby child care.

Elected and appointed women have also begun to make a difference by serving as role models for other women and, more directly, through their powers to hire and appoint. Because they are likely to belong to women's organizations and to have worked and socialized with other women, female officials know where to find qualified women to recommend for positions on boards and commissions, to hire for their own staffs, and to suggest to others with positions to fill in politics or government. Like men, women reach automatically into familiar networks for people with whom they share common experiences and can work comfortably. Moreover, political women in general make a point of hiring and promoting women. CAWP's 1981 national survey of officeholders found that large majorities of the women with staffs (state legislators, and federal and state appointees) actively recruited women to fill staff openings. A majority of women state legislators said that they specifically sought out women for staff positions.[39]

Women officials also take the time and trouble to encourage, educate, and advise other women about political life. They speak frequently to women's groups, counsel individual women, and lend their support to various efforts to bring other women into politics. CAWP's study concluded that political women "show evidence of a strong commitment when they take the time to educate women about political opportunities and to encourage women's political involvement. Contrary to the notion of the 'Queen Bee'—the woman who wants to keep all of the attention and power for herself to the exclusion of other women—the women in our studies and at our consultations welcome the chance to support other women."[40]

The pioneer elected women of the 1970s brought to office perspectives different from those of men. During the 1980s, one sometimes heard murmurs of disappointment from active feminist officeholders and constituency groups about some women more recently elected to office. Complaints included charges that these women are not feminists, not idealists committed to advancing women's issues and to social reform in general. Some recent entrants were described as being merely ambitious professional politicians, cautious game players toeing the line, careful about not alienating the men in power.

It is inevitable that, as more women enter politics, the characteristics of political women will become more diverse. Many differences between them and political men may disappear as women work their way into the mainstreams of party politics. Nevertheless, the evidence to date bears out claims that women make special contributions to the public world and suggests the potential for significant long-term impact if current trends continue. First, it appears that women in government will represent women's interests better than men have to date. They will do so collectively in caucuses and organizations, consciously as advocates of women's concerns, unconsciously as people with a shared history and set of life experiences. Second, women in politics will affect the political system by making it more open and responsive to larger sections of the citizenry and by bringing more women into positions in government and throughout public life. They will do so directly by hiring, promoting, and appointing women, and serving as mentors; indirectly by serving as role models and educators who encourage women's participation by example and admonition.

At a grander and more abstract level, questions about whether women will make fundamental differences in the public world must await a time when there are many more elected and appointed women establishing and implementing policy and expanding the public's image of an attorney general, an environmental commissioner, an insurance commissioner, a governor, a senator, a secretary of state, a secretary of defense, a chief justice, and a president. Only then will it be possible to provide a sound analysis of whether or how a full partnership of women and men in leadership might reshape policies and institutions, transform issue agendas, and change the nature and conduct of public business. Of course, there is great skepticism about idealistic projections for women's potential for transforming society. Nonetheless, some inspiring, energetic voices maintain that a vision of powerful change is not unrealistic. Their challenge and their question cannot be ignored: "If women do not become leaders in order to make a difference," they ask, "why bother?" In 1983, former Congresswoman Bella Abzug stated that position forcefully in a documentary film about women in politics:

> There's no point of women getting into politics or getting into public office if they are going to imitate and ape the white, male, upper-class power structure which has failed to recognize the needs of the majority of the people. We might just as soon let them do it. I don't want women to substitute themselves for what the male power structure has done. Women have another responsibility . . . which is enormous, and that is to find a way to change the nature of power so that it's more reflective of our pluralism and diversity.[41]

CONCLUSION

When Margaret Chase Smith was elected to the U.S. Senate in 1948, she won that seat in a social and political environment not encouraging to women with political ambitions. To some degree, she and the few other exceptional women in office before the 1970s may have been accepted precisely because they were anomalies—viewed as individual cases of unusual behavior, unthreatening because their untraditional behavior did not symbolize vast changes in the given order of the male-female hierarchy. By 1978, when Nancy Landon Kassebaum was elected to the Senate, it was assumed that she would not long remain the sole female senator elected to a full term. Indeed, while there would not be a swell in female Senate membership, before long a next woman and then another would inch in. Indeed, this has been the case—Paula Hawkins served from 1981 to 1987 and Barbara Mikulski was elected in 1986, both women entering the Senate in their own right.

Jeannette Rankin entered the House of Representatives in 1917 as the first congresswoman. Margaret Chase Smith's election to the Senate in 1948 made her the first and, for nearly 40 years (until Barbara

Mikulski's election), the only woman to have served in both houses of Congress. Because women had granted themselves permission to pursue political leadership and the social climate had changed by the time Margaret Chase Smith left the Senate in 1972—the same year Shirley Chisholm campaigned for the presidency—men and women were resettling the society in new proper places. The extraordinariness of Rankin, Smith, and a handful of others has given way to the more ordinary struggle of many political women to increase their leadership ranks. The singularity of a vice-presidential nomination, a governorship, a Supreme Court appointment, or a UN ambassadorship creates great excitement as it bursts forth; before long, however, it seems quite natural to have women in these powerful positions. Rather than facing resistance as examples of deviant behavior, women with power find relatively easy public acceptance. Long-held assumptions and certainties about women's lack of leadership abilities appear to diminish dramatically and almost instantaneously with the appearance of real women—Geraldine Ferraro, Ella Grasso, Sandra Day O'Connor, Jeane Kirkpatrick—in positions for which women had for centuries been considered unfit.

While the numbers of women and men in public office remain far from equal in the early 1990s, the possibilities for women's participation are far greater than ever before. For centuries, few had questioned the natural order of a world in which women were subordinate. Women's movement into politics represents a major difference in how society thinks about social roles and demonstrates that what is regarded as the natural order can change fundamentally. Even in 1960, it was virtually inconceivable for a young woman to imagine a career in political leadership. The odds still favor men, but, in 1992, young women can and do take it as their equally rightful possibility to run the world, and perhaps to change it for the common good.

MILESTONES FOR WOMEN IN POLITICS, 1971–1991*

1971 The NWPC is formed in July at a Washington, D.C., meeting of more than 300 feminists. Its aims are to increase women's access to political power in the major parties and to encourage and support

---

*Center for the American Woman and Politics (CAWP), Eagleton Institute of Politics, Rutgers University. Information in this chronology comes from a variety of news reports, printed materials, and documents collected in the CAWP library and available to the public through CAWP's fact sheets and monographs. A full time line of women's participation in American politics is in preparation and will be published by CAWP.

women committed to women's rights who seek elective and appointive office.

The CAWP is founded as part of the Eagleton Institute of Politics at Rutgers—the State University of New Jersey. For the first time, a university establishes a research and educational center to examine women's roles, status, and influence in politics and government.

Ann Armstrong of Texas is the first woman to cochair the Republican National Committee.

For the first time in the 150-year history of the U.S. Senate, girls are appointed as Senate pages.

1972 Congresswoman Shirley Chisholm of New York enters the presidential primaries and runs for the Democratic presidential nomination. She receives 151.95 delegate votes on the first ballot before Senator George McGovern is nominated at the national convention.

Frances ("Sissy") Farenthold, an attorney, former state legislator, and twice candidate for the Democratic gubernatorial nomination in Texas, receives over 400 votes to become runner-up in the balloting for the vice-presidential nomination at the Democratic National Convention.

A record number of female delegates (40 percent) participate in the Democratic National Convention. These women press the party to support representation of women at future national conventions in proportions consistent with their numbers in the population.

The WEDS project is started by the NWPC. Its purpose is to assist and train women in running for election as delegates to both major-party conventions.

Jean Westwood is named by presidential nominee George McGovern to chair the Democratic National Committee. The first woman to hold that position, she serves until just after the election, when she is replaced by Robert Strauss.

Yvonne Braithwaite Burke, a Democrat from California, is the first black woman to cochair a national party convention.

Ann Armstrong, at the Republican National Convention, is the first woman keynote speaker at the national convention of any major political party.

Women comprise 30 percent of delegates at the Republican National Convention, a large increase over the 1968 figure of 17 percent. Republican women win approval of Rule 32, which requests each state to "endeavor" to have equal representation of men and women in delegations at future conventions.

1973 Sissy Farenthold is elected the first chair of the NWPC at its first biennial convention.

The National Women's Education Fund (NWEF) is founded in Washington, D.C. A nonpartisan resource organization, it offers training programs in campaign techniques and provides technical assistance and public information to increase the numbers and influence of women in politics.

Yvonne Braithwaite Burke becomes the first member of Congress to take maternity leave.

1974 Mary Louise Smith of Iowa is elected chair of the Republican National Committee. Smith is the first woman not to share the chair with a man.

Ella Grasso, a former Democratic congresswoman, is elected governor of Connecticut, the first woman ever elected governor of any state in her own right. (Three women had served before her as surrogates for or successors to their husbands.) Reelected in 1978, Grasso had to step down in 1980 because of a terminal illness. Since Grasso, seven other women governors have been elected: Dixy Lee Ray (D-WA) in 1976; Martha Layne Collins (D-KY) in 1983; Madeleine Kunin (D-VT) in 1984, 1986, and 1988; Kay Orr (R-NE) in 1986; Joan Finney (D-KS), Ann Richards (D-TX), and Barbara Roberts (D-OR)—all elected in 1990.

The Women's Campaign Fund (WCF) is founded. It is the first national PAC established exclusively to fund women's campaigns. Its purpose is to elect "qualified progressive women of both parties" to national, state, and local offices. It provides both financial contributions and technical consultation to candidates.

1976 Lindy Boggs, a Democrat, is the first woman to chair a national presidential nominating convention of a major political party.

Barbara Jordan, a congresswoman from Texas, is the first woman and the first black person to keynote a Democratic National Convention.

1977 Patricia R. Harris, the first black female cabinet member, is appointed by President Jimmy Carter as secretary of the U.S. Department of Housing and Urban Development.

The Congresswomen's Caucus is established by women in the U.S. House of Representatives to support legislation affecting women and to monitor federal government programs that influence opportunities available to women. In 1981, it is renamed the Congressional Caucus for Women's Issues and admits congressmen to its membership.

The National Women's Conference is held in Houston, Texas. This is the first time American women have come together in a federally sponsored meeting with elected delegates from every state and territory to discuss and vote on a national plan of action for women. The presiding officer of the conference is Congresswoman Bella Abzug from New York.

1978 Nancy Landon Kassebaum, a Kansas Republican, is elected to the U.S. Senate. Prior to Kassebaum's election, all of the women who served in the Senate had succeeded their husbands in Congress or had first been appointed to fill unexpired terms.

Dianne Feinstein, a Democrat, becomes mayor of San Francisco, California, when Mayor George B. Moscone is killed by an assassin. She is elected mayor in her own right the following year.

1979 Jane M. Byrne, a Democrat, is elected mayor of Chicago. She is the first woman elected to lead one of the nation's three largest cities.

1980 For the first time, a national party's nominating convention delegates include equal numbers of men and women. At the convention in New York, the Democratic party added to its charter a requirement that future conventions also have equal numbers of female and male delegates.

1981 Sandra Day O'Connor, a former Republican state legislator from Arizona who had served on the state appeals court, is appointed by President Ronald Reagan as the first woman ever to sit on the U.S. Supreme Court.

Jeane J. Kirkpatrick, a professor of political science, becomes the first woman appointed as U.S. ambassador to the United Nations.

Kathy Whitmire, a Democrat, is elected as the first woman mayor of Houston, Texas.

1982 The Democratic National Committee establishes the Eleanor Roosevelt Fund to provide money to Democratic women running for office.

1983 The Campaign Fund for Republican Women is formed to provide Republican women candidates with financial support.

1984 Geraldine A. Ferraro, an attorney, three-term congresswoman from New York, and secretary of the House Democratic Caucus, becomes the first woman ever to run on a major party's national ticket when she is selected by Walter F. Mondale as his vice-presidential running mate.

Ten women receive major-party nominations for the U.S. Senate. While this is by far the largest number of female nominees ever to run for the Senate, nine are defeated in races where they challenge incumbents. The one who succeeds is Senator Nancy Landon Kassebaum of Kansas, an incumbent winning reelection.

Arlene Violet, a Republican, is elected attorney general of Rhode Island. She is the first woman elected to serve as a state's attorney general.

1986 Kay Orr of Nebraska is the first Republican woman elected governor of a state. Her opponent in the general election is Democrat Helen Boosalis, former mayor of Lincoln. This is the first time two women have run against each other as major-party gubernatorial candidates.

Barbara Mikulski, five-term congresswoman from Maryland, is the first Democratic woman elected to the U.S. Senate since 1960 and the first Democratic woman ever elected to the Senate without previously filling out a husband's unexpired term.

1987 The national media treat both Congresswoman Patricia Schroeder and former UN Ambassador Jeane Kirkpatrick as serious potential candidates for the nation's highest office. While each woman considers running for president, and Congresswoman Schroeder explores a candidacy through a summer of nationwide public appearances, neither woman chooses to pursue her party's nomination through the primaries.

Susan Estrich, a professor of law, becomes the first woman to serve as campaign manager for a major-party presidential candidate when Governor Michael Dukakis of Massachusetts appoints her in October 1987.

1989–91 In Congress, the number of women serving as senators and representatives fluctuates between 15 and 20 throughout the 1970s and holds at 23 to 25 during most of the 1980s. However, in the 101st Congress (1989–91) women gain an all-time high of 31 seats. Even with this number, women hold only 6 percent of the 535 Senate and House seats.

1990 Dr. Antonia C. Novello, a physician with a master's degree in public health, becomes the fourteenth Surgeon General of the United States. The first female and first Hispanic American to be appointed to the nation's chief health-care position, Dr. Novello is sworn in by Supreme Court Justice Sandra Day O'Connor.

1991 In her first 90 days in office, Ann Richards, newly elected governor of Texas, appoints more women and members of minority groups to gubernatorial boards and commissions than had any previous governors of Texas during their entire terms in office.

ACKNOWLEDGMENT

Special thanks go to Lucy Baruch for help with updating figures, for careful reading, and for unwavering support.

NOTES

1. S. Evans, *Personal Politics* (New York: Vintage, 1980); and J. Freeman, *The Politics of Women's Liberation* (New York: McKay, 1975).

2. Freeman, 1975; S. Baxter and M. Lansing, *Women and Politics: The Visible Majority* (Ann Arbor: University of Michigan Press, 1983); and E. Klein, *Gender Politics: From Consciousness to Mass Politics* (Cambridge, Mass.: Harvard University Press, 1984).

3. M. Gruberg, *Women in American Politics: An Assessment and Sourcebook* (Oshkosh, Wis.: Academia Press, 1968).

4. R. B. Mandel, *In the Running: The New Woman Candidate* (Boston: Beacon Press, 1983).

5. J. J. Kirkpatrick, *Political Woman* (New York: Basic Books, 1974).

6. N. E. McGlen and K. O'Connor, *Women's Rights: The Struggle for Equality in the 19th and 20th Centuries* (New York: Praeger, 1983).

7. G. Gallup, Jr., "Women in Politics" (Survey 239-G), *The Gallup Poll: Public Opinion 1984* (Wilmington, Del.: Scholarly Resources Inc., 1985).

8. M. Johnson and K. Stanwick, "Profile of Women Holding Office, 1975," in *Women in Public Office: A Biographical Directory and Statistical Analysis,* First Edition, compiled by the Center for the American Woman and Politics (New York: R. R. Bowker Company, 1976); and M. Johnson and S. J. Carroll, "Profile of Women Holding Office, 1977," in *Women in Public Office: A Biographical Directory and Statistical Analysis,* Second Edition, compiled by the Center for the American Woman and Politics (Metuchen, N.J.: The Scarecrow Press, 1978).

9. M. Ivins, "Woman in the News: Kathy Whitmire," *Working Woman* (March 1987), 124.

10. N. Lynn, "American Women and the Political Process," in *Women: A Feminist Perspective,* ed. J. Freeman (Palo Alto, Calif.: Mayfield, 1979).

11. S. Chisholm, *The Good Fight* (New York: Harper and Row, 1973).

12. Chisholm, 1973; and S. Tolchin and M. Tolchin, *Clout: Womanpower and Politics* (New York: Coward, McCann and Geoghegan, 1974).

13. "In her own right" became a common way of describing the achievement of a growing number of political women who have come into office directly as a result of their own personal aspirations, initiative, and political career paths. The phrase distinguishes these women from others, usually of an earlier generation, who arrived in office via "matrimonial connection," typically as widows, often only serving a short time to fill out the term of a deceased husband, although sometimes then running for the seat themselves and remaining in office for many terms. Until recently, the "widow's route" to office was common among women in Congress (Gertzog [1984] discusses this route to Congress). Moreover, the only three women who had served as state governors before Ella Grasso's election in 1974 had reached office via the matrimonial connection: Nellie Tayloe Ross, governor of Wyoming 1925–27, was elected to replace her deceased husband; both Miriam ("Ma") Ferguson, governor of Texas 1925–27 and again 1933–35, and Lurleen Wallace, governor of Alabama 1967–68, were elected as surrogates for husbands barred under state law from seeking reelection.

14. In broad outline and approach, the following profile of the new political woman (both numbers and demographics) is an adapted, expanded, and updated version of a similar discussion in Chapter 1 of Mandel, 1983.

15. Women's entry into politics since the early 1970s has taken place on a systemwide basis from local to national levels, in appointive as well as elective office, in political parties as well as in governmental positions, on campaign staffs and in political consulting firms, on lobbying and legislative staffs, in bureaucratic and administrative positions. Because elective office is the most visible part of the political system and most directly asks for a vote of approval from the general public, this profile of the new political woman is concentrated there. However, many of the observations and conclusions about trends and challenges faced by women seeking elective office apply generally to other areas of political life.

16. Gruberg, 1968.

17. R. L. Sivard, *Women . . . A World Survey* (Washington, D.C.: World Priorities, 1985); and United Nations, *The World's Women, 1970–1990* (New York: United Nations, 1991).

18. School boards are not included in this account of legislative and executive elective office.

19. Kirkpatrick, 1974; Johnson and Carroll, 1978; Mandel, 1983; S. J. Carroll and W. S. Strimling, *Women's Routes to Elective Office: A Comparison with Men's* (New Brunswick, N.J.: Center for the American Woman and Politics, Eagleton Institute of Politics, Rutgers University, 1983); and S. J.

Carroll, *Women as Candidates in American Politics* (Bloomington: Indiana University Press, 1985).

20. Carroll and Strimling, 1983.

21. In 1990, 964 black women were serving in elective offices as members of Congress, as state legislators, as county and municipal governing officials, and as mayors, according to figures compiled by the Joint Center for Political Studies (JCPS) in Washington, D.C. This number represents 21.9 percent of black elected officials and approximately 6 percent of women in these offices.

22. Carroll and Strimling, 1983.

23. Johnson and Carroll, 1978; and Carroll and Strimling, 1983.

24. Ibid.

25. Ibid.

26. Ibid.

27. Two 1980s efforts in Minnesota illustrate the type of activity that has taken place out of a commitment to increase the number of female candidates and to support political women. One project, Women Candidates Development Coalition, was established in 1986 to build a statewide, bipartisan women's network to identify and develop female candidates. Officers of the Coalition have gone from community to community to speak with women who lost their races in order to discover what would have helped them win, whether they plan to run again, and who else might be available for future candidacies. The second project, the Minnesota Women's Political Assembly, is a bipartisan coalition of various women's political groups (for example, the Minnesota Women's Political Caucus, the Minnesota Political Congress of Black Women, The Grand Old Party [GOP] Feminist Caucus of Minnesota, and the Democratic Farmer Labor Party [DFL] Feminist Caucus) which come together to promote and highlight women in politics through informal talent banks, education and information-sharing projects, and public relations efforts.

28. Center for the American Woman and Politics (New Brunswick, N.J.)—Series of Reports on *The Impact of Women in Public Office*: S. J. Carroll, D. L. Dodson, and R. B. Mandel, *The Impact of Women in Public Office: An Overview* (1991); D. L. Dodson and S. J. Carroll, *Reshaping the Agenda: Women in State Legislatures* (1991); and D. L. Dodson, ed., *Gender and Policymaking: Studies of Women in Office* (1991).

29. For a description of the history of the caucus, see I. N. Gertzog, *Congressional Women: Their Recruitment, Treatment, and Behavior* (New York: Praeger, 1984).

30. Mandel, 1983; and Carroll, 1985.

31. Carroll, 1985, 156.

32. Johnson and Carroll, 1978; and K. A. Stanwick and K. E. Kleeman, *Women Make a Difference* (New Brunswick, N.J.: Center for the American Woman and Politics, 1983).

33. Stanwick and Kleeman, 1983.

34. Results of this study, conducted under a grant from the Charles H. Revson Foundation, are reported in the CAWP series *The Impact of Women in Public Office* (see note 28). Included in the series are findings from a survey of a national sample of state legislators interviewed in the summer of 1988.

35. Carroll, Dodson, and Mandel, 1991.

36. Mandel, 1983; and Gertzog, 1984.

37. K. E. Kleeman and R. B. Mandel, "Women Officials: A Singular Bond," in *The Women's Economic Justice Agenda* (Washington, D.C.: The National Center for Policy Alternatives, 1987).

38. "Women Legislators Lead Stunning Revolt in WV," *National NOW Times* (May/June 1987), 4, 7.

39. Stanwick and Kleeman, 1983.

40. Ibid., 19.

41. *Not One of the Boys* (A documentary film about women in politics) (New Brunswick, N.J.: Center for the American Woman and Politics, 1984).

WOMEN OF A CERTAIN AGE

❖ ❖ ❖

Laura L. Carstensen and Monisha Pasupathi

> The whole meaning of our lives is in question. If we do not
> know what we are going to be, we cannot know what we are.
> Let us recognize ourselves in this old man or in that old
> woman. It must be done if we are to take upon ourselves the
> entirety of our human state.[1]

Medicare, social security, national health insurance, nursing-home
placement, and other pressing issues are receiving increasing attention
in the media. Rarely do we hear them framed as "women's issues."
On the contrary, age is treated as the great equalizer—men and
women, rich and poor, regardless of background, escape old age only
through premature death. It is true that both women and men suffer
the biological deterioration that advanced age brings, and both men
and women face ageist stereotypes and misconceptions. Both men
and women experience loss with age.

Aging, however, is not a process that occurs evenly for women
and men in the United States. In this chapter we will review briefly
some basic facts that distinguish older women from older men, illustrate the impact of these differences in everyday life, and suggest ways
people might modify the inevitability of deleterious outcomes and the
course of their own aging process.

THE FACTS

The fact that our elderly population is rapidly growing has become common knowledge. During the twentieth century, the proportion of elderly people in the population grew from 3 percent to 12 percent.[2] By the year 2040, 23 percent of the population will be over 65.[3] However, the fact that *most* of these people are women is largely ignored. At 65, women outnumber men by 100 to 83; by 85, women outnumber men by 100 to 39.[4] The over-85 age segment is the fastest growing segment of the population. Indeed, "the world of the very old is a world of women."[5]

These population statistics reflect the fact that women outlive men by about seven years. For reasons as yet unknown, the survivability of females is greater than males from conception on. The average life expectancy for white women in the United States is 79; for men it is 72. For most ethnic minorities in the United States, life expectancy is lower. For black women, the average life expectancy is 73 years; for black men it is 64 years. The difference of roughly seven years between men and women in longevity holds across ethnic groups.

In part because of the difference in longevity and in part because women traditionally marry older men, women are far more likely than men to be widowed in old age. In fact, even though 95 percent of Americans marry at some point during their lives, only 35 percent of women over 65 are married. After 85, only 21 percent of women are married. Moreover, when men *are* widowed, they are four times more likely to remarry than women who are widowed. For women, the average length of widowhood is 15 years; once widowed, women are at high risk for a number of age-related problems.

It is important to note that the jeopardy widowed women face is not the result of being without a man, but from widowhood itself. Women who have always been single fare much better than widows in late life; they are better off financially[6] and less likely to be depressed or lonely. Very little is known about older lesbians, but they are included in statistics about single women. Also included among single women are women who live in religious communities. Nuns enjoy a life expectancy six years longer than the average woman in the United States. Thus, it is not being *single* that puts women at risk; it is, as we will illustrate, the result of a complex system of structural inequities that exploit all women and especially married women.

Living alone is a risk factor for a number of negative outcomes in old age and widowed women are far more likely to live alone than other older people. Most men live out their lives living with a spouse in the community. Among elderly men, 76 percent of whites, 66 percent of Hispanics, and 63 percent of blacks live with a spouse. Among elderly women, these percentages are substantially lower— 41 percent of whites, 35 percent of Hispanics, and 27 percent of blacks live with a spouse.[7]

Twenty-five percent to 30 percent of older people will reside in nursing homes at some point in their lives.[8] These facilities are virtual worlds of women. Seventy-five percent of nursing-home residents are female.

Not surprisingly, older women are more likely than older men to be poor. Twenty-five percent of elderly white women are poor. Much higher poverty rates are found among minority women.

One more statistic—we hear a fair amount these days about caregivers of the elderly, what we don't hear is that the caregivers of the elderly are, for the most part, elderly women.

A CASE STUDY

What do these numbers really mean for the lives of elderly women? Consider the following scenario, a story that is more common than most of the us would like to admit.

Married since 1947, Helen and Paul—a white American, middle-class couple—are expecting to spend a relaxed and satisfying old age together. Paul retired from his engineering job a year ago with a good pension. Helen had worked on and off over the years in a day-care center. Because she worked only part time at a relatively low-paying job, she has not accrued any retirement benefits, but she does qualify for social security. Between Paul's pension and the couple's social-security benefits, they feel relatively secure and optimistic about their future. Their two sons, Michael and Robert, are both married and live out of state with children of their own. Both sons have jobs they like. Neither makes a lot of money, but they manage to make ends meet. Helen and Paul see their grandchildren once or twice a year and enjoy frequent telephone contact with them.

About one year after Paul retires, he begins to behave peculiarly. Always an active person, he now seems anxious in conversations with old friends and spends more and more time alone. One day Helen finds a note in Paul's pocket that gives directions from their house to the market only six blocks away. When she asks him what the instructions are for, he gets angry and accuses her of invading his privacy. During the next two months she finds him to be increasingly forgetful.

Occasionally, he acknowledges problems in performing familiar tasks, but usually he claims that it is "just old age."

One day, the doorbell rings. The local police bring Paul home. They tell Helen that they found Paul wandering in a park and that, while he could tell them his name, he could not remember his address. After looking up the address at the police station, the officers brought Paul home. They suggest to Helen that she take him to a physician for a thorough medical evaluation.

Helen calls Dr. Frierson, their longtime physician, and makes an appointment. After a lengthy workup, he informs Helen that Paul appears to be in the early stages of Alzheimer's disease, a chronic debilitating disease that ultimately ends in death. Helen is devastated, but is determined to do the best she can to make sure that Paul lives out his life as comfortably as possible.

Paul gets worse and worse. He has difficulty with basic grooming and bathing. She can dress him, but cannot bathe him without assistance. Paul is a large man and Helen cannot physically lift him. She hires help to come in three times a week to help Paul shower, but the aides quit regularly and Helen is forced to hire new people and sometimes go without assistance. Besides, she is quickly spending their savings to pay aides. As time passes, Paul loses the ability to tell night from day. He gets up many times throughout the night and wakes Helen. During the day, he naps frequently, but Helen cannot do the same. It is unusual for Helen to sleep more than three hours a night. She feels that she cannot afford to hire someone to stay in the evenings. She becomes increasingly depressed and physically exhausted.

Helen rarely sees her friends. She cannot bring Paul out with her because he becomes agitated in unfamiliar places. Her friends feel for her, but are uncomfortable coming to the house. It's hard for them to see Paul and, in some ways, Helen prefers that they stay away. Michael and Robert call regularly. They are obviously concerned for her so she tries to minimize the gravity of the situation. Susan, her daughter-in-law, tries especially hard to help. She even stops working full-time so that she can visit once a month and alleviate some of the burden, but she has young children so she cannot stay more than a day or two.

When Paul becomes incontinent, Helen realizes that she can no longer manage him at home. She looks at several nursing homes. Some are horrible—understaffed and overcrowded. Eventually, she finds a nice place where the staff are kind, the food is good, and Paul can have a room with a view of the park. They had saved about $200,000 toward their retirement so Helen feels that she can afford a decent place for him. The cost of the nursing home is $40,000 a year.

Helen assumes that her insurance will pay some of the nursing-home costs, but is told that less than 5 percent is covered. She decides that she has no choice, however, and admits Paul to the facility.

Helen visits every day even though Paul no longer recognizes her. She cannot stay away. She loves Paul very much and this is the only way left for her to show her love. Medicare pays for 80 percent of Paul's medical treatment, but virtually nothing toward the nursing-home expenses. She inquires about Medicaid, but is told that she has too much money to qualify for assistance. Rather, she must spend down their savings to $60,000 before Paul can qualify. Just a few years later, they qualify for Medicaid assistance. Seven years later, Paul dies.

Shortly after Paul's death Helen learns that Paul's pension pays only minimal survivor benefits. Helen, now 77 years old and alone, is living on far less income than she had anticipated. Her car engine fails one day. She decides to sell the car rather than pay the cost of repair. Then, one morning she slips on the sidewalk, breaks a hip, and is hospitalized. Her physician is pleased with her recovery progress and releases her after three weeks, but her cost of medical care, even with Medicare insurance, totals $40,000. Without savings to supplement her income, she can no longer make ends meet.

She considers asking her sons for financial assistance, but decides that the house is too big for her, anyway, and, after all, they have expenses of their own. She decides that if she sells the house, she can live more cheaply and perhaps leave some money for her grandchildren, as Paul had so hoped to do. She is surprised to see how high the rent is in her neighborhood. Eventually someone tells her about a housing unit, called the Rainbow House, in the center of the city and takes an apartment there.

In some ways, life is better now. Her financial concerns are somewhat alleviated and she is proud that she is not a burden on her children. She does not let them visit because she doesn't want them to see her apartment. It might concern them to see the neighborhood and she doesn't want to worry them. With her old furniture, her apartment is fairly comfortable, but the neighborhood is quite dangerous. Her friends from the old neighborhood telephone occasionally, but they do not visit. She leaves the building only when necessary. Unfortunately, Helen feels that she has nothing in common with the other tenants.

Helen's long-standing cardiac arrhythmia worsens. Normally, she would see her physician, but she can't get to Dr. Frierson without an expensive taxicab ride and she puts off finding a new physician in the neighborhood. Her diet is poor and, without exercise, her arthritis worsens.

One day, a worker from Adult Protective Services is called. A neighbor had reported that several newspapers had piled up outside Helen's door. The worker finds Helen weak and disoriented. She urges her to move into a state-funded nursing home nearby. When Michael and Robert find out how sick Helen is they want to help, but neither can afford to do very much. Michael visits once, but it breaks his heart to see his mother in the condition she is in and he never returns. Five years later, at the age of 85, Helen dies.

THE ISSUES

Sound extreme? Probably the worst thing you can do is to think that this cannot happen to you. A major part of the problem is that, in our society, older women and their problems are invisible. We are just beginning to fully realize the problems older people face. Only rarely do we hear that these issues are especially relevant to women. Instead, we hear in the media that older people wield more power than any other age group, are draining the social-security system, and hold positions of power. True, the U.S. government is a gerontocracy, but it is extremely important to realize that the power age affords is not evenly distributed across gender, class, or ethnicity.

Even aspects of aging that on the surface affect men and women equally, do not. For example, the incidence of Alzheimer's disease is equal for men and women, but since the chances increase with age, and women live longer, more women develop it. Moreover, because husbands are typically older than wives, elderly women are far more likely to care for a spouse who has dementia.

As our case study illustrates, caregiving takes its toll in many ways, affecting both physical and mental health. A large amount of literature documents the considerable physical and mental strain of caregiving.[9] Luck and fate may have some impact on who gets ill in old age, but they do not determine who becomes a caregiver. The vast majority of unpaid caregivers are women.[10] Wives care for their husbands; elderly daughters care for elderly mothers. The path of responsibility does not just flow directly down through bloodlines and generations. In families where there are only sons, daughters-in-law provide care. When daughters-in-law are not available, the burden is likely to fall on a granddaughter or a niece. Only rarely are caregiving responsibilities assumed by sons.[11]

Interestingly, when husbands do become caregivers, their experience is different from that of wives. For one, when husbands provide caregiving, they often receive help from other relatives and friends or hire professional help.[12] When women provide caregiving, they are reluctant to seek *any* help. Instead, they often try to protect other loved ones from the burden that they bear.[13] Subsequently, caregiving is typically more stressful for women than men.[14] The extent of the stress is evidenced in the fact that 50 percent of caregivers become clinically depressed.[15]

The cornerstone of the U.S. Department of Health and Human Services social policy is that caregiving falls in the private domain and is supported by the government *only as a last resort*.[16] Despite the fact that home-based care is relatively cheap, Congress imposes major restrictions on this funding, which forces families—in most cases, women—to provide an abundance of unpaid labor in order to provide home care. It is their only alternative to institutionalization of loved ones.[17]

In our story, Helen's daughter-in-law, Susan, helped her the most, compromising her career to do so. As noted above, this is common and occurs for a variety of reasons at different points in the life cycle. Young women often make career concessions by working part time or taking years off to care for children. Later in life, women often retire early to care for ailing spouses, parents, or siblings. Social security penalizes women for these work patterns. Because social-security benefits are based on income, working part time or taking years off reduces social-security entitlements.

The insidiousness of the disadvantages for women is apparent in two ways. First, since wives usually make less than husbands, they are the logical candidates for career compromises. Second, those compromises reduce the likelihood that they will accrue private pension benefits to supplement their already lower social security. Subsequently, elderly women are far more likely than elderly men to rely exclusively on minimal social security benefits. Elderly women receive approximately 24 percent less than elderly men in social-security benefits *and* have less private supplemental income.[18]

You can see the beginning of this process in our story when Susan begins working part time to help Helen. In the unwritten epilogue, Susan reaches old age having only worked part time. Subsequently, under current regulations, she will be entitled to lower social-security benefits. Moreover, as a widow, she will not have a private pension and will very likely live at poverty level. Sadly, even young women today, who work for most of their lives, will receive comparable retirement benefits to their mothers who were never employed.[19]

With Paul's illness, Helen's financial difficulties worsened considerably. A couple's entire life savings can be quickly exhausted providing medical intervention for a spouse, leaving a widow destitute. When Medicaid is required to pay for health care, as is the case in the vast majority of nursing-home placements, assets must be spent down before eligibility requirements are met.[20] Again, because of the shorter life span and accompanying morbidity of men, women are more likely to be left destitute after the death of their husbands. Interestingly, widowed women are worse off financially than single and divorced women.[21]

Many women come to old age poor, but others, like Helen, become poor for the first time in their lives in old age. A cogent argument can be made that public policy surrounding old age is inherently discriminatory because it fails to take into account the cumulative economic disadvantages women bring to old age. The poverty of old age is especially intractable due to very limited opportunities to generate more income.[22]

Among minorities, poverty is far more widespread than among whites. Over *half* of black and Hispanic elderly females not living with their families are living at or below poverty level.[23] These alarming statistics are not simply an artifact of past eras. It is estimated that 25 percent of young women today will live at or near the poverty level in old age.

Living alone increases the likelihood of institutionalization because no one is available to assist in daily care. Poverty drastically limits the available options for nursing homes or board-and-care facilities. Again, women are more likely than men to experience the consequences. In people 85 and over, one in four women lives in a nursing home, whereas only one in seven men lives in a nursing home.[24] The quality of nursing homes ranges from excellent to very poor and, not surprisingly, high quality care inevitably requires money. Here again we are confronted with the cumulative discrepancies between men and women in financial security garnered across the life span.

Less obvious are the combined ramifications of poverty and widowhood. For example, the health of low-income patients with heart disease is more likely to worsen[25] and, if they live alone, they are almost twice as likely to suffer another heart attack.[26] Once again, women are more likely to experience both risk factors.

Double jeopardy refers to being old and female; *triple jeopardy* refers

to being a member of a minority group, as well. The terms are problematic because they imply that the problems are additive when, in
fact, the problems older black women face are qualitatively different
from those older white women face.[27] But they are fitting in suggesting
that problems are greater for minority elderly. Reading the case study
in this chapter, you may have felt that we were presenting the worst-
case scenario. Not so. We provided you with a case study about people
who had come to old age privileged in many ways. Helen and Paul
were white and middle-class. They planned for their retirement, saved
thousands of dollars, and enjoyed excellent health care. To many
Americans, these are luxuries.

Virtually every risk factor we have discussed is greater for minority elderly. For example, non-Hispanic blacks and Puerto Ricans
are the least likely groups to have private health insurance.[28] Sixty-
four percent of black women living alone live below the poverty level.[29]
Elderly blacks are twice as likely as elderly whites to report fair or less
than fair health.[30]

In addition to problems that result from a lifetime of disadvantage, elderly minorities are more likely to face the disadvantages of
more current social crises. In the midst of a drug epidemic, which is
hitting the inner-city particularly hard, black grandmothers have become the most likely caregivers for grandchildren whose parents have
become addicted to drugs.[31] Native American grandparents are also
increasingly likely to assume primary caretaking roles for grandchildren, for reasons ranging from the desire to preserve native culture
to the drug dependency of parents.[32]

The picture we have painted is, indeed, pessimistic. If there is a
positive element to this at all it is that, despite the problems, older
women are doing quite well psychologically. For some reason, they
are less likely to be depressed[33] or lonely[34] than their younger counterparts. Instead, reading the literature on aging invokes the adage
"what doesn't kill you makes you stronger." Older women appear to
have impressive resilience despite the uneven odds.

The labeling of older women as a *special* or *needy* population is
ironic. Older women, by and large, face the cumulative disadvantages
of life-long discrimination and, *in spite of that*, cope reasonably well.
The problem is not a needy population; rather, the problem stems
from massive structural inequities. Government policy does not adequately address the concerns of minorities, women, or elderly people.
Those inadequacies in policy translate into cumulative disadvantages
that are dramatically evident in old age.

In theory, the inequities can be changed. The first step is to recognize the problem. Subsequent steps fall in two domains: personal planning and political restructuring. We offer the following suggestions: At the individual level, women must plan for their futures. Find out about health-insurance policies, survivor benefits, and retirement income. Plan for an old age without a spouse. Most women do not think about widowhood until they are nearing old age even though only a small minority of married women live out their lives with their spouses. Carefully think through alternative living arrangements. The second domain involves public policy. Write letters to state and local representatives. Insist on a national health-insurance plan. Affordable health care is possible if it is made a national priority. Medicaid laws can be changed to reduce the inherent discrimination toward women. We can reduce the likelihood of problems if we become informed about the future.

We need to act. Older women, who have a lifetime of experience on which to draw, may be our best spokespersons. We'll leave you with a last word from Maggie Kuhn, founder of the Gray Panthers:

> What can we do? Those of us who have survived to this advanced age? We can think and speak, we can remember. We can give advice, and make judgments. We can dial the phone, write letters and read. We may not be able to butter our bread, but we can still change the world.[35]

ACKNOWLEDGMENTS

Preparation of this chapter was facilitated by grants AG07476 and AG08816 from the National Institute on Aging. Many thanks go to Edwin L. Carstensen, Marty Lynch, Julio Garcia, Diana Pierce, Chantal Piot-Ziegler, Lillian Rabinowitz, and Susan Turk for their critical and constructive comments on an earlier draft of this chapter. Correspondence concerning this chapter should be directed to Laura L. Carstensen, Ph.D., Department of Psychology, Bldg. 420, Jordan Hall, Stanford University, Stanford, CA 94305.

Notes

1. S. de Beauvoir, *The Coming of Aging* (New York: Putnam, 1972), 12.

2. National Center for Health Statistics, *Vital and Health Statistics: Current Estimates from the National Health Interview Survey, 1990* (DHHS Publication No. PHS 92–1509) (Washington, D.C.: U.S. Government Printing Office, 1991).

3. Special Committee on Aging, United States Senate, *Aging America: Trends and Projections* (Serial No. 101–E) (Washington, D.C.: U.S. Government Printing Office, 1989).

4. Ibid.

5. G. Hagestad, "The Family: Women and Grandparents as Kinkeepers," in *Our Aging Society: Paradox and Promise*, ed. A. Pifer and L. Bronte (New York: W. W. Norton, 1986), 147.

6. Special Committee on Aging, 1989.

7. Ibid.

8. C. Lesnoff-Caravaglia, "The Five Percent Fallacy," *International Journal of Aging and Human Development* 2 (1978–79): 187–192.

9. D. E. Biegel, E. Sales, and R. Schulz, *Family Caregiving in Chronic Illness* (Newbury Park, Calif.: Sage Publications, 1991); L. George and L. P. Gwyther, "Caregiver Well-being: A Multidimensional Examination of Family Caregivers of Demented Adults," *The Gerontologist* 26 (1986): 253–259; and D. Gallagher, J. Rose, P. Rivera, S. Lovett, and L. Thompson, "Prevalence of Depression in Family Caregivers," *The Gerontologist* 29 (1989): 449–456.

10. S. E. England, S. M. Keigher, B. Miller, and N. Linsk, "Community Care Policies and Gender Justice," in *Critical Perspectives on Aging: The Political and Moral Economy of Growing Old*, ed. M. Minkler and C. Estes (Amityville, N.Y.: Baywood Publishing, 1991), 227–244.

11. A. Horowitz, "Sons and Daughters as Caregivers to Older Parents: Differences in Role Performance and Consequences," *The Gerontologist* 25 (1985): 612–617.

12. S. H. Zarit, N. K. Orr, and J. M. Zarit, *The Hidden Victims of Alzheimer's Disease: Families Under Stress* (New York: New York University Press, 1982).

13. Ibid.

14. A. S. Barusch and W. M. Spaid, "Gender Differences in Caregiving: Why Do Wives Support Greater Burden?" *The Gerontologist* 29 (1989): 667–675.

15. Gallagher et al., 1989.

16. England et al., 1991.

17. Ibid.

18. T. Arendell and C. Estes, "Older Women in the Post-Reagan Era," in *Critical Perspectives on Aging: The Political and Moral Economy of Growing Old*, ed. Minkler and Estes, 209–226.

19. Older Women's League, "Heading for Hardship: Retirement Income for American Women in the Next Century," *Mothers' Day Report*, 1991.

20. Spend-down rules have changed a great deal over the last few years. As of 1992, states vary considerably in the level of assets individuals are allowed to keep before they are eligible for Medicaid assistance.

21. Special Committee on Aging, 1989.

22. G. J. Duncan, *Years of Poverty, Years of Plenty: The Changing Economic Fortunes of American Workers and Families* (Ann Arbor: Institute for Social Research, University of Michigan, 1984).

23. Special Committee on Aging, 1989.

24. American Association of Homes for the Aging, "Fact Sheet: Nursing Homes" (Washington, D.C.: 1991).

25. R. B. Williams, J. C. Barefoot, R. M. Califf, T. L. Haney, W. B. Saunders, D. B. Pryor, M. A. Hlatky, I. C. Siegler, and D. B. Mark, "Prognostic Importance of Social and Economic Resources Among Medically Treated Patients with Angiographically Documented Coronary Artery Disease," *New England Journal of Medicine* 267(4) (1992): 520–524.

26. R. B. Case, A. J. Moss, N. Case, M. McDermott, and S. Eberly, "Living Alone After Myocardial Infarction: Impact on Prognosis," *New England Journal of Medicine* 267(4) (January 22/29, 1992): 515–519.

27. P. L. Dressel, "Gender, Race and Class: Beyond the Feminization of Poverty in Later Life," in *Critical Perspectives on Aging: The Political and Moral Economy of Growing Old*, ed. M. Minkler and C. Estes (Amityville, N.Y.: Baywood Publishing, 1991).

28. National Center for Health Statistics, *Health United States 1990* (DHHS Publication No. PHS 91–1232) (Washington, D.C.: U.S. Government Printing Office, 1991).

29. Special Committee on Aging, 1989.

30. U.S. Department of Health and Human Services, 1990.

31. M. Minkler, "Forgotten Caregivers: Grandparents Raising Infants and Young Children in the Crack Cocaine Epidemic," *Symposium Presented at the 44th Annual Scientific Meeting of the GSA*, San Francisco (1991).

32. J. Weibel-Orlando, "Grandparenting Styles: Native American Perspectives," in *The Cultural Context of Aging: Worldwide Perspectives*, ed. J. Sokolovsky (New York: Bergin & Garvey Publishers, 1991), 109–125.

33. D. Blazer, "Depression in Late Life: An Update," in *Annual Review of Geriatrics and Gerontology*, ed. M. P. Lawton (New York: Springer, 1989), 197–215.

34. T. A. Revenson, "Social and Demographic Correlates of Loneliness in Late Life," *American Journal of Community Psychology* 12 (1984): 338–342.

35. M. Kuhn, *No Stone Unturned: The Life and Times of Maggie Kuhn* (New York: Ballantine, 1991), 212–213.

SOMETHING OLD, SOMETHING NEW: WOMEN'S POVERTY IN THE 1990s

Diana M. Pearce

Mary came from a fairly typical middle-class family in which her father worked as a mid-level executive and her mother stayed at home for almost all of her growing-up years. She finished high school and went straight to college, leaving home and living in the dormitories. After graduation, she went to Washington, D.C., and worked for the federal government for several years before getting married to an older man, a Ph.D. agricultural researcher. She left paid employment with the birth of her first child and did not return until after her third child was born, and then only part time (in a job deliberately structured for wives reentering the workforce, but which was dead end). Taking a job was necessitated by her husband's increasingly unstable employment. His intermittent employment coupled with his refusal to share child care or other housework led to escalating tensions and resulted, within a few years, in their separation and divorce. Although she was able to keep the house because it had been bought with her own money (from a settlement from a bad accident in which she had sustained permanent injuries), she sometimes had to borrow money from friends and relatives to buy heating oil or even groceries. Her efforts to obtain child support from her ex-husband were met with threats of violence, as well as threats to sue her for support (since she was working and he was not). Her children began to get into trouble in school and the family social worker urged her to quit work and go on welfare. Instead, she left her part-time job and, using her premarriage experience, moved into a regular career-track government job; she eventually sought and obtained a transfer out of the area, in part to escape the continued threats from her ex-husband.

This story describes how many women come to experience poverty. It also happens to be, with a few minor details changed, my sister's story. It could, of course, be your story—or your sister's, daughter's, mother's, or friend's. It is typical, but not universal: It does not describe the experience of elderly women (although she may yet experience elderly poverty); the stigmatizing experience of going on welfare, even if briefly; or the experience of being a poor woman in a community in which many families experience lifelong poverty.

It is not typical in several ways. First, Mary had three children; two-thirds of poor women maintaining families alone have only one or two children.[1] Three or more is fairly unusual, despite newspaper features suggesting otherwise (a misleading source of information on the poor that I call *Sunday Supplement Sociology*). Second, she owned a house, and it was in her name. Three out of four women householders rent and pay an average of almost 60 percent of their income for housing.[2] Third, she had a college education. Only about half of women in poverty have finished high school, and less than one-sixth have had any college at all.[3]

However, in five very important ways, she was typical. First, she got married. Most women, in fact about 95 percent of women, get married at some time before they are 65.[4] Second, she had children—again, over 90 percent of women who marry have children.[5] Getting divorced is not as common, but since about 50 percent of marriages end in divorce, she is hardly atypical, either. Fourth, she was in her early thirties when she experienced poverty, which puts her in the largest group of poor mothers maintaining families alone. Over 40 percent of such mothers are 25 to 34 years old, and only 20 percent are less than 25 years old.[6] Finally, although most women who become single parents probably experience poverty-level incomes at some point, as with Mary, most do *not* go on welfare. According to one study, only one-fifth of women who become single parents go on welfare within two years of becoming a single parent;[7] even among unmarried teen mothers, who experience poverty rates of 80 percent and higher, only 30 percent go on welfare within three years of the birth of their child.[8]

What is striking about Mary's story and those of so many others like her is that she did what most women do and, moreover, she did it in the right order. She finished her schooling before entering the work force and she got married before having children—but she still ended up experiencing poverty. Even the ways in which she was atypical balanced each other out; that is, while she had three children, she also had a college education and several years of premarriage and prechildren work experience.

It would, of course, be much easier to understand if the typical Mary story involved dropping out of high school, early and multiple childbearing, lack of marriage, long-term welfare dependency, and little or no labor-force participation. It would further simplify understanding if she were a member of a disadvantaged racial or ethnic group, such as African American, Hispanic, or Native American. Because all of these characteristics are, in fact, highly correlated with poverty, it would be easy to assume that the high and persistent levels of poverty experienced by women are the result of their having made different choices from nonpoor women, perhaps influenced by a culture or underclass milieu in which they reside, and leave it at that. Such a description is not typical of poor women and thus we are left with a much more difficult task in understanding women's poverty. We have to ask why my sister was poor. We cannot ascribe her poverty, or indeed most of women's poverty, to different values, behaviors, and choices; for most poor women, like Mary, have made many of the same choices that nonpoor women make. Instead, we must look beyond individual characteristics and locate the complexities of women's poverty within the context of what is happening in the American economy and specifically within its job structure; within the structural inequalities experienced by women; and, for women of color, within the historical and contemporaneous experience of persistent poverty and racially or ethnically based inequality.

DEMOGRAPHIC CHANGES AND WOMEN'S POVERTY

Determining the cause(s) of women's poverty is halfway to determining the cure(s); equally important, however, is determining which factors can be influenced by public policy and which cannot. This distinction was the key to the effectiveness of reforms that were instigated under the Social Security Act of 1935,[9] our first major antipoverty legislation. Undergirding many of the programs was the then-radical recognition of some new facts of life, brought home by the Depression: Some unemployment is not due to individual actions or bad character and, in fact, is inevitable. For the elderly, there was an equally important recognition of the right to support after and as a reward for years of working, and a much less clearly articulated recognition of the need for the elderly not to be dependent on their adult children.

Both recognitions were the result of a somewhat belated understanding of the consequences of a shift to an urban industrialized and capitalist society. That is, it was finally accepted that industrial capitalism produced unemployment, especially during economic downturns; it also failed to provide for those too old, disabled, or sick to work. To deny these facts simply meant a lot of hardship and poverty for the unemployed, elderly, and disabled.

Today, the fact of life gradually being recognized and accepted is that single-parent families are a common family form. About one out of five families with children is maintained by a woman alone.[10] The combination of a 50 percent divorce rate and the fact that one out of four children is born out of wedlock means that living in a single-parent family has become extremely common.[11] One demographer estimates that 50 percent of white children and 90 percent of black children will experience living in a single-parent family at some time during their growing-up years.[12]

Assuming that the large numbers of families maintained by a single mother is a new phenomenon, there has been enormous effort expended to find the causes for this change, usually labeled pejoratively as the breakdown in the family, the demise of the intact family, the explosion of broken families, and so on. In spite of numerous efforts, however, researchers have been unable to attribute this widespread phenomenon to such public policies as levels of welfare benefits or ease of getting welfare, or type of divorce law.[13]

On the other hand, women's employment outside the home, women's education, the less stigmatizing label attached to single parenthood, male unemployment, and decreased tolerance of domestic violence and male dominance are all factors that have contributed to the increase in single-parent households. There are undoubtedly other factors as well, but, as in the 1930s, we are faced with a model that involves everything and everybody; that is, all of the forces and characteristics of modern life in an advanced industrialized and urbanized society are the same ones that make it possible for couples to divorce and for mothers and children to survive economically as single-parent families, though often in or near poverty.

There are some who would turn the clock back in terms of law, sex roles, and women's employment—in essence, returning to the nineteenth century when women (except lower-class and immigrant women) had few opportunities for employment outside the home and there was virtually no welfare to support single-parent families. Even then, women became single mothers either because they were widowed or, less commonly, because they left men who were abusive, alcoholic, or not supporting the family; but, because they could not work to support their families and because there was no child care and virtually no public welfare, they often lost their children and thus did not become independent single-parent families. (Even if they did work outside the home, they still often lost their children because they were neglecting them (some even "boarded" their children at orphanages and worked as domestics).[14]

To recognize that single-parent families in modern society are inevitable should not be taken as an implicit endorsement of this family form without reservations. Other things being equal, both economically and emotionally two adults are probably better than one for raising children. However, few would disagree that "other things" are often anything but "equal"; certainly violence, physical and sexual abuse, and constant tension, arguments, and rancor are better lived without if the choice is between such things and single parenthood—even if the latter means poverty.

To be agnostic on the question of single parenthood is not to be neutral on the question of impoverishment of single-parent families. That is, while we can do very little to decrease the numbers of single-parent families (and most of that is at the individual level, not at the public-policy level), we can do a lot about how poor they are. We know that single parenthood and poverty are not inevitably linked. Two types of comparisons, one with other (poor) groups in the United States historically and the other with single parents in other countries today, make this clear.

Take, for example, two groups that once experienced disproportionately high levels of poverty in the United States: the unemployed and the elderly. Once we decided to do something about unemployment, we created a system, unemployment insurance, that has largely worked (particularly pre-1980) to keep many unemployed workers out of poverty, at least until their benefits are exhausted. Likewise, we created a series of programs—social security, Medicare, and elderly housing—that have dramatically reduced poverty among the elderly (although least effectively for elderly widows).

It is possible, of course, that the poverty of single-parent families is more intractable than that of other groups. Yet, compared to European countries, one of the most striking facts about American society today is how much poorer single-parent families are in the United States and how much we are concentrating poverty among women-maintained families. In European countries, mainly through income-support programs—both means-tested (like our welfare system, but less stigmatized) and universal (such as child allowances that go to *all* children)—the poverty rates of children in single-parent families are reduced to rates that range from 2 percent to 16 percent, compared to 54 percent in the United States.[15] Contrary to the alarms raised by some conservatives, these policies have not increased the prevalence of single parents; indeed, none of these societies has nearly as high a rate of single parenthood as has the United States.[16]

Before we turn to solutions, it is necessary to untangle some of the complexities of women's poverty. Basically, women's poverty revolves around two factors that are distinct for women: their disadvantaged position in the labor force and the burden—economic as well as emotional—of children. Each of these, in turn, is embedded in two larger phenomena: economic trends and women's inequality generally. Let us now consider each of these factors.

THE DISTINCTIVE CHARACTER OF WOMEN'S POVERTY: WOMEN'S LABOR MARKET DISADVANTAGE

While employment is often touted as an all-encompassing key that will unlock women's poverty, the dismal labor-market picture for women suggests that jobs are as much a part of the problem as they are the solution. Three key aspects of this situation deserve attention: occupational sex segregation, women's lower wages, and the disproportionate numbers of women in part-time, temporary, and dead-end jobs.

OCCUPATIONAL SEX SEGREGATION

Although the concentration of women in a few occupations has decreased slowly in recent years, it is still very high and much higher than that of men. About 30 percent (compared to 40 percent a decade ago) of women are in the ten most common occupations for women: bookkeeper/accounting clerk, waitress, nurse, nursing aide/orderly, child-care worker, cashier, elementary school teacher, secretary, retail salesworker, and health technologist (e.g., dental hygienist).[17] All but two of these are nonprofessional and all are poorly paid relative to comparable male-dominated professions requiring similar levels of education, skill, and responsibility.[18]

At the other end of the scale, there is even less positive news regarding women in nontraditional occupations, that is, occupations in which fewer than 25 percent of the workers are women. While women have made substantial inroads in a few professions, such as law and medicine, there has been little change in others, such as engineering and some hard sciences, and losses in some of the craft occupations, such as carpentry, in which the percentage of women has dropped over the 1980s from 1.7 to 1.3. (Even newer occupations, such as airplane mechanic, have gone from 3.8 percent to 2.8 percent female through the 1980s.)[19] Altogether, the proportion of women who are in nontraditional occupations has remained virtually un-changed over the last decade at about 9 percent of women workers.[20]

LOWER WAGES

Two-thirds of minimum-wage workers are women. Overall, women who are employed full-time, year-round earn 71 cents for each dollar earned by men; the figure for black women workers (compared to all men) is 62 cents, and for Hispanic women workers, is 57 cents.[21] While this is an overall improvement from the 59 cents women earned a decade ago, it is much less of an improvement than it first appears when compared to the wage ratio in 1955, which was 64 cents.[22] The variations reflect not only what is happening to women's wages but what is happening to men's wages as well; in fact, most of the im-provement in the wage ratios between men and women workers over the last decade is the result of declining men's wages—due largely to sectoral shifts—rather than to increased wages for women.[23]

PART-TIME, TEMPORARY, OR DEAD-END JOBS

To talk about the wage gap is only half the story for women, literally, for only about half of women work full-time *and* year-round; women workers account for almost two-thirds of part-time workers.[24] Whether by choice or not—and the economic consequences are the same—women who hold jobs that are part time and part year find not only that their earnings are lower, but also that their hourly wages are less and they are likely to have no fringe benefits, including paid holidays, sick leave, and health insurance. Overall, their working conditions are worse and their job security virtually nonexistent.[25] Often by design, their hours and wages are inadequate and their job tenure too short to qualify for unemployment insurance when their job ends, which it frequently does in a relatively short amount of time.

These three characteristics—occupational segregation; lower wages; and part-time, temporary, or dead-end jobs—are the structural inequalities experienced by women in the labor market. It is against these and interacting with them that general economic trends are acting. Since most of these have been discussed elsewhere, they will be only briefly sketched here. Some of the most striking trends through the 1980s include the following:

- There has been a sectoral shift from primary manufacturing and heavy industry to a service-sector economy, including information processing as well as more traditional services.

- There has been an increase in low-wage employment, that is, wages paying less than what would be necessary for someone working full-time to support a family of three above the poverty line. This trend has been termed the *Great U-Turn*.[26]

- Unemployment compensation, created as part of the Depression-era New Deal to prevent unemployed workers from falling into poverty, has been drastically cut: At the height of the current recession (1991–1992), only about 40 percent of unemployed workers are receiving unemployment compensation benefits, compared to about 60 percent at the height of the 1975 recession.[27] During much of the mid- to late-1980s, only about one-third of unemployed workers received benefits.

- There has been an increase in income inequality. For decades, one could summarize American economic inequality with the *5 and 20 rule:* The bottom 20 percent received about 5 percent of aggregate income, while the top 5 percent received about 20 percent; actually, in 1947, the bottom 20 percent of families had 5.0 percent of the income, but the top 5 percent had only 17.2 percent of the income. In 1970, the bottom fifth had increased their share to 5.5 percent of aggregate income, while the share of the top 5 percent had gone down to 14.4 percent, reflecting a gradual reduction in income inequality during the post-war years. That trend reversed itself dramatically in the 1980s and, by the end of the decade, the bottom 20 percent was receiving just 4.6 percent of the income, a loss of almost one-sixth of its share, while the top 5 percent increased its share by about one-fourth, to 17.9 percent of aggregate income.[28]

- Women workers have steadily increased their participation in the labor force, from 34.5 percent of women in paid employment in 1960 to 61.5 percent in 1990.[29] It is expected that by the year 2000, half of all workers will be female.

Putting together these trends with the structural inequality experienced by women workers, created by occupational segregation and wage discrimination, one gets a clear picture of women's labor-market disadvantage. As new workers, women entering or reentering the work force in recent years have disproportionately taken the new jobs: 60 percent of the jobs taken by the increased number of women entering the labor force during the 1975–1985 decade, were low-wage jobs (i.e., paying at or below the poverty wage for a three-person family and assuming full-time, year-round work; that is roughly about $6.00 per hour in today's terms).[30]

Besides being low wage, many of these jobs are seasonal or temporary and do not last long enough (or pay enough) to make the worker eligible for unemployment insurance when the job ends. The average low-wage job, as defined earlier, lasts 1.75 years.[31] Of the women who maintained households alone, worked part of the year, and experienced unemployment part of the year, almost three times as many received welfare as received unemployment compensation during their period of unemployment (30 percent vs. 11 percent).[32] The receipt of unemployment insurance has dropped dramatically for this group of women over the last decade, from 14 percent to 11 percent, almost a one-third drop.

Given the low wages and part-time and part-year nature of employment for women workers, especially women householders, it is not surprising that poverty rates are not much reduced by going into paid employment. The families of one out of three women who are maintaining households alone are poor; if she is employed, the poverty rate drops to about 22 percent; among black women, employment drops the poverty rate from 48 percent to 32 percent, and among Hispanic women householders, the drop is from 48 percent to 28 percent. Only if she manages to hold a job full-time and for the whole year is her poverty rate reduced substantially, to 7 percent (11 percent for black women householders, and 14 percent for Hispanic women householders). By contrast, the poverty rate for married-couple households in which the husband works is only 4.2 percent (and 2.3 percent if he worked full-time, year-round).[33] Even when the householder is not employed, *the poverty rate for married-couple households in which the husband did not work at all is less than the poverty rate for black and Hispanic women-maintained households in which the householder worked full-time year-round.*[34]

THE DISTINCTIVE CHARACTER OF WOMEN'S POVERTY: CHILDREN

Having the economic responsibility for children greatly increases the likelihood of poverty, particularly for women. Of women-maintained families with children (less than 18 years old), 44.5 percent are poor;

56.1 percent of black and 58.2 percent of Hispanic women-maintained families with children are poor. If it is a family without children (e.g., two adult sisters living together), the poverty rate is less than 10 percent.[35] Again, the contrast with married-couple households with children is striking: only 7.8 percent are poor (14.3 percent of black and 20.8 percent of Hispanic married-couple families with children are poor). Moreover, the disparity between women-maintained families with children and all other families has increased; in 1970, the poverty rate for women-maintained families with children was 3.4 times the rate of all other families; today it is more than 5 times as great.

For at least one reason, poverty associated with the economic burden of children should be decreasing. In general, women are having fewer children, and average family size has steadily decreased over the last few decades, from 2.33 children in 1970 to 1.85 children per family in 1990. Likewise, poor women's families have also decreased in size: The average number of children in a woman-maintained family in 1970 was 2.90; in 1992, it is 2.15. Moreover, the proportion of families with four or more children is quite small: Only 15 percent of poor families have four or more children. Indeed, poor married-couple families tend to have more children than poor women-maintained families, averaging 2.47 children per family.

Given that the number of children is clearly not the issue, we must turn to the cost of children. There are two sides to this issue: how much the cost of children is borne by the single mother versus by others (the absent father, the state, etc.) and the actual costs of raising a child—for such things as food, shelter, and health care.

Other sources of funds to cover the cost of children are minimal and have not even kept up with inflation. Child support is only paid to 37 percent of children with absent fathers and, when they do pay, the average annual payment per family, not per child, was only $2,995 in 1989.[36] This was an increase over the average annual payment in 1981 of $2,106, but, when we adjust for inflation, it was actually only a slight increase of 4 percent. Women in poverty, of course, receive even less child support. Only about one-fourth receive child support, averaging $1,889 per family in 1989; although this amounts to over one-third of the income of families receiving child support, it does not lift very many out of poverty. Of 3.2 million single-parent families with an absent father, only 140,000 would be lifted out of poverty if all of child support due was paid.[37]

Women who turn to public assistance find that that too has

declined, in real terms, over the 1980s. In the average state, the total of welfare benefits plus the cash value of food stamps only reaches to three-fourths of the poverty level. Over the last decade, the value of those benefits has declined by about 20 percent, and, over the last three decades, the decline has been such that in real terms, welfare benefits are less, in the average state, than they were in 1960.

There are two possible reasons why poverty rates are so high, in spite of the decreasing numbers of children: (1) The children are younger, and (2) housing costs have risen. Younger children have always meant higher poverty rates; thus, the poverty rate for single mothers with children under six years of age was 59.4 percent in 1990, substantially the same as in 1970 (the earliest date for which we have such figures).[38] In addition, because of the high cost of child care, averaging $3,000 per year for the average preschool child, many women cannot earn enough to pay for child care as well as the rent and other essentials. In essence, she must earn an extra $1.50 per hour, more if she is not working full-time, just to pay for the child care. Therefore, many single mothers of very young children are not employed or work only part-time. On the other hand, because no allowance is made for child care, many employed single mothers are not considered poor, even though, once they have paid child care, they have less than a poverty-level income.

Housing costs have increased dramatically in the last decade in absolute terms, much faster than wages or other income sources available to women and their families. This has had three repercussions: First, because single mothers' income has increased very little, the proportion of income that goes to housing has risen from an average of 38 percent to 58 percent.[39] Second, doubling up has increased, particularly among poor women-maintained families, with about one out of four women-maintained families sharing their housing with another family; over half of these families are poor (unpublished 1990 Census Bureau data analyzed by the author).

Finally, some women-maintained families simply cannot pay the rent, or even half of it, and become homeless. One-third to 40 percent of the homeless are homeless families with children, most of which are single-mother families, and it is likely that there are many more not counted (living in abandoned cars, tents, garages, battered women's shelters, etc.). Thus, about one million persons (depending upon your estimate of total numbers of homeless) in women-maintained families experience homelessness each year. Because poverty counts are based on household surveys and do not include those living in shelters, in institutions, or on the streets, many of these women and their children are not counted among the poor.

SUMMARY AND CONCLUSIONS

Of course, the two sets of factors that make women's poverty distinctive—the economic burden of children and women's disadvantaged labor-market status—are only analytically separable. When a woman's wages are inadequate, she cannot pay rent on housing that is large enough for her and her child(ren). When child and other income support is lacking, women are forced into jobs, but the cost and availability of child care often limit her occupational choices and work hours. Moreover, our public policies reinforce the very inequalities that lead to poverty and this is especially true for single parents. There are almost no programs or policies that provide after-school care, for example. This makes it difficult for women to take full-time, better-paying jobs. Welfare programs, in addition to stigmatizing the recipients, offer little access to training or education beyond basic literacy; furthermore, they hurry women into employment, no matter how low the wages or how poor the future prospects, thus continuing the cycle of poverty.

Most painful of all, single mothers are asked to make difficult and unfair choices: work to support the family (be a good worker), but at a job without benefits, thus forgoing health care even when one needs it; or, stay at home to take care of the children, some of whom may be sick, disabled, or traumatized by abuse (be a good parent), and risk societal condemnation for being lazy. Pay the rent (but leave the kids on their own), pay the child care (and hope to postpone eviction), or eat at soup kitchens (and hope the kids do not get too hungry during the day, especially on nonschool days). Often something has to give.

Two areas of public policy will be critical in the 1990s and essentially will determine whether the feminization of poverty is reversed or continues to grow. The first area has to do with paid employment. Many jobs, particularly entry-level jobs in expanding sectors, such as service and information processing, have disappeared during the 1980s. Public policy may simply let that continue and worsen or it can begin to limit employers' ability to structure jobs that not only exploit workers but also make it extremely difficult for them to be both good workers and good parents.

There are four ways that public policy can restructure employment to help alleviate women's poverty. The first, and simplest, is to raise and index the minimum wage. For almost two decades, a full-time, year-round job at the minimum wage would provide enough support for a family of three at the poverty level; now, minimum-wage work will barely support a two-person family at the poverty level.

The second area of public-policy concern should be the limited occupational choices facing women. While there have been many programs developed to facilitate women's entry into nontraditional occupations, few have achieved meaningful numbers and many have simply disappeared. Particularly for noncollege-bound women, there has been little change and, without greater desegregation of occupations, achieving increased earnings and pay equity in more traditional occupations will continue to be difficult.

Third, public policy must reverse the trend toward part-time, part-year, or temporary jobs, which has become the employment ghetto of the 1990s for women workers. This means that benefits received by full-time employees should be extended to part-time employees, such as health insurance, sick leave, and so on. It also means that employers should be restricted from creating jobs with deliberately high turnover, the costs of which are borne almost entirely by workers. Such practices have seriously eroded unemployment insurance, which was originally intended to protect workers against unemployment that was not their fault, but that of business downturns, obsolescence, or capricious employers. Roughly two-thirds of today's workers, when they lose their jobs, do not have this cushion against unemployment.

Finally, it is time for employers to create family-friendly and woman-accepting work environments. Policies that provide child-care support, family and medical leave, unemployment insurance for women who become unemployed as a result of sexual harassment, and simply the flexibility to allow workers to deal with day-to-day crises of being parents (e.g., not being fired for talking to one's child on the telephone) are critical.

The second area of critical concern for women in the 1990s is housing. As women maintaining households alone are forced to spend increasing proportions of income securing housing, their ability to respond to other needs, especially emergency medical care, becomes quite tenuous. For example, what starts as an earache in a young child can easily snowball: If paying for emergency health care precludes making the rent, homelessness can result or, alternatively, if the cost of rent precludes health care, and the ear infection leads to deafness, long-term problems of disability will occur. Thus, when there is little or no margin—that is, too little is left after paying the rent—almost anything can become problematic. As mentioned earlier, increasing numbers of families are reacting to increased housing costs by doubling up, leading to another set of problems and issues: overcrowding, abuse and violence, as well as increased homelessness (due to the unstable nature of doubling-up arrangements).

As with all issues, the structural and interrelated nature of women's poverty affects housing as well; the affordability of housing for women can be increased by either increasing housing subsidies or by raising incomes, mainly through earnings, of women-maintained families. Because of the presence of children, many women with housing problems are reluctant to come forward (for fear they will lose their children to foster care because the housing they have is inadequate, overcrowded, unheated, or nonexistent).[40] Unfortunately, there has been little policy attention directed toward developing alternative models of housing ownership (such as cooperatives or limited equity cooperatives) to control housing costs. Likewise, community-enhanced models of housing, which integrate child care and job training (particularly in nontraditional occupations), would begin to address not only women's poverty but also women's structural inequalities.

Note that some issues are missing from this list, long as it is. For example, nothing has been said about child support, welfare-benefit levels, or such universal programs as child allowances to tax credits (such as the Earned Income Tax Credit [EITC], which reduces taxes for employed low-income families with children). There are three reasons for these omissions. First, they are all now, and are likely to continue to be, insignificant and limited as a means of moving poor women out of poverty. As a society, we are simply not willing to give enough or, in the case of child support, compel absent fathers to give enough, to move more than a very small number of poor women across the poverty line, and then not by much. Even discussions of a refundable child tax credit or expanded tax exemptions would not amount to a substantial hedge against poverty, and some even exclude poor families who receive welfare.

Second, most poverty policy discussions, to the extent that they acknowledge gender at all, end up prescribing income-support programs for women-maintained families (although usually substantially increased, but see the earlier discussion for the political realism of that), and jobs or employment programs for men and their families. Thus, this omission is intended to *gender integrate* the discussion of employment solutions to poverty, so that, in fact, women may benefit from them. Of course, employment solutions (including the training and education programs that lead to jobs) are not only more likely to lead out of poverty but also are more likely to lead to permanent exits from poverty. Income-support programs and tax provisions, on the other hand, are not only historically much less in amount, they are subject to frequent rounds of cutbacks, as we have recently seen. For example, in 1991, 40 states froze or cut back welfare or other income-support programs for the poor (such as general assistance and housing subsidies).[41]

Finally, these programs were omitted from the discussion in this chapter because they are based on a faulty premise; that is, that income supports for these families go to women who are doing nothing. If income-support programs, including tax credits, child support, and welfare, were instead viewed as providing the basics needed and deserved for children and their parents to live decent, healthy lives, then they would be worth supporting. In the latter case, there would be two effects: First, the income supports would be adequate in amount; for example, in the range of what we give foster parents to raise children. Second, they would not be taxed away; that is, mothers could enter employment and not lose by doing so (as of 1992, a dollar of welfare benefits is deducted for each dollar of earnings).

Putting together both the necessary items on the agenda, employment and housing, and the omitted ones, it is clear that addressing women's poverty is about addressing the structural inequalities faced by women, the changing employment and housing picture that developed in the 1980s (and is continuing in the 1990s), and, for women of color, the racism that perpetuates poverty for all people of color.

Many of the issues discussed here are quantitatively worse for black and Hispanic women; where data were available, these differences, or the lack of them, have been noted. This should not be taken to mean that poverty, labor-market disadvantage, or the economic aspects of children (child care, housing, etc.) are simply additive for women of color. Clearly, the historic high rates and the more recent growth of unemployment experienced particularly by black men (and women of color as well) due to racism and racial discrimination give the high rates of poverty and its persistence a different character than that experienced by many white women. At the same time, though difficult and maybe impossible to untangle, gender, as well as race, clearly contributes to the poverty experienced by women of color, and neither issue should be neglected in addressing poverty experienced by these women.

Neither the feminization of poverty nor women's poverty is inevitable. A first step is to reorder our thinking. Just as we switched a half-century ago from talking about *the unemployed* to talking about *unemployment*, and thereby restructured our policies, today we must turn from talking about *the poor* to talking about *poverty*. The second, and crucial step, is to recognize that poverty is gendered, as well as racialized, with different causes and cures when it is experienced by women compared to men and by different racial and ethnic groups. Our task is not about finding out how poor women are different or how *they* need to be changed, but to recognize the universal and embedded nature of women's poverty in the gender, racial, and class inequalities that characterize American society today.

NOTES

1. U.S. Bureau of the Census, "Current Population Reports" (Series P-60, No. 168), *Money Income and Poverty Status in the United States: 1989* (Advance data from the March 1990 Current Population Survey) (Washington, D.C.: U.S. Government Printing Office, 1990).

2. Low Income Housing Information Service, 1989.

3. U.S. Bureau of the Census, 1990.

4. S. M. Bianchi and D. Spain, *American Women in Transition* (New York: Russell Sage Foundation, 1986), 12.

5. Ibid., 66.

6. U.S. Bureau of the Census, "Current Population Reports" (Series P-60, No. 175), *Poverty in the United States: 1990* (Washington, D.C.: U.S. Government Printing Office, 1991).

7. N. Mudrick, "The Use of AFDC by Previously High-and-Low-Income Households," *Social Service Review* 52 (1978): 111.

8. Committee on Ways and Means, U.S. House of Representatives, *Overview of Entitlement Programs, 1991 Green Book: Background Material and Data on Programs within the Jurisdiction of the Committee on Ways and Means* (Washington, D.C.: U.S. Government Printing Office, 1990).

9. "The Social Security Act: The First Twenty Years," *Social Security Bulletin* (August 1955): 1–10.

10. U.S. Bureau of the Census, *Poverty*, 1991.

11. This may not actually be as much a change as we think. Because of poor public health and high industrial-accident rates, the rate of marriage dissolution was about as high a century ago as today (A. J. Cherlin, *Marriage, Divorce, Remarriage* [Cambridge, Mass.: Harvard University Press, 1981]). The difference was that a century ago it was due to death,

rather than divorce. Also, recent research has shown that many single parents moved in with their parents, creating a three-generation family and hiding the true rate of single parenthood (L. Gordon and S. McLanahan, "Single Parenthood in 1900" [DP #919–90] [Madison: Institute for Research on Poverty, University of Wisconsin–Madison, 1990]).

12. L. Bumpass, "Children and Marital Disruption: A Replication and Update," *Demography* 21 (February 1984): 71–82.

13. I. Garfinkel and S. McLanahan, *Single Mothers and Their Children: A New American Dilemma* (Washington, D.C.: The Urban Institute Press, 1986).

14. Gordon and McLanahan, 1990.

15. T. M. Smeeding, "Cross National Perspectives on Income Security Programs," for "The War on Poverty: What Worked?" Testimony for the Congress of the United States, Joint Economic Committee, September 25, 1991: 4 and Table 3.

16. G. S. Goldberg and E. Kremen, *The Feminization of Poverty: Only in America?* (New York: Praeger, 1990). Although single parenthood rates in other Western countries probably are a function of the complexity of factors that have been discussed here for the United States (see text) and thus little influenced by public policy, if single-parenthood rates *were* influenced by public policy, particularly the generosity of income support, the evidence suggests that the relationship is the opposite of that posited by conservatives. That is, societies with the most generous income-support programs and lowest impoverishment rates of single parents have the *lowest* levels of single parenthood.

17. Bureau of Labor Statistics, *Employment and Earnings* (Washington, D.C.: Bureau of Labor Statistics, January 1991).

18. Julianne Malveaux finds similar overall distributions of black women in occupational categories, but concentrations of black women within very specific occupations, often ones with lower overall earnings; see J. Malveaux, "Similarities and Differences in the Economic Interests of Black and White Women," *Review of Black Political Economy* 14(1) (Summer 1985); and discussion in J. Malveaux, "Gender Differences and Beyond: An Economic Perspective on Diversity and Commonality Among Women," in *Theoretical Perspectives on Gender Differences,* ed. D. Rhode (New Haven, Conn.: Yale University Press, 1990).

19. U.S. Department of Labor, Bureau of Labor Statistics, *Employment and Earnings* (January 1983); and Bureau of Labor Statistics, 1991.

20. Ibid.

21. U.S. Bureau of the Census, "Current Population Reports" (Series P-60,

No. 174), *Money Income of Households, Families and Persons in the United States: 1991* (Washington, D.C.: U.S. Government Printing Office, 1991).

22. National Committee on Pay Equity, Briefing Paper #1, "The Wage Gap" (Washington, D.C., 1989).

23. U.S. Bureau of the Census, *Money Income*, 1991; National Committee on Pay Equity, 1989.

24. U.S. Bureau of the Census, *Money Income*, 1991; National Committee on Pay Equity, 1989; 55 percent of black, 51 percent of Hispanic, and 50 percent of white women workers are employed full-time year-round.

25. J. Smith, "The Paradox of Women's Poverty: Wage-Earning Women and Economic Transformation," Special Issue: Women and Poverty, *Signs* 10 (1984): 291–310.

26. B. Harrison and B. Bluestone, *The Great U-Turn* (New York: Basic Books, 1988), 5.

27. Center for Budget and Policy Priorities, *Unemployment Insurance* (Washington, D.C.: Center for Budget and Policy Priorities, 1991).

28. U.S. Bureau of the Census, "Current Population Reports" (Series P-60, No. 80), *Income in 1970 of Families and Persons in the United States* (Washington, D.C.: U.S. Government Printing Office, 1971); and U.S. Bureau of the Census, 1990.

29. Census figures quoted in J. Matthaei, *An Economic History of Women in America: Women's Work, the Sexual Division of Labor, and the Development of Capitalism* (New York: Schocken Books, 1982); and U.S. Bureau of the Census, *Money Income*, 1991. Although historically black women have participated in the paid labor force at a higher rate than other groups, the low labor-force participation rate of black single mothers has reversed this trend: in 1990, 62 percent of white women, 59 percent of black women, and 54 percent of Hispanic women were in paid employment.

30. D. Pearce, "Chutes and Ladders: Playing the Low-Wage Employment Game" (Paper presented at the American Sociological Association Annual Meeting, Cincinnati, Ohio, August 1991).

31. Ibid.

32. D. Pearce, "Women, Working and Poverty: Toward the Year 2000," in *Risks and Challenges: Compendium on Women, Work and the Future* (Washington, D.C.: Wider Opportunities for Women, 1990). Figures are U.S. Bureau of the Census, 1990.

33. U.S. Bureau of the Census, *Money Income*, 1991.

34. Ibid.

35. Ibid.

36. U.S. Department of Commerce, Bureau of the Census, *Child Support and Alimony: 1989* (Series P-60, No. 173) (Washington, D.C.: U.S. Government Printing Office, 1991).

37. Ibid.

38. U.S. Bureau of the Census, *Poverty*, 1991.

39. Low Income Housing Information Service, 1989.

40. See D. Pearce, "The Herstory of Homelessness: Women and Homelessness" (Unpublished paper, Women and Poverty Project, Wider Opportunities for Women, Washington, D.C., 1990).

41. Center on Budget and Policy Priorities, *1991 Survey of State Budget Cuts of Programs Aiding the Poor* (Washington, D.C.: Center on Budget and Policy Priorities, 1992).

POORER AND SICKER: LEGACIES OF THE 1980s, LESSONS FOR THE 1990s

❖ ❖ ❖

Diana B. Dutton

In 1988, American women had a shorter average life expectancy than women in 15 other countries. A decade ago, we were behind only seven other countries. In 1980, the United States ranked twentieth in infant mortality; by 1991, we'd slipped to twenty-fourth.

What happened? The answer lies not in averages for the entire population, which have mostly been improving, but in what's happened to the disadvantaged. By many health measures, the poor and people of color were left behind in the 1980s. This slowdown has lowered American health statistics for the population as a whole and underlies the slipping position of the United States relative to other countries.

Who are the disadvantaged? Increasingly, women and children. About half of all people below poverty level are children and youth under age 22. The other half are adults, two-thirds of whom are women. In 1989, the official federal poverty threshold for a family of four was $12,672, barely a subsistence income; even above this level, many families scrape to get by. One out of five U.S. children—and nearly one of two black children—lives below the federal poverty level.[1] Over half of those living in poverty are in families headed by women. Women and children are also the fastest-growing segment of the burgeoning homeless population, although the majority are still single black men.

So women have a very personal stake in how the United States treats its underprivileged. In this chapter, we look first at evidence that low-income and minority groups have fallen behind on various health indicators, then turn to what happened during the 1970s and 1980s that caused these trends, and, finally, consider what might be done in the 1990s to reverse them. Since trends are easiest to see visually, this chapter includes a number of graphs that track the health of low- versus upper-income groups over time or, if health measures are not reported by income, of blacks versus whites. Blacks have the lowest economic status of any major racial group: In 1989, blacks were three times as likely to be poor as whites (31 percent vs. 10 percent) and had a median family income of $19,329 vs. $33,915 for whites.[2] Yet race is an imperfect proxy for economic status because the large majority of blacks (69 percent in 1989) are not below poverty level, and poverty is generally a stronger determinant of health than race.[3] It is also important to remember that two-thirds of all Americans below the poverty level are white. While blacks are more likely than whites to be poor, they represent only 13 percent of the population and so are well outnumbered by whites among the poor.

It isn't just the poor whose health depends on socioeconomic factors. No matter where one stands on the economic ladder, those a step up tend to have better health, while those beneath have worse health. Although not all of the reasons for this gradient are known, it appears in nearly every measure of illness. Economic position clearly has a powerful impact on everyone's health.[4]

Yet shifting trends in death and disease over the last three decades suggest that the relationship between economic level and health is not fixed, but responds to changing social policies. The enactment in the mid-1960s of public programs like Medicaid and Medicare expanded access to health care dramatically and led to significant health gains among previously underserved groups. As federal health expenditures escalated, many of these programs were cut back despite growing poverty and shrinking private insurance coverage. In virtually every measure of health, as we'll see, trends for the disadvantaged were improving during the 1970s and then slackened or worsened in the 1980s. In looking at graphs showing these trends, bear in mind that population statistics tend to be quite stable; even small differences mean that many people changed a little or that a smaller number of people changed a great deal. A slight upward tilt in the trend in death rates, for example, represents thousands of additional deaths every year as long as the tilt continues.

SLOWING HEALTH GAINS AMONG THE DISADVANTAGED

Infant and maternal death rates illustrate the slackening health trends of minorities in the 1980s and the persisting gap between blacks and whites. It is well known that black babies are twice as likely as white babies to die in their first year; less well known is the fact that black mothers are *four* times as likely as white mothers to die during pregnancy or childbirth. As Figures 1 and 2 show, black infant and maternal death rates were both falling rapidly during the 1960s and 1970s and the black-white gap was narrowing steadily until the 1980s, when rates for blacks flattened out and the gap remained largely unchanged. In 1989, while the white infant mortality rate continued to fall, the black rate actually rose by 6 percent—the first time in 30 years it had risen. This rise was outweighed by the declining white rate, however, and the overall infant mortality rate fell to the lowest level ever (9.8 infant deaths/1000 live births).[5] This paradoxical achievement underscores the growing gulf between the haves and have-nots in U.S. society.

It also belies the worsening trends in low birthweight. Low birth-

FIGURE 1   Infant mortality rates by race: United States, 1960–1989.

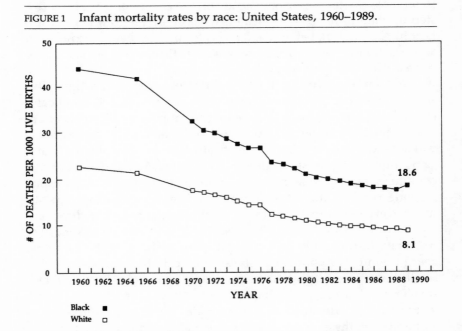

SOURCE: *Health U.S. 1991, 1983, 1978.*

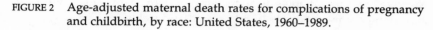

FIGURE 2   Age-adjusted maternal death rates for complications of pregnancy and childbirth, by race: United States, 1960–1989.

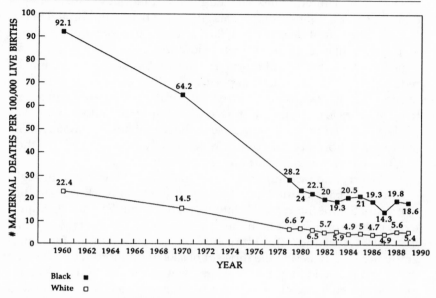

SOURCE: *Health U.S. 1991, 1987, 1985.*

weight is an important predictor of infant mortality; babies born with very low birthweight account for more than half of all infant deaths in the first year, and the babies that survive have much higher rates of lifelong disabilities such as mental retardation, cerebral palsy, vision and hearing impairment, and delayed development. In 1989, more U.S. babies were born with low birthweight than in any year since 1978, and the black-white birthweight gap was the widest ever recorded since the government began collecting such statistics in 1969.[6] The United States now ranks twenty-eighth in the world in percentage of low-birthweight births, worse than Greece and the former Soviet Union and tied with Chile and Paraguay. This humiliating record in preventing prematurity and low birthweight is largely responsible for the rising infant death rate among blacks and for the slipping international ranking of the United States in both infant mortality and adult life expectancy. Commenting on the continuing decline in overall infant mortality in the United States, the president of the March of Dimes Birth Defects Foundation said, "I take cold comfort at the slight improvement in the infant mortality rate. The reality beneath the survival of these babies is increasingly grim. The babies who are surviving are increasingly handicapped and sickly."[7]

Has the United States pushed its infant mortality rate as low as it can go? Hardly. Japan's rate is less than half that of the United States (4.8 vs. 10.0 infant deaths per 1000 live births in 1988) and Sweden's is just over half (5.8)—both well below the 1988 U.S. rate even for white infants (8.5).[8] Infant mortality rates for blacks could certainly be reduced as well. The racial gap virtually disappears in populations like the U.S. military, where extreme poverty is eliminated and access to health care is guaranteed. In fact, infant mortality rates for families of black enlisted men are very close to those of whites nationally.[9] The high infant mortality rate of blacks nationally is due mainly to their lack of adequate income and access to health care.

Poverty and race influence survival not only at birth but throughout the life span. In the United States, the typical black woman dies five years before the typical white woman (at ages 74 and 79, respectively); the typical black man dies eight years before the typical white man (at ages 65 and 73).[10] From 1984 on, life expectancies for whites gradually lengthened while those of blacks grew shorter; by 1989, the racial gap had widened by 0.7 years for women and by 1.7 years for men. Meanwhile, death rates in many poor and minority communities were exploding. One study concluded that black men living in Harlem were less likely to survive to age 65 than men living in Bangladesh.[11] Although violence and substance abuse were partly responsible for Harlem's extraordinarily high death rates, the chief causes were heart disease and other illnesses—conditions that afflict women as often as men. Again, studies have attributed race-related differences in mortality primarily to the lower economic level of blacks in the United States.[12]

Chronic disease, already the major killer of the disadvantaged, also reveals a widening gap between poor and nonpoor, blacks and whites. The most dramatic example is breast cancer, the fourth highest cause of death among women. Death rates from breast cancer have been climbing steadily among black women, while remaining virtually unchanged among white women (Figure 3).[13] In 1950, the breast-cancer death rate for black women was 17 percent lower than for white women; by 1988, it was 17 percent higher. Death rates for almost every chronic condition, including heart disease, cancer, and stroke, the three other leading killers of women, are higher among low-income and minority groups. Most chronic conditions are also more common among such groups (some are two or three times as common), and have been increasing more rapidly.[14]

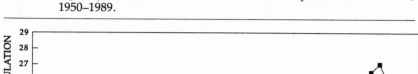

FIGURE 3   Age-adjusted death rates for breast cancer, by race: United States, 1950–1989.

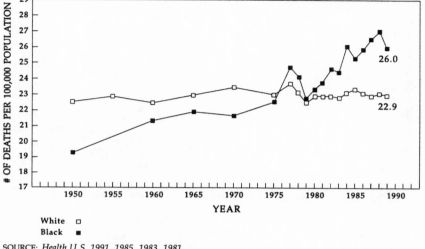

YEAR

White ☐
Black ■

SOURCE: *Health U.S. 1991, 1985, 1983, 1981.*

Rates of infectious disease have also been rising. AIDS has ravaged many poor communities and is spreading most rapidly among minorities. AIDS is a particular problem for women (see the chapter by O'Leary et al.). Tuberculosis (TB) cases in the United States have increased 16 percent since 1985—in 1990, 26,000 Americans were diagnosed with TB.[15] The spread of TB is linked to the rise in poverty, homelessness, and AIDS in the 1980s, and has hit the poor and minorities hardest: TB is nearly *eight* times more common among blacks than whites.[16] Fatality rates from many infectious diseases have also been climbing. From 1982 on, death rates from influenza and pneumonia (the sixth leading cause of death among both women and men) have been rising among whites as well as blacks, reversing their historical downward trend (see Figure 4). The racial gap in this measure, like others, narrowed sharply during the 1960s and 1970s, but failed to improve in the 1980s, leaving death rates nearly 50 percent higher among blacks than whites.

More global measures of health, like the number of days people restrict their activity due to poor health, confirm these worsening trends. During the 1980s, restricted activity increased sharply among low-income people aged 45 to 64, the prime working-age category,

FIGURE 4 Age-adjusted death rates for influenza and pneumonia, by race: United States, 1950–1989.

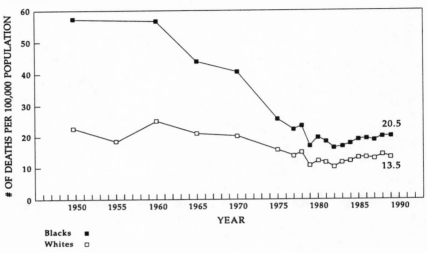

Blacks ■
Whites □

SOURCE: *Health U.S. 1991, 1985, 1983, 1981.*

FIGURE 5 Number of restricted activity days per person per year, by income, for people aged 45 to 64: United States, 1982, 1989.

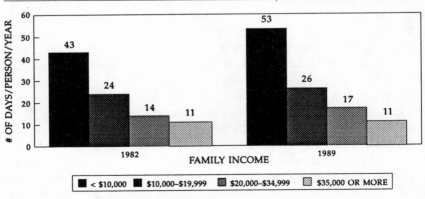

SOURCE: NCHS Series 10:176, 1990; 10:150, 1985.

while remaining flat among upper-income people (Figure 5). In 1989, low-income adults of this age, who should have been at their peak earning capacity, spent almost *two months* of the year with restricted activity—more than four times as much time as the affluent. Likewise, almost half of all low-income adults aged 45 to 64 rated their health "fair" or "poor," compared with less than 7 percent of the affluent.[17] The majority of these low-income adults, it bears remembering, were women.

For many measures, the health gap widens with age, yet substantial disparities are found even among children. Poor children have a higher prevalence of many disorders, including congenital infections, anemia, lead poisoning, and hearing and vision problems. They are confined to bed almost twice as often as affluent children and have four times as many hospital days.[18] Whatever it is about poverty that is detrimental to health apparently takes effect very early in life and cumulates as the years of deprivation take their toll. By almost every account, conditions for poor children worsened significantly during the 1980s.

SHIFTING PATTERNS OF CARE

Access to health care also became less equitable in the 1980s. Figure 6 shows how the likelihood of seeing a doctor has changed over the last 25 years. In 1964, the more money people made, the more likely they were to see a doctor. Since lower-income groups tended to be sicker, this was widely viewed as unfair. Access expanded greatly in the 1970s and, by 1981, the poor were almost as likely as the affluent to see physicians. The pattern changed again in the 1980s, however, and, by 1989, as in 1964, the chances of seeing a doctor once again increased directly with income.[19] Although there is no way of knowing what the right number of physician visits is, visit rates should bear some relation to the underlying medical need. By 1989, the highest income group had more than twice as many physician visits per restricted activity day (one indicator of need) as the lowest—a much greater disparity than in 1981.[20]

Physician visits alone, of course, don't reflect the adequacy of the care provided. As one expert testified before Congress,

> Simply counting the number of visits people make to doctors each year is not sufficient. The term "physician visit" can mean many things. It can be a hurried visit to a "Medicaid mill" in which a patient is ping-ponged among a series of doctors,

FIGURE 6   Probability of seeing a physician within the last year, by family
income: United States, 1964, 1981, 1990.

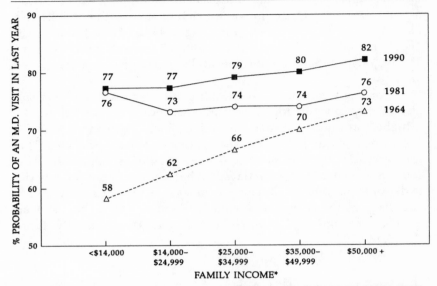

*Age-adjusted income categories for 1990. Categories for 1981 are less than $7,000; $7,000–$9,999; $10,000–$14,999; $15,000–$24,999; $25,000 or more. Corresponding categories in 1964 were less than $2,000; $2,000–$3,999; $4,000–$6,999; $7,000–$9,999; $10,000 or more.

SOURCE: *Health U.S. 1991, 1987.*

nurses and others to maximize reimbursement income. It can be hours spent waiting in a crowded, noisy hospital out-patient clinic or a few minutes with a doctor you've never seen before. At the other end of the scale—and far more desirable personally and medically—is the kind of visit you and I are accustomed to: seeing a doctor we know by name and who knows us and our families. Implicit in this relationship is the physician's assumption of personal responsibility for attending to an individual's medical care needs.[21]

Waiting hours to be seen in a clinic full of sick people is especially hard on single mothers with kids in tow and on working women with limited time off.

The poor clearly receive inadequate preventive care. Disparities in three widely recommended forms of preventive care—breast-cancer screening, well-baby checkups, and dental care—are shown in Figure

7. Lack of access to breast exams, which Medicaid doesn't cover in many states, may be contributing to the rising breast-cancer death rates of low-income and minority women. In one study, periodic screening using mammography and breast palpation eliminated the traditional racial difference in survival.[22] Equally disturbing is the disparity in well-baby care; in 1988, nearly 13 percent of low-income infants *never* saw a doctor for a check-up during their first year, compared with less than 3 percent of high-income infants. Undetected medical problems in children can have serious consequences, and regular health monitoring is strongly advised, especially in the early years. The poor also get less dental care and have more dental problems; one study of children in low-income families found that about 40 percent had untreated dental caries.[23]

A shocking proportion of poor and minority women receive inadequate prenatal care. In 1989, 40 percent of all black women had no prenatal care in the first trimester of pregnancy, along with similar percentages of low-income women, Native Americans, Mexican Americans, and other Latina women.[24] Until 1980, access to prenatal

FIGURE 7   Percentage of infants under age 1 who have never had well-baby visits; percentage of women over age 40 who have never had a breast exam; and percentage of all ages who have never had a dental visit, by family income and race: United States, 1986–1988.

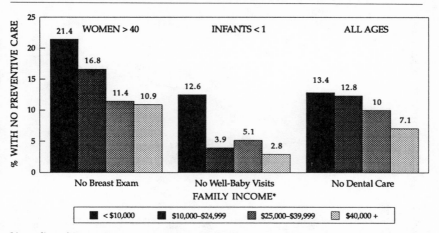

*Age-adjusted income categories are for well-baby visits, assessed in 1988. Categories for breast exams (1987) and dental care (1986) are less than $10,000; $10,000–$19,999; $20,000–$34,999; $35,000 or more.

SOURCE: Advance Data, No. 188, 1990; *Health U.S. 1990*; NCHS Series 10:172, 1989.

care had been improving among minority women, but the proportion of black women with late or no prenatal care began to climb in the 1980s and the black-white gap increased (Figure 8). The importance of prenatal care in preventing premature birth and related complications is well documented. Prenatal care is highly cost-effective; it has been estimated that each dollar spent on prenatal care reduces hospital and later expenses by nearly $11. Even among drug-using mothers, prenatal care appears to cut prematurity rates by half or more.[25] Declining access to prenatal care was probably the main reason why black infant and maternal mortality rates stopped improving in the 1980s.

Children's immunizations against common infectious diseases (measles, mumps, rubella, diphtheria, pertussis, tetanus, and polio) also fell during the 1980s, especially among nonwhites, and the white-

FIGURE 8 Percentage of women receiving inadequate prenatal care, by race: United States, 1970–1989.

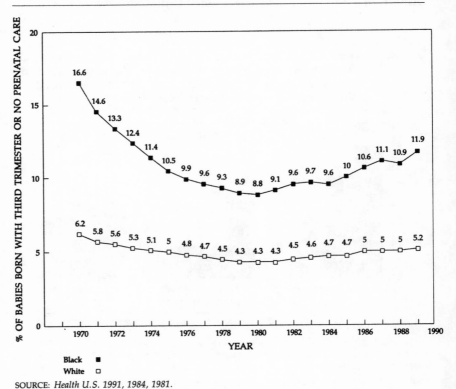

SOURCE: *Health U.S. 1991, 1984, 1981.*

nonwhite gap widened for all vaccines except diphtheria-pertussis-tetanus (DPT) and polio. By 1985, immunization rates for all of these diseases were about 20 percent lower among nonwhite than white children; after 1985, the government stopped reporting immunization statistics. Many of these diseases have been in resurgence. Twice as many children contracted pertussis in 1991 as in 1981, and there were five times as many rubella cases in 1991 as in 1988.[26] Measles, thought to be virtually eradicated in the early 1980s, is once again epidemic among preschoolers, teenagers, and unvaccinated adults. Total measles cases in the United States jumped from 1,497 in 1983 to over 30,000 in 1990, with more than 60 deaths.[27] The worst outbreaks have been in poor inner-city areas where vaccine shortages are routine and immunization levels low. Childhood immunizations are another highly cost-effective form of prevention, with an estimated savings of at least $10 in hospital and other expenses for every dollar spent.[28]

By most measures, in short, the health of the disadvantaged clearly worsened during the 1980s, and access to medical care remained inadequate or declined. Why did the gains achieved during the late 1960s and 1970s come to such an abrupt halt?

Growing Economic Inequality

Part of the explanation for the lack of continued improvement undoubtedly has to do with the changing economic situation in the United States. The economy was expanding in the 1960s and early 1970s, and unemployment was falling. In 1965, President Lyndon Johnson launched his War on Poverty, a broad-ranging federal effort that included, among other programs, Medicaid, Medicare, Head Start, federal aid to education, college loans and scholarships, higher social-security benefits, rent supplements, and food stamps. Such antipoverty programs, along with the strong economy, brought the poverty rate down from 19 percent in 1964 to 11 percent in 1973.

As the 1970s wore on, the economy began to weaken and, by the early 1980s, a major recession had begun, unemployment rates were soaring, and there was mounting concern over the federal deficit. The newly elected President Reagan promised to get the economy moving again by cutting taxes, reducing domestic spending, and enacting policies favorable to business and investors. Private enterprise, unfettered by burdensome regulations, was to replace government in solving social problems. With the economy in full gear, Reagan claimed, benefits to those at the top of the economic ladder would trickle down to the rungs beneath. Everyone would get bigger slices of the economic pie, he promised, because the pie itself would expand.

The economy did finally recover by the mid-1980s, but the trickle went up, not down, and the only people who got bigger slices of the pie were those at the top. Economic inequality in the United States increased sharply under Reagan, reversing the gradual trend toward income equality that had prevailed since the 1950s.[29] In 1989, the typical black family's income was *lower* than it was in 1975, adjusting for inflation, while the typical white family's income was over $3,000 higher. The gap between rich and poor is larger today than it's ever been since government data collection began in 1947: The top 1 percent of households is worth more than the bottom 90 percent combined.[30]

The pool of Americans in poverty also widened and deepened in the 1980s. The number of people in poverty increased 24 percent between 1978 and 1988. In 1990, another 2.1 million Americans joined the ranks of the poor, bringing the poverty rate to 13.5 percent, higher than any time in the 1970s.[31] Average wages declined during the 1980s and many jobs no longer kept people out of poverty. In 1988, nearly half of all poor adults—and almost 40 percent of welfare mothers— worked either full- or part-time, an increase of 27 percent in the number of working poor since 1978. By 1992, one out of every ten Americans was on food stamps, the highest proportion ever.[32]

Poor families with children have been hurt most by these trends. Record numbers of children have fallen below the poverty level, and children are now more likely than any other age group to be poor. Worst off are those in female-headed families. In 1989, nearly two-thirds of white children in single-parent families were below the poverty level, and 80 percent of black and Hispanic children. Young families with children today are living on just two-thirds of the income similar families had in 1973.[33] Federal policies bear much of the responsibility. Together, federal and state programs lift almost half of the elderly out of poverty, compared with less than 5 percent of children. Federal expenditures per child through the major child-oriented programs are less than one-tenth of total federal expenditures per person over age 65.[34] As a result, poor families with children have been losing ground relative to the affluent, while the poor elderly are mostly protected. The average income of the poorest fifth of families with children fell 14 percent during the 1980s, whereas the incomes of middle- and upper-income families with children rose; the incomes of elderly childless households, by contrast, rose across the board (Figure 9).

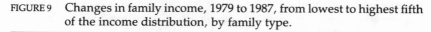

FIGURE 9   Changes in family income, 1979 to 1987, from lowest to highest fifth of the income distribution, by family type.

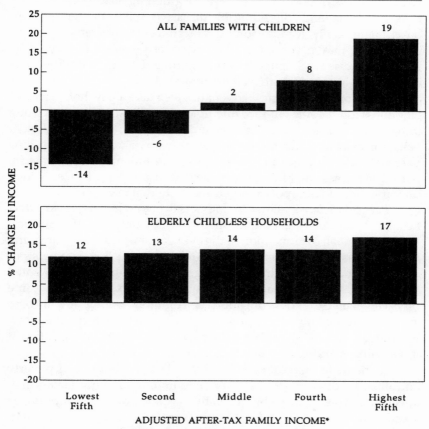

*Income is adjusted for family size, government benefits, inflation, and taxes.

SOURCE: Select Committee on Children, U.S. House of Representatives, 1989.

THE CYCLE OF POVERTY AND ILLNESS

Poverty and illness create a vicious cycle: being poor tends to under-mine health and, in turn, poor health makes it even harder to escape from poverty. Poverty can affect health in myriad ways, both at home and at work.[35] Lower-status jobs tend to be more hazardous and physically strenuous, as well as less rewarding emotionally and eco-nomically. Accidents on the job are more common among lower-

income workers, even within specific job categories. Inadequate housing presents numerous threats to health. Crowding leads to greater
stress and less opportunity for rest, heightening susceptibility to illness, accidents, and communicable disease (see the chapter by Dornbusch). Nationally, lead poisoning is far more common among lower-
income and minority children. Urban poverty areas are plagued by
pollution, noise, accidents, drugs, and crime. Higher mortality levels
in poor neighborhoods are well documented.

Many of these physical adversities also take a psychological and
emotional toll. People who are unemployed, for instance, report being
unhappy and dissatisfied with life and suffer from insomnia. Violent
behavior increases and family relationships break down. In 1982, 69
percent of the counties in Wisconsin where unemployment rose reported increases in child abuse, whereas 71 percent of those where
unemployment fell reported a decline in child abuse.

People's *relative* status in the social hierarchy may also affect
health. Being "on the bottom" involves not only specific physical
hardships but also humiliation in the eyes of the world and a damaging
loss of self-esteem and perceived control over one's life. Coping strategies may include smoking, drinking, and drug abuse, which entail
health risks. A more affluent life-style often allows more leisure-time
physical exercise. Poor nutrition is common among low-income
groups. National nutrition surveys indicate that 95 percent of all low-
income preschool children are deficient in iron, about half are deficient
in vitamins A and C, and one-fourth are deficient in calcium.

Inadequate medical care is another link in the cycle of poverty
and illness. Although medical care is only one of many factors that
affect health—and probably a relatively minor one—its importance
should not be minimized, for it can prevent disease, relieve suffering,
improve physical function, and save lives. In the 1980s, as we've seen,
access remained flat or declined among lower-income groups, despite
their worsening health, depriving them of care that might have cush-
ioned the consequences of their deteriorating economic situation.

THE RISE AND FALL OF PUBLIC PROGRAMS

Federal domestic policy also underwent a profound change between
the 1970s and 1980s. Most of the War on Poverty programs of the
1960s mushroomed during the 1970s. Enrollment in Medicaid, which
had been created to eliminate financial barriers to care for the poor,
grew from 18 million people in 1972 to 22 million in 1980, while
expenditures nearly quadrupled to $23 billion. Medicare grew even

faster and, by 1980, covered 29 million elderly at a cost of $37 billion.[36] Federal programs to reduce geographic barriers also expanded, most notably the Community Health Center program, which set up clinics in underserved urban and rural poverty areas, and the National Health Service Corps (NHSC), which subsidized physicians locating in underserved areas.

Community Health Centers defined a broader role for medicine. The most ambitious, like the center in Mound Bayou, Mississippi, an extremely poor region of the Mississippi Delta, offered not only standard medical care but also basic social and environmental services, ranging from sanitation and housing to transportation and education. Child care was available at the center for both patients and employees. For nutritional deficiencies, center doctors wrote prescriptions for food, while staff helped organize a cooperative vegetable farm. The hope was to create self-sustaining initiatives that would enable the community to lift itself out of impoverishment and dependency.[37] While not all of Mound Bayou's pioneering programs survived, its achievements have been impressive. The infant mortality rate dropped 40 percent during the center's first four years, hundreds of residents obtained better housing and sanitary water, and over 100 people earned postsecondary school degrees, including 13 physicians, because of health-center-sponsored programs—in a community where the average adult education had previously been fourth grade.

Community Health Centers multiplied during the 1970s, although federal-funding restrictions forced them to abandon their more innovative activities. By 1982, there were 872 centers throughout the United States serving 4.2 million people, mostly the poor and minorities. Nearly half of the centers' patients were uninsured, and NHSC subsidies helped cover their costs.[38] Numerous evaluations showed that these centers increased access in poor communities and improved health, providing high-quality care that was also more efficient and economical than conventional medicine.

Other federal programs were aimed specifically at needy women and children, including the food program for Women, Infants, and Children (WIC) and the Maternal and Child Health (MCH) program. Studies found that WIC food supplements for pregnant women lowered the risk of prematurity and improved infant health, saving $3 during the child's first year for every $1 spent. MCH services raised immunization levels among poor children and improved hearing and vision.[39] The combined impact of these various public programs was reflected in the steadily improving health trends of poor and minority groups during the 1960s and 1970s.

The Reagan administration had a different agenda. Reagan was eager to reduce domestic spending and, with medical costs spiraling, health programs were a prime target. In the early 1980s, federal spending on Medicaid and Medicare was cut by $4 billion and $13 billion, respectively, below what it would have been, leading nearly every state to limit Medicaid services, eligibility, or physician payment levels. An estimated 700,000 children lost Medicaid coverage in 1982, as did 567,000 elderly between 1981 and 1984.[40] Congress, fearing by the mid-1980s that federal cutbacks had gone too far, mandated phased expansion of Medicaid to all poor pregnant women, infants, and children. Yet the proportion of poor and near poor covered by Medicaid continued to drop and, by 1990, Medicaid served only 40 percent of the poor and near poor, down from 65 percent in 1976. More children became eligible, but, by 1987, only 56 percent of all poor children were enrolled in Medicaid—well below the 73 percent covered in 1975.[41] In 1991, beset by another recession, most states cut Medicaid funding further. The steady chipping away at physician payment levels led growing numbers of doctors to refuse Medicaid patients; 70 percent of California pediatricians responding to a 1991 survey said they restricted or refused new Medicaid patients.[42]

Federal assistance for poor women and children was also slashed in the 1980s. Reagan tried to abolish the WIC food program and to suppress data on its health benefits and cost-effectiveness. Congressional support for WIC prevailed, but the program has been chronically underfunded and still reaches less than half of those eligible.[43] Now, Bush wants to kill a $3 million program that lures WIC participants to farmers' markets to buy fresh fruits and vegetables while boosting sales for struggling farmers. Federal MCH funds were cut by 18 percent in 1981, and almost every state reduced prenatal and delivery services for pregnant women. Not until 1985 did funding return to its 1981 level, and it has remained about the same despite significant growth in the number of poor women and children without insurance.[44]

The Reagan administration also cut federal funding for Community Health Centers sharply in the early 1980s and terminated the NHSC program (the latter was reinstated in 1990, although with funding that met only about a quarter of the need). Over 250 community clinics—one-third of the total—had to limit services or close, leaving people in some of the poorest areas with nowhere to go for basic medical care. Reagan also slashed aid for the disabled and removed many people from the disability rolls, prompting an outpouring of public criticism and numerous court challenges. (In 1992, the Bush administration finally agreed to reopen some of these cases.)[45]

INCREASING NUMBERS OF UNINSURED

As public programs were scaled back, private insurance coverage also shrank. In 1989, nearly 39 million Americans, or 16 percent of the population, had no health coverage at all—the largest number since before the creation of Medicare and Medicaid. About half of the uninsured were women, and the majority were poor. As Figure 10 shows, despite Medicaid and other public programs, the lower people's income, the less likely they are to be insured. As a result, the poor spend a disproportionate share of their income on medical care. In 1977, low-income Americans spent *eight* times as much of their income on medical expenses as the affluent; the figure is surely even higher today.[46] Moreover, income disparities in insurance coverage widened substantially between 1976 and 1989. Among the poor, the proportion of people without insurance nearly doubled, whereas it actually declined slightly among upper-income groups (see Figure 10). In 1990, more than *half* of all families with incomes under $20,000 had no medical coverage. Lack of insurance has been linked to lower rates of hospital and ambulatory care and worse health outcomes.[47]

People with present or past illness have had growing difficulty getting coverage. In 1989, nearly 900,000 Americans were denied

FIGURE 10   Percentage of people under 65 with neither public nor private health insurance, by family income: United States, 1976, 1980, 1989.

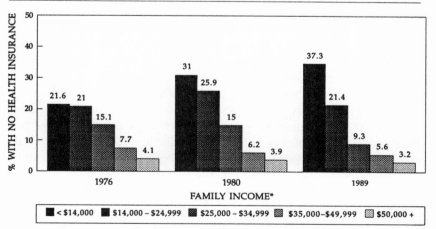

*Age-adjusted income categories for 1989. Categories for 1980 are less than $7,000; $10,000–$14,999; $25,000 or more. Categories for 1976 are less than $3,000; $7,000–$9,999; $15,000 or more.

SOURCE: *Health U.S. 1990, 1985, 1978*

health insurance because of poor health.[48] Although insurance was originally supposed to provide a means of sharing the risk of illness as widely as possible, commercial insurers have found numerous ways to exclude the sick, by limiting benefits, canceling policies, or raising premiums when people become ill. More and more victims of AIDS, cancer, and other serious illnesses are discovering that their insurance evaporates just when they need it most. By excluding the sick, insurers can lower premiums, attract more clients, and increase profits—but they are denying coverage to the very people who need it to pay for their care.

GROWING COST BURDEN FOR PATIENTS

Even people who did have insurance found their protection eroding during the 1980s and their out-of-pocket costs growing. *Cost-sharing*— the portion of medical bills that insurance doesn't cover—has increased dramatically. In 1991, the average family paid $2,100 for premiums and costs not covered by private insurance, more than twice what it paid in 1980. The Medicaid program originally prohibited cost-sharing; in the early 1980s, 26 states imposed copayments, deductibles, or other cost-sharing requirements on Medicaid recipients. Cost-sharing in the Medicare program has risen so steeply that the elderly now spend 61 percent *more* of their income on out-of-pocket medical expenses than they did before Medicare was enacted in 1965![49]

This escalation in cost-sharing is the result of efforts by the major public and private funders—government, large employers, and commercial insurers—to limit health spending; if people have to pay, the reasoning goes, they'll use less health care. The problem is that cost-sharing discourages mainly low-income groups, even if the cost is small. When $1.50 to $2.00 was charged for physician visits in Saskatchewan, for instance, visits declined three times as much among the poor and aged as among the population as a whole. If cost-sharing eliminates needed services, it doesn't necessarily save money. In California's 1972 copayment experiment, which imposed a $1 charge on some Medicaid recipients, doctor visits declined by 8 percent, but hospitalization rose by 17 percent, resulting in a net *increase* in total costs.[50]

LESSONS FOR HEALTH CARE IN THE 1990s

In the 1990s, many conditions look worse than they did a decade ago. The economy is again in the midst of a serious recession, unemployment rates are high, and medical costs continue to soar. Americans are frustrated and worried. What can we learn from the policies of the 1970s and 1980s?

First, it's clear that American health care became less efficient as well as less equitable during the Reagan/Bush era. True efficiency in health care delivery requires matching services to need. During the 1980s, cutbacks in public funding, shrinking insurance coverage, and escalating patient cost-sharing diverted resources away from those in greatest need and gave them to the relatively healthy well-to-do. If we allow these trends to continue, we can expect further erosion in access and health status. To reverse them, we must allocate resources according to health needs, not ability to pay, and redirect services to the groups with the greatest need. We can start by making sure that programs like Medicaid, Community Health Centers, WIC, and Head Start at least have enough funding to meet the needs of all who are eligible.

Second, funding cutbacks that deprive people of needed care are not only inhumane but they may actually end up costing more money than they save. Cutbacks that reduce prenatal care, for example, make no sense even in strictly economic terms. Prenatal-care costs are trivial compared with those of the developmental disorders and other problems that prenatal care helps prevent. (Neonatal care for one premature infant costs about $25,000 and can exceed $100,000 for a very tiny infant. Institutional care for a developmentally disabled child costs $69,000 to $200,000 or more *a year*.) It is estimated that California would save up to $346 million annually in reduced hospital and future costs if it provided prenatal care to women who now go without it.[51]

The cutbacks of the 1980s also took a toll in human suffering and lost productivity that will never be fully known. Many of the poor depend on Medicaid and have gone without care or been left destitute when they lost coverage. One study followed a group of California Medicaid recipients who lost eligibility in 1982 and found that they got less care and suffered significant deterioration of previously controlled chronic disease.[52] There were five deaths in the group cut from Medicaid and none in a control group that stayed on Medicaid. One death was from a perforated ulcer, for which the patient delayed seeking care because he couldn't pay the emergency-room fees. Two other patients died of hypertensive hemorrhage and heart attack after discontinuing prescribed medications, which they could no longer afford.

Third, the Community Health Centers model demonstrated how medicine could address the roots as well as the symptoms of disease among the poor. Medical care alone, even if equitably distributed, will not break the cycle of poverty and illness. Patterns of care in Britain's National Health Service have been considerably more equal than in the United States for over three decades, yet health disparities persist. A government study attributed these disparities primarily to the numerous social inequalities that affect health and called for a wide range of social-policy measures to combat them.[53] Community Health Centers sought to initiate such measures. Understandably, they didn't solve all the health problems of the poor and not all centers have been uniformly successful. Yet, by redrawing traditional medical boundaries, Community Health Centers were able to break into the cycle of poverty and illness at multiple points, treating nonbiologic as well as biologic causes and fostering both human and economic development. Although this is not the only (nor perhaps even the most effective) way to achieve social change, Community Health Centers showed that it was possible to work with communities as well as individuals to remedy conditions that compromise health. With the battery of social ills we face today, the need for broadening medicine's boundaries is greater than ever.

The final lesson is that government programs targeting the poor, no matter how successful, will always be vulnerable to shifting political agendas. Even though public programs were making real headway in the 1970s in improving the health of low-income groups, their effectiveness was crippled in the 1980s by funding cutbacks. Probably the only way to achieve lasting improvements for the poor is to enact basic reforms that will guarantee all Americans access to a decent standard of health care. A universal national health insurance system, similar to Canada's, would do more than any other proposed reform to narrow the health gap between rich and poor. In the process, it will make health care for everyone more rational, equitable, and efficient.

PROPOSED HEALTH-CARE REFORMS

To understand why a national health insurance system is more likely to close the health gap than any other approach, let's look at how the three main reforms that have been proposed would affect the disadvantaged. One approach is former President Bush's minimalist reform: *tax credits* for low- and middle-income people to help them buy private health insurance. A second approach, favored by President Bill Clinton, often called *play or pay*, would also broaden insurance coverage by requiring employers either to insure their workers (play), or pay a tax that would fund a federal insurance program. The third approach is national health insurance, also called a *single-payer system*, which would replace existing public and private insurance programs with a single universal plan run by the government and financed through the tax system.

For women, children, and other groups left behind in the 1980s, there are five key questions.

1. WILL UNIVERSAL COVERAGE BE GUARANTEED?

The only way to guarantee uninterrupted coverage for all Americans is to break the present link between employment and health insurance and establish a government-run financing system that would cover all citizens regardless of employment. Breaking the employment-insurance link is especially important for women because so many work in low-paying or part-time jobs, often in small businesses, which don't provide health benefits. Leaving insurance tied to employment will hurt poor children even more. In 1987, nearly two-thirds of poor families with only one working adult weren't even *offered* employment-based health coverage for their children (if they were, 80 percent to 90 percent or more took it).[54] In Canada, everyone has a National Health Program card and can receive care from any provider simply by showing this card.

Tax credits and play-or-pay plans, which both leave health insurance tied to employment, are unlikely to achieve universal coverage. Bush's tax credit plan, according to administration estimates, would leave about 5 million people uncovered.[55] If present trends continue, most of these people will be sick, poor, or both. Moreover, critics say the proposed tax credit is too low anyway to buy good coverage. In play-or-pay plans, a federal insurance program would be credited to cover part-time or unemployed workers, but loss of coverage could still occur in some cases when employment changed or ended, and people might feel locked into unwanted jobs—as some do now—if their prospects of future coverage were uncertain. There is also the danger that employers as well as insurers might discriminate against workers apt to have higher health expenses, such as those with previous illness.

Loss of insurance coverage and denial of claims represent a growing threat for many Americans. About half of all personal bankruptcies in the United States are reportedly due to medical costs; that simply doesn't happen in Canada. As one Canadian official put it,

"No one in Canada need mortgage his future because of a need for hospital services."[56]

2. WILL FINANCIAL AND STRUCTURAL BARRIERS TO CARE BE ELIMINATED?

Americans regularly name out-of-pocket cost as their number one concern about health care. Making people pay for care is a particularly bad way to discourage overutilization because the groups most likely to be deterred are precisely those most in need of care. In a large controlled trial of the effects of cost-sharing, low-income people who had to pay a portion of their medical bills used fewer services and had worse health by several measures than those with free care.[57] Ideally, no one would face cost-sharing; at the very least, the poor and near-poor should be fully protected.

If a tax credit plan is adopted, people who buy insurance will probably face increased cost-sharing as insurers seek to curb rising demand for care (people who can't get insurance will be no better off than at present). Cost-sharing would probably also increase under a play-or-pay plan, as insurers and providers tried to limit consumer health spending. By contrast, most single-payer plans would limit cost-sharing or prohibit it entirely.[58]

The incentives fostered by tax credit and play-or-pay plans could create further hurdles for the poor. Play-or-pay plans encourage providers to compete for patients in the hope of improving efficiency, but it won't be the poor for which most will be competing because reimbursement rates, which are unlikely to vary by income, probably won't cover the extra costs of caring for the more serious and complex problems of low-income patients. In fact, competitive providers will have an incentive to avoid such high-cost groups, just as many commercial insurers now shun the sick. California's disastrous experience with competing prepaid health plans for the poor in the 1970s led to outright fraud.[59] To avoid such problems, single-payer systems downplay or forbid price competition, but do allow providers to compete by improving quality or convenience.

Insurance coverage alone will not remedy the dearth of basic medical-care providers in many low-income urban and rural areas. Tax credit and play-or-pay plans would both leave Medicaid intact, yet fewer and fewer physicians are willing to see Medicaid patients, as noted earlier, while the emergency rooms of public hospitals are strained to the breaking point. With either of these approaches, increased funding for programs like Community Health Centers and the NHSC would be critical to attract providers to underserved areas and to enable them to serve uninsured patients.

With national health insurance, Medicaid would cease to exist and the poor would be covered under the same system as everyone else. Providers would be drawn to underserved areas because for the first time *all* the poor would be insured and doctors could count on being paid at reasonable rates (although high-poverty areas might still require subsidies). As managed-care plans and other gatekeeper arrangements proliferate, even middle-class families face growing constraints on their medical options. These barriers would also be eliminated by a single-payer system similar to Canada's, in which everyone has free choice of providers.

3. WILL SERVICES COVERED BE COMPREHENSIVE AND INCLUDE DISEASE PREVENTION?

The present U.S. health-care system is not geared toward prevention. Most health-insurance policies don't cover preventive services, and most hospital emergency rooms, where the poor often end up, don't provide them. As we've seen, many poor women and children lack essential preventive and primary care such as prenatal care, breast-cancer screening, and early-childhood examinations. By contrast, countries with universal health insurance—all of which spend far less than the United States does on health care—achieve nearly complete participation of children in preventive health care and, as a result, have better overall health status and survival rates.[60]

A single-payer plan would guarantee everyone access to a comprehensive set of benefits, including a broad range of preventive services. Many single-payer proposals would prohibit cost-sharing on preventive care, thus eliminating financial barriers. Some would require community-based disease prevention to reduce hazards in the social and physical environment.[61] Play-or-pay plans would also cover preventive services (the scope might vary), but cost-sharing provisions might limit access among lower-income groups. A tax-credit plan would do absolutely nothing to promote prevention, since most insurers would presumably continue to exclude preventive care from benefit packages.

Whatever plan is adopted, facilities that offer preventive and primary care must be made available in low-income neighborhoods. Community Health Centers provide a wide range of services under one roof, maximizing convenience for patients and enabling health providers to coordinate the care delivered. Arizona's managed-care system for Medicaid patients, which delivers comprehensive care through health maintenance organizations (HMOs), achieves rates of cancer screening (Pap smears and mammograms) among poor women comparable to those of women with private health insurance, without any special motivational programs. Mobile mammography vans operating from primary health-care centers have also helped to increase breast-cancer screening among underserved women.[62]

4. WILL HEALTH-CARE COSTS BE CONTROLLED?

The United States now spends 40 percent more per person on health than Canada does, and nearly three times as much as Great Britain. What do we get for all that money? Not better health, unfortunately. There is no evidence that people's health in countries that spend much less than we do on medical care is any worse than ours; by most measures, in fact, it is better and getting more so every year. What we clearly do get is a lot of waste. Costly procedures are performed unnecessarily, and huge sums are spent on highly specialized and often futile care for the terminally ill. Fraud and billing abuses by providers eat up an estimated 10 percent of the U.S. health budget.[63] Meanwhile, medical innovation continues, generating more expensive technologies and procedures that drive costs inexorably upward.

This relentless cost escalation is doing more than just wasting money. It is distorting medical priorities and misallocating health resources. As high-cost procedures proliferate, they devour a growing share of public budgets and squeeze out low-cost yet effective preventive and primary-care services. We end up spending vast amounts for problems that could have been prevented for a fraction of the cost. For instance, we spend roughly $2 billion—57 percent of the costs incurred for all newborns—caring for the 7 percent of babies born with low birthweight, instead of trying to ensure that these babies were born healthy by getting their mothers into prenatal care.[64] Public programs are forced either to limit services or help fewer people. Families and individuals are saddled with rising medical bills. Without some way to control costs, medical priorities will become increasingly skewed and out-of-pocket costs will continue to escalate. The needy will be deprived of cost-effective care, the U.S. ranking in population health statistics will continue to fall, and the return on our health-care dollars will dwindle.

Tax credit and play-or-pay plans offer no realistic way of controlling costs. By broadening insurance coverage, tax credits would stimulate more health spending, but largely of the wrong type (prevention would typically not be covered) and among the wrong groups (the sick and poor are likely to be excluded). Play-or-pay plans rely on competition among providers or insurers to control costs, yet the evidence to date suggests that competition is as likely to increase costs as reduce them. Trying to create incentives for consumers, providers, or insurers to limit spending hasn't worked and probably won't. What clearly does work are global budgets—deciding first how much money should be spent on health and then how to spend it. That's how virtually all other industrialized countries have managed to curb their costs—and most spend less than *half* of what the U.S. does per person on health care. It's time for us, too, to put our health-care system on a budget. Only a national single-payer system would create an overall budget for health, allowing total spending to be controlled. States or regions could then decide how to use their share to pay for the mandated benefits, working with insurers and providers to eliminate wasteful procedures. According to one independent estimate, a single-payer plan, similar to the Canadian system, could save the United States more than a trillion dollars over the next decade.[65]

5. WILL ADMINISTRATIVE COMPLEXITY AND WASTE BE MINIMIZED?

Anyone who has ever filled out a health-insurance claim form knows just how aggravating and time consuming this process can be. And these costs—the time individuals spend dealing with all the bureaucracy and paperwork—aren't even included in calculations of how much the American health system wastes on administration. It's estimated that nearly a quarter of the total U.S. health budget goes to managers, insurers, marketers, lawyers, and other paper-pushers—*two to five times* as much as Canada spends on health-care administration. Similarly, administrative costs in government-run programs like Medicare and Medicaid are less than a quarter of those of private insurers (3 percent vs. 13 percent).[66] Again, there's no mystery here. It's simply much more efficient to have a single way of doing things rather than a jumble of different rules, regulations, and procedures. Only a single-payer system would streamline the present bloated morass, saving consumers endless paperwork and diverting the resources presently wasted on administration into more productive activities.

In sum, tax credits and play-or-pay plans would pump more money into the existing system while failing to correct its most glaring flaws. Only a universal health-insurance system, similar to those in Canada and other industrialized countries, is likely to achieve the basic changes necessary to reverse the worsening health trends of the disadvantaged. Moreover, only a single-payer plan would, for the first time, permit meaningful cost control, and thus represents the only approach likely to produce lasting change.

There is widespread public support for such a system. National surveys indicate that roughly two-thirds of Americans, given brief descriptions of the Canadian system, would prefer it to the American system. Polls comparing opinions in 10 nations in 1990 showed that Canadians were the most satisfied with their health system and Americans the least. Nearly 90 percent of Americans said that the U.S. system needed fundamental changes or complete rebuilding. In a 1992 national survey, nearly 60 percent of Americans expressed support for a national health-insurance system, and almost as many said they would pay $600 a year to finance it.[67] The irony is that by controlling medical and administrative costs, most single-payer plans would *reduce* health spending, not increase it, while extending coverage to the entire population. Any of the various proposed single-payer plans would represent a giant step forward in the quest for affordable health care for all Americans.[68]

LARGER LESSONS

The economic and social policies of the 1970s and 1980s also had a profound impact on health. Again, there are valuable lessons to be learned. The first, and perhaps most important for anyone concerned about women and children, is that trickle-down economics didn't work. Inequalities in income, health, and wealth all increased substantially during the 1980s, living standards for middle- and lower-income Americans deteriorated, and growing numbers of working people fell below the poverty level. By the end of the decade, the "safety net" of public programs that was supposed to protect those on the bottom was in shreds.

Were these trends inevitable? Certainly not; they are the result of deliberate governmental choices. Even if modern industrialized economies do tend to produce growing inequality—and this is debatable—governments can do much to moderate the consequences. When Canada experienced similar trends toward inequality during the 1980s, the government strengthened its antipoverty programs and held the poverty rate flat. Indeed, through public assistance and tax policies, governments in Canada and most European countries have managed to reduce their poverty rates for families with children to roughly half those in the United States.[69]

When large numbers of people lose jobs, as happened in the early 1980s and is happening again, and they get no financial assistance with housing, food, or health care, their toehold on a decent life crumbles. Rates of crime, disease, disability, and death begin to rise. Broad and coordinated interventions are required to combat the social disintegration that occurs and to help people get back on their feet.[70] The Bush administration has done exactly the opposite, encouraging financially strapped states to cut public-assistance programs even further under the guise of "welfare reform." The principal victims will once again be women and children.

This should not happen. It's a national disgrace that the richest country in the world has turned its back on its most vulnerable citizens. In 1986, America's Catholic bishops released a pastoral letter on the U.S. economy, which stated: "The obligation to provide justice for all means that the poor have the single most urgent claim on the conscience of the nation." As our cities decay around us and racial unrest increases, more and more Americans are expressing similar views. In a national poll conducted after the 1992 riots in Los Angeles, nearly two-thirds of those interviewed said we were spending too little on improving the conditions of poor and black Americans—almost double the percentage who felt that way four years ago. Women are especially concerned about the underprivileged. In a 1992 Gallup poll, 50 percent more women than men said the problem of poverty and homelessness should be an "extremely important" government priority.[71]

Indeed, we can't afford *not* to help the poor improve their conditions. As a group of the country's major corporate executives stated in 1987,

> This nation cannot continue to compete and prosper in the global arena when more than one-fifth of our children live in poverty . . . and we continue to squander the talents of millions of our children. . . . We believe that to succeed in helping children at risk, we must respond to the needs of the whole child from prenatal care through adulthood. Such efforts must also involve the children's parents, who may themselves be disadvantaged and in need of support services to help them learn how to prepare their children for a better future.[72]

In short, we must not only reestablish an adequate safety net but also make a national commitment to provide the full range of opportunities that would enable disadvantaged citizens to become productive members of society.

What would that entail? A fascinating survey by Louis Harris and Associates posed this question to a cross-section of black members of the so-called underclass—those living in extreme poverty—in eight major U.S. cities. Their top three responses were "better job opportunities," "more schooling available," and "more job training."[73] But is our society prepared to help them fulfill these goals? Harris found that it was—overwhelmingly so. More than 9 in 10 Americans endorsed special school programs for underclass children and incentives for business to locate workplaces in high-poverty areas. More than 8 in 10 Americans favor linking welfare to job-training programs, but would couple this with benefits for the working poor, including childcare, transportation, and health-care costs.

It's time for our leaders, in both government and the private sector, to heed these opinions. Women in particular must get Washington to hear their concerns about the poor. The first step is making sure suitable jobs are available. After the Los Angeles riots, more than three-quarters of those interviewed said that investing in jobs and job-training programs was a better way of preventing future turmoil than strengthening police forces. Some local job-training programs are highly effective, but most lack adequate funding. Many people believe federal action is also necessary. Senator David Boren (D-Oklahoma) has introduced a bill to create a modern version of the Works Progress Administration (WPA), the enormously successful public-works program that rescued millions of people from poverty during the 1930s Depression and left the nation with improved roads, schools, and airfields.[74] Although many welfare recipients would undoubtedly need further training, the end result would be not only more productive workers but also much-needed improvements on our crumbling infrastructure.

Workfare programs, which require welfare recipients with children over age 3 to find a job or get more schooling or job training, seek to ease the transition to work by offering suitable training and guaranteeing participants child care and Medicaid eligibility for a year. Early results are encouraging, but it remains to be seen whether states will be able to offer the services called for given growing budget deficits.[75] In the long run, major educational interventions could have an even greater payoff. The *New York Times* urged "massive new commitments to Head Start, to primary and secondary education, to training high school dropouts and welfare mothers, to more higher education of different kinds, to workplace training."[76] Such an investment in the needy could pay for itself many times over by lowering rates of crime and disease while adding skilled workers to the work force.

Strengthening child-support laws would also help poor children, many of whom live in female-headed families. Congress is presently considering a radical change in the way the country collects child-support payments from absent fathers. Proposed legislation would transfer responsibility for child-support collection from the states to the Internal Revenue Service, guaranteeing each family up to $4,000 a year and creating 300,000 new public-service jobs to give unemployed fathers a way of making their payments.[77] Also helpful would be children's allowances for all families, regardless of income, similar to those in most industrialized countries. Although a universal family-support program would not, by itself, meet the needs of most poor children, such a policy might attract broader political support than programs aimed at the poor and would reflect society's commitment to the welfare of all children.[78]

In short, there is much the United States can do about poverty and the tragic loss of human potential it causes. The economic and social policies of the 1960s and 1970s proved we could tackle some of poverty's toughest challenges and cut the poverty rate nearly in half. We could do the same in the 1990s. Steps like those outlined could revitalize our economy, restore our national pride, and heal our collective conscience. And, they might well do more to improve population health statistics than anything conventional medicine could achieve.

CONCLUSION

Given the marked shift in health trends between the 1970s and 1980s, it is evident that the high rates of death and disease among the poor and people of color are not an immutable feature of social disadvantage, as the Bush administration has maintained, but are directly affected by federal policy.[79] The Reagan/Bush era was not kind to the poor. Federal economic policies lowered the living standards of all but the ultrarich, and allowed more Americans to sink below the poverty level. Federal social policies slashed public assistance of all types. Federal health policies cut or eliminated the programs that had done the most to expand access in the 1970s. There can be little doubt that these policies underlie the worsening health trends of the disadvantaged during the 1980s and hence this country's slipping international ranking in most health statistics. Ronald Reagan said that government was the problem, not the solution, and, for the 1980s, he was largely right. But trends in the 1960s and 1970s showed it could be otherwise, and it can again. With proper leadership, government programs can play a vital role in narrowing the health gap between rich and poor and in altering the conditions that create that gap.

The legacy of the 1980s is now apparent. By neglecting those at the bottom of the economic ladder, federal policies undermined the viability of the country as a whole. Now is our chance to set things right. We can redistribute health care to those who need it most and will reap the greatest benefit. More broadly, we can call for economic policies that will narrow inequalities and domestic policies that will improve the social and environmental circumstances that compromise health and exacerbate illness. In the final analysis, the short-run costs of such an approach may be outweighed by long-run efficiencies; it's wasteful and, in fact, futile to treat people's ailments and then send them back into the same environment that made them sick. This is the most fundamental form of disease prevention, and perhaps ultimately the only truly effective one.

ACKNOWLEDGMENTS

For helpful comments on earlier drafts, thanks go to Randy Bean, Halsted Holman, Michael Holman, Vincent Iacopino, Sherri Matteo, Louise Pilote, Tom Robinson, Carol Schaffer, Miriam Shuchman, David Thom, Randy Thomas, Michael Ward, and Andrew Zolopa.

NOTES

1. National Center for Health Statistics, *Health, United States, 1991* (Hyattsville, Md.: Public Health Service, 1992), 22 (hereafter cited as *Health U.S. 1991*).

2. Bureau of the Census, *Statistical Abstract of the United States, 1991* (Washington, D.C.: U.S. Department of Commerce), 38. Moreover, according to the Census Bureau, white families typically have ten times as much accumulated wealth as black families (R. Pear, *New York Times*, January 11, 1991, 1).

3. For example, blacks and whites with similar levels of income and education differ only slightly in reported health; by contrast, for both races, reported health status differs widely between people with high vs. low levels of income or education. See National Center for Health Statistics (cited hereafter as NCHS), "Health of Black and White Americans, 1985–87," *Vital and Health Statistics* (Series 10, No. 171) (Hyattsville, Md.: Public Health Service, 1990), 55.

4. Comparisons of illness by income, education, occupation, and race all show much the same thing: the lower the status, the higher the rates of

death and disease. Although comparisons by income involve a two-way effect—being poor can lead to worse health, and bad health can also lower income—gradients by income are generally similar to those by race and prior education, implying that all of the gradients reflect primarily the adverse effects of poverty on health rather than vice versa.

5. *Health U.S. 1991*, 141.

6. Ibid., 128; and S. Rosenbaum, C. Layton, J. Liu, *The Health of America's Children* (Children's Defense Fund, 122 C Street N.W., Washington, D.C. 20001, 1991).

7. J. Howse, quoted in R. Pear, " U.S. Reports Rise in Low-Weight Births," *New York Times*, April 22, 1992, A12.

8. *Health U.S. 1991*, 148.

9. J. Rawlings and M. Weir, "Race- and Rank-Specific Infant Mortality in a U.S. Military Population," *American Journal of Diseases of Children* 146 (March 1992): 313–316. Consistent with this, numerous studies have shown that infant-mortality rates among blacks with adequate prenatal care are far lower than for blacks nationally and, in fact, similar to rates for whites. See J. Murray and M. Bernfield, "The Differential Effect of Prenatal Care on the Incidence of Low Birth Weight among Blacks and Whites in a Prepaid Health Care Plan," *New England Journal of Medicine* 319 (1988): 1385–1391.

10. *Health U.S. 1991*, 140.

11. C. McCord and H. Freeman, "Excess Mortality in Harlem," *New England Journal of Medicine* 322 (1990): 173–177.

12. Low family income (or things correlated with income) account for more than one-third of the excess mortality of blacks nationally, even after accounting for the effects of smoking, drinking, blood pressure, cholesterol, obesity, and diabetes. See M. Otten, S. Teutsch, D. Williamson, and J. Marks, "The Effect of Known Risk Factors on the Excess Mortality of Black Adults in the United States," *Journal of the American Medical Association* 263 (1990): 845–850.

13. By contrast, the incidence of breast cancer, which is somewhat lower among black than white women, has been rising since the 1950s for women of both races, and the black-white gap has remained about the same (*Health U.S. 1991*, 198). Studies suggest that black women's poorer survival from breast cancer, like other conditions, stems mainly from their lower economic status. See H. Dayal, R. Power, and C. Chiu, "Race and Socio-Economic Status in Survival from Breast Cancer," *Journal of Chronic Diseases* 35 (1982): 675–683; and H. Freeman, "Race, Poverty, and Cancer," *Journal of the National Cancer Institute* 83 (1991): 526–527.

14. NCHS, "Current Estimates from the National Health Interview Survey, 1989," *Vital and Health Statistics* (Series 10, No. 176) (Hyattsville, Md.: Public Health Service, 1990).

15. *Health U.S. 1991*, 187.

16. NCHS, "Advance Report of Final Mortality Statistics, 1989," *Monthly Vital Statistics Report* (Vol. 40, No. 8, Supplement 2) (Hyattsville, Md.: Public Health Service, January 7, 1992), 30.

17. NCHS, "Americans Assess Their Health: United States, 1987," *Vital and Health Statistics* (Series 10, No. 174) (Hyattsville, Md.: Public Health Service, 1990), 26. Self-rated health has been shown to correlate closely with longevity and other objective health indices. See J. Ware, Jr., "Monitoring and Evaluating Health Services," *Medical Care* 23 (1985): 705–709.

18. L. Egbuonu and B. Stargield, "Child Health and Social Status," *Pediatrics* 69 (1982): 550–557.

19. Average *number* of physician visits shifted accordingly. All else being equal, we'd expect people who are sicker to make more visits. During the 1980s, visits increased only slightly among the poor, despite their worsening health, and markedly among the rich, and, by 1989, visit rates had almost equalized (*Health U.S. 1990*, 1983).

20. In 1989, people with family incomes under $10,000 had 26 visits per 100 restricted-activity days, compared to 53 visits for people with incomes of $35,000 or more. In 1981, the corresponding ratios were 20 vs. 32 (NCHS, Series 10, No. 176, 1990).

21. D. Rogers, testimony before the Senate Subcommittee on Health and Scientific Research, Committee on Labor and Human Resources, 1980.

22. N. Natarajan, T. Nemoto, C. Mettlin, and G. Murphy, "Race-Related Differences in Breast Cancer Patients," *Cancer* 56 (1985): 1704–1709; B. Skura, "Barriers to Care: The Case of Breast Cancer," *Health/PAC Bulletin* (Summer 1991): 29–33; L. Boss and F. Guckes, "Medicaid Coverage of Screening Tests for Breast and Cervical Cancer," *American Journal of Public Health* 82 (1992): 252–253; and S. Shapiro, W. Venet, P. Strax, et al., "Prospects for Eliminating Racial Differences in Breast Cancer Survival Rates," *American Journal of Public Health* 72 (1982): 1142–1145.

23. *Healthy People 2000* (Washington, D.C.: Public Health Service, U.S. Department of Health and Human Services, 1990), 31.

24. *Health U.S. 1990*, 9; *Health U.S. 1991*, 37.

25. On the content and benefits of prenatal care, see Public Health Service, *Caring for Our Future: The Content of Prenatal Care* (Washington, D.C.: Public Health Service, 1989); and Institute of Medicine, *Prenatal Care* (Washington, D.C.: National Academy Press, 1988). Cost-benefit estimate is from

W. Lazarus, *Back to Basics 1988: Strategies for Investing in the Health of California's Next Generation,* report of the Southern California Child Health Network (712 Wilshire Blvd., Suite 1, Santa Monica, Calif. 90941, 1988). For the effects of prenatal care among drug-using mothers, see J. Feldman, H. Minkoff, S. McCalla, and M. Salwen, "A Cohort Study of the Impact of Perinatal Drug Use on Prematurity in an Inner-City Population," *American Journal of Public Health* 82 (1992): 726–727.

26. J. Liu and S. Rosenbaum, "Medicaid and Childhood Immunizations: A National Study" (Children's Defense Fund, 122 C Street N.W., Washington, D.C. 20001, January 1992).

27. "Measles Vaccination Levels among Selected Groups of Preschool-Aged Children—United States," *Morbidity and Mortality Weekly Report* 40 (January 18, 1991): 36–39; and P. Hilts, "U.S. Measles Epidemic Tied to Flawed System," *New York Times,* January 1, 1991, C19. See also Liu and Rosenbaum.

28. Liu and Rosenbaum, 8.

29. "Measuring the Distribution of Income Gains," *CBO Staff Memorandum* (Washington, D.C.: Congressional Budget Office (hereafter cited as CBO), March 1992).

30. For black and white income figures, see Bureau of the Census, *Statistical Abstract of the United States, 1991* (Washington, D.C.: U.S. Department of Commerce, 1991, 454. On the the widening gap, see "Gap between Rich, Poor Widens," *San Francisco Examiner,* December 31, 1989, A6; see also, S. Nasar, "The 1980s: A Very Good Time for the Very Rich," *New York Times,* March 6, 1992, A1. The ultrarich reaped the greatest gains, with the top 1 percent, all of them millionaires or more, receiving an extraordinary 70 percent of the total growth in after-tax income between 1977 and 1989 (CBO, 1992).

31. *World Almanac and Book of Facts 1992,* ed. M. Hoffman (New York: Pharos Books, 1992), 134; see also R. Lewis, "Poverty Traps More Workers," *San Francisco Chronicle,* April 15, 1990, A8.

32. The proportion of people working in low-paying jobs grew sharply during the 1980s, despite the expanding economy, after having been stable in the 1970s and declining during the 1960s (U.S. Bureau of the Census, "Current Population Reports" (Series P-60, No. 178), "Workers with Low Earnings: 1964 to 1990" (Washington, D.C.: U.S. Government Printing Office, 1992). Measured in constant 1982 dollars, the average hourly wage for all nonfarm, nonsupervisory workers was $8.03 in 1970, $7.78 in 1980, and $7.53 in 1990 (Edward Luttwak, "The Riots: Underclass vs. Immigrants," *New York Times,* May 15, 1992, A15). See also Spencer Rich, "Nearly 40% of Welfare Mothers Work, Study Says," *San Francisco Chronicle,* May 23, 1992,

A5. On food stamps, see "More than One in 10 Americans Rely on Food Stamps," *Peninsula Times Tribune*, June 4, 1992, A5.

33. "Vanishing Dreams" (Children's Defense Fund, 122 C Street N.W., Washington, D.C. 20001, 1992); and "Report Says Poor Children Grew Poorer in 1980s," *New York Times*, March 24, 1992, A7. For each race, moreover, the proportion of children living in single-parent families has roughly doubled in the last 30 years. In 1969, only about 7 percent of white children were in single-parent families, but by 1989 nearly 17 percent were. For black children, the proportion jumped from 33 percent in 1969 to 61 percent in 1989, and for Hispanic children from 18 percent in 1974 to 29 percent in 1989 (R. McLeod, "California's Children Faring Badly," *San Francisco Chronicle*, March 23, 1992, A11); see also, R. McLeod, "New Federal Study Says Middle Class is Shrinking," *San Francisco Chronicle*, February 20, 1992, 2.

34. J. Axinn and M. Stern, "Age and Dependency: Children and the Aged in American Social Policy," *Milbank Memorial Fund Quarterly/Health and Society* 63 (Fall 1985): 665; and S. Preston, "Children and the Elderly in the U.S.," *Scientific American* 251 (December 1984): 45.

35. Detailed references for this section are given in D. Dutton, "Social Class, Health, and Illness," in *Applications of Social Science to Clinical Medicine and Health Policy*, ed. L. Aiken and D. Mechanic (New Brunswick, N.J.: Rutgers University Press, 1986): 31–62.

36. *Health U.S. 1990*. Medicaid provides financial coverage for most medical bills for certain groups of people—adults (mostly women) and children in single-parent families through the Aid to Families with Dependent Children (AFDC) program, and also the disabled, aged, and, in some states, people below specified income levels. Because these categories don't include everyone below the poverty level, and eligibility even within categories varies widely among states, the Medicaid program covers less than half of all of the poor in the United States.

37. J. Geiger, "Community Health Centers: Health Care as an Instrument of Social Change," in *Reforming Medicine: Lessons of the Last Quarter Century*, ed. V. Sidel and R. Sidel (New York: Pantheon, 1984): 11–32.

38. For 1982 data on Community Health Centers, see Geiger, 1984. On percentage uninsured, see "House Passes Bill for Continuing Community Health Center Funds," *The Nation's Health* (April 1986): 1. Federal reimbursement restrictions in the 1970s also forced these centers to become "competitive" with private medicine, which meant they had to compromise their original mission further by attracting more paying patients and serving fewer of the uninsured. See A. Sardell, *The U.S. Experiment in Social Medicine: The Community Health Center Program, 1965–1986* (Pittsburgh: University of Pittsburgh Press, 1988). Community Health Centers

might have realized even greater cost savings had the scope of reimbursable services not been narrowed. Government programs will pay thousands of dollars when a child is hospitalized with infectious diarrhea because that is a "legitimate" medical expense, but won't pay $25 to dig a well or $75 to build an outhouse, which might have prevented the illness.

39. On the benefits of MCH services, see U.S. General Accounting Office (hereafter cited as GAO), *Early Childhood and Family Development Programs Improve the Quality of Life for Low-income Families* (Pub. No. HRD-79-40) (Washington, D.C.: U.S. Government Printing Office, 1979). On the benefits of WIC, see GAO, *Early Intervention: Federal Investments Like WIC Can Produce Savings* (Pub. No. HRD-92-18) (Washington, D.C.: U.S. Government Printing Office, April 7, 1992); *S.O.S. America! A Children's Defense Budget* (Children's Defense Fund, 122 C Street N.W., Washington, D.C. 20001, 1990); see also, M. Kotelchuck, J. Schwartz, M. Anderka, and K. Finison, "WIC Participation and Pregnancy Outcomes: Massachusetts Statewide Evaluation Project," *American Journal of Public Health* 74 (1984): 1086–1092; and L. Hicks, R. Langham, and J. Takenaka, "Cognitive and Health Measures Following Early Nutritional Supplementation: A Sibling Study," *American Journal of Public Health* 72 (1982): 1110–1118.

40. D. Rowland et al., "Medicaid: Health Care for the Poor in the Reagan Era," *Annual Review of Public Health* 9 (1988): 427–450; National Health Law Program, "In Poor Health: The Administration's 1985 Health Budget" (2639 S. La Cienaga Blvd., Los Angeles, Calif. 90034); and "Health Care Found in 'Deterioration,'" *San Francisco Chronicle*, Oct. 18, 14.

41. *U.S. Children and Their Families: Current Conditions and Recent Trends, 1989,* Report of the Select Committee on Children, Youth, and Families (hereafter cited as Select Committee), U.S. House, 101st Congress, 1st Session, Nov. 14, 1989, 127. Figures on the poor and near poor are from D. Altman, Health Services Research Seminar, Stanford University, January 6, 1992.

42. "States Drastically Cut Programs Aiding Poor in 1991, Report Says," *New York Times*, December 19, 1991, A15; and M. Peaslee, "Medi-Cal Participation Survey Results," report for the Children's Research Institute of California (P.O. Box 448, Sacramento, Calif. 95812, 1991).

43. The attempted suppression of WIC data is described in E. Marshall, "USDA Admits 'Mistake' in Doctoring Study," *Science* 247 (1990): 522. WIC coverage is reported in Select Committee, 276.

44. S. Rosenbaum, D. Hughes, and K. Johnson, "Maternal and Child Health Services for Medically Indigent Children and Pregnant Women," *Medical Care* 26 (1988): 315–331; and "Farmers Market Nutrition Program Is at Risk," *San Jose Mercury*, May 18, 1992, A7.

45. Rosenbaum et al., 1991; N. McKenzie and E. Bilofsky, "Shredding the

Safety Net: The Dismantling of Public Programs," *Health/PAC Bulletin* (Summer 1991): 5–11; R. Pear, "U.S. to Reconsider Denial of Benefits to Many Disabled," *New York Times*, April 19, 1992, 1.

46. Data on coverage are from *Health U.S. 1991*, p. 291; also, Center for National Health Program Studies, "The Vanishing Health Care Safety Net: New Data on Uninsured Americans" (Cambridge Hospital, 1493 Cambridge St., Cambridge, Mass. 02139, 1992). Figures on spending by income are based on unpublished data from the National Medical Care Expenditure Survey provided by Dan Walden, National Center for Health Services Research, Hyattsville, Md., 1984.

47. Proportion of uninsured families with incomes under $20,000 is from "Medicaid Expansions Cut Levels of Low-Income Uninsured," *The Nation's Health* (March 1992): 4. For data linking insurance to hospitalization, ambulatory care, and health outcomes, see B. Bloom, "Health Insurance and Medical Care," *Advance Data* 188 (1990): 1–5; H. Freeman, R. Blendon, L. Aiken, S. Sudman, C. Mullinix, and C. Corey, "Americans Report on Their Access to Health Care," *Health Affairs* 6 (1987): 6–18; and P. Braveman, G. Oliva, M. G. Miller, R. Reiter, and S. Egerter, "Adverse Outcomes and Lack of Health Insurance Among Newborns in an Eight-County Area of California, 1982 to 1986," *New England Journal of Medicine* 321 (1989): 508–512. Coverage also varies by race. More than one-third of all Mexican Americans are uninsured (probably because many work in low-paying jobs), compared with 22 percent of blacks and 12 percent of whites (*Health U.S. 1990*).

48. "Persons Denied Private Health Insurance Due to Poor Health," NMES Data Summary 4 (AHCPR Pub. No. 92-0016, 1992) (available from AHCPR Clearinghouse, U.S. Department of Health and Human Services); and J. Garrison, "Health Care Crisis: Firms Are Dumping Sick People," *San Francisco Chronicle*, April 5, 1992, 1. In addition, recent court rulings have given large employers who insure their own employees wide leeway to cut back on existing coverage when people get sick, and have also made it harder for patients under all kinds of health-insurance plans to sue to get benefits they believe were unjustly denied.

49. J. Feder, "The Proposal Won't Save Money," *New York Times*, January 25, 1992, A15; see also C. Sullivan and T. Rice, "The Health Insurance Picture in 1990," *Health Affairs* (Summer 1991): 104–113; GAO, *Medicare and Medicaid: Effects of Recent Legislation on Program and Beneficiary Costs* (Pub. No. HRD-87-53) (Washington, D.C.: U.S. Government Printing Office, April 1987), 34–42; and K. Trumbull, "Older Americans Are Spending 61 Percent More on Health Care than 30 Years Ago," *Peninsula Times Tribune*, February 26, 1992, A6.

50. R. G. Beck, "The Effect of Co-Payment on the Poor," *Journal of Human Resources* 9 (1974): 129–142. The Saskatchewan experience is described in

M. Barer, R. Evans, and G. Stoddart, *Controlling Health Care Costs by Direct Charges to Patients: Snare or Delusion?* (Toronto: Ontario Economic Council, 1979). The California Medicaid copayment experiment is described in J. Helms, J. Newhouse, and C. Phelps, "Co-Payments and Demand for Medical Care: The California Medicaid Experience," *Bell Journal of Economics* 10 (1979).

51. Lazarus, *Back to Basics 1988*, 1988. Cost figures are from L. Crain, D. Mangravite, R. Allport, M. Schour, and K. Biakanja, "Health Care Needs and Services for Technology-Dependent Children in Developmental Centers," *Western Journal of Medicine* 152 (April 1990): 434–438.

52. N. Lurie, N. Ward, M. Shapiro, and R. Brook, "Termination from Medi-Cal—Does It Affect Health?" *New England Journal of Medicine* 331 (1984): 480–483.

53. A. M. Gray, "Inequalities in Health. The Black Report: A Summary and Comment," *International Journal of Health Services* 12 (1982): 349–380.

54. P. J. Cunningham and A. C. Monheit, "Insuring the Children: A Decade of Change," *Health Affairs* (Winter 1990): 76–88. One survey found that only 55 percent of working women in their mid-40s or older had coverage through their employers, compared with 72 percent of men (F. Barringer, "Insurance Gap Is Seen Among Older Women," *New York Times*, May 7, 1992, A8). The overwhelming majority of uninsured people (85 percent in 1990) live in families headed by a worker ("States Continue Trend Toward Allowing Basic Benefits Laws," *The Nation's Health* [May–June 1992]: 11). Even many two-worker families, if their combined income is low, have no health insurance (C. Schur and A. Taylor, "Choice of Health Insurance and the Two-Worker Household," *Health Affairs* [Spring 1991]: 155–163).

55. "President Presents Health Care Reform Plan: Reaction from APHA Is Sharp," *The Nation's Health* (March 1992): 1.

56. D. Timbrell, president of the Ontario Hospital Association, in C. Farnsworth, "Canadians Defend Care System Against Criticism," *New York Times*, February 17, 1992, C8.

57. See R. Brook, J. Ware, W. Rogers, E. Keeler, A. Davies, C. Donald, G. Goldberg, K. Lohr, P. Masthay, and J. Newhouse, "Does Free Care Improve Adults' Health?" *New England Journal of Medicine* 309 (1983): 1426–1433; E. Keeler, R. Brook, G. Goldberg, C. Kamberg, and J. Newhouse, "How Free Care Reduced Hypertension in the Health Insurance Experiment," *Journal of the American Medical Association* 254 (1985): 1926–1931; and N. Lurie, C. Kamberg, R. Brook, E. Keeler, and J. Newhouse, "How Free Care Improved Vision in the Health Insurance Experiment," *American Journal of Public Health* 79 (1989): 640–642. In this trial (the Rand Health Insurance Experiment), cost-sharing was proportionate to income,

whereas in the real world it is generally highly regressive, and the poor end up spending a far larger share of their income on health expenses than the affluent.

58. For an argument in favor of the play-or-pay approach, see A. Enthoven and R. Kronick, "A Consumer-Choice Health Plan for the 1990s," *New England Journal of Medicine* 320 (1989): 29–37. An excellent single-payer proposal is described in K. Grumbach, T. Bodenheimer, D. Himmelstein, and S. Woolhandler, "Liberal Benefits, Conservative Spending: The Physicians for a National Health Program Proposal," *Journal of the American Medical Association* 265 (1991): 2549–2554.

59. It isn't difficult for providers to avoid high-cost groups: publicity can be directed at affluent clientele, sick patients can be underserved and encouraged to switch providers, clinics can be located far from poor areas, and so on. California Prepaid Health Plans engaged in various dubious marketing practices, including high-pressure door-to-door salesmen and misrepresentation of services, and some tried to screen out bad risks (V. Goldberg, "Some Emerging Problems of Prepaid Health Plans in the Medi-Cal System," *Policy Analysis* [1976]: 55–68). While this experience is often blamed on bureaucratic mismanagement and other idiosyncratic factors, Rand Health Insurance Experiment results suggest that even mainstream prepaid plans do less well by the poor than fee-for-service settings— perhaps because of similar cost-cutting incentives.

60. B. Williams and A. Miller, *Preventive Health Care for Young Children: Findings from a 10-Country Study and Directions for a United States Policy* (Arlington, Va.: National Center for Clinical Infant Programs, 1991).

61. E. R. Brown, "Health USA: A National Health Program for the United States," *Journal of the American Medical Association* 267 (1992): 552–558.

62. See B. Kirkman-Liff and J. Kronenfeld, "Access to Cancer Screening Services for Women," *American Journal of Public Health* 82 (1992): 733–736; and C. McCoy, B. Nielsen, E. Trapido, J. Zavertnik, E. Khoury, and H. McCoy, "Increasing Breast Cancer Screening Among the Medically Underserved—Dade County, Florida, September 1987–March 1991," *Morbidity and Mortality Weekly Report* 40 (1991): 261–263.

63. For international health comparisons, see G. Scheiber, J-P. Poullier, and L. Greenwald, "Health Care Systems in Twenty-Four Countries," *Health Affairs* (Fall 1991): 22–38. On fraud and billing abuses, see GAO, *Health Insurance: Vulnerable Payers Lose Billions to Fraud and Abuse* (Pub. No. HRD-92-69) (Washington, D.C.: U.S. Government Printing Office, May 1992).

64. National Commission to Prevent Infant Mortality, "Troubling Trends Persist: Shortchanging America's Next Generation" (330 C Street S.W., Washington, D.C. 20201, 1992).

65. "RWJF Study Finds National Health Insurance Could Save Billions," *Advances* (Newsletter of the Robert Wood Johnson Foundation, Winter 1992).

66. For comparisons with Canada, see GAO, *Canadian Health Insurance: Lessons for the United States* (Pub. No. HRD-91-90) (Washington, D.C.: U.S. Government Printing Office, June 1991); see also S. Woolhandler and D. Himmelstein, "The Deteriorating Administrative Efficiency of the U.S. Health Care System," *New England Journal of Medicine* 324 (1991): 1253–1258. For administrative costs of Medicare and Medicaid, see K. Levit, H. Lazenby, S. Letsch, and C. Cowan, "National Health Care Spending, 1989," *Health Affairs* (Spring 1991): 120.

67. R. Blendon, R. Leitman, I. Morrison, and K. Donelan, "Satisfaction with Health Systems in Ten Nations," *Health Affairs* (Summer 1990): 185–192; and P. Anderson, "Survey: Americans Want National Health Plan, Would Pay for It," *Peninsula Times Tribune* May 16, 1992, 1.

68. Single-payer national health-insurance plans have been introduced into Congress by Senator Bob Kerrey (D-Neb) (Brown, 1992), and by Representatives Marty Russo (D-Ill) and Ron Dellums (D-Cal). Although these plans differ in many details, they would all incorporate current funding sources into a single program that would finance comprehensive services for everyone, control costs, and match resources with need. In the absence of federal leadership in health-care reform, a number of states are pushing ahead with their own plans for extending coverage to the uninsured and reestablishing planning mechanisms to control costs. Initiatives underway in Oregon, Minnesota, Florida, Vermont, and other states are being closely watched as potential models for national reform.

69. T. Smeeding and B. Torrey, "Poor Children in Rich Countries," *Science* 242 (1988): 873–877; and "The Rich Get Richer: And What to Do About It," *New York Times*, April 19, 1992, 10.

70. For an insightful review of these issues, see L. Schorr, *Within Our Reach: Breaking the Cycle of Disadvantage* (New York: Doubleday, 1988).

71. Polls conducted after the Los Angeles riots are reported in R. Toner, "Los Angeles Riots Are a Warning, Americans Fear," *New York Times*, May 11, 1992, 1; and in J. DeParle, "The Civil Rights Battle Was Easy Next to the Problems of the Ghetto," *New York Times*, May 17, 1992, E1. Gallup poll results are in L. Grunwald, "If Women Ran America," *Life* (June 1992): 39–46.

72. Committee for Economic Development, *Children in Need: Investment Strategies for the Educationally Disadvantaged* (477 Madison Avenue, New York, N.Y. 10022, 1987).

73. L. Harris, "Examine These Myths of the 80s," *New York Times*, May 19, 1989, A15.

74. J. DeParle, "Nostalgia and Need Conjure Up Thoughts of the WPA," *New York Times*, May 3, 1992, E6. Successful job-training programs are described in P. Kilborn, "Jobs Program Makes Carpenters of Urban Young," *New York Times*, June 8, 1992, 1.

75. Early results from workfare programs in California suggest that they raised the earnings of people on welfare and reduced the amount they received in public aid, although both effects were small. Perhaps more importantly, many mothers felt that their children's sense of self-worth and commitment to education had improved as a result of their participation in the program (J. DeParle, "Welfare Plan Linked to Jobs Is Paying Off, a Study Shows," *New York Times*, April 23, 1992, 1; and J. Marshall, "The Hidden Benefits of Workfare," *San Francisco Chronicle*, May 14, 1992, A6). The 1988 Family Support Act authorized up to $1 billion a year in federal matching funds for workfare programs, but many states are facing such severe budget shortages that workfare programs can serve only a fraction of the eligible population, and child care for program participants remains in short supply, despite the 1988 law's mandate that it be provided.

76. "The Rich Get Richer," 10.

77. The bill was introduced by Thomas Downey, a liberal Long Island Democrat, and Henry Hyde, a conservative Illinois Republican (J. DeParle, "Radical Overhaul Proposed In System of Child Support," *New York Times*, May 13, 1992, A8).

78. For a compassionate discussion of the plight of poor women and children in the United States, see R. Sidel, *Women and Children Last* (New York: Penguin, 1992).

79. For example, the administration's Office of Management and Budget, seeking to delay implementation of new occupational-health regulations, argued that the regulations might lead employers to cut jobs or wages, leaving workers poorer, hence sicker. OMB noted that "the positive effect of wealth on health has been established both theoretically and empirically. Richer workers on average buy more leisure time, more nutritious food, more preventive health care and smoke and drink less than poorer workers." (Under pressure from Congress, OMB later retreated from its demand for a delay.) A. Clymer, "O.M.B. Retreats on Work-Health Issue," *New York Times*, March 30, 1992, A8.

HEALTH ISSUES FOR WOMEN IN THE 1990s

❖ ❖ ❖

Iris F. Litt

HEALTH STATUS OF WOMEN

Women are traditionally viewed as being healthier than men because they live longer, although it is not clear how much of this advantage is due to biologic or social and cultural influences.

While it is true that the average life expectancy of women is seven years longer than that of men,[1] there are many illnesses that are unique to women or affect them more, and others that are more serious in women or for which there are different risk factors or interventions.[2] Moreover, *quantity* of life is different from *quality* of life and it is now apparent that the majority of women who live to old age do so in a state of dependency and disability because of chronic diseases that are more common in women.

As disabled elderly, women are less likely to have a spouse or children available to care for them and are more apt to need long-term health care than are men. Accordingly, women's health must be examined not merely as the absence of disease but in the context of the definition of health, given by the World Health Organization, "the achievement of optimal physical, psychological, economic and social well-being."[3]

Changing social roles and responsibilities interact with biologic features to affect the health and well-being of women. Women have always had dual roles, as wives and mothers. Increasingly, through the 1980s and early 1990s, they have entered the paid labor force and assumed additional responsibilities that carry the risk of additional health problems. Currently, 52 percent of women are employed outside the home. While the majority work in the service fields, there is evidence of diversification and some upward mobility. Consequently, women's work roles are emerging as one of the most important factors concerning their health status.[4]

In this chapter, we will examine the causes, preventive measures, and possible remedies of women's health problems, and consider the implications of these factors for public policy.

GENDER DIFFERENCES IN HEALTH STATUS

Health status is generally monitored by mortality and morbidity statistics. *Mortality* describes the causes of death and *morbidity* describes how frequently a reportable disease occurs in a population.

MORTALITY

As seen in Table 1, which outlines the ten leading causes of death for women in 1988, 28 percent of deaths among women were caused by heart disease, previously considered almost exclusively a disease of men. In fact, men have heart attacks at an earlier age than women, largely because of the protective effect of estrogen on women. This protection is lost after the menopause unless replacement estrogen is taken. Thus, for both women and men over age 65, the three leading causes of death are the same: heart disease, cancer, and stroke.

The types of cancer differ between men and women, with the most conspicuous differences related to cancers of the reproductive organs. Contrary to general impressions, however, "female" cancers are no longer common types of cancer in women. Since 1986, there have been more deaths in women from lung cancer than from breast cancer,[5] and more deaths from cancer of the colon and rectum than from cancers of the ovaries, uterus, or cervix. The fact that mortality data are usually collected at a single point in time means that these figures may mask other dramatic changes that have occurred recently with regard to death in women. For example, the death rate from lung cancer in women has increased sixfold in the past 30 years. From 1980 to 1986, the rate of lung cancer increased steadily from 28.4 to 37.2 per 100,000 per year for females.[6] During the same period of time, there was a slight fall in the rate of lung cancer for men, suggesting that factors like environmental pollution are not to blame for this increase.

TABLE 1

LEADING CAUSES OF DEATH FOR WOMEN, 1988

CAUSE OF DEATH	NUMBER OF DEATHS
1. Heart disease (28 percent of all deaths in women)	379,754
2. Cancer	226,960
Lung	55,000 ±
Breast	44,500 ±
Colorectal	13,000 ±
Ovarian	12,500
Endometrial	5,500
Cervical	4,500
3. Cerebrovascular disease	90,758
4. Pneumonia/influenza	40,828
5. Chronic obstructive pulmonary disease	33,914
6. Accidents	31,279
Automotive	
Domestic violence	
7. Diabetes	23,393
8. Atherosclerosis	13,759
9. Septicemia	11,793
10. Nephritis	11,512

Modified from Pharmaceutical Manufacturers Association, *New Medicines in Development for Women* (Washington, D.C.: Pharmaceutical Manufacturers Association, 1991).

Clearly, it is the increase in smoking among women during this period that is responsible for this devastating finding.

Another worrisome mortality statistic is that deaths from AIDS among women are increasing at a much faster rate than in men. It is now the seventh leading cause of death among women of all races in the 25 to 34 year age group and the fourth leading cause of death for black women.[7] In New York City, it is now the leading cause of death among women ages 25 to 44 years.[8] The true number of women with AIDS is, as yet, unknown because the official criteria for diagnosing the disease have been established on the basis of male symptoms. As a result, cervical cancer, a common cause of death among women with AIDS, is not listed in criteria for its diagnosis. The disparity in rates of increase reflects, in part, the fact that the incidence of AIDS in the heterosexual community has been grossly underestimated in the United States.

MORBIDITY

Table 2 describes those health problems that are unique to women. These obviously reflect biologic differences between the sexes and focus on those illnesses of reproductive organs and characteristics. The health problems listed in Table 3 are less obvious, but equally important, because they represent the illnesses that are currently recognized as being more common in women than in men. For these, there is no simple biologic explanation for their predilection for women. Research is needed to better understand this phenomenon and eventually to reduce the disproportionate burden of illness faced by women.

Morbidity data are considered in terms of incidence and prevalence. The *incidence* of an illness is its rate of occurrence in a given period of time, usually a year. The *prevalence* is the total number of cases in the population under study at any one point in time. These data are tracked by government agencies interested in public health, as well as by categorical private professional or lay organizations, such as the American Cancer Society, for example. Health-care delivery systems and insurance companies also provide morbidity data. The reliability of these figures depends upon how accurately and consci-

TABLE 2

PREVALENCE OF HEALTH PROBLEMS

HEALTH PROBLEM	PREVALENCE
Gynecologic	
Cancers	
Endometrial	33,000/yr
Cervical	13,000/yr
Ovarian	20,700/yr
Infections	
Pelvic inflammatory disease	(750,000 in 1990)
Human papilloma virus	15% to 40% of women
Vulvovaginal candidiasis	13 million
Amenorrhea	3%
Infertility	4.9 million (15 to 44 years)
Endometriosis	10% to 20% (15 to 44 years)
Postmenopausal symptoms	6.2 million
Breast	176,000

SOURCE: Pharmaceutical Manufacturers Association, *New Medicines in Development for Women* (Washington, D.C.: Pharmaceutical Manufacturers Association, 1991).

TABLE 3

HEALTH PROBLEMS THAT ARE MORE COMMON IN WOMEN THAN IN MEN

HEALTH PROBLEMS	NUMBER OF WOMEN (%)
Musculo-skeletal-connective tissue	37 million
Osteoporosis	20 million (80)
Juvenile rheumatoid arthritis	61,000 (86)
Osteoarthritis	11.7 million (74)
Rheumatoid arthritis	1.5 million (71)
Systemic lupus erythematosus	450,000 (90)
Cardiovascular	
Hyperlipidemia	(82% of women aged 45 to 74 years vs. 71% of men)
Hypertension	16 million (58)
Kidney/urologic	
Incontinence	9.6 million (80)
Neurologic	
Migraine	12 million (70)
Glaucoma	1.5 million (67)
Psychiatric	
Depression	(9.7% of women vs. 4.7% of men)
Bulimia	7 million (87)
Respiratory	
Acute bronchitis	5.3 million (60.5)
Asthma	6.02 million (53)
Influenza	66 million (54)

SOURCE: Pharmaceutical Manufacturers Association, *New Medicines in Development for Women* (Washington, D.C.: Pharmaceutical Manufacturers Association, 1991).

entiously organizations and agencies report the illnesses they see. While government agencies are subject to penalties for the failure of responsible individuals or institutions to report such figures, other agencies are not. Because not all conditions can be tracked, these data are necessarily limited to those deemed sufficiently important to be reported for public-health or other reasons.

Some data of potential importance to understanding women's health status may, under the current system, be difficult to access. For example, it would not be possible to find the numbers of women with premenstrual syndrome (PMS), eating disorders, or osteoporosis, or who use oral contraceptives, and so on. Even for those conditions that *are* reportable, it is not possible to know how many women have more than one condition. Moreover, since women are less often insured and less likely to receive health care when ill, their illnesses may never get diagnosed and never enter any data base. In addition, because more data are reported from public institutions than from private doctors' offices (particular about sensitive issues such as sexually transmitted diseases and suicide attempts), poor women are more likely to be overrepresented in some data bases. Since there are more poor women reported than affluent, the recorded data about the health of women may be skewed by this reporting bias.

Neither mortality nor morbidity data adequately address the issue of quality of life. Clearly, what might be a relatively minor ailment for an individual with support and resources can become a major problem for a poor single mother or an elderly woman caring for her disabled spouse. In addition, since the quality of a younger woman's life is often determined by the number and spacing of her children, the availability of safe and effective birth control is an important health issue that is not reflected in any data base.

DETERMINANTS OF WOMEN'S HEALTH STATUS

While our knowledge is limited by the inadequacy and accuracy of the methods used to collect information about women's health status, it has grown considerably during the late 1980s and early 1990s. We are now aware that it is an oversimplification to consider the health status of women as if they are a homogeneous group. In fact, their health status varies in relation to their socioeconomic status, ethnicity, age, and occupation, as well as being influenced by biologic factors.

BIOLOGY

It is clear that the biologic differences between men and women will, in some way, influence their respective health status. But, in addition to illnesses of reproductive organs or hormones, there are other more subtle differences between women and men. These include certain genetic diseases or features that only occur in women (e.g., Turner's syndrome). Other genetically determined diseases are more common in women than men (among these are diabetes mellitus and systemic lupus erythematosus).

Biologic differences are found in terms of physical growth and development. For example, when puberty is completed, women are generally shorter, have more body fat, wider hips, smaller hearts, less lung capacity, looser ligaments, fewer red blood cells, and, therefore, less oxygen-carrying capacity than males. These differences, for example, affect their athletic capabilities, giving them an advantage in swimming and a disadvantage in long-distance running. These differences may also have less apparent effects. For example, the increase in fatness of puberty in females is normal and healthy, but it interacts with the present societal emphasis on thinness as the supposed ideal for the female form. Clearly, the high rates of dieting and of unhealthy eating behaviors among adolescent women in our society have their origins in this biologic fact.

SOCIOECONOMIC STATUS

Poverty affects health in direct and indirect ways. Not having enough money for the necessities of life like food and shelter will directly impact on health by causing malnutrition, or increasing susceptibility to infectious diseases, exposure, and overcrowding. In the United States, poverty is also associated with receipt of little or no preventive or therapeutic health care. As a result, the poor suffer disproportionately from preventable diseases, have higher infant mortality rates, more disability from chronic illness, and more accidents and violence.[9] Because many women live in poverty, they bear a disproportionate share of these health burdens.

For women, however, having financial resources does not guarantee good health care. Even with private health insurance, it is often difficult to get payment for preventive procedures, like mammograms, or for psychiatric care, which is typically capped on these policies. Moreover, the inadequate research on women's health (as discussed later in this chapter) and the biases among physicians about the health status of women contribute to poorer health care for women of all socioeconomic strata.

ETHNICITY

In addition to genetically transmitted diseases that may vary with ethnicity, this variable may affect health in other ways. In our society, however, it is often difficult to disentangle the effects of ethnicity from those of poverty, which for most minority groups in the United States are intertwined.

Language is often a barrier to receiving health care. For example, one study found that Hispanic women who did not speak English were less likely to get a mammogram for early detection of breast cancer than were those who spoke English.[10]

For women, ethnic differences have been reported in the incidence of AIDS (more common in blacks and Latinas), eating disorders (more common in whites), homicides (higher rate in blacks), sexually transmitted diseases (more common in blacks), osteoporosis (less common in blacks than whites), and so on.

AGE

During adolescence, gender differences in health emerge that result from the biologic events of puberty, from different psychosocial experiences, and from the interactions of both.

The pubertal differences between the sexes were discussed earlier. Those differences are also responsible for the development of a higher incidence of thyroid disease and scoliosis, as well as the more obvious breast and gynecologic disorders in female adolescents.

Among the psychosocial problems, the higher incidence of eating disorders and depression that continue throughout the life span of women are first seen in the mid-adolescent years. For example, suicidal depression at some time has been reported in 30 percent of adolescent women vs. 10 percent of their male peers. A recent survey of 12- to 14-year-olds showed that 1 in 11 females had already experienced suicidal thoughts, compared with 1 in 25 males.[11]

Physicians begin to prescribe more mood-altering medications, such as tranquilizers and sedatives, to women than men from the time patients are 13 years of age.[12] Drug abuse has, on the other hand, been traditionally viewed as a problem of male adolescents. While it remains true that there is more drug and alcohol use and abuse among teen males, the gender gap is narrowing.[13] In fact, there are now more female adolescent new smokers than males. Because of its significant role in the causation of life-threatening disease in later life, the increase in smoking by adolescent females, which now exceeds that for males, must be regarded as a critical area for preventive research.

Similarly, although there are more violent deaths among male than female adolescents, homicide is one of five leading causes of death among adolescent women. The incidence of sexual, emotional, and physical abuse is much higher in teenaged women. Females are four times more likely to be sexually abused than males (a rate of 3.5/1000).[14]

Pregnancy during adolescence is associated with serious socioeconomic, as well as health, consequences for women and their children. Because of political and religious pressures in the United States, it is difficult for minors to obtain contraception without parental consent. For this reason, the United States has the highest rate of adolescent pregnancy among industrialized countries of the world. A related problem is the high incidence of sexually transmitted disease among adolescents, responsible for acute illness and, often, for sterility in women.

For adult women, health problems often include some of those seen among adolescents, such as problems related to reproductive function, but there is an increased incidence of collagen-vascular diseases, cancers, and diseases of the endocrine or hormonal system at this life stage. For the nearly 50 percent of women who have entered the paid labor force, these preexisting health problems are further complicated by problems related to occupational status. Exposure to industrial hazards, complications of work requiring repetitive motion and use of equipment designed for and by men, and psychologic pressures of environments that may discriminate against women are currently some of the additional health-risk factors for women. In fact, one study found that a woman's satisfaction with her primary work role is the most significant determinant of her health status.[15] Another report shows that occupation is one of the most important causes of premature death among women.[16] Violence has become one of the leading causes of death and disability for women under the age of 34 years, with homicide becoming one of the top five.

For middle-aged women, there is increased health risk from the changes that relate to the menopause. Coronary artery disease, strokes, breast cancer, lung cancer and cancer of the colon and rectum, and the beginning of osteoporosis become significant issues at this time in life. One of the most urgent areas for additional research is the prevention of these life-threatening diseases. The role of estrogen-replacement therapy and the prevention or cessation of smoking are two critical factors that require further study.

Older women are at increased risk for a variety of life-threatening diseases, such as congestive heart failure, stroke, myocardial infarction (heart attacks), hypertension (high blood pressure), and chronic obstructive pulmonary disease. The most serious threat to the quality of their lives, however, relates to their increased risk for development of chronic illnesses, such as Alzheimer's disease, parkinsonism, and the sensory deficits such as blindness and deafness. Their increased risk for arthritis and osteoporosis (fractures) further limits their mobility and health status.

COST

It has been estimated by the Department of Commerce and the Department of Health and Human Services that health-care spending cost $738 billion in 1991. They predict that it will rise to $817 billion in

1992, thus constituting 14 percent of the GNP.[17] This percentage has been rising at a rate of 1 percent each year since 1989. For comparative purposes, the cost of the national health insurance plan for Canada is only 8.6 percent of the GNP. It is reasonable to estimate that health care for women represents about one-half to three-quarters of the total expenditure (based on the 1988 figure of $464 billion given in Table 4). As seen in Table 4, although the total cost of health care for women currently exceeds that spent on men, relatively little is expended on research or prevention efforts. Until this fact is acknowledged and remedied, women will continue to require a disproportionately large

TABLE 4

ESTIMATED COST OF WOMEN'S HEALTH PROBLEMS

HEALTH PROBLEM	ESTIMATED COST
Arthritis	$36 billion/yr
Osteoporosis	>$10 billion for care of fractures (1987)
Cancers	$104 billion (1990)[1]
Atherosclerosis	$34.2 billion (1987, direct costs)
Congestive heart failure	$4.7 billion (1987, direct costs)
Coronary artery disease	$14 billion (1987, direct costs)
Hypertension	$13.7 billion (1991, estimate)
Stroke	$25 billion/yr
Urinary tract infections	$4.4 billion/yr[2]
Alzheimer's disease	$88 billion (1985)
Migraine	$50 billion+/yr (workdays lost and medical expenses)
Eye disorders	$16 billion+/yr
Depression	$27 billion+/yr[3]
Asthma	$6.8 billion (1986)[4]
Chronic obstructive pulmonary disease	$10.2 billion (1988)
Diabetes	$20.4 billion/yr

[1]Approximately ⅓ for direct medical costs, <⅔ for mortality costs, and ⅒ for lost productivity/morbidity
[2]Includes physician, hospitalization, and lost productivity
[3]15% of this is the amount lost due to suicides
[4]⅓ of this is for direct medical costs

Modified from Pharmaceutical Manufacturers Association, *New Medicines in Development for Women* (Washington, D.C.: Pharmaceutical Manufacturers Association, 1991).

share of the health-care dollar in the United States while experiencing a poorer quality of life because of their higher illness burden.

BARRIERS TO IMPROVED HEALTH FOR WOMEN

ACCESS TO CARE   Access to health care, according to Pechansky and Thomas,[18] consists of the following five relationships:

1. Availability: the relationship between supply and need
2. Accessibility: the relationship between location and population
3. Affordability: the relationship between service prices and client resources
4. Accommodation: the relationship between organization of the resources and use patterns of clients
5. Acceptability: the relationship between provider and practice characteristics and client attitudes, preferences, and expectations

For each of these relationships, there is evidence that access is problematic for women patients. Most significant among the problems of access, however, is that of cost.

Thirty-seven million Americans have no health insurance and an additional 7,000,000 to 10,000,000 have inadequate coverage.[19] Because insurance coverage is often linked to employment and because women are more likely to be part-time employees, temporary or service workers, or unemployed heads of households, they number prominently among the uninsured. Under the current system in the United States, therefore, in which access to health care is based largely on private insurance provided through employment, women are at a clear disadvantage. In an analysis provided by Hartmann of the system of employer-provided insurance coverage, it was shown that during the 1980s there was a 3 percent decrease in the proportion of married couples with children who had health insurance through their employers, but the drop for single mothers was 10 percent.[20] By 1987, 50 percent of single mothers had no health insurance for their children. Including the insurance provided by Medicaid, which serves twice as many women as men, children of single mothers are twice as likely not to have health insurance as children of married couples. In addition to the obvious psychologic implications of lack of health coverage for their children, children's illness is a leading cause of parents' absence from work, a particular problem and reason for job loss for single parents, most of whom are women.

There are many adverse effects of being uninsured, the most

studied of which is its impact on pregnancy outcome. Prenatal care is the most important determinant of good pregnancy outcome, including a decrease in stillbirths, miscarriages, prematurity, and maternal anemia. Pregnancy outcome is notoriously worse for adolescents than for older women, one explanation for which is the fact that adolescents get prenatal care late or not at all. Contributing to this problem is the fact that the majority of adolescent females lack health-insurance coverage for maternity-related care, either because of exclusions in their parents' policies, the necessity to notify policy holders and thus violate the adolescent's right to confidentiality, or the absence of any form of health insurance.[21] The cost to society of providing care to sick and premature infants born to mothers unable to access prenatal care for financial reasons far exceeds that which would be required to provide the needed coverage.

Access may also be affected by ethnicity and socioeconomic status. It is obviously difficult to separate the effects of poverty and of acculturation from that of lack of health insurance, but one study showed that Hispanic women who were predominately Spanish speaking and lacked health insurance were one-quarter as likely as English-speaking Hispanic women (who were twice as likely to have health insurance) to have had a mammogram for the early detection of breast cancer.[22]

Any measures that enhance women's employability are important steps toward improving their health status insofar as they enhance the likelihood that they will have access to health insurance. A major step toward achieving this goal is the passage of a universal national health plan, provided there is adequate support for the health needs of women and provided there is nonpoliticized choice of and access to the full range of health-care options and protection of the rights that women require in U.S. society.

HEALTH-CARE RATIONING

When health resources are scarce, decisions about their allocation are necessary. As health cost containment becomes critical, as it is in the early 1990s, there is increasing pressure to limit expenditures. The few data available suggest that women suffer under conditions of health-care rationing. For example, one criterion for the decision to undertake an expensive medical procedure is age. Often, the younger patient will be given preference in allocation of costly or limited resources, such as transplantation. Age is, therefore, one important limiting factor in medical decision making. Because women are disproportionately represented among the elderly, this criterion has a greater impact in disqualifying women than men from care.[23]

Age is not the only explanation, however, for the gender inequality in distribution of costly medical interventions. One study of patients with end-stage kidney disease showed that a female patient had 25 percent less chance than a male with the same disease to receive a kidney transplant.[24] In fact, among those in the 46- to 60-year age category, a woman's chance was half that of a man. In addition, despite the fact that the risk of having coronary artery disease is only three times higher for men than women, women were 6.5 times less likely to be referred by their physicians for cardiac catheterization than men with the same clinical symptoms and findings. Women are less likely to be referred for cardiac bypass surgery when their coronary artery disease is diagnosed, largely because of data showing that they have a greater chance of dying following the procedure. This poorer outcome results from the fact that women are typically operated on when their disease has progressed further than is the case for men,[25] and should not be used as a reason to limit women's access to this procedure.

Traditional social-value judgments also enter into these decisions. "A general perception that men's social role obligations or their contributions to society are greater than women's may fuel these disparities."[26] Viewed as the primary financial supports of their families, our society has typically placed a greater value on the lives of men and appears more willing to pay to support their health-care costs.

LEGAL AND POLICY ISSUES THAT AFFECT HEALTH-CARE DELIVERY TO WOMEN

REPRODUCTIVE RIGHTS

Political and religious impediments to access to the necessary range of reproductive options represents one of the most serious health problems facing women in the United States today.

The most recent setback in this long and often-fought battle to allow women to make well-informed decisions about their reproductive health is the U.S. Supreme Court's upholding of the restrictive Title X regulations in the case of *Rust v. Sullivan*.[27] This so-called *gag rule* bars health-care providers in family-planning clinics that receive federal funds (which effectively includes all facilities available to the poor) from mentioning, let alone counseling or referring women for abortions. This decision interferes not only with the right to free speech of physicians and other health workers but also with their professional and moral duty to provide their patients with information about all medical options. Because physicians in the private practice of medicine are not constrained in terms of the information they provide to patients who can afford their care, the gag rule clearly discriminates against poor women and the young who must attend federally funded clinics or get no care at all. Limitation of payment for abortion in federal Medicaid recipients is another way in which the government has interfered with this vital right of women.

States vary in the extent to which they limit reproductive decision making by women; some require spousal notification or parental consent for performance of abortion or prescription of contraceptives to a minor. It is likely that the U.S. Supreme Court will use the restrictive Pennsylvania, Utah, or Louisiana cases as the basis for eventually overturning *Roe v. Wade*.

A pro-choice Congress is the only hope for preservation of the limited reproductive rights women now have. The protections now afforded by *Roe v. Wade* must become codified under federal law. The Freedom of Choice Act has been introduced into both houses of Congress in order to reverse the ban on abortion counseling (the gag rule). It has been passed in the Senate and action in the House is expected soon. Elected officials at every level of local, state, and federal government must support women's health rights, as battles will be fought across this spectrum of the system.

PRODUCT LIABILITY LAWS

Fear of product liability lawsuits, as well as the cost involved, has caused the pharmaceutical industry to withdraw from developing new, safer, forms of contraception. In 1991, Norplant became the first new contraceptive to be introduced in the United States in 20 years. Fear of antichoice extremism has forced the French manufacturers of RU-486, a potentially noninvasive safer method of inducing an early abortion, to withhold the drug from the U.S. market. The 1992 Labor–Health and Human Services–Education Appropriations bill includes funding for the National Institutes of Health (NIH) Women's Health Initiative, one small part of which is for contraceptive research. A model for needed legislation is that of the 1988 Vaccine Injury Compensation Act.

A related issue is the need for better surveillance of products such as breast implants and tampons, which have not received ade-

quate review under past Food and Drug Administration (FDA) procedures.

RESEARCH

Half of the U.S. population is female, women's health problems currently constitute more than two-thirds of health-care costs, and
women contribute equally with men through their tax dollars to the
budget of the NIH, which directs most medical research in the United
States; yet, only 13 percent of the medical research in this country is
on women's health.

The image of women as the healthy sex (based on their longer
life expectancy) has helped to exclude them from much of medical
research, except that which relates to "female problems." Those illnesses that affect reproductive function and structure have typically
colored the picture of women's health status and guided the content
and process of health-care delivery to women, to the detrimental
exclusion of other conditions. Indeed, the exclusion of women from
research studies has severely limited our knowledge of the extent of
health problems in women. Women have been ignored or intentionally
excluded from research for a variety of reasons, some of which are
well intentioned.

Fear among researchers that a woman may be pregnant and not
know it or may become pregnant during a study has led to wholesale
exclusion of women from research that involves the testing of any
drug deemed potentially harmful to an unborn fetus. The possibility
of periodic pregnancy testing and that women are capable of giving
informed consent with appropriate warnings and safeguards, is not
considered, often out of concern about a lawsuit. In other cases,
women are excluded from drug research because of concern about the
effect of changing hormones during the menstrual cycle and their
potential effect on drug metabolism. This is another understandable,
but potentially controllable, rationale. Moreover, the effect of hormonal fluctuations on drug metabolism is never considered in the
prescribing of drugs. Physicians never consider the stage of the menstrual cycle and adjust the dose accordingly. A recent study under-
scored the importance of this consideration.[28] It showed that by
prescribing the same daily dose of an antidepressant a woman has too
high a blood level in the first half of the cycle and a less than therapeutic
level in the premenstrual half of the cycle. From this observation, it is
appropriate to conclude that drug doses are, indeed, influenced by
women's hormone levels. Rather than being the basis for excluding

women from research, however, it is imperative that this biologic fact be addressed in both the design of research testing of new drugs to be prescribed ultimately to women and in the prescribing information provided to physicians, as well as to patients. We cannot simply generalize from research on male subjects to female patients.

Increased spending for research on identified health problems of women is a reasonable beginning, but woefully inadequate to redress the deficits of the past. We need exploratory epidemiologic surveys designed to redefine health in ways more consistent with the experience of women. Existing instruments and diagnostic criteria derived from and by males must be reexamined to eliminate bias against women. New paradigms for thinking about women's health are indicated and more women researchers and health-care providers are necessary. Such a large-scale overhaul of the medical research system of this country requires commitment and funding. This funding must come from the public sector, as well as from the pharmaceutical and health-care industries.

INFLUENCING POLICY AND THE POLITICAL PROCESS

To influence the political process, policymakers as well as candidates for local, state, and federal office must be aware of, sensitive to, and knowledgeable about the health status of women, its improvement, and its implications for their well-being. Accordingly, they must be responsive to questions about access, research needs, and health policy.

In the area of access, they should favor some form of national health insurance, specifically being aware of the need for adequate coverage for preventive procedures such as mammograms, for psychiatric and contraceptive care, and opposed to rationing provisions that are potentially discriminatory against women. They must be sensitive to the need to cover all women at every stage of life and to the importance of not linking health insurance to employment status. They should be aware that tax credits for purchase of private health insurance are inadequate for poor women.

They must be aware of the need to increase the funding for research on women's health problems through federal and private funding, the latter linked to the need for protection against legal suit of pharmacologic companies. A related issue is the importance of bringing more women into the sciences and health fields by increasing role models in leadership positions in these fields in both academic and industrial settings.

When asked what can be done to decrease the problem of adolescent sexually transmitted disease and pregnancy, the candidate should be aware of the importance of improved quality and earlier introduction of sex education in the schools, elimination of parental notification requirements for access to contraception or abortion, and the need for increased funding for research on more effective interventions and improved availability of contraceptives.

The recent revelations about the questionable safety of breast implants has far-reaching implications and mandates that we ensure safer and more effective preventive and therapeutic interventions for women. Accordingly, candidates must be aware of the need to guarantee inclusion of women in drug-research studies; support wider FDA control of devices, products, and drugs used by women; and advocate control of cigarette and alcohol advertising aimed at young women.

As in all other aspects of their well-being, women's participation in the paid labor force has important health implications. Accordingly, the candidate need be sensitive to the need for paid dependent care leave (e.g., support The Family Leave Act) and for adequate child and dependent care and recognize the role of gender bias in hindering advancement and pay equity.

NOTES

1. U.S. Department of Health and Human Services, Public Health Service, Centers for Disease Control, *Monthly Vital Statistics Report* 40(8) Suppl. 2, January 7, 1992.

2. P. Cotton, "Is There Still Too Much Extrapolation from Data on Middle-Aged White Men?" *Journal of the American Medical Association* 263 (1990): 1051–1052.

3. World Health Organization Constitution, WHO Basic Documents (Geneva: World Health Organization, 1948).

4. L. M. Verbrugge, "Work Satisfaction and Physical Health," *Journal of Community Health* 7 (1982): 262–283.

5. *Mortality and Morbidity Weekly Report* 39(48), December 7, 1990: 875, 881.

6. Ibid.

7. H. Hartmann, "Women's Health in the United States," Institute for Women's Policy Research. Presented by the Campaign for Women's Health, July 12, 1991.

8. Department of Health, New York City, 1992 (personal communication).

9. Children's Safety Network, "A Data Book of Child and Adolescent Injury" (Washington, D.C.: National Center for Education in Maternal and Child Health, 1991).

10. J. A. Stein and S. A. Fox, "Language Preference as an Indicator of Mammography Use among Hispanic Women," *Journal of the National Cancer Institute* 21 (1990): 1715–1716.

11. C. Garrison, K. Jackson, C. Addy, et al., "Suicidal Behaviors in Young Adolescents," *American Journal of Epidemiology* 133 (1991): 1005–1014.

12. D. B. Kandel and J. A. Logan, "Patterns of Drug Use from Adolescence to Young Adulthood: 1. Periods of Risk for Initiation, Continued Use, and Discontinuation," *American Journal of Public Health* 74 (1984): 660–666.

13. L. D. Johnston, J. G. Bachman, and P. M. O'Malley, "Drug Use, Drinking, and Smoking: National Survey Results from High School, College and Young Adult Populations, 1975–1988," NIDA, USDHHS, PHS, Alcohol, Drug Abuse, and Mental Health Administration. DHHS Publ. No. (ADM) 89-1638, 1989.

14. National Center on Child Abuse and Neglect, *Study Findings—Study of National Incidence and Prevalence of Child Abuse and Neglect* (Washington, D.C.: USDHHS, 1991).

15. J. H. LaRosa, "Executive Women and Health: Perceptions and Practices," *American Journal of Public Health* 80 (1990): 1450–1454.

16. G. Doebbert, K. R. Riedmiller, and K. Kizer, "Occupational Mortality of California Women, 1979–1981," *Western Journal of Medicine* 149 (1988): 734–740.

17. *New York Times*, January 6, 1992.

18. R. Pechansky and J. W. Thomas, "The Concept of Access: Definition and Relationship to Consumer Satisfaction," *Medical Care* 19 (1981): 127–140.

19. U.S. Congress, Office of Technology Assessment, *Adolescent Health–Volume I: Summary and Policy Options* (OTA-H-468) (Washington, D.C.: U.S. Government Printing Office, April 1991), 25–27.

20. Hartmann, 1991.

21. Ibid.

22. Stein and Fox, 1990.

23. N. S. Jecker and R. A. Pearlman, "Ethical Constraints on Rationing Medical Care by Age," *Journal of the American Geriatrics Society* 37 (1989): 1067–1075.

24. Council on Ethical and Judicial Affairs, American Medical Association, "Gender Disparities in Clinical Decision Making," *Journal of the American Medical Society* 266 (1991): 559–562.

25. Ibid.

26. *Rust v. Sullivan*, 499 U.S., 111 S.C.T.1759, 114 LED.2d 233 (1991).

27. Ibid.

28. *Newsletter of the Association of Women Psychiatrists* 9(1), October 3, 1990.

SOME POLITICAL IMPLICATIONS OF THE STANFORD STUDIES OF HOMELESS FAMILIES

Sanford M. Dornbusch

The American public cares about homelessness, but most of our information comes from disturbing news articles that emphasize the numbers, the obtrusiveness, and the personal deficiencies of homeless individuals. There have been few attempts to portray family homelessness and its complexity, despite the fact that homeless people include children and teenagers as well as adult women and men; families as well as single and attached individuals. The Stanford Studies[1] focused on homeless families and the children in those families, keeping in mind that the majority of homeless families are headed by women.

The experience of homelessness for women has been shown to be quite different from that for men. Historically, homeless women have been invisible to most researchers and service providers, in part because women did not tend to occupy the same skid-row locations as homeless men and also because women went to greater lengths to conceal their plight. The deinstitutionalization policies of the 1950s, together with the declining availability of low-income housing and the changing economic situation of the succeeding decades, put many of the most poverty-stricken women over the edge and onto the streets.[2]

Women with children who become homeless face even greater obstacles to solving their problems than other homeless groups. As we will see, their lack of available and affordable housing and child care; inadequate job and, in the case of some minority groups, language skills; and insufficient access to medical care for themselves and their children are among the most critical factors affecting these families' ability to get out of homelessness.

CHARACTERISTICS OF HOMELESS FAMILIES

HOMELESS FAMILIES CONTRASTED WITH HOMELESS INDIVIDUALS

By definition, the distinction between homeless individuals and homeless families is the presence of children. At least one adult, usually female, in every homeless family plays the parental role. Homeless parents, compared with unattached individuals, were predominately female, younger, and more likely to be on the margins of the economy—less educated and less likely to have a history of full-time employment. Disadvantaged minorities, African American and Hispanic, formed a larger proportion of the homeless families in our studies than of the homeless individuals.

Homeless parents, compared with homeless unattached individuals, were less likely to have histories of drug abuse, alcoholism, or mental illness. Only 34 percent of homeless parents reported any history of substance abuse, and only 5 percent had previously been treated for mental illness or any type of emotional problem. In part, the lower rates of substance abuse and mental illness among homeless families were a result of differences in the forces that pushed individuals, compared with families, into homelessness. This result was also explained by gender differences in the composition of the two groups. Overall, women had lower rates of substance abuse than did men. Thus, compared with the predominately male group of homeless individuals, substance abuse in homeless families played a relatively minor role.

Families and individuals also differed in the length of time they were homeless. Families tended to be homeless for shorter periods of time (about one month) than did individuals (about one year). In addition, homeless families were more likely to have been homeless only once, with Hispanic families of Mexican descent being least likely to have experienced multiple periods of homelessness.

Homeless families and unattached individuals differed in many ways. Accordingly, the results of previous studies of homeless individuals are not necessarily applicable to homeless families, especially when those families are headed by women.

DEMOGRAPHIC CHARACTERISTICS OF THE HOMELESS FAMILIES

Among the homeless families we studied, Hispanics of Mexican descent and African Americans were overrepresented, while non-Hispanic whites were underrepresented when compared with the entire population of the two counties in our studies. Thirty-six percent of the homeless families were Hispanics of Mexican descent, 29 percent were non-Hispanic whites, and 25 percent were African Americans. In the two counties, 20 percent of the total population were Hispanics (including non-Mexicans), 70 percent were non-Hispanic whites, and 4 percent were African Americans. Although African Americans constituted the smallest proportion of the homeless families in the two counties, they were the most overrepresented ethnic group.

About half of the homeless families (52 percent) were headed by single parents, the majority of whom were women. In 30 percent of homeless families, both biological parents were present. Fifteen percent of the families included a stepparent or partner. However, the substantial proportion of two natural-parent homeless families contradicts popular stereotypes of homeless families being almost exclusively single-parent units.

Another popular stereotype is that homeless families are the result of early parenthood. In our studies, only 29 percent of homeless mothers were under 18 when their first child was born. Even among homeless families headed by single mothers, the proportion who were teen mothers was only 30 percent. Thus, most families' homelessness could not be explained by early parenthood.

The average number of children in homeless families (2.3) was not much different from the average number of children in poor American families, although there were slight ethnic differences in the number of children per family. Hispanics of Mexican descent, on average, had the largest number of children (2.8) compared with 2.3 for African Americans and 1.9 for non-Hispanic whites. The national statistics for families below the poverty line are similar within each ethnic group: 2.5 for Hispanics of Mexican descent, 2.3 for African Americans, and 2.2 for non-Hispanic whites.

How Families Become Homeless

POVERTY AND THE LACK OF AFFORDABLE HOUSING

In the United States today, there is a lack of affordable housing. Many families have incomes that are too low to pay high rental and housing purchase prices. According to Harvard's Joint Center for Housing

Studies, in 1987, young single-parent renters paid on average 81 percent of their income for housing. Even a two-parent family in which both parents work full-time at low-paying jobs is a candidate for homelessness. Because women earn less than men, single-mother families are especially at risk.

The federal government set a minimum of $13,359 as the amount a family of four needed to earn in 1990 to be above the poverty line. At least 97 percent of the homeless families in our studies lived below that poverty line. Some received government assistance while others worked at low-paying jobs. The minimum wage has not kept pace with the rising cost of living or, in particular, the rising cost of housing. One formerly homeless mother explained, "The way rents are, you could get a $5.00 an hour job and still be on the street." Another mother receiving Aid to Families with Dependent Children (AFDC) expressed the inadequacy of federal help this way: "Rents are too expensive. AFDC only gives me $560.00 a month to live on. I can only afford a studio, but a studio is only for one person, not a mom with kids."

Women face additional problems when they attempt to increase their income by entering the job market. When poor women were asked about their employment history, we found that most had worked at unskilled blue-collar jobs, if they had worked at all. Many had no previous work experience, staying at home with their young children while the father brought home the income. The loss of his job, his desertion of the family, his incarceration, or his abusive behavior created a new problem for these women. They needed to support their families, but were ill-prepared to do so.

One group, women of Mexican descent, was particularly low in job skills. They had previously thought of themselves as wives and mothers. They were poorly educated and their largely rural backgrounds gave them little familiarity with the contemporary occupational structure. One clearly identifiable need of these women is instruction in English. They were less likely than their husbands to get outside of the barrio, and Spanish was the language of the home and of the street. When they tried to enter the labor force, their lack of fluency in English made it harder for them to get a job that would pay a wage large enough to support a family. Though California has passed a referendum specifying English as the official language, instruction in English is not readily available for adults and the current budget discussions envisage eliminating the few existing programs.

Although low incomes and lack of affordable housing were crucial elements in creating homelessness among families, they were not enough to explain why some poor, at-risk families did not become homeless. How can we explain this?

One powerful difference between the homeless and the housed was the presence of social support from families and friends. However, the number of relatives in the area who were available for support was not the key. Rather, the support network's ability to provide resources, such as housing, over a long period without excessive crowding, made a critical difference.

Middle-class families seldom become homeless, not merely because they start with greater resources and can stand longer bouts of unemployment, but because their relatives and friends have more space and money with which to provide assistance. Lower-class families require government aid sooner, but it is not because of an atmosphere of passive acceptance of homelessness. The women who typically head homeless families are desperately trying to avoid homelessness, but they no longer can count on their social-support network.

ETHNIC DIFFERENCES IN THE PATTERNS OF ENTRY INTO HOMELESSNESS

There appeared to be somewhat different patterns of entry into homelessness among the three ethnic groups. While the patterns do not fit every family, they give a broader picture of the complexities that may lead to homelessness.

Hispanics of Mexican descent had much less information about services that help homeless families than did other ethnic groups. For example, over half of these families had never heard of the Homeless Assistance Program. Homeless parents from this group were more likely to be married, to have both parents present, to have more children, to be less educated, to have lived a shorter time in this geographic area, and to have received less government aid. They were the most likely to be experiencing homelessness for the first time, had the lowest rates of alcohol and drug abuse, and were least likely to give individual, personal reasons for becoming homeless.

African-American families were the most informed about the service-delivery system. They were more likely to be single parents, to have never married, to have received government aid, and to be long-term residents of the area. The pattern of homelessness for this group was associated with long-term poverty, participation in the welfare system, and the problems of single parenthood.

Compared with other ethnic groups, non-Hispanic white parents were more likely to have histories of substance abuse and mental illness. In addition, it was only among non-Hispanic whites that a history of substance abuse significantly distinguished those families who had experienced homelessness from the at-risk families who had not. More than any other group, they gave personal reasons for becoming homeless.

Physical and Mental Health of Homeless Families

CHILDREN'S HEALTH

Overall, homeless children did not have acute or chronic illness more often than did poor, housed children. However, those children who lived in inappropriate places—and 34 percent of families reported living in such places as garages, outdoors, cars, and empty public buildings—did have more chronic or recurring illnesses (14 percent vs. 5 percent for homeless children who had never lived under such conditions). These problems tended to involve the eyes, ears, and musculoskeletal and urogenital systems.

Homeless and formerly homeless parents reported that their children's health had indeed suffered as a result of their living situation. In addition, parents who reported declines in their children's health were likely to have been homeless more than once; to have been homeless for longer periods of time; and to have reported an increase in their own depression, anxiety, and stress. Children's emotional distress, however, was not related to their parents' reports of distress.

PARENTS' HEALTH

Homeless parents did not differ greatly from formerly homeless or at-risk parents on the frequency of acute or chronic illnesses, although they were more likely to suffer from acute illnesses such as trauma; respiratory and skin diseases; and chronic disorders of the cardiovascular, musculoskeletal, and neurological systems as well as eye problems. Homeless parents reported worse health than their children, and levels of emotional distress among parents was much higher than among the formerly homeless or those at risk of homelessness.

MEDICAL SERVICES FOR FAMILIES

Homeless children were less likely to receive medical treatment than were poor, housed children. Eight percent of homeless children had untreated medical problems (compared with 6 percent of formerly homeless and 4 percent of at-risk children) and 31 percent were not receiving regular health care (compared with 7 percent of formerly homeless and 14 percent of at-risk children). Among homeless children under the age of 6, 18 percent had not received all their immunizations, compared with 3 percent of all children nationally. Homeless children have little access to dental care and, on average, were last seen by a dentist about four years ago.

Thirty-five percent of homeless parents and 22 percent of their children lacked medical insurance. For both parents and children, those who did not have medical insurance were more likely to have untreated medical problems and not get regular health care. Dental services were even less available than medical treatment for homeless families. Consequently, homeless families postponed needed dental services because they could not afford treatment.

Formerly homeless families had links to medical and dental services that homeless and at-risk families lacked. Although formerly homeless parents and children received the most medical services and reported the least medical need, homeless parents and children received the fewest medical services and reported the greatest medical need. Thirty-eight percent of this group reported needing medical services and 51 percent reported needing dental care, compared with 15 percent and 23 percent of formerly homeless families.

NONMEDICAL EFFECTS OF HOMELESSNESS

Of course, there are many other, nonmedical effects of homelessness on children. Most of the children were concerned with adult responsibilities far beyond their years, such as paying rent and buying food. They were aware of the reasons for their situations and quite realistic about their immediate needs. Despite their problems, the children were more likely to be compassionate than hardened. One mother told the story of her son asking for $0.30 to give a homeless man; the mother gave it to him, even though she only had $1.30 in her pocket.

At the same time, the restrictive rules of the shelters, along with the lack of privacy, presented problems, particularly for the older children, who were more negative in their evaluations of shelter environments. While they were appreciative of having a place to sleep and food to eat, their comments revealed the stress of their living situations. Perhaps the most worrisome effect is that homelessness seemed to reduce the future dreams and occupational expectations of the children. One 11-year-old girl, for example, wanted to be a "lawyer, doctor, or engineer," but thought she would probably end up in a much lower paying job, such as bus driver. A homeless 12-year-old boy, when asked what he wanted to be when he got older, replied, "I won't have a job. I'll do nothing, just sit around, if I have a place to sit around, if I'm not dead." A 7-year-old told his vision of the future: "When I grow up, I'll live in a place with furniture."

THE EDUCATION OF HOMELESS CHILDREN

Surprisingly, a large proportion of homeless children were enrolled in school. Eighty-nine percent of shelter children and 88 percent of homeless children were enrolled, indicating considerable flexibility on the part of schools to accommodate these families. On the down side, two central problems emerged that continue to threaten the education of homeless children: frequent changes of schools and the lack of transportation to those schools.

Homeless families move frequently as they search for housing, and most reported moving at least three times in the last year. The majority of homeless children, most of whom were in elementary school, had already attended four or more schools. Added to poor attendance, the result was little continuity in the children's educational experiences. Attempts to provide schools on-site at homeless shelters may give temporary relief, but do not solve the problem of continuity of education.

Transportation is an additional burden. In addition to the lack of school buses for both sheltered and nonsheltered children, there were no discounts for bus passes for the more expensive public transportation systems. Younger children often found traveling on public buses frightening, especially if multiple transfers were necessary.

It is clear that the recent improvements that eliminate barriers to school enrollment for homeless children need to be extended to other educational issues. Homeless parents need assistance in getting their children to school each day, keeping their children in the same school even when the family has to move, and providing a quiet place for their children to study.

GETTING OUT OF HOMELESSNESS

Why do some families get out of homelessness while others do not? Just as there are no single descriptions of *the homeless family*, there is no single answer to this question. When asked, formerly homeless families said they were helped most by an increase in income, the support of family and friends, and access to affordable housing. The very same factors that propelled these families into homelessness played a powerful role in helping them emerge from their situations.

While service providers agreed that these three factors were critical, they also included knowing how to use the social-services system, being homeless only a short time, and internal strengths and motivations on the part of the families.

Access to affordable housing seemed as important as increased income in helping families get out of homelessness. Those few families who found a subsidized housing program, shared housing, or a flexible landlord, got out of homelessness. The current waiting list for Section 8 housing, the largest subsidized housing program in the state of California, is closed. Families wait months and years before they receive housing. Requirements for Section 8 housing limit the number of persons per room and also state that children of different genders cannot share a bedroom. For families with three or four children, this often makes it impossible to find housing, even with a government subsidy. Thus, families with fewer children had a better chance to get out of homelessness.

Both homeless and formerly homeless families stressed the importance of affordable housing. Many families were upset by the lack of assistance in hunting for affordable housing. Even if they were able to find affordable rents and come up with the necessary cash for the first month's rent and deposit, they often faced landlord discrimination against AFDC families and against homeless families without strong credit histories. Yet, a frequent response about how homeless families found affordable housing was, "The landlord helped." Landlords who were willing to trust homeless families and be flexible about methods of payment, such as receiving the deposit in installments, made a major difference for some of the families.

In California, formerly homeless families most frequently cited the California AFDC Homeless Assistance Program as giving them the help they needed to find temporary shelter while they looked for permanent housing. Even after finding housing, the program provides financial assistance in the form of first month's rent and security deposit, allowing families precious time to attend to the next immediate need of finding a steady income. Unfortunately, in the early 1990s, the Homeless Assistance Program has been severely reduced.

The additional concern of service providers, that families know how to use the social-services system, emerged as our most powerful finding. Families who were not fluent in English were much less likely to have even heard of programs like the AFDC Homeless Assistance Program or Section 8 housing. Lack of English fluency was a substantial barrier to understanding and using the system.

Within the sample of formerly homeless families, only 18 percent of the Hispanics of Mexican descent reported problems speaking English. In the homeless sample, however, the proportion who had problems speaking English was much larger (76 percent). Even among those who had lived in the United States ten years or longer, 39 percent of the homeless families of Mexican descent reported some problems with English. Our additional analyses showed that fluency in English was more important in a family's ability to get government aid than was actual length of time spent in the United States.

The Importance of Child Support and Child Care

CHILD SUPPORT

Child support and child care are two additional factors that affect homeless women's ability to improve their situations. When asked about child support from absent fathers, many of the women reported being unable to locate the fathers and expected to receive no child support from them. It is clear that the lack of enforcement of child-support orders has accentuated the feminization of poverty. After divorce, the former husband often is better off economically, while the mother and children suffer abrupt declines in income. Child support, if paid, would seldom provide adequately for children, and much of the time it is not paid. In addition, a large proportion of the single mothers have never been married, and that group finds it almost impossible to gain legal rights to child support.

A surprising anomaly in the welfare system makes it even less likely that truant fathers will be found or forced to comply with child support. When a family is on AFDC, all child-support payments made by the father are given to the government as repayment for AFDC support. There is no economic motive for women on welfare to assist the government in locating the missing spouse. Indeed, there were some cases where the women noted how much better off they were in *not* receiving child support and getting occasional under-the-table payments from the missing father. That money could be kept without reducing AFDC payments.

Moreover, the welfare reforms of 1988 recognized that some aspects of the system were discriminating against couples that stay together. In our 1991 study of homeless families, we found that single-parent families still are far more likely to get government aid than are two-parent families in similar economic circumstances. Similarly a woman on AFDC who has a man living in the household will receive less aid if she and he marry.

Because single-parent families are far more frequent among some ethnic groups (such as African-American families) than among families in other groups, we examined the pattern of support in each of our study's groups. This analysis showed that very poor families among Hispanics of Mexican descent, non-Hispanic whites, and African Americans all remained less likely to receive government aid if there were two parents present with their children. Thus, the welfare system's attack on two-parent households is a general problem, not linked to any single ethnic group.

These glitches in the system should not obscure the fact that women who do receive government aid report that the amount is woefully inadequate to meet their needs. With average rents high enough to take 70 percent to 80 percent of their total income, most mothers do not have enough money to feed their children. As one forthright woman put it to a group of county officials, "You see before you a welfare cheat. Each month I ask myself whether I should let my children be hungry or be a criminal. It only takes a few seconds for me to decide. I hate to do it, but I am constantly forced to earn money off the books, lie about my income, and feed my kids."

Local, state, and federal officials are currently considering the reduction and capping of already inadequate welfare payments. As inflation advances, the demands on welfare mothers will become even more pressing. The current welfare system is not working, and one element of needed reform is assistance to single mothers and very poor families, regardless of the presence or absence of a male in the household. There are millions of working-poor households that, given some assistance, could make it. As it stands, our welfare system works against the attempts of these families to improve their lives, discourages marriage, and encourages men to leave the household.

CHILD CARE AS A NECESSITY

The enormity of the problem of child care has been and continues to be discussed at length by families, employers, researchers, and policymakers. As the real wage of the typical worker has fallen, the increased labor-force participation of women has been the major mechanism for keeping up the standard of living for families. The solutions for this problem will be expensive and not without value conflicts of great ferocity. The women at the bottom don't pose the same policy dilemmas, however. Their male partners cannot support the family, and government expenditures to assist the family are already built into the system. Therefore, the money spent on child care may be offset by the increased ability of the family to survive on its own.

A common lament among homeless women is the lack of child care for their young children. Their immediate need is housing and they find it almost impossible to search for a place to live with small children in tow. In addition, these women, as noted, need training if they are to be competitive in the labor market. Again and again, we heard women say that they needed child care in order to attend school or training programs.

Finally, as has been recognized by recent federal legislation, women cannot afford to get off welfare and work if they have to pay for child care. Recent reforms move in the right direction, assisting some mothers on welfare during their first year of training and work. But the problem is not limited to those mothers or to the first year. Essentially, poor women cannot work and pay for child care. Our society has to face the trade-offs when child care is unavailable and whole families become dependent.

SERVICES FOR HOMELESS FAMILIES AND THEIR CHILDREN

IMPROVING SERVICE DELIVERY

A substantial proportion of service providers coordinated their efforts with other agencies, but there was still a high level of frustration over the lack of integration of services for homeless families. The most frequent form of coordination was referral, but agencies also collaborated in the joint provision of services.

Service providers often felt overloaded with the needs of too many families. Given the scarcity of resources and the lack of steady funding, they had to make difficult choices, such as working more intensively with fewer families. Collectively, the 60 agencies we studied reported that they turned away at least 650 homeless families each month because of lack of resources.

In addition, there was a need for more bilingual staff at agencies that serve non-English-speaking clients. Women of Mexican descent and their children pay an additional price for their lack of fluency in English. Even for those women who had been in the United States for more than ten years, low proficiency in English is associated with getting fewer services from government agencies.

Finally, some parts of the service-delivery system were not geared toward prevention. Families in crisis were often not helped until they were actually homeless. Service providers told us that regulations often hamper their activities, preventing early action to assist families. Providers believed that there was a need for funds that could be quickly employed to help families before they became homeless, rather than responding later when the families were already homeless. They felt that preventive services would cost less and be more effective. Although some homeless prevention programs exist in the two counties studied, the families that were interviewed were often unaware of those resources.

IMAGES OF HOMELESS FAMILIES

Service providers, who had direct experience with homeless families, believed that the usual cause of family homelessness was a combination of bad luck and difficult circumstances. They saw family homelessness as the product of external events, such as a factory closing, an apartment house being demolished, or becoming ill while not having adequate medical insurance.

The low-income public, compared to the service providers, were more than twice as likely to believe that homeless families were mentally ill, drug abusers, alcoholics, undocumented aliens, and unwilling to work. The low-income public emphasized personal problems and the deficiencies of homeless families far more than did the service providers.

However, there was one point on which both service providers and the low-income public agreed: Each group saw the lack of affordable housing as the single greatest factor associated with homelessness for families. Homeless families' lack of affordable housing was noted by 83 percent of the service providers and by 55 percent of the low-income public. The homeless families themselves concurred with the significance of affordable housing and said they needed assistance in their search for such housing.

WHERE DO WE GO FROM HERE?

Our studies point to a number of steps that can be taken to help these families get and stay out of homelessness. Those who got out of homelessness were more likely to have been helped into subsidized housing, to be receiving assistance from government and social agencies, and to have had more contact with service providers.

The more resources that are available, the larger the proportion of homeless families who will be thrown a lifeline. The current system favors those who know its inner workings. People who have long associations with the welfare system and who have never been homeless, we found, have more knowledge of the services available for the homeless than do those who are currently homeless.

We must develop a new system, one that works for the people it is meant to serve and one that is particularly sensitive to the needs of women and their families. Some of the ingredients of that new system are the following: (1) We must help families of the working poor, regardless of the number of parents present in the home: Too many aspects of the current system emphasize aid for single parents and discourage marriage and long-term parental relationships. Subsidizing the working poor whose salaries are inadequate to support the family will increase political support because grants are available for those who are actively participating in the labor force. (2) Government payments for child support must be made directly to the parent and billed to the absent spouse. Court orders for child support are too seldom enforced. By having the government act as the intermediary, we increase the number of families and children receiving child support while simultaneously increasing the pressure on the absent spouse to fulfill legal obligations. (3) We must provide long-term assistance for those who are unable to work. Our current emphasis on workfare has tended to ignore those who require general assistance because they are simply unable to work. Physical and mental disabilities are real in their consequences, and the needs of this group must supersede well-intentioned efforts to increase labor-force participation. (4) We must train those who are inadequately prepared to compete in the workplace. There is a need to increase vocational skills especially for women who are the sole breadwinners after divorce or desertion. Access to training, when needed, should be taken for granted, and the training should be appropriate for current demands for more skilled labor. (5) We must teach English to those who are not fluent in English. Immigrant women, in particular, have long been more segregated from the English-speaking population than have been immigrant men. Both women and men, therefore, require fluency in English in order to become aware of and receive available government services and to compete actively and effectively in the search for jobs. (6) We must provide child-care services to encourage vocational and educational training and labor-force participation of working parents. We have been startled by the inability of so many homeless parents to act effectively for their own welfare and that of their families. They are handicapped by their inability to find even temporary child care that would permit them to search for housing, get training, and go for job interviews. (7) We must be concerned for and sensitive to the needs of parents and their children. In the midst of bureaucratic regulations and legislative initiatives, there must be room for the exceptions, the families and children who don't fit into the usual categories. We are dealing with real people and not abstractions or statistics.

What is good for children helps their parents. A family policy that emphasizes the welfare of children will also help the women who do most of the childrearing in the United States. Our society rests on more than compassion. It needs the economic and social contributions of millions who are currently left out. A system of social assistance must give priority to those who cannot work, to those who are working and are not able to get a wage adequate for family subsistence, and to the children who are today's dependents and tomorrow's productive workers.

NOTES

1. In 1990, the Santa Clara County Help House, the Homeless Coalition, and the San Mateo County Hunger and Homeless Action Coalition asked the Stanford Center for the Study of Families, Children and Youth to do an in-depth, objective study of homeless families and children. These grassroots homeless coalitions wanted to know who these families were and what homelessness was doing to them. In 1991, we completed nine studies of homeless families in two northern California counties. Families at risk of homelessness, homeless families, and formerly homeless families were included in the studies, totaling 1,021 parents and 1,720 children in 809 families.

2. For a detailed examination of women's experience of homelessness, see Stephanie Golden, *The Women Outside: Meanings and Myths of Homelessness* (Berkeley: University of California Press, 1992).

WOMEN AND AIDS

Ann O'Leary, Loretta Sweet Jemmott, Mariana Suarez-Al-Adam, Carolyn AlRoy, and M. Isa Fernandez

Since the advent of the AIDS pandemic, the World Health Organization has estimated that between eight and ten million people have become infected with the human immunodeficiency virus (HIV) globally, with between one and two million affected in the United States thus far. While gay men constituted the first wave of the epidemic in the United States, women are now becoming infected in increasing numbers, and numerous considerations specific to women have arisen in recent years. These considerations include differences in how the disease progresses over time and how it is treated, issues in the prevention of infection, and effects of stigmatization. This chapter presents the epidemiologic profile of women with AIDS and HIV infection, and describes the medical considerations pertinent to female infection, prevention of infection, and, finally, an examination of media discourse regarding women and AIDS.

THE MAGNITUDE OF THE PROBLEM

Within the United States, women are a rapidly growing segment of the population infected with HIV, the virus that causes AIDS. Their representation among people with AIDS, expressed as a percentage of the total, has increased from about 3 percent in 1981, when the first cases were reported to the Centers for Disease Control, to 12 percent in 1990.[1] In the United States, the proportion of women who have contracted AIDS by heterosexual transmission has increased from 11 percent in 1984 to 34 percent in 1990. It is estimated that women may ultimately make up half of all the AIDS cases in the United States as they do in the Caribbean and central Africa.[2] Further, women comprise the fastest growing risk group for HIV infection in the United States and around the world.[3]

Because the latency between exposure to HIV and the development of AIDS is generally several years, the epidemiologic profile characterizing people with AIDS is different from that characterizing the newly infected, a point that is important to keep in mind when considering AIDS statistics. Because women are becoming infected with disproportionately increasing frequency, it is likely that the percentage of HIV-infected women who have not yet become symptomatic is much greater than that for those who have already developed AIDS. In the United States, the initial route for infection of women was the sharing of needles used to inject drugs. Heterosexual transmission, which appears to be considerably more efficient when the infected partner is male, has also been a prominent source of female infection.

For women in AIDS epicenters, particularly the greater metropolitan New York area, AIDS has become a threat of crisis proportion. AIDS is now the leading cause of death among black women of reproductive age in New York and New Jersey.[4] It is the leading killer of women aged 20 to 29 in New York City and may soon be the leading cause of death for all women of reproductive age.[5] In 1988, approximately 6 per 1,000 women who gave birth in New York State carried the AIDS virus,[6] and, in some areas of New York City, more than 2 percent of women giving birth were infected.[7] As the thousands of women who are now infected begin to show symptoms, the magnitude of the AIDS problem for women will become increasingly salient.

WHO IS AT RISK?

At present, AIDS affects predominately the inner-city poor, the majority of whom are people of color. Among women with AIDS in 1990, 51 percent were infected through injected drug use and 29 percent through heterosexual contact, with heterosexual transmission increasing over time.[8] Black and Hispanic women are disproportionately affected; of women with AIDS, about 50 percent are black and about 20 percent are Hispanic. About 73 percent of mothers with HIV-infected children receive public assistance.[9] Partly because of its association with illicit drug use, the correctional system is an arena severely affected by HIV. In one study, close to 20 percent of females entering the New York State correctional system were found to be infected.[10] Commercial sex workers are also at high risk for HIV infection.[11]

Adolescents are another group at high risk for contracting HIV. In the inner city, runaway and delinquent youths report high levels of risky behavior, including trading sex for money and crack, and sharing needles used to inject drugs.[12] However, adolescent females who report enjoyment of sex with condoms and greater skill at communicating with partners do report higher levels of condom use and are at lower risk for contracting AIDS.[13]

MEDICAL ASPECTS OF AIDS IN WOMEN

Infection with HIV initiates a lengthy process of immune-system destruction, which culminates in the development of one or more critical opportunistic conditions for the diagnosis of AIDS.[14] A lengthy period with no symptoms precedes the development of AIDS; during this time, blood can be screened for the presence of the antibody directed against the virus, which indicates that infection has occurred. Unfortunately, antibodies are not produced immediately and some alarming reports of up to three-year latencies have been published.[15] HIV infection is considered at this time to be virtually universally fatal.

It has recently become apparent that illnesses related to and indicative of HIV infection occur differently for men and women.[16] Thus, it is probable that statistics concerning illness rates for women underestimate the true prevalence both because they are diagnosed later than men and because they have decreased access to health care. Women die more quickly than men after receiving an AIDS diagnosis. Disorders of the reproductive system are among the distinguishing features of HIV in women. Severe, chronic, and persistent vaginal yeast infections are a frequent early sign of HIV infection.[17] Sexually transmitted diseases (STDs) are often more severe in those with HIV infection, and human papillomavirus, the epidemic-level STD that is the cause of cervical and uterine cancer, has an accelerated course with more rapid progression to cancer among women with HIV.[18] Similarly, syphilis, chancroid, and pelvic inflammatory diseases (PID) are more severe in their symptomatology and more resistant to treatment in HIV-infected women. Concern that the unique medical manifestations of AIDS in women have produced misdiagnosis and late diagnosis of HIV-related illnesses has resulted in a recent revision by the Centers for Disease Control of the criteria for AIDS diagnosis. The revised system includes those conditions that are more common among women and rely more heavily on indices of depletion of CD4 lymphocytes, the immune-system cells that are the targets of HIV.[19]

Unfortunately, women have received inadequate attention in basic AIDS research and studies of drug treatments. The vast majority of subjects enrolled in drug studies have been men.[20] In addition, azidothymidine (AZT; an antiviral medication that slows replication of the HIV virus) has not been sufficiently tested on women, including pregnant women or their unborn fetuses. Federal regulations that were originally instigated to protect the fetus require both parents' written consent to proceed with the drug trials.[21] For many women who are HIV-positive, the prospective fathers often are not present or available. Many research institutes are unwilling to change this regulation because they worry that by not including the father's consent they will risk loss of federal funding.

VERTICAL TRANSMISSION: CHILDREN AND AIDS

AIDS affects primarily women of reproductive age. As many as 78 percent of women with AIDS were of reproductive age, according to mid-1991 statistics from the Centers for Disease Control.[22] In the past few years, public opinion has focused on the perceived threat of vertical or perinatal transmission of the AIDS virus from mother to child. Indeed, vertical transmission is a serious concern. Children who are seriously afflicted with AIDS may contract *pneumocystis carinii* pneumonia (PCP) during the first year of life, die within the first or second year, and suffer most of their lives.[23] As of 1990, in the United States, 5,900 babies a year are born to mothers who are infected with HIV.[24] However, most experts estimate that vertical transmission occurs only 20 percent to 30 percent of the time.[25] In addition, perhaps only 15 percent to 20 percent of these women give birth to babies who fit the worst-case scenario of HIV infection: early infection, chronic hospitalization, and death before the age of 2.[26]

Although most babies with HIV-positive mothers will not get AIDS, all of them receive the HIV antibodies from their mothers. However, these passive antibodies usually disappear by the child's first birthday. Vertical transmission can occur in one of three ways: (1) in the uterus (in utero), (2) during delivery (HIV has been isolated in cord blood and fetal tissues),[27] or (3) after birth. Infants may catch HIV by ingesting breast milk containing particles of infected maternal blood, and infected mothers are advised not to breastfeed their infants (except where alternatives to breast milk do not exist—for example, in Third World countries that do not have clean water supplies or powdered milk available). However, perinatal infection is thought to take place primarily in utero. Unfortunately, while researchers are attempting to develop procedures for determining whether fetuses are infected, none is available at the present time, and it is unlikely that those tests will have good reliability when they are developed.[28] Interestingly, the likelihood of fetal infection may vary depending on when the mother becomes infected with HIV; those who are infected during conception or pregnancy may be more likely to pass the virus than those with preexisting infection.[29]

An issue that has received a modest amount of research attention is the possible effect of pregnancy on the course of the mother's disease. Normal pregnancy is accompanied by immune-system changes that are generally considered to be suppressive; therefore, it is reasonable to suppose that the course of HIV illness may be accelerated by pregnancy. Unfortunately, research has been inconsistent in its answers to this question. While some have suggested that pregnancy may be deleterious,[30] others have concluded that it is not.[31]

There is discernible prejudice against, and little concern and support for, black and Latina HIV-positive women who choose to give birth. Choosing to continue with pregnancies that may involve perinatal transmission of AIDS is viewed by many as tantamount to child abuse. In addition, many of these women are likely to experience incapacitating illness and death after the child is born. Whether the child is born infected, that child may be deprived of his or her mother due to sickness or death. While it is true that HIV-positive mothers may not be able to take care of their children, the hostility directed at these women is very likely due to their minority status. Levine and Dubler refer to *Steel Magnolias*,[32] a popular movie in which Julia Roberts portrayed a young heroine with ailing health who decides to continue with her pregnancy, despite the fact that she may not survive childbirth. If the heroine were black or Latina and was dying of AIDS, they argue, it is unlikely that she would be viewed as admirable, or would be very popular.

A matter of some controversy is the recommendation by some experts that women residing in high HIV-incidence areas be given routine prenatal screening for HIV infection. While there are clear public-health benefits to be gained from such a strategy, many are concerned that monitoring pregnant women or women considering pregnancy with the intention of persuading them to abort or prevent conception may give way to coercive counseling. John Arras argues for an educational model of noncoercive counseling,[33] in which a peer educator informs the client of the risks and issues associated with having an HIV-positive baby. In addition, obtaining informed consent for testing and counseling is crucial, as many women may need to protect their privacy about their HIV status. If such information is released, health and life insurance, mortgages, and house purchases may be jeopardized as well as the potential loss of a sexual partner providing home and food.[34]

Given the socioeconomic backdrop and special issues with which women of color are confronted, there are many reasons that these women choose to give birth, even when they are aware of the potential costs. These reasons include the following: (1) Many religions, such as Catholicism, espouse that it is immoral under any circumstance to abort an "unborn child." (2) It may be the last opportunity for a woman who is aware of her HIV status to have a child. (3) Abortion may not be legal or affordable to these women. (4) For inner-city black and Latina women who have little education and very limited job opportunities, having a child may be an important source of self-esteem and life meaning. Children may also be the primary or only source of unconditional love and acceptance, especially for women who have AIDS.

Since there are many issues relating to the decision to continue with pregnancy, HIV-infected women should be accorded the right to make their own decisions and enjoy reproductive freedom, whether they choose to have their children or to terminate their pregnancies.

PREVENTION

In the absence of a cure or preventive vaccination against HIV, behavior change remains the only available means for combating the epidemic. The only accepted method for preventing sexual transmission of HIV, apart from abstinence, is the use of latex condoms. The efficacy of condoms may be enhanced by the addition of the spermicide nonoxynol-9, which has antiviral properties. It is important to note that other STDs, many of which constitute severe epidemics in the inner city,[35] can also be prevented through condom use.

Perhaps the most critical feature of behavior change necessary for preventing sexual transmission of HIV is that it requires the cooperation of another person, namely, the woman's sex partner. Unfortunately, many of the women most at risk depend on their male partners for economic security. Some women also fear that they will lose desired partners if they insist on condom use, since condoms may be taken to indicate unfaithfulness on the part of the woman, lack of trust concerning the man's own faithfulness, or infection with HIV or other STDs. Young women sometimes report attempting to become pregnant in order to cement bonds with men who may not be committed to the relationship at the time. Of particular concern is the plight of the woman experiencing domestic violence and coerced sex, for whom the recommendation of condom use may be impossible to execute. While the female condom will give women some control over the safety of their encounters, many of the problems that women experience in their attempts to be safe will persist because the presence of the female condom is quite obvious to her partner.

Nevertheless, some behavioral interventions that have been developed for same- or mixed-sex groups appear to carry some promise of effecting behavior change[36] or intended behavior change[37] among female participants. Female and male adolescent runaways attending 20 or more sessions of an intervention program in youth shelters have also reported reductions in risk-related activities.[38]

An issue that has become the subject of much debate but woefully little research is the recommendation that women use spermicide alone when the protection afforded by a condom is not a possible option. Particularly in situations in which women perceive themselves as helpless to prevent unprotected encounters, as in cases of rape and domestic violence, many service providers in the community are recommending this measure, which obviously does not depend on male cooperation. Arguments in favor of this recommendation include the in vitro virucidal effects of nonoxynol-9,[39] the speculation that the lubrication afforded by spermicidal gels may prevent tearing of the skin during episodes of coerced sex, and some very preliminary correlational studies indicating its possible effectiveness in preventing HIV infection.[40] However, because frequent use of nonoxynol-9 has been shown to disrupt the outer lining of the cervix and vagina in some women,[41] it is possible that transmission may be *facilitated* in some cases by this strategy. Furthermore, some intervention specialists express concern about giving complex or mixed messages, particularly given the extreme paucity of data regarding the effectiveness of this strategy.

SPECIAL CONSIDERATIONS OF BLACK AND LATINA WOMEN

Because the majority of women who currently are infected with HIV are from nondominant cultures, we next consider special issues for women from the two cultural/ethnic groups most severely affected by the epidemic: black women and Latina women.

BLACK WOMEN

Blacks are, as previously mentioned, disproportionately burdened by AIDS.[42] Only 12 percent of the nation's population is black, yet 27 percent of persons with AIDS have been black. Although AIDS is emerging as a leading killer of both black and white women of child-bearing age, more cases of AIDS have been reported among black women than among white women.[43] Black women account for about 52 percent of female AIDS cases, whereas white women account for only 27 percent. More than one-half of the children under 13 years of age who have AIDS are black. Compared with white pediatric AIDS cases, black cases are more likely to have a mother who was exposed to HIV as a result of intravenous drug use or heterosexual contact.[44]

Populations with higher rates of STDs are at increased risk for HIV infection and, in general, inner-city black women have dispro-portionately higher rates of chlamydia, syphilis, gonorrhea, and PID.[45] Like the rise of STDs, risk of HIV infection is heightened by unpro-tected sexual activity. In addition, the presence of an STD and asso-ciated lesions may facilitate transmission of HIV. Inasmuch as intravenous drug users are thought to play an important role in the transmission of HIV infection to heterosexuals, the prevalence of in-travenous drug users in urban areas greatly heightens the risk of HIV infection for black women who reside in that environment. Although the women themselves may not use intravenous drugs, they may have sexual relationships with men who do.

The failure to use condoms is perhaps the most common HIV-risk-associated behavior among women of childbearing age.[46] A large percentage of sexually active black women report inconsistent use of condoms.[47] Jemmott and Jemmott found that only 20 percent of sex-ually active unmarried black women undergraduates at an inner-city commuter university in New Jersey reported always using condoms during coitus in the previous three months.[48] On average, the women reported failing to use condoms 60 percent of the time they had coitus in the previous three months. Belcastro found that 42 percent of black undergraduate women as compared with 27 percent of white under-graduate women reported never using condoms.[49] Data from the 1982 and 1988 National Surveys of Family Growth have suggested that among women 15 to 44 years of age, black women were less likely to use condoms than were white women in both 1982 and 1988.[50]

Only very limited data are available about most sexual behaviors other than contraceptive use among black women.[51] Some evidence suggests that white women are more likely than black women to have had only one nonmarital sexual partner. On the other hand, sexually experienced black women undergraduates were less likely than their white counterparts to have had six or more partners.[52] Similarly, Wyatt, Peters, and Guthrie found that among white women aged 18 to 36, 52 percent reported having had 11 or more sexual partners since age 18; whereas, among black women, the figure was only 29 percent.[53] Even less research has examined patterns of sexual behavior among poor black women in U.S. inner cities; the information that does exist is often contradictory. Houston-Hamilton has observed that poor black women may have more limited sexual repertoires than white women.[54] They may equate intimacy specifically with vaginal sex or penetration. An emphasis on vaginal sex may be related to an orientation to procreation rather than erotic sex, an orientation supported by conservative religious values.

An important issue that continues to emerge regarding condom use among black women is the belief that condoms interfere with sexual pleasure. Jemmott and Jemmott reported results of a survey that highlighted the importance of hedonistic beliefs and certain normative influences on black women's decisions about using condoms.[55] Studying 103 black women college students from a university in Newark, New Jersey, they found that the key hedonistic beliefs related to attitudes toward condoms were that sex is more fun when a condom is not used, sex does not feel as good if a condom is used, and condoms are too much trouble to carry around. These results suggest that interventions to increase condom use among women should attempt to modify women's perceptions of adverse effects of condoms on sexual pleasure.

AIDS-prevention efforts in the black community must also overcome the low level of trust in health-care professionals and health services.[56] Black women's wariness of self-disclosure is part of their larger survival strategy. AIDS-prevention efforts must address that survival strategy in order to break down denial, which is driven by fear of racial and sexual backlash if women admit to being at risk. Furthermore, denial does not just exist on an individual level, it must be viewed as a broader phenomenon. Unless the communities in which black women live can afford to face the impact of AIDS free from further discrimination and free from the fear that by addressing the problem of AIDS the black community will open itself to furthering the traditional association of blacks, disease, and immoral behavior, denial of the risk of AIDS and the ensuing conspiracy of silence about it will continue. The choice of who delivers the message that AIDS is an issue of importance to the black community and that individuals' or organizations' political beliefs about the etiology of AIDS will determine how or whether that message is received and acted upon. Distrust may contribute to delay in women seeking services, a lack of planning for health care and other social needs, an orientation toward the present, and beliefs that there are proper ways of behavior that produce the desired results.

LATINA WOMEN

The AIDS epidemic has had a devastating impact on Hispanic women. Although AIDS education and prevention campaigns have been launched by both public and private entities, these efforts have been slow to reach the Latina community. Many of these programs are not effective because they do not adequately address the numerous demographic, socioeconomic, cultural, and linguistic factors that influence Latinas' attitudes, beliefs, behaviors, and access to health information and services.[57] The implications of these factors for curbing the further spread of HIV infection among Latinas are subsequently described.

As a group, Hispanic women are younger and have lower educational attainment than white women in the general U.S. population.[58] They also tend to have lower annual incomes and live in poorer families than non-Hispanics. Latinas are also overrepresented among women heads of households and among women in lower socioeconomic classes. They suffer from problems often associated with poverty, such as unemployment, illicit drug use, physical and sexual abuse, discrimination, and homelessness.

Many Latinas, particularly those living in the northeastern United States and Puerto Rico, report high rates of illicit drug use. These areas have high HIV rates, and women, including Latinas, are at higher risk for infection through heterosexual contact and needle sharing than are Latinas in other parts of the country. In fact, more than half of the Latinas with AIDS are intravenous drug users. An additional 20 percent became infected through heterosexual sex with a partner who was an intravenous drug user. These high rates of drug use among Latinas and their sex- and needle-sharing partners and the associated sequelae of illicit drug use pose additional challenges for HIV-prevention efforts in the Northeast and Puerto Rico.

A higher proportion of Latinas are in their reproductive years as compared with white women. Childbearing among Hispanic women starts earlier and continues later than it does for white women; fertility rates (number of births per 1,000 women age 16 to 44) is higher among Hispanic women (91.5) than it is among non-Hispanic women (64.3).[59] Despite higher birth rates, Latinas use prenatal care less often than white women. When they do use prenatal care, it tends to be later in pregnancy.[60] Thus, Latinas with HIV infection may be more likely than white women to become pregnant and unwittingly transmit the virus to the fetus during pregnancy. Many first learn of their HIV-positive status upon delivery or so late into their pregnancy as to negate any reproductive choice.

The literature has characterized Hispanic women as having traditional cultural values, religious beliefs, and gender roles in which they are willing to sacrifice themselves for their children and are passive and subordinate to men.[61] These findings must be interpreted with caution because they are not derived from controlled studies and often do not account for demographic and socioeconomic variables. Data indicate that Hispanics have strong family orientations and that mothers play important and unique roles within the family structure.[62]

It is also widely believed that Latinas have a strong religious orientation and that Roman Catholic doctrine has tremendous influence on their life decisions. It is often assumed that Latinas will follow papal decrees regarding birth control and condom use. However, contemporary studies indicate that Hispanic women use contraception and that Catholicism does not necessarily promote traditional reproductive behavior.[63]

These factors have implications for HIV-prevention efforts in both research and service delivery. There is a need for innovation and prevention programs that capitalize on the cultural strengths, such as the powerful role of Latina mothers, and discard untested stereotypes. Nontraditional sources such as community-based organizations, neighborhood or tenant groups, and formal or informal community leaders should be involved in prevention efforts. Alternative education strategies such as *telenovelas*, street theater, Spanish-language radio, and television programs should be considered.

In addition, prevention programs must incorporate the socioeconomic, cultural, and linguistic factors specific to the subpopulation of Latinas being reached. Differences among the different subgroups cannot be ignored. For instance, programs designed to reach Puerto Rican women living in the Northeast will need to address illicit drug use and migration issues that may be less relevant to Latinas in the Southwest.

GENERAL ISSUES FOR MINORITY WOMEN

A great need exists for research aimed at developing and implementing AIDS risk-reduction interventions for black and Latina women. Such interventions are likely to be most effective if they are (1) based on a sound theoretical framework and (2) sensitive to the cultural values of the participant.[64] Mays and Cochran have suggested that tailoring advice to the cultural and political realities of the target community is essential to the success of risk-reduction interventions aimed at ethnic minority women.[65] In particular, they have asserted that prevention approaches for ethnic minority individuals should focus on the individual as a responsible member of a familial or social network. Ethnically based values of cooperation, unity, and collective responsibility may be particularly powerful motivators of behavior change among blacks.[66]

Another factor thought to be important is the ethnicity of the change agent. The basic idea is that risk-reduction interventions may be most effective if they are implemented by individuals with whom the participants can identify. Following this line of argument, Peterson and Marin have reasoned that programs for ethnic minority intravenous drug users, for instance, should include ethnic minority staff,[67] who may be more accepted by minority addicts because of their knowledge of minority cultural values.

Culturally determined values influence how individual perceptions of AIDS are created, how attitudes toward high-risk behavior are formed, and how habits that characterize high-risk behavior may be altered. The cultural values that inform sexuality among ethnic minority women cannot be understood out of the context of racism, sexism, and economic oppression, which have shaped gender relations and family structure. Researchers and historians continue to have difficulty in distinguishing cultural and religious variables from the structural variables that affect black women's choices.[68] Although economic and social survival exert strong influences on both sexual and risk-taking behavior in the black community, there has been little exploration of the social or economic determinants of attitudes toward sex and drug use among black women.[69] Too often, the behavior of black and Latina women is filtered through cultural stereotypes.

AIDS education that promotes "safer sex" may threaten behavior patterns that black and Latina women link with their survival. The suggestion that women should explore new forms of sexual behavior (e.g., nonpenetrative sexual techniques) as a means of prevention of HIV transmission may be received ambivalently by women subject to victim-blaming because of stereotypes about their sexual behavior.[70] AIDS educators must keep in mind that sexual choices express not only cultural values and expectations but adaptive means of living with racism, sexism, and economic disenfranchisement. Introducing behavioral concepts that propose to alter or go against cultural values or ignore structural variables can lead to social conflict, especially in communities undergoing rapid acculturation. Proposed changes in gender roles or sexual behavior may create guilt over acting against traditional community norms and set in motion changes that will alter the locus of power in sexual relationships. The sex lives of many minority women are currently characterized by a lack of power, by multiple forms of *otherness* that are imposed on them from within and without their community. If they are to be supported to undertake behavior changes, their otherness has to be diminished, and behavior changes must be linked to the attitudes and beliefs that support their concepts of cultural and economic survival.

WOMEN AND AIDS IN PUBLIC REPRESENTATION

Stigmatization and discrimination are near-universal experiences for those infected with HIV. The behaviors associated with transmission in the early stages of the epidemic—intravenous drug use and sex, including homosexual relations and commercial sex work—are themselves heavily stigmatized. Sadly, the AIDS epidemic has affected those already most marginalized in U.S. society. The epidemic has come to exacerbate racism, sexism, classism, and homophobia. Media portrayals of women in the AIDS epidemic, including those designed for purposes of education and prevention, have frequently exhibited sexual stereotyping and scapegoating. For example, one widely distributed poster depicting a little girl reads, "She has her father's eyes and her mother's AIDS," implying a greater contribution from the mother than the father to the child's condition. Commercial sex workers have frequently been cited as major sources of transmission to men,[71] despite the fact that it is considerably more likely that they will be infected by their clients than vice versa. Juhasz has argued that a general strategy of "containment"[72] of threatening female sexuality has been manifest in the AIDS media through the framing of distinctions between "safe" and "unsafe" women, the latter being the poor, black, unmarried, and sexually liberated. Those in the United States who would limit sexual freedom for any reason have used AIDS to their advantage, asserting or implying that the disease constitutes divine reprisal for the excesses of the sexual revolution.[73] The over-representation of children with AIDS in the media, virtually all of whom carry the label "innocent victim," also serves to reinforce the position that the adult with AIDS (especially the mother who selfishly gave birth to a terminally ill child) is a shameful and deserving casualty of this nightmarish disease.

Despite these discouraging aspects of public discourse concerning women and AIDS, the epidemic is not without the potential for beneficial effect. AIDS has forced into the public arena discussion of topics formerly ignored—STDs, drug use, and the woeful inadequacy of the U.S. health-care system—and has made more salient many aspects of life for the inner-city poor. Feminist contribution to AIDS discourse has the capacity to present such material in ways that can contribute to our common wisdom and provide solutions to these difficult social issues.

CONCLUSIONS

This chapter has presented some of the aspects of HIV and AIDS that are pertinent for women. As the AIDS epidemic progresses in the United States, women, particularly poor black and Latina women, are affected in rapidly growing numbers. Among the challenges that we face are the need for increased research and clinical attention to the medical aspects of HIV in women, innovative and effective education and prevention strategies, and public discourse that is sympathetic to those affected and sensitive to the social and political conditions that contribute to the epidemic. The years of AIDS have just begun; the disease will be with us for a long time to come. Despite its tragic consequences, it provides us with challenges that bring great potential for growth—for the women's health movement and for health-care reform, for female-centered discourse concerning sexuality and pleasure, and for our development as a humane society.

ACKNOWLEDGMENTS

This work was facilitated by grants 1-RO1-MH45238 and 5-U10-MH48013 from the National Institute of Mental Health to the first author. The authors wish to thank Carlos Allende-Ramos, Cheryl Simpson, and Sandy Yingling for helpful comments on the manuscript.

NOTES

1. T. V. Ellerbrock, T. J. Bush, M. E. Chamberland, and M. J. Oxtoby, "Epidemiology of Women with AIDS in the United States, 1981–1990," *Journal of the American Medical Association* 265 (1991): 2971–2975.

2. H. W. Haverkos and R. Edelman, "The Epidemiology of Acquired Immunodeficiency Syndrome Among Heterosexuals," *Journal of the American Medical Association* 260 (1988): 1922–1929.

3. S. Y. Chu, J. W. Buehler, and R. L. Berkelman, "Impact of the Human Immunodeficiency Virus Epidemic on Mortality in Women of Reproductive Age, United States," *Journal of the American Medical Association* 264 (1990): 225–229; and J. Chin and J. Mann, "HIV Infection and AIDS in the 1990's," *American Journal of Public Health* 11 (1990): 127–142.

4. Ibid.

5. B. Almond and C. Ulanowsky, "HIV and Pregnancy," *Hastings Center Report* (March/April 1990): 16–21.

6. M. Gwinn, M. Pappaioanou, J. R. George, W. H. Hannon, S. C. Wasser, M. A. Redus, R. Hoff, G. F. Grady, A. Willoughby, A. C. Novello, L. R. Petersen, T. J. Dondero, and J. W. Curran, "Prevalence of HIV Infection in Childbearing Women in the United States," *Journal of the American Medical Association* 265 (1991): 1704–1708.

7. L. F. Novick, D. Berns, R. Stricof, R. Stevens, K. Pass, and J. Wethers, "HIV Seroprevalence in Newborns in New York State," *Journal of the American Medical Association* 261 (1989): 1745–1750.

8. Ellerbrock et al., 1991.

9. V. T. Shayne and B. J. Kaplan, "Double Victims: Poor Women and AIDS," *Women and Health* 17 (1991): 21–37.

10. P. F. Smith, J. Mikl, B. I. Truman, L. Lessner, J. S. Lehman, R. W. Stevens, E. A. Lord, R. K. Broaddus, and D. L. Morse, "HIV Infection Among Women Entering the New York State Correctional System," *American Journal of Public Health* 81 (1991): 35–40.

11. Centers for Disease Control, "Antibody to Human Immunodeficiency Virus in Female Prostitutes," *Morbidity and Mortality Weekly Report* 36 (1987): 157–161; and J. B. Cohen, P. Alexander, and C. Wofsy, "Prostitutes and AIDS: Public Policy Issues," *AIDS and Public Policy Journal* 3 (1988): 16–22.

12. J. A. Inciardi, A. E. Pottieger, M. A. Forney, D. D. Chitwood, and D. C. McBride, "Prostitution, IV Drug Use, and Sex-for-Crack Exchanges Among Serious Delinquents: Risks for HIV Infection," *Criminology* 29 (1991): 221–235; and M. J. Rotheram-Borus, C. Koopman, C. Haignere, and M. Davies, "Reducing HIV Sexual Risk Behaviors Among Runaway Adolescents," *Journal of the American Medical Association* 266 (1991): 1237–1241.

13. J. A. Catania, M. M. Dolcini, T. J. Coates, S. M. Kegeles, R. M. Greenblatt, S. Puckett, M. Corman, and J. Miller, "Predictors of Condom Use and Multiple Partnered Sex Among Sexually Active Adolescent Women: Implications for AIDS-Related Health Interventions," *Journal of Sex Research* 26 (1989): 514–524.

14. For an excellent review of the medical and clinical aspects of HIV infection, see R. R. Redfield and D. S. Burke, "HIV Infection: The Clinical Picture," *Scientific American* 259 (4) (1988): 90–98.

15. D. T. Imagawa, H. L. Moon, S. M. Wolinsky, K. Sano, F. Morales, S. Kwok, J. J. Sninsky, P. G. Nishanian, J. Giorgi, J. L. Sahey, B. Visscher, and R. Detels, "Human Immunodeficiency Virus, Type 1 Infection in Homosexual Men Who Remained Seronegative for Prolonged Periods," *New England Journal of Medicine* 320 (1989): 1458–1463.

16. Reviewed in S. C. Smeltzer and B. Whipple, "Women and HIV Infection," *Image: Journal of Nursing Scholarship* 23 (1991): 249–256.

17. J. L. Rhoads, C. D. Wright, R. R. Redfield, and D. S. Burke, "Chronic Vaginal Candidiasis in Women with Human Immunodeficiency Virus Infection," *Journal of the American Medical Association* 257 (1987): 3105–3107.

18. M. A. Byrne, D. Taylor-Robinson, P. E. Munday, and J. R. W. Harris, "The Common Occurrence of Human Papillomavirus Infection and Intraepithelial Neoplasia in Women Infected by HIV," *AIDS* 3 (1989): 379–382; and L. K. Schrager, G. H. Friedland, D. Maude, K. Schreiber, A. Adachi, D. J. Pizzuti, L. G. Koss, and R. S. Klein, "Cervical and Vaginal Squamous Cell Abnormalities in Women Infected with Human Immunodeficiency Virus," *Journal of Acquired Immune Deficiency Syndrome* 2 (1989): 570–575.

19. Centers for Disease Control, "1992 Revised Classification System for HIV Infection and Expanded AIDS Surveillance Case Definition for Adolescents and Adults" (Atlanta, Ga.: Center for Infectious Diseases, Centers for Disease Control, draft, November 15, 1991).

20. C. Levine, "Women and HIV/AIDS Research," *Evaluation Review* 14 (1990): 447–463.

21. G. Kolata, "U.S. Rule on Fetal Studies Hampers Research on AZT," *New York Times*, August 25, 1991.

22. P. A. Pizzo and K. M. Butler, "In the Vertical Transmission of HIV, Timing May Be Everything," *New England Journal of Medicine* 325 (1991): 652–654.

23. J. D. Arras, "AIDS and Reproductive Decisions: Having Children in Fear and Trembling," *The Milbank Quarterly* 68 (1990): 353–382.

24. Ibid.

25. Ibid.; C. Levine and N. N. Dubler, "HIV and Childbearing: 1. Uncertain Risks and Bitter Realities: The Reproductive Choices of HIV-infected Women," *The Milbank Quarterly* 68 (1990): 321–351; and Pizzo and Butler, 1991.

26. Arras, 1990.

27. C. A. Campbell, "Women and AIDS," *Social Sciences and Medicine* 30 (1990): 407–415.

28. Arras, 1990.

29. Pizzo and Butler, 1991.

30. Centers for Disease Control, "Recommendations for Assisting in the Prevention of Perinatal Transmission of Human T-lymphotropic Virus Type III/Lymphadenopathy-associated Virus and Acquired Immunodeficiency Syndrome," *Morbidity and Mortality Weekly Report* 34 (1985): 721–726, 731–732; and R. J. Biggar, S. Pahwa, H. Minkoff, H. Mendes, A. Willoughby, S. Landesman, and J. J. Goedert, "Immunosuppression in Pregnant Women Infected with Human Immunodeficiency Virus," *American Journal of Obstetrics and Gynecology* 161 (1989): 1239–1244.

31. H. L. Minkoff, "AIDS in Pregnancy," *Current Problems in Obstetrics, Gynecology and Fertility* 12 (1989): 205–228.

32. Levine and Dubler, 1990.

33. Arras, 1990.

34. Almond and Ulanowsky, 1990.

35. S. O. Aral and K. K. Holmes, "Sexually Transmitted Diseases in the AIDS Era," *Scientific American* 264 (1991): 62–69; H. M. Bauer, Y. Ting, C. E. Greer, J. C. Chambers, C. J. Tashiro, J. Chimera, A. Reingold, and M. M. Manos, "Genital Human Papillomavirus Infection in Female University Students as Determined by a PCR-based Method," *Journal of the American Medical Association* 265 (1991): 472–477; and R. B. Rothenberg, "Those Other STDs," *American Journal of Public Health* 81 (1991): 1250–1251.

36. J. B. Jemmott, L. S. Jemmott, and G. T. Fong, "Reductions in HIV Risk-associated Sexual Behaviors Among Black Male Adolescents: Effects of an AIDS Prevention Intervention," *American Journal of Public Health* 82 (1992): 372–377.

37. J. J. Flaskerud and A. M. Nyamathi, "Effects of an AIDS Education Program on the Knowledge, Attitudes, and Practices of Low Income Black and Latina Women," *Journal of Community Health* 15 (1990): 343–355.

38. Rotheram-Borus et al., 1991. Among the theoretical approaches that have been applied in this area are Social Cognitive Theory (A. Bandura, "A Social Cognitive Approach to the Exercise of Control over AIDS Infection," in *Adolescents and AIDS: A Generation in Jeopardy*, ed. R. DiClemente [Beverly Hills, Calif.: Sage, 1992]); and A. O'Leary, "Self-efficacy and Health: Behavioral and Stress-physiological Mediation," *Cognitive Therapy and Research* 16 [1992]: 229–245) and the Theory of Reasoned Action (L. S. Jemmott and J. B. Jemmott, "Applying the Theory of Reasoned Action to

AIDS Risk Behavior: Condom Use Among Black Women," *Nursing Research* 40 [1991]: 228–234).

39. Reviewed in B. B. North, "Effectiveness of Vaginal Contraceptives in Prevention of STDs," in *Heterosexual Transmission of AIDS*, ed. N. J. Alexander, H. L. Gabelnick, and J. M. Spieler (1990), 273–290.

40. L. Zekeng, R. Oliver, S. Godwin, P. Feldblum, and L. Kaptue, "HIV Infection and Barrier Contraceptive Use Among High-Risk Women in Cameroon" (unpublished report, 1992).

41. S. Niruthisard, R. E. Roddy, and S. Chutivongse, "The Effects of Frequent Nonoxynol-9 Use on the Vaginal and Cervical Mucosa," *Sexually Transmitted Diseases* 4 (1991): 176–179.

42. Centers for Disease Control, *HIV/AIDS Surveillance Report* (Atlanta, Ga.: Center for Infectious Diseases, Centers for Disease Control, January 1992).

43. Chu et al., 1990.

44. Centers for Disease Control, 1992.

45. T. A. Bell and K. K. Holmes, "Age-specific Risks of Syphilis, Gonorrhea, and Hospitalized Pelvic Inflammatory Disease in Sexually Experienced U.S. Women," *Sexually Transmitted Diseases* 7 (1984): 291; R. A. Hatcher, F. H. Stewart, J. Trussell, D. Kowal, F. Guest, G. K. Stewart, and W. Cates, *Contraceptive Technology, 1990–1992* (New York: Irvington Publishers, Inc., 1990); C. Hayes, *Risking the Future* (Washington, D.C.: National Academy Press, 1987); S. Hofferth and C. Hayes, *Risking the Future*, Volume 2 (Washington, D.C.: National Academy Press, 1987); E. F. Jones, J. D. Forrest, N. Goldman, S. Henshaw, R. Lincoln, J. L. Rosoff, C. F. Westoff, and D. Wulf, *Teenage Pregnancy in Industrialized Countries* (New Haven, Conn.: Yale University Press, 1986); W. Pratt, W. Mosher, C. Backrach, and M. Horn, "Understanding U.S. Fertility: Findings from the National Survey of Family Growth, Cycle III," *Population Bulletin* 39 (1984): 1–42; and M. Zelnick and J. F. Kantner, "Sexual Activity, Contraceptive Use and Pregnancy Among Metropolitan-area Teenagers: 1971–1979," *Family Planning Perspectives* 12 (1980): 230–238.

46. Jemmott and Jemmott, 1991.

47. P. A. Belcastro, "Sexual Behavior Differences between Black and White Students," *Journal of Sex Research* 21 (1985): 56–67; and Jemmott and Jemmott, 1991.

48. Jemmott and Jemmott, 1991.

49. Belcastro, 1985.

50. W. D. Mosher and W. F. Pratt, "Contraceptive Use in the United States,

1973–1988," *Advance Data from Vital and Health Statistics*, no. 182 (Hyattsville, Md.: National Center for Health Statistics).

51. J. M. Reinisch, S. A. Sanders, and M. Ziemba-Davis, "The Study of Sexual Behavior in Relation to the Transmission of Human Immunodeficiency Virus," *American Psychologist* 43 (1988): 921–927; C. Turner, H. Miller, and L. Moses, *AIDS: Sexual Behavior and Intravenous Drug Use* (Washington, D.C.: National Academy Press, 1989).

52. Belcastro, 1985.

53. G. E. Wyatt, S. Peters, and D. Guthrie, "Kinsey Revisited, I: Comparisons of Sexual Socialization and Sexual Behavior of White Women over 33 Years," *Archives of Sexual Behavior* 17 (1988): 201–239; and G. E. Wyatt, S. Peters, and D. Guthrie, "Kinsey Revisited, II: Comparisons of Sexual Socialization and Sexual Behavior of Black Women over 33 Years," *Archives of Sexual Behavior* 17 (1988): 289–332.

54. A. Houston-Hamilton, *Implications of Sexual and Contraceptive Practices/Attitudes for Prevention of Heterosexual Transmission in Blacks* (NIDA Technical Review Meeting, January 1988).

55. Jemmott and Jemmott, 1991.

56. S. B. Thomas and S. C. Quinn, "The Tuskeegee Syphilis Study, 1932–1972: Implications for HIV Education and AIDS Risk Education Programs in the Black Community," *American Journal of Public Health* 81 (1991): 1498–1505.

57. H. Amaro, "Hispanic Women and AIDS," *Psychology of Women Quarterly* 12 (1988): 423–443; P. J. Guarnaccia, R. Angel, and J. L. Worobey, "The Factor Structure of CES-D in the Hispanic Health and Nutrition Examination Survey: The Influence of Ethnicity, Gender and Language," *Social Science and Medicine* 29 (1989): 85–94; and G. Marin and V. O. B. Marin, *Research with Hispanic Populations, Applied Social Research Methods Series*, Volume 23 (Newbury Park, Calif.: Sage, 1991).

58. Bureau of the Census, "Persons of Spanish Origin in the United States," *Current Population Reports* (Series P-20, No. 403) (Washington, D.C.: U.S. Government Printing Office, 1986).

59. S. J. Ventura, *Birth of Hispanic Parentage, 1983 and 1984*, Vital and Health Statistics, Series 21, Data from the National Vital Statistics System (Washington, D.C.: U.S. Government Printing Office, 1987).

60. A. Giachello, "Hispanics and Health Care: Hispanics and the Social Service System," in *Hispanics in the United States: A New Social Agenda*, ed. P. S. J. Cafferty and W. C. McCready (New Brunswick, N.J.: Transaction Books, 1985).

61. G. Canino, "The Hispanic Woman: Sociocultural Influences on Diagnosis

and Treatment," in *Mental Health of Hispanic Americans*, ed. R. Becerra, M. Karno, and J. Escobar (New York: Grune and Stratton, 1982); and C. Rivera, "Hispanics and the Social Service System," in *Hispanics in the United States*, ed. Cafferty and McCready.

62. Marin and Marin, 1991.

63. Ibid.

64. J. Fisher and W. Fisher, "Changing AIDS Risk Behavior," *Psychological Bulletin* 111 (3) (1992): 455–474; and M. Fishbein and S. Middlestadt, "Using the Theory of Reasoned Action as a Framework for Understanding and Changing AIDS-Related Behaviors," in *Primary Prevention of AIDS: Psychological Approaches*, ed. V. Mays, G. Albee, and S. Schneider (Newbury Park, Calif.: Sage, 1989).

65. V. M. Mays and S. D. Cochran, "Issues in the Perception of AIDS Risk and Risk Reduction Activities by Black and Hispanic/Latina Women," *American Psychologist* 43 (1988): 949–957.

66. Ibid.

67. J. L. Peterson and G. Marin, "Issues in the Prevention of AIDS Among Black and Hispanic Men," *American Psychologist* 43 (1988): 871–877.

68. E. E. Jones, "Psychotherapy and Counseling with Black Clients," in *Handbook of Cross-Cultural Counseling and Therapy*, ed. P. Pederson (New York: Praeger, 1973).

69. E. Fox-Genovese, *Within the Plantation Household* (Chapel Hill: University of North Carolina Press, 1988).

70. D. Hine and K. Wittenstein, "Female Slave Resistance: The Economics of Sex," in *The Black Woman Cross-Culturally*, ed. F. Steady (Cambridge, Mass.: Schenkman Publishing Company, 1981), 189–344.

71. D. King, "Prostitutes as Pariah in the Age of AIDS: A Content Analysis of Coverage of Women Prostitutes in the *New York Times* and the *Washington Post* September 1985–April 1988," *Women and Health* 16 (1990): 155–175.

72. A. Juhasz, "The Contained Threat: Women in Mainstream AIDS Documentary," *Journal of Sex Research* 27 (1990): 25–46.

73. P. Treichler, "AIDS, Homophobia and Biomedical Discourse: An Epidemic of Signification," in *AIDS: Cultural Analysis/Cultural Activism*, ed. D. Crimp (Cambridge, Mass.: The MIT Press, 1988), 31–70.

THE ABORTION DEBATE: PSYCHOLOGICAL ISSUES FOR ADULT WOMEN AND ADOLESCENTS

❖ ❖ ❖

Nancy E. Adler and Jeanne M. Tschann

One of the most controversial issues in the United States today is that of abortion. Controversy over this issue involves moral, religious, emotional, and political considerations. Much of the discussion has focused on the "rights" of the woman versus the "rights" of the fetus,[1] but psychological issues have recently entered this debate.

In this chapter, following a brief review of the legal status of abortion in the United States, we will describe some of the psychological issues involved in the abortion debate and present the relevant findings from psychological research on abortion.

LEGAL STATUS OF ABORTION IN THE UNITED STATES

Historian James Mohr has traced the origin of abortion laws during the 1800s.[2] At the beginning of the nineteenth century, there were no laws regulating abortion. However, there was increasing concern about the upsurge in the number of abortions being performed and about the consequences of the abortions. The initial laws that were passed were largely to protect women against poisoning, which was often a side effect of the available methods of the day. At that time, also, the American Medical Association was trying to professionalize the practice of medicine and wanted to cast out the so-called "irregular" doctors who were not "scientifically trained." These doctors were the ones who were primarily providing abortions. By limiting abortions, such doctors would be driven out of business. Physicians led the crusade to prohibit abortion and tried to enlist the efforts of the clergy. However, few clergymen became involved in the fight for restrictive legislation. The common religious belief was that the soul does not infuse until quickening and because abortions were performed prior to quickening, it was not seen as a religious matter. A more receptive group was state legislators, many of whom were concerned that the increasing use of abortion by white, middle-class Protestant women would change the population balance. States began enacting restrictive abortion legislation that generally stayed on the books until 1973 when *Roe v. Wade* was decided by the U.S. Supreme Court. Until then, in most states, abortion was allowed only if continuation of the pregnancy threatened the life of the mother. Some states, such as California, allowed such "therapeutic" abortions if continuation of the pregnancy threatened the physical or mental health of the mother and required a doctor to certify that the procedure was needed. The vast majority of procedures that were done were performed on the basis of threat to mental health.

Roe v. Wade struck down state restrictions on abortion. The ruling stated that the abortion decision was protected by the right of privacy, but that the state has legitimate interests in protecting both the woman's health and potential human life. These are interests that grow with development and reach a "compelling point at later stages of gestation." Thus, in the first trimester, when abortion is safer than normal childbirth, the abortion decision is protected by the right of privacy and rests with the woman and her physician. Later in pregnancy, states may regulate abortion to ensure that maternal health is protected. Finally, in the third trimester, the viability of the fetus permits states to exercise their interests in protecting potential life, and regulation and prohibition of abortion is permitted except where abortion is necessary to preserve the life or health of the mother. It is interesting to note that, in contrast to the nineteenth century, during which the medical profession lobbied for restrictions on abortion, in the 1960s and 1970s physicians were in the forefront in the arguments to overturn restrictions on abortion. The medical community had become aware of the costs of illegal abortion in terms of maternal injury and death.

Abortion practices changed dramatically in the United States after 1973. The number of illegal procedures decreased greatly, as did rates of maternal mortality. While it is difficult to assess the exact number of procedures that were done prior to 1973, estimates range from 200,000 to 1.2 million per year. Since 1973, the rates rose from about 800,000 in 1973 to over 1.5 million in 1980 and have remained at between 1.5 and 1.6 million annually since then.[3]

PSYCHOLOGICAL ISSUES REGARDING ABORTION

Psychologists have conducted research on various aspects of abortion, including factors associated with unwanted pregnancy, decision making regarding abortion, and psychological responses following abortion. Many of the studies were not designed primarily to study abortion, but to test specific psychological theories.[4] Until the early 1990s, there was little discussion of such studies in political, policy, or legal debates on abortion. This changed when individuals and organizations opposed to abortion began to invoke psychological reasons for limiting access to the procedure. Among their claims was the assertion that abortion leads to psychopathology and should be limited because it is a hazard to women's mental health.

This issue came to national attention in 1987 when President Reagan asked Surgeon General C. Everett Koop to issue a report on the medical and psychological impact of abortion. Surgeon General Koop wrote a report, but then declined to release it, stating that there was not sufficient scientific evidence to reach a conclusion. During this time, because conflicting claims were being made about the research on the psychological effects of abortion, the American Psychological Association (APA) convened an expert panel. The panel was charged with reviewing the literature on the psychological effects of abortion and determining which, if any, conclusions could be reached on the basis of this literature.

The APA panel identified a large number of articles on psychological responses following abortions. However, the literature was marked by wide variation in the quality of the data. For example, a number of studies were conducted prior to *Roe v. Wade* and examined women undergoing illegal or "therapeutic" abortions for which the woman had to qualify on the basis that continuation of the pregnancy would pose a threat to her physical or mental health. These experiences are so different from current conditions that the conclusions of such studies cannot be applied to the experiences of women undergoing safe, legal, unrestricted abortion. Additionally, many of the studies were of highly self-selected populations, such as women seeking mental-health services. Such samples are unlikely to be representative of the broader population of women having abortions. Finally, some researchers made only subjective evaluations of women's psychological states, did not provide sufficient information about their research techniques, or acquired data that could not be subjected to statistical analysis. These are all flaws that seriously compromise the conclusions reached by most of the studies.

The APA panel decided to focus only on scientifically sound studies and it set three criteria for including a study in its review. These criteria provide a minimum level of scientific rigor and permit reasonable ability to generalize to the experiences of women in the United States who are undergoing abortions. The first criterion set by the panel was that the study had to have clearly defined its subject population and to have used data-collection techniques that could provide objective data. Specification of the study participants and of data-collection procedures is important because it allows for future studies to be conducted on similar populations using the same data-collection methods and it provides information about groups to whom results may apply. The second and third criteria were set to ensure that the conclusions reached from studies reasonably reflect the experiences of U.S. women at the present time. These criteria were that the sample had to be of women who had undergone legal abortion under nonrestrictive conditions and who were in the United States. Applying these criteria provides a set of the most rigorous scientific studies on abortion for U.S. women. The following discussion on the psychological effects of abortion is based largely on the conclusions reached by the APA panel.[5]

IMPACT OF ABORTION

The debate over the psychological impact of abortion centers around the frequency and severity of negative psychological responses. Some have asserted that the experience of abortion is traumatic for women and results in post-abortion trauma syndrome, similar to the post-traumatic stress disorder (PTSD) evidenced by Vietnam veterans. Evidence regarding the occurrence of psychopathology comes largely from clinical case studies of women who have sought mental-health treatment or from selected samples of women identified on the basis of their having experienced negative responses following abortion.

As with other issues, it is important to be aware of the *relative frequency* of various kinds of outcomes. Presentations of case studies of negative outcomes of abortion provide a numerator, but we need to know the size and type of sample used as the denominator. If a study presents 10 women who have had serious negative responses following abortion, we would interpret this very differently depending on whether those 10 were from a sample of 30 randomly selected women, a sample of 3,000 randomly selected women, or a sample that was not randomly selected at all but was of a group of women who had been chosen because they had a negative response.

While case studies and specially selected samples demonstrate that some women will experience severe distress or psychopathology, they do not demonstrate that the negative responses are due to the abortion or that such responses are common enough to be considered to be a syndrome. These issues are discussed in more detail in the next section.

DETERMINING CAUSALITY

It is not possible to determine the effects of abortion itself (i.e., the termination of one's pregnancy). Abortion cannot be separated from the entire experience of having become pregnant and then having terminated the pregnancy. Negative responses following this experience could be due to a number of factors. First, women who experience an unwanted pregnancy may be at higher risk for negative psychological states to begin with.[6] This may be particularly true for adolescents, who are less likely to use contraception and are more likely to become pregnant if they have low self-esteem, are more passive, or are more conflicted over sexual activity.[7] To the extent that this occurs, poor self-image contributes to pregnancy and *precedes* rather than follows from abortion. Dagg, in his review of the abortion literature, concludes that symptoms of distress and negative emotion following abortion "seem to be continuations of symptoms present before the abortion and more a result of the circumstances leading to the abortion than a result of the procedure itself."[8]

Second, the experience of an unwanted pregnancy is itself likely to be upsetting and could engender negative responses. Such an experience may contribute to a woman's sense of lack of control or low self-worth. Some women may be upset that they permitted themselves to get pregnant. Women who blame themselves for an unwanted pregnancy tend to show more negative responses following its termination.[9] The occurrence of the pregnancy may also trigger a cascade of events (e.g., abandonment by the partner or punishment by the parents) that may themselves be stressful and upsetting.

The experiences women have in obtaining an abortion may al~ contribute to responses afterward, apart from the impact ᴼᶠ mination. As noted earlier, women who had illegaˡ have experienced situations in which they were viᵼ risking serious complications, and undergoing a paiᵢ without anesthesia. In recent times, women having abortions increasingly have had to make their way through angry mobs in order to get their procedure.[10] Such experiences can be upsetting, making it difficult to attribute responses following the abortion to the actual termination of the pregnancy or to the experience the woman had in obtaining the abortion.

The conditions under which the pregnancy occurred are also likely to influence a woman's response to its termination. Women who terminate pregnancies that initially were wanted are more likely to show negative responses than those for whom the pregnancy was unwanted.[11] Similarly, those who reported that the pregnancy was "highly meaningful" to them showed greater distress following its termination. Women who terminate a pregnancy following results of genetic diagnostic screening appear to be at heightened risk of negative responses;[12] in this instance, the pregnancy that is terminated is likely to have been wanted and there is a greater sense of loss than for women who are terminating unintended and unwanted pregnancies.[13]

Other circumstances surrounding the reason for the pregnancy must also be taken into account. For example, responses following termination of pregnancies that occurred as the result of rape cannot be attributed solely to the abortion since responses to rape are highly negative and remain over time. One study of rape victims showed that 94 percent were diagnosed as suffering from PTSD shortly after the experience; 47 percent were still suffering from it 3 months later, and 16.5 percent still had PTSD 17 years later.[14]

RESEARCH FINDINGS ON RESPONSES FOLLOWING ABORTION

The discussion in the previous section describes the difficulty of attributing negative responses following abortion solely to the termination of pregnancy. For the most part, however, such reactions are rare. In well-designed studies with representative samples of women having abortions, the incidence of severe negative responses is low.[15] The emotions that are most commonly and most strongly reported following abortion are positive: relief and happiness.[16] In addition, studies that have included measures of psychological distress both prior to and following abortion have shown women's distress is generally lower after the abortion, and emotional distress continues to diminish over time.[17] This suggests that the abortion serves to reduce distress associated with the experience of an unwanted pregnancy and does not generally create new or additional distress for most women.

The claim by anti-abortion groups that the experience of unwanted pregnancy terminated by abortion causes psychopathology can be evaluated by two pieces of evidence. The first has to do with the fact that large numbers of women have had abortions. Over 1.5 million abortions are performed each year in the United States.[18] Given the frequency of this event, if a substantial proportion of women suffered psychopathology as a result of this experience, there would be a sizeable number of women with psychiatric disorder. Further, the incidence of psychopathology should have increased between 1973 when 744,000 procedures were done and 1988 when 1.6 million were performed, but a comparable increase in psychopathology has not occurred. There is no evidence from the mainstream mental-health professionals that a noticeable number of women are developing symptoms associated with abortion.

Importantly, the Diagnostic and Statistical Manual of Mental Disorders (DSM-III-R), the official diagnostic manual of the American Psychiatric Association that provides definitions for all psychiatric disorders, does not list abortion as one of the events associated with PTSD. The diagnostic manual defines this disorder as one that follows "a psychologically distressing event that is outside the usual range of human experience." Examples given are experiences of rape or assault, military combat, torture, and (less frequently) experiences of natural disasters (e.g., earthquake or tornado) or accidental disasters (e.g., fire or automobile crash). The diagnostic manual differentiates such "traumas" from more common life experiences that may be stressful, but do not result in such a syndrome. Examples of common life experiences that are given include bereavement and chronic illness. From all available evidence, the experience of abortion would be described as a normal (though stressful) life experience rather than as a trauma.

The second piece of evidence demonstrating that abortion is not generally associated with psychopathology comes from studies using measures that have cut-off points indicating pathological versus non-pathological states (based on testing with known pathological populations). These studies have shown that, as a group, abortion patients obtain average scores well below the cut-off points for psychopathology.[19]

In contrast, studies of women who were denied legal abortions (prior to legalization or in other countries) found that the vast majority of those who delivered and kept the child experienced long-term negative effects, both for the woman as well as for the child. It is difficult to do similar studies today because most women who wish to terminate their pregnancies can do so.

Some researchers have evaluated the effects of abortion by comparing responses of women following abortion to those of women following term birth. This is useful, although not a wholly adequate comparison because the vast majority of women who are carrying pregnancies to term are likely to have had wanted pregnancies. Women having a term birth are likely to have more positive responses if the pregnancy is wanted than if it is not. Even though comparisons of abortion patients to women with term births will thus overestimate negative effects of abortion, such comparisons have shown few adverse consequences for abortion versus birth for the vast majority of women.[20]

Two studies in the United States have compared women who have had abortions with those who carried to term. One compared women who were undergoing a first trimester abortion, a second trimester abortion, or a term birth at the same hospital.[21] The groups were similar in terms of age, number of previous live births, marital status, and ethnicity. Thirteen to 16 months later, the women completed the Minnesota Multiphasic Personality Inventory (MMPI), a personality measure that assesses various types of adjustment and psychopathology, and the Symptom Checklist (SCL), a measure that assesses psychological and psychosomatic symptomatology. Few differences among the groups were found. The only differences reaching statistical significance were that the term birth group scored higher on the paranoia subscale of the MMPI than did women having either early or late abortions and that women having an early abortion had fewer somatic complaints on the SCL than did women in the groups having late abortion or term birth. Otherwise, the groups were, in the authors' words "startlingly similar." If anything, the early abortion patients showed the most favorable psychological responses.

A similar conclusion emerged from a study by Zabin, Hirsch, and Emerson.[22] Adolescents completed questionnaires at three points in time: while they were waiting for results of a pregnancy test, and again one and two years later. Measures were taken on self-esteem, trait anxiety (one's general tendency to be anxious), state anxiety (current feelings of anxiety), and locus of control (the extent to which individuals feel that they are in control of events that happen to them). Comparisons were made between the adolescents who had a negative pregnancy test, those who had a positive test and then carried to term, and those who had a positive pregnancy test and then had an abortion.

The comparisons over time and across groups are revealing. First, while waiting for the pregnancy test result, all three groups of adolescents showed high state anxiety, which dropped dramatically over the two years. No differences across groups of adolescents were shown on these scores. The measure of general tendency to be anxious also declined over the two years: The groups did not differ on trait anxiety at first testing, but one year later the negative pregnancy test group had higher trait anxiety than the abortion group, and two years later both the negative pregnancy test and the term birth groups showed higher trait anxiety than did the abortion group. Scores on self-esteem improved over the two years for all three groups. While the groups were essentially the same at first testing, two years later the abortion group had more positive self-esteem than did the negative pregnancy group. Similarly, the three groups of adolescents had similar locus of control at first testing, but differences emerged over time. The abortion group and the negative pregnancy group both felt more in control of things that were happening to them after two years, but the childbearing group did not feel more in control. Furthermore, when the three groups were compared, the childbearing group felt less in control than did the abortion group, both one and two years later. As with the previous study, this study found that abortion patients showed, if anything, a more positive psychological profile after abortion than did the comparison groups.

PSYCHOLOGICAL ISSUES IN ABORTION FOR ADOLESCENTS

The debate about abortion is intensified in relation to adolescent abortion. In addition to restrictions that have been proposed on abortion for all women in some states, additional restrictions have been placed on abortion for adolescents. Most of these restrictions involve the need for parental notification and consent. The need for such restrictions is frequently based on assumptions about the psychological maturity and vulnerability of the adolescent. In the following sections we present statistics on the frequency of adolescent abortion and then consider two issues underlying the parental-consent mandates.

ADOLESCENT ABORTION

A little over one-quarter of all abortions are to adolescents.[23] These numbers reflect the rates of sexual activity and of unintentional pregnancy in this age group. There have been substantial increases in the proportion of females who have sexual intercourse during their teenage years. The percentage of females aged 15 to 19 who have had intercourse has risen from 28 in 1971 to 53 in 1988.[24] This change has been reflected in increased rates of pregnancy among adolescents over the past 25 years, which have remained at around 110 per 1,000 adolescents over the past decade.[25] In any given year, over 10 percent of all adolescents, and about 25 percent of those who are sexually active, will become pregnant. Translating this into absolute numbers, over 1 million adolescents will conceive each year. In 1985, for example, 1,031,000 teenagers became pregnant. Thirteen percent of these (n = 137,120) either miscarried or had a stillbirth. Of the remainder, 477,710 (46 percent) had a live birth and 416,170 (40 percent) terminated the pregnancy. Adolescent pregnancies are more likely than those among adults to be unintended and, because of this, a higher proportion of adolescents terminate pregnancies than do older women.[26]

ISSUES OF PARENTAL CONSENT

States have been passing legislation mandating that adolescents obtain the consent of one or both parents or use a "judicial bypass" (a procedure by which a judge may grant permission for the abortion). The need for parental consent for abortion is predicated on two assumptions: (1) abortion poses a risk to the adolescent, and (2) adolescents are not capable of making an informed decision evaluating the risks and benefits of abortion. We will now examine these two assumptions.

RISK TO ADOLESCENTS FROM ABORTION   The California Legislature passed a parental-consent bill in 1987 (which is undergoing court challenge), which stated that "the medical, emotional, and psychological consequences of an abortion are serious and can be lasting, particularly when the patient is an immature minor." The review presented earlier in this chapter demonstrated that, overall, women were at relatively little risk of serious negative psychological effects of abortion. (There is also little evidence for serious medical risk from abortion, particularly compared to childbirth, but a review of that evidence is beyond the scope of this chapter.) One might reasonably ask, however, if adolescents are at higher risk than adults, is the degree of risk sufficient to necessitate special protection for adolescents?

The studies cited in this chapter, with one exception,[27] included women of all ages. Some studies have examined whether younger or older women have more negative responses following abortion. Several of these studies found younger women to have more negative responses,[28] while others have found no relationship between age and negative post-abortion responses.[29]

There are reasons why adolescents might be at increased risk for negative responses following abortion. For example, they may be more likely to feel pressure from others (particularly from parents) to have an abortion. Torres and Forrest surveyed abortion patients regarding their reasons for having an abortion.[30] Those under age 18 were more likely than the older abortion patients to cite their parents' desire for them to have an abortion as a reason for doing so. To the extent to which they act in response to parental pressure to terminate a pregnancy that is at least partially wanted, adolescents may be at relatively greater risk for negative responses following the abortion.[31] In addition, unmarried adolescents who have an abortion may be dealing with the double stigma of revealing that they are sexually active as well as the fact that they are having an abortion. Their responses following abortion may be due to other people's responses to their sexual activity as well as to the abortion.

Although adolescents may be at somewhat greater risk than older women for negative responses to abortion, the absolute degree of risk does not appear to be great. As noted earlier, adolescent abortion patients showed a more positive psychological profile one and two years following abortion than did the adolescents who carried to term or who were not pregnant.[32] As with older women, there may be individuals who are at high risk of developing adverse responses following abortion, but the risk for the general population appears to be small.

ADOLESCENTS' COMPETENCE TO CONSENT TO ABORTION   The second assumption underlying parental-consent legislation is that adolescents are not capable of making an adequately informed decision that takes into account risks and benefits. There is very little research directly on this topic, but several studies suggest that adolescents are capable of making informed decisions in this area. Our own research has examined the extent to which adolescents engage in "rational" decision making in their choice and use of contraceptive methods.[33] A number of authors have characterized adolescents as too immature and impulsive to engage in rational decision making, and have assumed that the theoretical decision models that have been used with adults could not be applied to adolescents. We tested this question in a study of 350 sexually active adolescents.[34] We examined their beliefs, values, intentions, and behaviors regarding several methods of contraception and then followed their behavior over the next year. We found that the adolescents were consistent in their reasoning and behavior. Their intention to use a given method of contraception was associated with their beliefs about the consequences of using that method, the values they placed on those consequences, and their perception of social expectations regarding their using that method. In addition, adolescents intending to use a method, compared to those not intending to use it, were more likely to actually use the method during the next year, particularly if it were one over which they had control (i.e., pill use for females and withdrawal for males).

Much of the debate over adolescents' ability to consent to abortion has focused on cognitive development. One question that emerges is how strongly an adolescent's general level of cognitive ability relates to her ability in a specific domain. In considering adolescents' competence to provide consent for abortion, one study found that "the level of sophistication demonstrated by a minor solving a specific problem is thought to be influenced not only by general level of cognitive development but also by context-specific factors including: domain-relevant knowledge and experience; cognitive problem solving skills, affect during decision making; and social support."[35] Because of this, it is particularly important to have studies of adolescents' decision-making skills specifically in the context of abortion. One such study has already been done.[36] These researchers examined 75 adolescents seeking pregnancy tests, grouping them by age: 15 years or younger, 16 to 17 years, and 18 years or older. They further divided each of these groups into those who considered abortion and those who did not.

The researchers examined cognitive competence in terms of criteria for legal competence to consent, comparing the abilities across the age groups for adolescents who did and did not consider abortion. The researchers assessed (1) volition, that is, whether the decision making was based on the adolescent's own desires rather than being coerced or unduly influenced, and (2) cognitive competence, including an overall assessment of the quality of the young woman's reasoning and its clarity and content, the extent to which the adolescent considered relevant consequences of her choice, and the richness or variety of consequences that the adolescent considered in weighing costs and benefits. The critical comparison for purposes of evaluating whether adolescents who consider abortion are competent to consent is the comparison of adolescents over 18 (who are not subject to parental consent) with the two younger groups. The researchers found that all three age groups were similar in both volition and cognitive competence.

Although further research is needed, currently available studies suggest that younger adolescents who are considering abortion are as able as those over age 18 to reason adequately about the risks and benefits of abortion. Studies of minors' abilities to provide consent in different situations, including consent to medical treatment, have findings that are consistent with the findings regarding consent for abortion. In his review of the research on the legal competence of minors to provide consent, Mulvey concluded that "children are *more similar* to adults than the law assumes in both the choices made and the logical processes followed."[37]

IS MANDATED PARENTAL CONSENT EFFECTIVE?

Mandated parental consent is intended to have several effects on the family and the adolescent's decision-making process regarding abortion. Several states have contended that parental consent supports parental authority and promotes family harmony.[38] Parental consent is also intended to improve adolescents' decision making about abortion and to increase parental involvement.[39] Although there is little research regarding these issues, what does exist suggests that requiring parental consent does not have these positive effects.

PROMOTION OF FAMILY HARMONY   Adolescents who have emotional support from parents and partner have been found to have more positive responses following abortion.[40] Interestingly, Bracken, Hachamovitch, and Grossman found that responses following abortion did not depend on whether a woman had actually told her partner or parents, but a woman had more positive responses if she felt she had or would have support from them.[41] The majority of adolescents, particularly young adolescents, voluntarily tell their parents of the abortion: In one study, 55 percent of all adolescents and 75 percent of those 15 or younger told their parents about the abortion.[42] However, some of those who do not voluntarily tell their parents may have reason not to do so. Clary found that 30 percent of adolescents who choose not to tell their parents are fearful of negative responses, such as retaliation or physical punishment.[43] Recent estimates based on a national probability sample are that 20 percent to 56 percent of children ages 13 to 17 are physically abused by their parents, and that 6 percent to 13 percent experience severe physical abuse.[44] For such adolescents, the requirement of parental notification is not helpful, and could provoke an abusive episode.

PARENTAL INVOLVEMENT IN DECISION MAKING   There are two key questions regarding parental involvement in decision making. The first question is whether parental-consent legislation increases actual levels of parental involvement in the abortion decision, and the second is whether such involvement is beneficial for the adolescent and her family. In 1992, there is no research assessing whether parental notification improves adolescents' decision-making process, but there is some evidence on whether parental involvement has increased as a result of parental-notification legislation.

Most states allow judicial bypass, and many adolescents have used it. In a Minnesota sample, 43 percent of the adolescents at abortion clinics used the judicial bypass procedure.[45] A study that compared rates of parental notification in Minnesota, which requires notification, and in Wisconsin, which does not, found that the rates of parental notification were not significantly different for the two states.[46] These studies suggest that mandated parental notification does not increase parental involvement in adolescent decision making about abortion.

Ironically, the results of petitions for judicial bypass underscore research conclusions that adolescents are capable of making informed decisions. In the overwhelming majority of cases, adolescent petitions for abortion are granted. For example, of 477 cases heard in Massachusetts between 1981 and 1985, 10 percent of the adolescents were appealing parental refusal to give consent to the abortion and 90 percent wanted to avoid notifying their parents.[47] Only one adolescent of 477 was denied her request for abortion. Similarly, in Minnesota, of the 3,500 adolescents petitioning for judicial bypass during 1985 to 1990, only nine were denied abortions.[48]

Given these figures, one might question the contribution of parental-consent laws. It is possible that some adolescents will consult their parents who would not otherwise do so and that this will benefit them. However, there are several costs as well. There is a financial cost to the courts and the public of the notification hearings. In addition, it may be difficult and upsetting for an adolescent to have to go before a judge about this very personal issue. It also adds delay.[49] At a minimum, this increases the period of time that the adolescent is likely to experience as the most stressful and difficult. For adolescents who present late in the first trimester, it may increase the chances that they will have to undergo a second-trimester procedure, which carries with it a higher risk of physical and emotional problems. Finally, an extreme cost is shown in the publicized case of Becky Bell, an adolescent who sought an illegal abortion rather than notify her parents and who subsequently died of complications from that procedure.

The available research suggests that it is better for an adolescent to involve her parents in her decision if they will be supportive of her. However, the adolescent is in the best position to evaluate whether parental involvement is wise. Such a decision ought to be made with guidance from a neutral adult who can help the adolescent anticipate consequences if she does or does not tell her parents. This can best be done in the context of counseling within a health-care setting, which is a more comfortable and supportive environment than a court.[50]

SUMMARY

Insofar as psychological issues are raised in the debate over abortion, we need to be aware of the scientific basis underlying different positions. Individual examples are often gripping and convincing (be they about a woman who suffered psychopathology following abortion or an adolescent who suffered as a result of a parental-consent requirement). However, in forming policy, we need to have data on representative samples to know the frequency and distribution of different types of responses. We have good data on some questions, but not on all.

In terms of psychological responses following abortion, the research evidence is consistent and persuasive. While abortion may be difficult and upsetting for many women, a substantial body of research provides convincing evidence that it is not an *abnormally* stressful or traumatic experience. In fact, most women feel relief and happiness following abortion. Lunnenborg, in a recent book on positive aspects of the abortion experience, notes that abortion can have a positive impact on a woman's mental health, providing her with an enhanced sense of control over her own life, increased self-esteem, and greater maturity.[51]

For some women (for example, those terminating a wanted pregnancy or with a history of prior psychiatric illness), the experience may be followed by a psychopathological reaction. Such women need support and treatment. However, the proportions do not appear to be out of the range of reactions that occur with a wide range of normal life stresses. As former Surgeon General C. Everett Koop noted, problems of serious psychological difficulties following abortion, while they could be overwhelming to a particular woman, were "minuscule from a public health perspective."[52]

We also need, in assessing the impact of abortion, to consider the alternative to abortion. Once an unwanted pregnancy occurs, the alternatives are limited. Carrying to term has a number of negative consequences associated with it, particularly for adolescents. Term delivery carries with it more serious physical risks and there are a number of adverse long-term consequences associated with adolescent motherhood.[53] Under current laws, where women of all ages can choose the resolution to the crisis of an unwanted pregnancy that they believe to be the best for them, there are relatively few adverse psychological consequences of choosing either abortion or term birth. If, however, women are coerced into one or the other form of resolving the pregnancy (either coerced abortion or coerced motherhood), far more adverse responses would be likely. In this context, it is interesting to note that the demands for parental notification and consent have been proposed and implemented for abortion, but not for pregnancy. We might ask whether an adolescent who is not capable of understanding the risks and benefits of having an abortion is capable of understanding the risks and benefits of term birth and motherhood.

More research is needed about the processes by which adolescents make decisions about pregnancy, abortion, and motherhood. Because there are few studies of adolescent decision making in these areas, we have little information on which to base policy. In addition, studies have not had sufficient diversity in adolescents' age or ethnicity to allow for comparisons among age groups or among those of different ethnicity. While the currently available research suggests that adolescents who are seeking abortions are capable of making adequately informed choices, research efforts need to be expanded. Comparisons should be made with adolescents who are carrying to term as well as with those who have different experiences in obtaining the procedure. In addition, we should see if the decision-making process relates to later responses, for both adolescents who obtain abortion and those who carry to term.

Finally, more resources (including research and intervention) need to be directed at pregnancy prevention. It would be far better for everyone if unwanted pregnancies were avoided. Perhaps our discomfort with the whole area of adolescent sexuality (evidenced, for example, in the cancellation of the American Teenager study, which would have provided critical information about the sexual behavior of adolescents from a nationally representative sample) has prevented us from adequately addressing this problem. Our failure to do so is demonstrated in U.S. statistics. The rate of adolescent pregnancy is higher in the United States than in any other developed country. As noted earlier, the pregnancy rate in the United States for adolescents has remained at around 110 per 1,000 adolescents. The rate was 15 per 1,000 in the Netherlands, 33.2 in Sweden, and 34 in Denmark. In Canada, which is more similar to U.S. culture, the pregnancy rate is less than half of ours, at 45.4 per 1,000.[54] Discussion of approaches to preventing unwanted pregnancy is beyond the scope of this chapter, but is central to considerations of abortion for both adolescent and adult women, and should be part of any debate on this issue.

4THE ABORTION DEBATE ❖ 209

NOTES

1. R. M. Baird and S. E. Rosenbaum, eds., *The Ethics of Abortion* (Buffalo, N.Y.: Prometheus Books, 1989).

2. J. C. Mohr, *Abortion in America: The Origins and Evolution of National Policy* (New York: Oxford University Press, 1978).

3. S. K. Henshaw and J. Van Vort, "Abortion Services in the United States, 1987 and 1988," *Family Planning Perspectives* 22(3) (1990): 102–142.

4. L. Cohen and S. Roth, "Coping with Abortion," *Journal of Human Stress* 10(3) (1984): 140–145; B. Major, C. Cozzarelli, A. M. Sciacchitano, M. L. Cooper, M. Testa, and P. M. Mueller, "Perceived Social Support, Self-efficacy, and Adjustment to Abortion," *Journal of Personality and Social Psychology* 59 (1990): 452–463; and B. Major, P. Mueller, and K. Hildebrandt, "Attributions, Expectations and Coping with Abortion," *Journal of Personality and Social Psychology* 48(3) (1985): 585–599.

5. N. E. Adler, H. P. David, B. N. Major, et al., "Psychological Responses after Abortion," *Science* 248 (1990): 41–44. Reprinted in *Le Journal International de Medicine* 158 (May 2, 1990): 23–27.

6. W. B. Miller, "Sexual and Contraceptive Behavior in Young Unmarried Women," *Primary Care* 3 (1976): 427–433.

7. For review, see N. E. Adler, "Contraception and Unwanted Pregnancy," *Behavioral Medicine Update* 5 (1984): 28–34; and C. Chilman, *Adolescent Sexuality in a Changing American Society: Social and Psychological Perspectives* (Washington, D.C.: U.S. Department of Health, Education, and Welfare, Public Health Service, National Institutes of Health, 1979).

8. P. K. B. Dagg, "The Psychological Sequelae of Therapeutic Abortion—Denied and Completed," *American Journal of Psychiatry* 148(5) (1991): 578–585.

9. Major et al., 1985.

10. S. K. Henshaw, "The Accessibility of Abortion Services in the United States," *Family Planning Perspectives* 23(2) (1991).

11. Major, Mueller, and Hildebrandt (see note 4) found that women who reported beforehand that they had at least some intention of becoming pregnant had more negative responses following abortion than did those who indicated that they had had no intention of conceiving.

12. B. D. Blumberg, M. S. Golbus, and K. H. Hanson, "The Psychological Sequelae of Abortion Performed for a Genetic Indication," *American Journal of Obstetrics and Gynecology* 122(7) (1975): 799–808.

13. N. E. Adler, "Unwanted Pregnancy and Abortion: Definitional and Research Issues," *Journal of Social Issues* 48(3) (1992): 19–35.

14. E. B. Foa, B. O. Roghbaum, D. S. Riggs, and T. B. Murdock, "Treatment of Posttraumatic Stress Disorder in Rape Victims: A Comparison Between Cognitive-behavioral Procedures and Counseling," *Journal of Consulting and Clinical Psychology* 59(5) (1991): 715–723.

15. N. E. Adler et al., 1990; and Dagg, 1991.

16. N. E. Adler, "Emotional Responses of Women Following Therapeutic Abortion," *American Journal of Orthopsychiatry* 45(3) (1975): 446–454; A. Lazarus, "Psychiatric Sequelae of Legalized First Trimester Abortion," *Journal of Psychosomatic Obstetrics and Gynecology* 4 (1985): 141–150; and J. D. Osofsky and H. Osofsky, "The Psychological Reaction of Patients to Legalized Abortion," *American Journal of Orthopsychiatry* 42 (1972): 48–60.

17. Adler, 1975; Cohen and Roth, 1984; and Major et al., 1985.

18. S. K. Henshaw, L. M. Koonin, and J. C. Smith, "Characteristics of U.S. Women Having Abortions, 1987," *Family Planning Perspectives* 23(2) (1991).

19. R. Athanasiou, W. Oppel, L. Michaelson, T. Unger, and M. Yager, "Psychiatric Sequelae to Term Birth and Induced Early and Late Abortion: A Longitudinal Study," *Family Planning Perspectives* 5 (1973): 227–231; Cohen and Roth, 1984; and Major et al., 1985.

20. H. David, N. Rasmussen, and E. Holst, "Postpartum and Postabortion Psychotic Reactions," *Family Planning Perspectives* 13(2) (1981): 88–93.

21. Athanasiou et al., 1973.

22. L. Zabin, M. B. Hirsch, and M. R. Emerson, "When Urban Adolescents Choose Abortion: Effects on Education, Psychological Status, and Subsequent Pregnancy," *Family Planning Perspectives* 21(6) (1989): 248–255.

23. Henshaw et al., 1991.

24. J. D. Forrest and S. Singh, "The Sexual and Reproductive Behavior of American Women, 1982–1988," *Family Planning Perspectives* 22 (1990): 206–214.

25. S. L. Hofferth and C. P. Hays, eds., *Risking the Future: Adolescent Sexuality, Pregnancy, and Childbearing* (Washington, D.C.: National Academy Press, 1987).

26. S. K. Henshaw and J. Van Vort, "Teenage Abortion, Birth and Pregnancy Statistics: An Update," *Family Planning Perspectives* 21(2) (1989): 85–88; and Forrest and Singh, 1990.

27. Zabin et al., 1989.

28. Adler, 1975; M. B. Bracken, M. Hachamovitch, and G. Grossman, "The

Decision to Abort and Psychological Sequelae," *The Journal of Nervous and Mental Disease* 158 (1974): 154–162; and Osofsky and Osofsky, 1972.

29. Cohen and Roth, 1984; O. T. Moseley, D. R. Follingstad, H. Harley, and R. Heckel, "Psychological Factors That Predict Reaction to Abortion," *Journal of Clinical Psychology* 37 (1981): 276–279.

30. A. Torres and J. D. Forrest, "Why Do Women Have Abortions?" *Family Planning Perspectives* 20(4) (1988): 169–177.

31. However, parental-consent laws will not alleviate this potential problem because in these instances the parents have given consent.

32. Zabin et al., 1989.

33. N. E. Adler, *Risking Pregnancy: Impulsivity, Rationality, and the Adolescent Mind* (San Francisco: American Psychological Association, 1991).

34. N. E. Adler, S. M. Kegeles, C. E. Irwin, and C. Wibbelsman, "Adolescent Contraceptive Behavior," *Journal of Pediatrics* 116(3) (1990): 463–471.

35. B. Ambuel and J. Rappaport, "Developmental Trends in Adolescents' Psychological and Legal Competence to Consent to Abortion," *Law and Human Behavior* 16 (1992): 129–154.

36. Ibid.

37. E. P. Mulvey, "Law and Mental Health Issues Affecting Minors: Research Directions," in *Law & Mental Health: Major Developments and Research Needs* (Rockville, Md.: U.S. Department of Health and Human Services, Public Health Service, Alcohol, Drug Abuse, and Mental Health Administration, 1991).

38. H. Rodman, "Should Parental Involvement Be Required for Minors' Abortions?" *Family Relations* 40 (1991): 155–160.

39. G. B. Melton, "Legal Regulation of Adolescent Abortion: Unintended Effects," *American Psychologist* 42(1) (1987): 79–83.

40. Moseley et al., 1981; J. M. Robbins and J. D. DeLamater, "Support from Significant Others and Loneliness Following Induced Abortion," *Social Psychiatry* 20(2) (1985): 92–99; and L. R. Shusterman, "Predicting the Psychological Consequences of Abortion," *Social Science and Medicine* 13A (1979): 683–689.

41. Bracken et al., 1974.

42. A. Torres, J. D. Forrest, and S. Eisman, "Telling Parents: Clinic Policies and Adolescents' Use of Family Planning and Abortion Services," *Family Planning Perspectives* 12 (1980): 284–292.

43. F. Clary, "Minor Women Obtaining Abortions: A Study of Parental No-

tification in a Metropolitan Area," *American Journal of Public Health* 72 (1982): 283–285.

44. L. C. Eagly, "What Changes the Societal Prevalence of Domestic Violence?" *Journal of Marriage and the Family* 53(4) (1991): 885–897.

45. R. W. Blum, M. D. Resnick, and R. Stark, "Factors Associated with the Use of Court Bypass by Minors to Obtain an Abortion," *Family Planning Perspectives* 22(4) (1990): 158–160.

46. R. W. Blum, M. D. Resnick, and R. Stark, "The Impact of a Parental Notification on Adolescent Abortion Decision Making," *American Journal of Public Health* 77 (1987): 619.

47. S. Yates and A. J. Pliner, "Judging Maturity in the Courts: The Massachusetts Consent Statute," *American Journal of Public Health* 78 (1988): 546–549.

48. Rodman, 1991.

49. Ibid.

50. F. F. Furstenburg, R. Herceg-Baron, D. Mann, and J. Shea, "Parental Involvement: Selling Family Planning Clinics Short," *Family Planning Perspectives* 14(3) (1982): 140–144.

51. P. Lunnenborg, *Abortion: A Positive Decision* (New York: Bergin & Garvey, 1992).

52. House Committee on Government Operations, *The Federal Role in Determining the Medical and Psychological Impact of Abortion in Women*, 1989, H. Rept. 101.392.

53. Ibid.; F. F. Furstenberg, J. Brooks-Gunn, and L. Chase-Landale, "Teenaged Pregnancy and Childbearing," *American Psychologist* 44 (1989): 313–320; and Hofferth and Hayes, 1987.

54. E. F. Jones, J. D. Forrest, N. Goldman, S. Henshaw, R. Lincoln, J. I. Rosoff, C. F. Wesloff, and D. Wulf, *Teenage Pregnancy in Industrialized Countries* (New Haven, Conn.: Yale University Press, 1986).

GENDER DILEMMAS IN SEXUAL HARASSMENT: POLICIES AND PROCEDURES

❖ ❖ ❖

Stephanie Riger

Anita Hill's charges of sexual harassment against Clarence Thomas at his confirmation hearings as a justice of the U.S. Supreme Court galvanized the country into a nationwide teach-in on this subject. Hill's testimony raised a multitude of questions about relations between the sexes, workplace decorum, and where to draw the line between flirtation and harassment. Perhaps the most frequently raised question was why Hill did not bring a complaint about Thomas's actions at the time they occurred.

Many organizations have established policies and procedures to deal with sexual harassment, yet few complaints are reported. Some have suggested that the lack of complaints is due to the absence of a problem, or the timidity or fearfulness of victims. This chapter proposes that the reasons for the lack of use of sexual harassment grievance procedures lie not in the victims, but rather in the procedures themselves. Women perceive sexual harassment differently than men do, and their orientation to dispute-resolution processes is likely to differ as well. The way that policies define harassment and the nature of dispute-resolution procedures may better fit male than female perspectives. This gender bias is likely to discourage women from reporting complaints.

Sexual harassment—unwanted sexually oriented behavior in a work context—is the most recent form of victimization of women to be redefined as a social rather than a personal problem, following rape and wife abuse. A sizeable proportion of women surveyed in a wide variety of work settings reported being subject to unwanted sexual attention, sexual comments or jokes, offensive touching, or attempts to coerce compliance with or punish rejection of sexual advances. In 1980, the U.S. Merit Systems Protection Board conducted the first comprehensive national survey of sexual harassment among federal employees: About 4 out of 10 of the 10,648 women surveyed reported having been the target of sexual harassment during the previous 24 months.[1] A recent update of this survey found that the frequency of harassment in 1988 was identical to that reported earlier: 42 percent of all women surveyed in 1988 reported that they had experienced some form of unwanted and uninvited sexual attention compared to exactly the same percentage of women in 1980.[2]

Women ranging from blue-collar workers[3] to lawyers[4] to airline personnel[5] have reported considerable amounts of sexual harassment in surveys. Among a random sample of private sector workers in the Los Angeles area, more than one-half of the women surveyed by telephone reported experiencing at least one incident that they considered sexual harassment during their working lives.[6] Some estimate that up to about one-third of women in educational institutions have experienced some form of harassment[7] and that "[u]nwanted sexual attention may be the single most widespread occupational hazard in the workplace today" (p. 75).[8]

It is a hazard faced much more frequently by women than men. About 40 percent of the women in the original U.S. Merit Systems Protection Board survey reported having experienced sexual harassment, compared with only 15 percent of the men.[9] Among working people surveyed in Los Angeles, women were nine times more likely than men to report having quit a job because of sexual harassment, five times more likely to have transferred, and three times more likely to have lost a job.[10] Women with low power and status, whether due to lower age, being single or divorced, or being in a marginal position in the organization, are more likely to be harassed.[11]

Sex differences in the frequency of harassment also prevail in educational environments.[12] A mailed survey of more than 900 women and men at the University of Rhode Island asked about a wide range of behavior, including the frequency of respondents' experience of sexual insult, defined as an "uninvited sexually suggestive, obscene or offensive remark, stare, or gesture."[13] Of the female respondents, 40 percent reported being sexually insulted occasionally or often while on campus, compared with 17 percent of the men. Both men and women reported that women are rarely the source of such insults. Similar differences were found in a survey of social workers, with 2½ times as many women as men reporting harassment.[14]

Despite the high rates found in surveys of sexual harassment of women, few complaints are pursued through official grievance procedures. One study found that 20 percent to 30 percent of female college students experience sexual harassment.[15] Yet academic institutions averaged only 4.3 complaints each during the 1982–1983 academic year,[16] a period roughly consecutive with the surveys cited by Dzeich and Weiner. In another study conducted at a university in 1984, of 38 women who reported harassment, only 1 reported the behavior to the offender's supervisor and 2 reported the behavior to an adviser, another professor, or employer.[17] Similar findings have been reported on other college campuses.[18]

Low numbers of complaints appear in other work settings as well. In a survey of federal workers, only about 11 percent of victims reported the harassment to a higher authority, and only 2.5 percent used formal complaint channels.[19] Similarly, female social workers reacted to harassment by avoiding or delaying the conflict or attempting to defuse the situation rather than by adopting any form of recourse such as filing a grievance.[20] The number of complaints alleging sexual harassment filed with the Equal Employment Opportunity Commission in Washington, D.C., has declined since 1984, despite an increase in the number of women in the work force during that time,[21] and surveys that suggest that the rate of sexual harassment has remained relatively stable.[22]

It is the contention of this chapter that the low rate of utilization of grievance procedures is due to gender bias in sexual harassment policies that discourages their use by women. Policies are written in gender-neutral language and are intended to apply equally to men and women. However, these policies are experienced differently by women than men because of gender differences in perceptions of harassment and orientation toward conflict. Although victims of all forms of discrimination are reluctant to pursue grievances,[23] women, who are most likely to be the victims of sexual harassment, are especially disinclined to pursue sexual harassment grievances for at least two reasons. First, the interpretation in policies of what constitutes harassment may not reflect women's viewpoints, and their complaints may not be seen as valid. Second, the procedures in some policies that are designed to resolve disputes may be inimical to women because they are not compatible with the way that many women view conflict resolution. Gender bias in policies, rather than an absence of harassment or lack of assertiveness on the part of victims, produces low numbers of complaints.

GENDER BIAS IN THE DEFINITION OF SEXUAL HARASSMENT

The first way that gender bias affects sexual harassment policies stems from differences between men and women in the interpretation of the definition of harassment. Those writing sexual harassment policies for organizations typically look to the courts for the distinction between illegal sexual harassment and permissible (although perhaps unwanted) social interaction.[24] The definition of harassment in policies typically is that provided by the U.S. Equal Employment Opportunity Commission guidelines:

> Unwelcome sexual advances, requests for sexual favors, and other verbal or physical conduct of a sexual nature constitute sexual harassment when (1) submission to such conduct is made either explicitly or implicitly a term or condition of an individual's employment, (2) submission to or rejection of such conduct by an individual is used as the basis for employment decisions affecting such individual, or (3) such conduct has the purpose or effect of unreasonably interfering with an individual's work performance or creating an intimidating, hostile, or offensive working environment.[25]

The first two parts of the definition refer to a quid pro quo relationship involving people in positions of unequal status, as superior status is usually necessary to have control over another's employment. In such cases, bribes, threats, or punishments are used. Incidents of this type need happen only once to fall under the definition of sexual harassment. However, courts have required that incidents falling into the third category, "an intimidating, hostile, or offensive working environment," must be repeated in order to establish that such an environment exists;[26] these incidents must be both pervasive and so severe that they affect the victim's psychological well-being.[27] Harassment of this type can come from peers or even subordinates as well as superiors.

In all three of these categories, harassment is judged on the basis of conduct and its effects on the recipient, not the intentions of the harasser. Thus, two typical defenses given by accused harassers—"I was just being friendly," or "I touch everyone, I'm that kind of person"—do not hold up in court. Yet behavior may have an intimidating or offensive effect on some people but be inoffensive or even welcome to others. In deciding whose standards should be used, the courts employ what is called the *reasonable person rule,* asking whether a reasonable person would be offended by the conduct in question. The dilemma in applying this to sexual harassment is that a reasonable woman and a reasonable man are likely to differ in their judgments of what is offensive.

Definitions of sexual harassment are socially constructed, varying not only with characteristics of the perceiver but also those of the situational context and actors involved. Behavior is more likely to be labelled harassment when it is done by someone with greater power than the victim,[28] when it involves physical advances accompanied by threats of punishment for noncompliance,[29] when the response to it is negative,[30] when the behavior reflects persistent negative intentions toward a woman,[31] the more inappropriate it is for the actor's social role,[32] and the more flagrant and frequent the harasser's actions.[33] Among women, professionals are more likely than those in secretarial-clerical positions to report the more subtle behaviors as harassment.[34]

The variable that most consistently predicts variation in people's definition of sexual harassment is the sex of the person making the definition. Men label fewer behaviors at work as sexual harassment.[35] Men tend to find sexual overtures from women at work to be flattering, whereas women find similar approaches from men to be insulting.[36] Both men and women agree that certain blatant behaviors, such as sexual assault or sexual bribery, constitute harassment, but women are more likely to see as harassment more subtle behavior such as sexual teasing or looks or gestures.[37] Even when they do identify behavior as harassment, men are more likely to think that women will be flattered by it.[38] Men are also more likely than women to blame women for being sexually harassed.[39]

These gender differences make it difficult to apply the reasonable person rule. Linenberger proposed ten factors that permit an "objective" assessment of whether behavior constitutes sexual harassment, regardless of the perception of the victim and the intent of the perpetrator.[40] These factors range from the severity of the conduct to the number and frequency of encounters, and the relationship of the parties involved. For example, behavior is less likely to be categorized as harassment if it is seen as a response to provocation from the victim. But is an objective rating of provocation possible? When gender differences are as clear-cut and persistent as they are in the perception of what behavior constitutes sexual harassment, the question is not one of objectivity, but rather of which sex's definition of the situation will prevail. Some have asserted that there is a "hierarchy of credibility" in organizations, and that credibility and the right to be heard are differentially distributed: "In any system of ranked groups, participants take it as given that members of the highest group have the right to define the way things really are" (p. 241).[41] Because men typically have more power in organizations,[42] this analysis suggests that in most situations the male definition of harassment is likely to predominate. As Catherine MacKinnon put it, "objectivity—the non-situated, universal standpoint, whether claimed or aspired to—is a denial of the existence or potency of sex inequality that tacitly participates in constructing reality from the dominant point of view."[43] "The law sees and treats women the way men see and treat women."[44] This means that men's judgments about what behavior constitutes harassment, and who is to blame, are likely to prevail. Linenberger's ten factors thus may not be an objective measure, but rather a codification of the male perspective on harassment. This is likely to discourage women who want to bring complaints about more subtle forms of harassment.

GENDER BIAS IN GRIEVANCE PROCEDURES

Typically, procedures for resolving disputes about sexual harassment are written in gender-neutral terms so that they may apply to both women and men. However, men and women may react quite differently to the same procedures.

Analyzing this problem requires looking at specific policies and procedures. Educational institutions will serve as the context for this discussion for three reasons. First, they are the most frequent site of surveys about the problem, and the pervasive nature of harassment on campuses has been well documented.[45] Second, although sexual harassment is harmful to women in all occupations, it can be particularly devastating to those in educational institutions, in which the goal of the organization is to nurture and promote development. The violation of relationships based on trust, such as those between faculty and students, can leave long-lasting and deep wounds, yet many surveys find that those in positions of authority in educational settings are often the source of the problem.[46] Third, educational institutions have been leaders in the development of sexual harassment policies, in part because of concern about litigation. In *Alexander v. Yale University* (1977) the court decided that sexual harassment constitutes a form of sex discrimination that denies equal access to educational opportunities, and falls under Title IX of the Educational Amendments of

1972.[47] The Office of Civil Rights in the U.S. Department of Education now requires institutions that receive Title IX funds to maintain grievance procedures to resolve complaints involving sexual discrimination or harassment.[48] Consequently, academic institutions may have had more experience than other work settings in developing procedures to combat this problem. A survey of U.S. institutions of higher learning conducted in 1984 found that 66 percent of all responding institutions had sexual harassment policies, and 46 percent had grievance procedures specifically designed to deal with sexual harassment complaints, with large public schools more likely to have them than small private ones.[49] These percentages have unquestionably increased in recent years, given the government funding regulations. Although the discussion here is focused on educational contexts, the problems identified in sexual harassment policies exist in other work settings as well.

Many educational institutions, following guidelines put forward by the American Council on Education[50] and the American Association of University Professors,[51] have established policies that prohibit sexual harassment and create grievance procedures. Some use a formal board or hearing, and others use informal mechanisms that protect confidentiality and seek to resolve the complaint rather than punish the offender.[52] Still others use both types of procedures. The type of procedure specified by the policy may have a great impact on victims' willingness to report complaints.

COMPARISON OF INFORMAL AND FORMAL GRIEVANCE PROCEDURES

Informal attempts to resolve disputes differ from formal procedures in important ways (see Table 1).[53] First, their goal is to solve a problem, rather than to judge the harasser's guilt or innocence. The assumptions underlying these processes are that both parties in a dispute perceive a problem (although they may define that problem differently), that both share a common interest in solving that problem, and that together they can negotiate an agreement that will be satisfactory to everyone involved. Typically, the goal of informal processes is to end the harassment of the complainant rather than judge (and punish, if appropriate) the offender. The focus is on what will happen in the future between the disputing parties, rather than on what has happened in the past. Often policies do not specify the format of informal problem solving, but accept a wide variety of strategies of reconciliation. For example, a complainant might write a letter to the offender,[54] or someone might talk to the offender on the complainant's behalf. The offender and victim might participate in mediation, in which a third party helps them negotiate an agreement. Many policies accept

TABLE 1

A COMPARISON OF FORMAL AND INFORMAL GRIEVANCE PROCEDURES

	PROCEDURES	
ELEMENTS	INFORMAL	FORMAL
Purpose	Problem solving or reconciliation	Judge guilt or innocence
Time focus	What will happen in the future	What happened in the past
Format	Usually unspecified	Usually specified
Completion	When complainant is satisfied	When hearing board decides
Control	Complainant	Hearing board
Compliance	Voluntary	Punishment is binding

a wide array of strategies as good-faith attempts to solve the problem informally.

In contrast, formal procedures generally require a written complaint and have a specified procedure for handling cases, usually by bringing the complaint to a group officially designated to hear the case, such as a hearing board. The informal process typically ends when the complainant is satisfied (or decides to drop the complaint); the formal procedure ends when the hearing board decides on the guilt or innocence of the alleged harasser. Thus, control over the outcome usually rests with the complainant in the case of informal mechanisms, and with the official governance body in the case of a hearing. Compliance with a decision is usually voluntary in informal procedures, whereas the decision in a formal procedure is binding unless appealed to a higher authority. Formal procedures are adversarial in nature, with the complainant and defendant competing to see whose position will prevail.

A typical case might proceed as follows: A student with a complaint writes a letter to the harasser (an informal procedure). If not satisfied with the response, she submits a written complaint to the sexual harassment hearing board, which then hears both sides of the case, reviews available evidence, and decides on the guilt or innocence of the accused (a formal procedure). If the accused is found guilty, the appropriate officer of the institution decides on punishment.

GENDER DIFFERENCES IN ORIENTATION TO CONFLICT

Women and men may differ in their reactions to dispute-resolution procedures for at least two reasons. First, women typically have less power than men in organizations.[55] Using a grievance procedure, such as appearing before a hearing board, may be inimical because of the possibility of retaliation for a complaint. Differences in status and power may affect the way that people handle conflict:

> As soon as a group attains dominance it tends inevitably to produce a situation of conflict and . . . it also, simultaneously, seeks to suppress conflict. Moreover, subordinates who accept the dominant's conception of them as passive and malleable do not openly engage in conflict. Conflict . . . is forced underground.[56]

This may explain why some women do not report complaints at all. When they do complain, however, their relative lack of power or their values may predispose women to prefer informal rather than formal procedures. Beliefs about the appropriate way to handle disputes vary among social groups.[57] Carol Gilligan's distinction between an orientation toward rights and justice[58] compared with an emphasis on responsibilities to others and caring is likely to be reflected in people's preferences for ways of handling disputes.[59] Neither of these orientations is exclusive to one sex, but, according to Gilligan, women are more likely to emphasize caring. Women's orientation to caring may be due to their subordinate status.[60] Empirical support for Gilligan's theories is inconcluve;[61] yet the fact that most victims of sexual harrassment state that they simply want an end to the offending behavior rather than punishment of the offender[62] suggests a "caring" rather than "justice" perspective (or, possibly, a fear of reprisals).

In the context of dispute resolution, an emphasis on responsibilities and caring is compatible with the goals of informal procedures to restore harmony or at least peaceful coexistence among the parties involved, whereas that of justice is compatible with formal procedures that attempt to judge guilt or innocence of the offender. Thus women may prefer to use informal procedures to resolve conflicts, and indeed most cases in educational institutions are handled through informal mechanisms.[63] Policies that do not include an informal dispute resolution option are likely to discourage many women from bringing complaints.

PROBLEMS WITH INFORMAL DISPUTE-RESOLUTION PROCEDURES

Although women may prefer informal mechanisms, they are problematic for several reasons.[64] Because they do not result in punishment, offenders suffer few negative consequences of their actions and may not be deterred from harassing again. In institutions of higher learning, the most common form of punishment reported is a verbal warning by a supervisor, which is given only "sometimes."[65] Dismissal and litigation are almost never used. It seems likely, then, that sexual harassment may be viewed by potential harassers as low-risk behavior, and that victims see few incentives for bringing official complaints.

The confidentiality usually required by informal procedures prevents other victims from knowing that a complaint has been lodged against a multiple offender. If a woman knows that another woman is bringing a complaint against a particular man who has harassed both of them, then she might be more willing to complain also. The secrecy surrounding informal complaint processes precludes this information from becoming public and makes it more difficult to identify repeat offenders. Also, complaints settled informally may not be included in reports of the frequency of sexual harassment claims, making these statistics underestimate the scope of the problem. Yet confidentiality is needed to protect the rights of the accused and may be preferred by those bringing complaints.

These problems in informal procedures could discourage male as well as female victims from bringing complaints. Most problematic for women, however, is the assumption in informal procedures that the complainant and accused have equal power in the process of resolving the dispute. This assumption is likely to put women at a disadvantage. Parties involved in sexual harassment disputes may not be equal either in the sense of formal position within the organization (e.g., student versus faculty) or status (e.g., female versus male students), and position and status characteristics that reflect levels of power do not disappear simply because they are irrelevant to the informal process. External status characteristics that indicate macro-level social stratification (e.g., sex and age) help explain the patterns of distribution of sexual harassment in the workplace.[66] It seems likely that these external statuses will influence the interpersonal dynamics within a dispute-resolution procedure as well. Because women are typically lower than men in both formal and informal status and power in organizations, they will have less power in the dispute-resolution process.

When the accused has more power than the complainant (e.g., a male faculty member accused by a female student), the complainant is more vulnerable to retaliation. Complainants may be reluctant to use grievance procedures because they fear retaliation should the charge be made public. For example, students may fear that a faculty member will punish them for bringing a complaint by lowering their grades or withholding recommendations. The person appointed to act as a guide to the informal resolution process is usually expected to act as a neutral third party rather than advocate for the complainant, and may hold little formal power over faculty: "Relatively few institutions have persons empowered to be (nonlegal) advocates for the complainants; a student bringing a complaint has little assurance of stopping the harassment and avoiding retaliation."[67] The victim then is left without an advocate to face an opponent whose formal position, age, and experience with verbal argument is often considerably beyond her own. The more vulnerable a woman's position is in her organization, the more likely it is that she will be harassed;[68] therefore, sexual harassment, like rape, involves dynamics of power and domination as well as sexuality. The lack of an advocate for the complainant who might equalize power between the disputing parties is particularly troubling. However, if an advocate is provided for the complainant in an informal process, fairness and due process require that the defendant have an advocate as well. The dilemma is that this seems likely to transform an informal, problem-solving process into a formal, adversarial one.

OTHER OBSTACLES TO REPORTING COMPLAINTS

BELIEF THAT SEXUAL HARASSMENT OF WOMEN IS NORMATIVE

Because of differences in perception of behavior, men and women involved in a sexual harassment case are likely to have sharply divergent interpretations of that case, particularly when a hostile environment claim is involved. To women, the behavior in question is offensive, and they are likely to see themselves as victims of male actions. The requirement that an attempt be made to mediate the dispute or solve it through informal processes may violate their perception of the situation and of themselves as victims of a crime. By comparison, a victim of a mugging is not required to solve the problem with the mugger through mediation.[69] To many men, the behavior is not offensive, but normative. In their eyes, no crime has been committed, and there is no problem to be solved.

Some women may also consider sexual harassment to be normative. Women may believe that these sorts of behaviors are simply routine, a commonplace part of everyday life, and thus not something that can be challenged. Younger women—who are more likely to be victims[70]—are more tolerant of harassment than are older women.[71]

Indeed, Lott et al. concluded that "younger women in particular have accepted the idea that prowling men are a 'fact of life'" (p. 318). This attitude might prevent women from labelling a negative experience as harassment. Surveys that ask women about sexual harassment and about the frequency of experiencing specific sexually harassing behaviors find discrepancies in responses to these questions.[72] Women report higher rates when asked if they have been the target of specific harassing behaviors than when asked a general question about whether they have been harassed. Women are also more willing to report negative reactions to offensive behaviors than they are to label those behaviors as sexual harassment.[73]

Normative beliefs may deter some male victims of harassment from reporting complaints also, because men are expected to welcome sexual advances if those advances are from women.

NEGATIVE OUTCOMES FOR VICTIMS WHO BRING COMPLAINTS

The outcome of grievance procedures does not appear to provide much satisfaction to victims who bring complaints. In academic settings, despite considerable publicity given to a few isolated cases in which tenured faculty have been fired, punishments are rarely inflicted on harassers, and the punishments that are given are mild, such as verbal warnings.[74] Among federal workers, 33 percent of those who used formal grievance procedures to protest sexual harassment found that it "made things worse."[75] More than 65 percent of the cases of formal charges of sexual harassment filed with the Illinois Department of Human Rights involved job discharge of the complainant.[76] Less than one-third of those cases resulted in a favorable settlement for the complainant, and those who received financial compensation got an average settlement of $3,234.[77] Similar findings in California were reported by Coles,[78] with the average cash settlement there of $973, representing approximately one month's pay. Although a few legal cases have resulted in large settlements,[79] these studies suggest that typical settlements are low. Formal actions may take years to complete, and in legal suits the victim usually must hire legal counsel at considerable expense.[80] These small settlements seem unlikely to compensate victims for the emotional stress, notoriety, and financial costs involved in filing a public complaint. Given the consistency with which victimization falls more often to women than men, it is ironic that one of the largest settlements awarded to an individual in a sexual harassment case ($196,500 in damages) was made to a man who brought suit against his female supervisor,[81] perhaps because sexual aggression by a woman is seen as especially egregious.

EMOTIONAL CONSEQUENCES OF HARASSMENT

In academic settings, harassment can adversely affect students' learning and, therefore, their academic standing. It can deprive them of educational and career opportunities because they wish to avoid threatening situations. Students who have been harassed report that they consequently avoid taking a class from or working with a particular faculty member, change their major, or leave a threatening situation.[82] Lowered self-esteem follows the conclusion that rewards, such as a high grade, may have been based on sexual attraction rather than one's abilities.[83] Decreased feelings of competence and confidence and increased feelings of anger, frustration, depression, and anxiety all can result from harassment.[84] The psychological stress produced by harassment is compounded when women are fired or quit their jobs in fear or frustration.[85]

Meek and Lynch proposed that victims of harassment typically go through several stages of reaction,[86] at first questioning the offender's true intentions and then blaming themselves for the offender's behavior. Women with traditional sex-role beliefs are more likely to blame themselves for being harassed.[87] Victims then worry about being believed by others and about possible retaliation if they take formal steps to protest the behavior. A victim may be too frightened or confused to assert herself or punish the offender. Psychologists who work with victims of harassment would do well to recognize that not only victims' emotional reactions but also the nature of the grievance process as discussed in this chapter may discourage women from bringing formal complaints.

Prevention of Sexual Harassment

Some writers have argued that sexual harassment does not occur with great frequency or, if it once was a problem, it has been eliminated in recent years. Indeed, Morgenson, writing in the business publication *Forbes*,[88] suggested that the whole issue had been drummed up by professional sexual harassment counselors in order to sell their services. Yet the studies cited in this chapter have documented that sexual harassment is a widespread problem with serious consequences.

Feminists and union activists have succeeded in gaining recognition of sexual harassment as a form of sex discrimination.[89] The law now views sexual harassment not as the idiosyncratic actions of a few inconsiderate males but as part of a pattern of behaviors that reflect the imbalance of power between women and men in society. Women in various occupations and educational settings have sought legal redress for actions of supervisors or coworkers, and sexual harassment has become the focus of numerous organizational policies and grievance procedures.[90]

Well-publicized policies that use an inclusive definition of sexual harassment, include an informal dispute resolution option, provide an advocate for the victim (if desired), and permit multiple offenders to be identified seem likely to be the most effective way of addressing claims of sexual harassment. However, even these modifications will not eliminate all of the problems in policies. The severity of the consequences of harassment for the victim, coupled with the problematic nature of grievance procedures and the mildness of punishments for offenders, makes retribution less effective than prevention of sexual harassment. Organizational leaders should not assume that their job is completed when they have established a sexual harassment policy. Extensive efforts at prevention need to be mounted at the individual, situational, and organizational level.

In prevention efforts aimed at the individual, education about harassment should be provided.[91] In particular, policymakers and others need to learn to "think like a woman" to define which behaviors constitute harassment and recognize that these behaviors are unacceptable. Understanding that many women find offensive more subtle forms of behavior such as sexual jokes or comments may help reduce the kinds of interactions that create a hostile environment. Educating personnel about the punishments involved for offensive behavior also may have a deterring effect.

However, education alone is not sufficient. Sexual harassment is the product not only of individual attitudes and beliefs, but also of organizational practices. Dzeich and Weiner described aspects of educational institutions that facilitate sexual harassment,[92] including the autonomy afforded the faculty, the diffusion of authority that permits lack of accountability, and the shortage of women in positions of authority. Researchers are beginning to identify the practices in other work settings that facilitate or support sexual harassment, and suggest that sexual harassment may be part of a pattern of unprofessional and disrespectful attitudes and behaviors that characterizes some workplaces.[93]

Perhaps the most important factor in reducing sexual harassment is an organizational culture that promotes equal opportunities for women. There is a strong negative relationship between the level of perceived equal employment opportunity for women in a company and the level of harassment reported:[94] Workplaces low in perceived equality are the site of more frequent incidents of harassment. This finding suggests that sexual harassment both reflects and reinforces the underlying sexual inequality that produces a sex-segregated and sex-stratified occupational structure.[95] The implementation of sexual harassment policies demonstrates the seriousness of those in authority; the language of the policies provides some measure of clarity about the types of behavior that are not acceptable; and grievance procedures may provide relief and legitimacy to those with complaints.[96] But neither policies nor procedures do much to weaken the structural roots of gender inequalities in organizations.

Reforms intended to ameliorate women's position sometimes have unintended negative consequences.[97] The presence of sexual harassment policies and the absence of formal complaints might promote the illusion that this problem has been solved. Assessment of whether organizational policies and practices promote or hinder equality for women is required to ensure that this belief does not prevail. A long-range strategy for organizational reform in academia would thus attack the chilly climate for women in classrooms and laboratories,[98] the inferior quality of athletic programs for women, differential treatment of women applicants, the acceptance of the masculine as normative, and a knowledge base uninfluenced by women's values or experience.[99] In other work settings, such a long-range approach would attack both sex-segregation of occupations and sex-stratification within authority hierarchies. Sexual harassment grievance procedures alone are not sufficient to ensure that sexual harassment will be eliminated. An end to this problem requires gender equity within organizations.

Although this chapter focused on educational institutions, the problems discussed here are prevalent in other work settings as well. The June 1992 issue of *Working Woman* magazine states that more than 60 percent of respondents in a survey of their readers said they have been harassed. According to these women, who are mostly in managerial and professional positions and working in male-dominated companies, harassment increases as women rise in the corporate hierarchy. Yet only one out of four women reported the harassment. In their words, filing a complaint of sexual harassment still amounts to "career suicide," and few believe that complaints are dealt with justly. Unless organizations develop effective strategies for combatting harassment, women will continue to suffer intimidation and bullying by harassers, and workplaces will lose millions of dollars in absenteeism, turnover, lowered productivity, and lawsuits.

ACKNOWLEDGMENTS

I am grateful to Dan A. Lewis, Jane Mansbridge, Jeanne Brett, Margaret Strobel, Christopher Keys, Arlene Eskilson, Alice Dan, Judith Kegan Gardiner, and anonymous reviewers for helpful comments and suggestions on an earlier draft of this chapter, and to Nicole Schultz and Linda Schaumann for outstanding research assistance.

Correspondence concerning this chapter should be addressed to Stephanie Riger, Professor of Psychology and Women's Studies (m/c 285), University of Illinois at Chicago, Box 4348, Chicago, Ill. 60680.

NOTES

1. U.S. Merit Systems Protection Board, *Sexual Harassment in the Federal Workplace: Is It a Problem?* (Washington, D.C.: U.S. Government Printing Office, 1981).

2. U.S. Merit Systems Protection Board, *Sexual Harassment in the Federal Government: An Update* (Washington, D.C.: U.S. Government Printing Office, 1988).

3. E. LaFontaine and L. Tredeau, "The Frequency, Sources, and Correlates of Sexual Harassment Among Women in Traditional Male Occupations," *Sex Roles* 15 (1986): 433–442; and D. E. Maypole and R. Skaine, "Sexual Harassment of Blue-collar Workers," *Journal of Sociology and Social Welfare* 9 (1982): 682–695.

4. N. Burleigh and S. Goldberg, "Breaking the Silence: Sexual Harassment in Law Firms," *ABA Journal* 75 (1989): 46–52.

5. S. Littler-Bishop, D. Seidler-Feller, and R. E. Opaluch, "Sexual Harassment in the Workplace as a Function of Initiator's Status: The Case of Airline Personnel," *Journal of Social Issues* 38 (1982): 137–148.

6. B. A. Gutek, *Sex and the Workplace* (San Francisco: Jossey-Bass, 1985).

7. S. Kenig and J. Ryan, "Sex Differences in Levels of Tolerance and Attribution of Blame for Sexual Harassment on a University Campus," *Sex Roles* 15 (1986): 535–549.

8. M. S. Garvey, "The High Cost of Sexual Harassment Suits," *Labor Relations* 65 (1986): 75–79.

9. U.S. Merit Systems, 1981.

10. A. M. Konrad and B. A. Gutek, "Impact of Work Experiences on Attitudes Toward Sexual Harassment," *Administrative Science Quarterly* 31 (1986): 422–438.

11. T. C. Fain and D. L. Anderton, "Sexual Harassment: Organizational Con-

text and Diffuse Status," *Sex Roles* 5/6 (1987): 291–311; LaFontaine and Tredeau, 1986; and W. L. Robinson and P. T. Reid, "Sexual Intimacy in Psychology Revisited," *Professional Psychology: Research and Practice* 16 (1985): 512–520.

12. L. F. Fitzgerald, S. L. Schullman, N. Bailey, M. Richards, J. Swecker, Y. Gold, M. Ormerod, and L. Weitzman, "The Incidence and Dimensions of Sexual Harassment in Academia and the Workplace," *Journal of Vocational Behavior* 32 (1988): 152–175.

13. B. Lott, M. E. Reilly, and D. R. Howard, "Sexual Assault and Harassment: A Campus Community Case Study," *Signs: Journal of Women in Culture and Society* 8 (1982): 296–319.

14. D. E. Maypole, "Sexual Harassment of Social Workers at Work: Injustice Within?" *Social Work* 31 (1986): 29–34.

15. B. Dziech and L. Weiner, *The Lecherous Professor* (Boston: Beacon Press, 1984).

16. C. Robertson, C. E. Dyer, and D. Campbell, "Campus Harassment: Sexual Harassment Policies and Procedures at Institutions of Higher Learning," *Signs: Journal of Women in Culture and Society* 13 (1988): 792–812.

17. M. E. Reilly, B. Lott, and S. Gallogly, "Sexual Harassment of University Students," *Sex Roles* 15 (1986): 333–358.

18. J. W. Adams, J. L. Kottke, and J. S. Padgitt, "Sexual Harassment of University Students," *Journal of College Student Personnel* 23 (1983): 484–490; D. J. Benson and G. Thomson, "Sexual Harassment on a University Campus: The Confluence of Authority Relations, Sexual Interest, and Gender Stratification," *Social Problems* 29 (1982): 236–251; J. B. Brandenburg, "Sexual Harassment in the University: Guidelines for Establishing a Grievance Procedure," *Signs: Journal of Women in Culture and Society* 8 (1982): 320–336; L. P. Cammaert, "How Widespread Is Sexual Harassment on Campus?" *International Journal of Women's Studies* 8 (1985): 388–397; P. M. Meek and A. Q. Lynch, "Establishing an Informal Grievance Procedure for Cases of Sexual Harassment of Students," *Journal of the National Association for Women Deans, Administrators, and Counselors* 46 (1983): 30–33; and B. E. Schneider, "Graduate Women, Sexual Harassment, and University Policy," *Journal of Higher Education* 58 (1987): 46–65.

19. J. A. Livingston, "Responses to Sexual Harassment on the Job: Legal, Organizational, and Individual Actions," *Journal of Social Issues* 38(4) (1982): 5–22.

20. Maypole, 1986.

21. G. Morgenson, "Watch That Leer, Stifle That Joke," *Forbes* (May 1989): 69–72.

22. U.S. Merit Systems, 1981; and U.S. Merit Systems, 1988.

23. K. Bumiller, "Victims in the Shadow of the Law: A Critique of the Model of Legal Protection," *Signs: Journal of Women in Culture and Society* 12 (1987): 421–439.

24. See C. F. Cohen, "Legal Dilemmas in Sexual Harassment Cases," *Labor Law Journal* (November 1987): 681–689, for a discussion of this distinction in legal cases.

25. U.S. Equal Employment Opportunity Commission, "Final Amendment to Guidelines on Discrimination Because of Sex under Title VII of the Civil Rights Act of 1964, as Amended, 29 CFR Part 1604," *Federal Register* 45 (November 10, 1980): 74675–74677.

26. D. E. Terpstra and D. D. Baker, "Outcomes of Sexual Harassment Charges," *Academy of Management Journal* 31 (1988): 185–194.

27. T. B. Trager, "Legal Considerations in Drafting Sexual Harassment Policies," in *Sexual Harassment on Campus: A Legal Compendium*, ed. J. Van Tol (Washington, D.C.: National Association of College and University Attorneys, 1988).

28. B. A. Gutek, B. Morasch, and A. G. Cohen, "Interpreting Social-sexual Behavior in a Work Setting," *Journal of Vocational Behavior* 22 (1983): 30–48; Kenig and Ryan, 1986; D. Lester, B. Banta, J. Barton, N. Elian, L. Mackiewicz, and J. Winkelried, "Judgments about Sexual Harassment: Effects of the Power of the Harasser," *Perceptual and Motor Skills* 63 (1986): 990; and P. M. Popovich, B. J. Licata, D. Nokovich, T. Martelli, and S. Zoloty, "Assessing the Incidence and Perceptions of Sexual Harassment Behaviors Among American Undergraduates," *Journal of Psychology* 120 (1987): 387–396.

29. P. H. Rossi and E. Weber-Burdin, "Sexual Harassment on the Campus," *Social Science Research* 12 (1983): 131–158.

30. T. S. Jones, M. S. Remland, and C. C. Brunner, "Effects of Employment Relationship, Response of Recipient, and Sex of Rater on Perceptions of Sexual Harassment," *Perceptual and Motor Skills* 65 (1987): 55–63.

31. J. B. Pryor and J. D. Day, "Interpretations of Sexual Harassment: An Attributional Analysis," *Sex Roles* 18 (1988): 405–417.

32. J. B. Pryor, "The Lay Person's Understanding of Sexual Harassment," *Sex Roles* 13 (1985): 273–286.

33. D. A. Thomann and R. L. Wiener, "Physical and Psychological Causality as Determinants of Culpability in Sexual Harassment Cases," *Sex Roles* 17 (1987): 573–591.

34. D. I. McIntyre and J. C. Renick, "Protecting Public Employees and Em-

ployers from Sexual Harassment," *Public Personnel Management Journal* 11 (1982): 282–292.

35. Kenig and Ryan, 1986; Konrad and Gutek, 1986; Lester et al., 1986; G. N. Powell, "Effects of Sex Role Identity and Sex on Definitions of Sexual Harassment," *Sex Roles* 14 (1986): 9–19; and Rossi and Weber-Burdin, 1983.

36. Gutek, 1985.

37. Adams et al., 1983; E. G. C. Collins and T. B. Blodgett, "Some See It . . . Some Won't," *Harvard Business Review* 59 (1981): 76–95; Kenig and Ryan, 1986; and U.S. Merit Systems, 1981.

38. D. Kirk, "Gender Differences in the Perception of Sexual Harassment" (Paper presented at the Academy of Management National Meeting, Anaheim, Calif., August 1988).

39. Kenig and Ryan, 1986; and I. W. Jensen and B. A. Gutek, "Attributions and Assignment of Responsibility in Sexual Harassment," *Journal of Social Issues* 38 (1982): 121–136.

40. P. Linenberger, "What Behavior Constitutes Sexual Harassment," *Labor Law Journal* (April 1983): 238–247.

41. H. S. Becker, "Whose Side Are We On?" *Social Problems* 14 (1967): 239–247.

42. R. M. Kanter, *Men and Women of the Corporation* (New York: Basic Books, 1977).

43. C. A. MacKinnon, "Feminism, Marxism, Method and the State: Toward Feminist Jurisprudence," in *Feminism and Methodology: Social Science Issues*, ed. S. Harding (Bloomington: Indiana University Press, 1987), 136.

44. Ibid., 140.

45. Dziech and Weiner, 1984.

46. Benson and Thomson, 1982; Fitzgerald et al., 1988; R. D. Glaser and J. S. Thorpe, "Unethical Intimacy: A Survey of Sexual Contact and Advances between Psychology Educators and Female Graduate Students," *American Psychologist* 41 (1986): 43–51; Kenig and Ryan, 1986; N. Maihoff and L. Forrest, "Sexual Harassment in Higher Education: An Assessment Study," *Journal of the National Association for Women Deans, Administrators, and Counselors* 46 (1983): 3–8; J. Metha and A. Nigg, "Sexual Harassment on Campus: An Institutional Response," *Journal of the National Association for Women Deans, Administrators, and Counselors* 46 (1983): 9–15; Robinson and Reid, 1985; and K. R. Wilson and L. A. Krause, "Sexual Harassment in the University," *Journal of College Student Personnel* 24 (1983): 219–224.

47. *Alexander v. Yale University*, 459 F. Supp. 1 (D. Conn. 1977), affirmed 631 F.2d 178 (2nd Cir. 1980).

48. M. Wilson, "Sexual Harassment and the Law," *The Community Psychologist* 21 (1988): 16–17.

49. Robertson et al., 1988.

50. American Council on Education, *Sexual Harassment on Campus: Suggestions for Reviewing Campus Policy and Educational Programs* (Washington, D.C.: American Council on Education, 1986).

51. American Association of University Professors, "Sexual Harassment: Suggested Policy and Procedures for Handling Complaints," *Academe* 69 (1983): 15a–16a.

52. See, e.g., Brandenburg, 1982, or Meek and Lynch, 1983.

53. For a general discussion of dispute resolution systems, see J. M. Brett, S. B. Goldberg, and W. L. Ury, "Designing Systems for Resolving Disputes in Organizations," *American Psychologist* 45 (1990): 162–170.

54. M. P. Rowe, "Dealing with Sexual Harassment," *Harvard Business Review* (May–June 1981): 42–46.

55. Kanter, 1977.

56. J. B. Miller, *Toward a New Psychology of Women* (Boston: Beacon Press, 1976), 127.

57. S. E. Merry and S. S. Silbey, "What Do Plaintiffs Want? Reexamining the Concept of Dispute," *Justice System Journal* 9 (1984): 151–178.

58. C. Gilligan, *In a Different Voice: Psychological Theory and Women's Development* (Cambridge, Mass.: Harvard University Press, 1982).

59. D. M. Kolb and G. G. Coolidge, *Her Place at the Table: A Consideration of Gender Issues in Negotiation* (Working paper series 88–5, Harvard Law School, Program on Negotiation, 1988).

60. Miller, 1976.

61. See, e.g., M. T. Mednick, "On the Politics of Psychological Constructs: Stop the Bandwagon, I Want to Get Off," *American Psychologist* 44 (1989): 1118–1123, for a summary of criticisms.

62. Robertson et al., 1988.

63. Ibid.

64. J. Rifkin, "Mediation from a Feminist Perspective: Promise and Problems," *Mediation* 2 (1984): 21–31.

65. Robertson et al., 1988.

66. Fain and Anderton, 1987.

67. Robertson et al., 1988.

0

68. Robinson and Reid, 1985.

69. B. Sandler, personal communication, 1988.

70. Fain and Anderton, 1987; LaFontaine and Tredeau, 1986; and McIntyre and Renick, 1982.

71. Lott et al., 1982; and Reilly et al., 1986.

72. Fitzgerald et al., 1988.

73. M. Brewer, "Further Beyond Nine to Five: An Integration and Future Directions," *Journal of Social Issues* 38 (1982): 149–175.

74. Robertson et al., 1988.

75. Livingston, 1982.

76. D. E. Terpstra and S. E. Cook, "Complainant Characteristics and Reported Behaviors and Consequences Associated with Formal Sexual Harassment Charges," *Personnel Psychology* 38 (1985): 559–574.

77. Terpstra and Baker, 1988.

78. F. S. Coles, "Forced to Quit: Sexual Harassment Complaints and Agency Response," *Sex Roles* 14 (1986): 81–95.

79. Garvey, 1986.

80. Livingston, 1982.

81. M. B. Brewer and R. A. Berk, "Beyond Nine to Five: Introduction," *Journal of Social Issues* 38 (1982): 1–4.

82. Adams et al., 1983; and Lott et al., 1982.

83. A. McCormack, "The Sexual Harassment of Students by Teachers: The Case of Students in Science," *Sex Roles* 13 (1985): 21–32.

84. Cammaert, 1985; P. Crull, "The Stress Effects of Sexual Harassment on the Job," *American Journal of Orthopsychiatry* 52 (1982): 539–543; J. A. Hamilton, S. W. Alagna, L. S. King, and C. Lloyd, "The Emotional Consequences of Gender-based Abuse in the Workplace: New Counseling Programs for Sex Discrimination," *Women and Therapy* 6 (1987): 155–182; Livingston, 1982; and Schneider, 1987.

85. Coles, 1986.

86. Meek and Lynch, 1983.

87. Jensen and Gutek, 1982.

88. Morgenson, 1989.

89. C. A. MacKinnon, *Sexual Harassment of Working Women: A Case of Sex Discrimination* (New Haven, Conn.: Yale University Press, 1979).

90. Brewer and Berk, 1982.

91. K. Beauvais, "Workshops to Combat Sexual Harassment: A Case Study of Changing Attitudes," *Signs: Journals of Women in Culture and Society* 12 (1986): 130–145.

92. Dziech and Weiner, 1984.

93. Gutek, 1985.

94. LaFontaine and Tredeau, 1986.

95. F. L. Hoffman, "Sexual Harassment in Academia: Feminist Theory and Institutional Practice," *Harvard Business Review* 56(2) (1986): 107–121.

96. Schneider, 1987.

97. See D. L. Kirp, M. G. Yudof, and M. S. Franks, *Gender Justice* (Chicago: University of Chicago Press, 1986).

98. Project on the Status and Education of Women, "The Campus Climate, A Chilly One for Women?" (Washington, D.C.: Association of American Colleges, 1982).

99. A. Fuehrer and K. M. Schilling, "The Values of Academe: Sexism as a Natural Consequence," *Journal of Social Issues* 41 (1985): 29–42.

THE POLITICS OF PORNOGRAPHY

❖ ❖ ❖

Madeleine Kahn

The current public debate about whether society should enact stricter legal controls over the production and dissemination of pornography is a matter of both immediate and far-reaching concern for women politicians and women voters. Fundamental to this debate are conflicting notions about the role public policy can play in legislating sexuality and sexual behavior; about the extent to which women are either consenting participants in or victims of both pornography and a patriarchal society; and about the uses to which our legal system can be put in support of the goal of greater social, political, and economic power for women. That this debate has divided feminists is further evidence of its importance as a policy issue: The resulting rhetoric of exclusion has caused feminism to abandon temporarily the inclusiveness that has been one of its greatest political strengths.

In this chapter, I argue for a return to that inclusiveness, which will allow us to address the very real abuses of some women in the pornography industry without surrendering to an image of women as helpless victims for whom all sex is brutalization or to the notion that we must acquiesce to the constraints of the patriarchy's image of women if we hope to be protected by its laws. First I lay out the traditional terms of the public debate over pornography, emphasizing the contrasting ideas about the power of images and symbols. Then I turn to the ways the traditional debate has been complicated by the

235

introduction of feminist goals. Finally, I propose a different way of framing questions about how pornography affects women in the hope that this new framework will allow us to take pragmatic steps to make our society a better place for women.

THE TRADITIONAL FRAMEWORK

Traditionally, pornography has seemed like a matter for public policy to only two groups in the United States: civil libertarians interested in maintaining or extending the protections of the First Amendment and religious groups concerned with upholding their religion's definition of public decency and private morality. Clearly, these two groups have defined pornography differently.

For civil libertarians, pornography is a representation of an idea.[1] It may be offensive or it may be liberating, depending on the context in which it is viewed or read and depending on the audience's interpretation. Some civil libertarians also see pornography as properly challenging the status quo. For them, the flouting of prevailing sexual mores prompts a healthy reexamination of our social and political assumptions about what is public and what is private, and what is a fit subject for representation and discussion. For these people, the obscenity trials of such books as Allen Ginsberg's *Howl,* John Cleland's *Fanny Hill,* and Henry Miller's *Tropic of Cancer* were important tests of the rights of authors to publish ideas that were contrary to prevailing political and social norms. But even those civil libertarians who are not interested in extending the reach of the First Amendment assume that the definition of obscenity is not absolute: Context and interpretation are everything. Thus, an explicit photograph of female genitals might be obscene in one context (such as in an advertisement for jeans) and not in another (such as in a medical textbook).

Moreover, for those interested in upholding the protections of the First Amendment, it is far preferable to risk permitting potentially obscene speech than to risk censoring potentially valuable political speech. For them, the remedy for speech that individual members of society find offensive is more speech. Only speech that is an incitement to harmful action should be censored.

In varying degrees, the trend in judicial decisions in the United States in this century, from Judge Woolsey's 1933 decision to allow *Ulysses* into the country to the 1973 Supreme Court ruling in *Miller v. California,* has been to deny that sexually explicit texts or images have any absolute meaning. In both of these cases, the judges were concerned to uphold the goals of existing obscenity laws: to promote public decency. Yet in both cases the judges assumed that obscenity is a matter of context and interpretation. Thus the same material can be put to different uses: What is pornographic to one viewer in one community has serious political value to another viewer in another community. Sexually explicit texts or images might be obscene and offensive to prevailing social values or they might have redeeming social and artistic value and might be part of an ongoing discussion about both sexuality and the things that sexuality affects.[2]

In contrast, those from the religious right, who are also concerned about public decency, believe that the meaning of a sexually explicit image is fixed, not open to interpretation or contextualization. This conviction stems from religious doctrine about sexual behavior. For example, if you believe that sex for pleasure rather than procreation is wrong, then any explicit depiction of sexual activity or even nudity is threatening and obscene.[3]

Equally important as these strict boundaries for proper sexual behavior, however, is the underlying religious conviction that having sexual desires or fantasies is as reprehensible as acting on them.[4] Because images prompt such fantasies, they are themselves temptations and contaminants, not representations of ideas available for discussion and interpretation. Thus, the context in which a sexually explicit image appears does not change its meaning; it is always obscene.

Until recently, these have been the terms of the public debate over what constitutes obscenity and what legal controls U.S. society should exert over such material. There have been two camps: those who believe that human nature and human sexuality are not monolithic and that texts and images are representations of ideas that are open to interpretation versus those who believe that we know absolutely what constitutes moral and immoral sexual behavior and that texts and images have one fixed meaning. Neither of these camps has been particularly concerned with the rights of women.

THE FEMINIST FRAMEWORK

In recent years, however, with the advent of the feminist antipornography movement and its challenge by the feminist anticensorship movement, these traditional terms have been used in a new discussion of pornography's effect on its male audience and of whether women need to be protected from those men through new laws like the 1983 amendment to the Human Rights Ordinance in Minneapolis defining pornography as sex discrimination.

Antipornography feminists view pornography as contributing to the subjugation of women in the United States. As Caryn Jacobs puts it,

> Pornography harms all women. Some of us sell our bodies to create the photographs, films, and live shows. Others of us have experienced the actions of men who have learned the lessons of pornography: forced sex, child molestation, wife-battering, and rape. All of us live in the poisoned atmosphere of misogyny to which pornography contributes.[5]

Like many other antipornography feminists, Jacobs focuses on eroticized violence and on the violence often used to force women to make pornographic movies or to imitate the acts depicted in them. Citing studies that show that viewing violent pornography causes men to engage in violent sexual behavior, those who want to increase public and legal controls on pornography elaborate upon Robin Morgan's assertion that "pornography is the theory, rape the practice."[6] They make a distinction between obscenity and pornography, arguing that obscenity, which is the merely sexually explicit, is not an issue for feminism, but pornography, which is "a broader, more comprehensive act, crushes a whole class of people through violence and subjugation: and sex is the vehicle that does the crushing," absolutely must be.[7]

Andrea Dworkin states that "[t]he role of violence in subordinating women has one special characteristic congruent with sex as the instrumentality of subordination: the violence is supposed to be sex for the woman too."[8] This reveals the fantasy of pornography and the promise that it makes to both men and women. To men, pornography says, "Women's only desire is to mirror your desire; women want from you only what you want to do to us. If you exercise your power over women through sex, women will love it, and you will be completely sexually satisfied." To women, pornography says, "You must desire only what men desire for you, or you will be punished." Pornography also makes a promise to women: "If you do what is asked of you, then you will be liberated, and you too will be completely sexually satisfied."[9]

With their amendment to the human rights ordinance in Minneapolis, Dworkin and Catharine MacKinnon got the opportunity to give this theory concrete form in law. The Minneapolis City Council had been trying to control the proliferation of pornographic bookstores and movie theaters by using zoning laws to restrict them to defined areas of the city. Those zoning restrictions were facing legal challenges, however, and when Dworkin and MacKinnon, testifying at the zoning hearings, urged the city to take a civil-rights approach to banning pornography, the City Council hired them to draft an amendment to the city's Human Rights Ordinance.[10]

The amendment they drafted proposed a new definition of pornography and a new legal approach to controlling it. Dworkin and MacKinnon's view is that pornography "sexualizes inequality and in doing so creates discrimination as a sex-based practice,"[11] and this is the heart of the amendment: Pornography is not just an idea, but a practice. In proposing and defending that ordinance, Dworkin and MacKinnon made two crucial extensions to the way even other antipornography feminists had seen pornography: They defined pornography as an action or practice, not as speech protected by the First Amendment, and they defined "trafficking" in pornography (that is, its production, sale, distribution, or exhibition) as discrimination against women and a violation of women's civil rights.[12]

Like the religious right, antipornography feminists claim that pornography is not speech and is not open to interpretation; it is itself an act or practice that harms women. "The enjoyment of pornography infringes on women's rights to bodily safety and equal participation in public life. Regulation is justified by these infringements on women's civil rights."[13] If pornography is not speech, then the question of regulating it does not come down to a battle between the First Amendment rights of pornographers and the First Amendment rights of women (a battle women are almost guaranteed to lose), and those filing suit don't have to prove that the pornography directly incited the harmful act. (This would be difficult to prove, as pornography rarely directly addresses its audience.)

In its efforts to avoid a battle over First Amendment rights, the proposed Minneapolis amendment is careful not to impose prior restraint on pornographic texts or images, so that the pornography is technically not being censored. Rather, individual women may file civil suits against pornographers for producing or distributing pornography. This would "allow women to advance equality by removing this concrete discrimination and hurting economically those who make, sell, distribute, or exhibit it."[14]

Proponents of this right to civil redress against those who traffic in pornography point to the precedent set by *New York v. Ferber* (1982) in which "the Supreme Court for the first time explicitly recognized that preventing or alleviating exploitation of those involved in pornography production is a valid goal of obscenity regulation."[15] The assumption in *Ferber* is that minors cannot give informed consent, so that any sexually explicit photographs of children are evidence of sexual exploitation. *Ferber* further assumes that the advertising, distribution, and selling of child pornography "provide the incentive for its production and, therefore [are] an integral part of that production."[16] Here the Court seems to have decided that it was not practical to try to stop the harm to children used in pornography by trying to enforce laws against such use. It was more effective to "undermine the profit motive that generates child pornography in the first place."[17] Proponents of the civil-rights ordinance claim that women are also incapable of giving informed consent when we are often both economically and physically coerced into working as prostitutes or pornographic models. They further point out that *Ferber*'s claim that the state's great interest in preventing harm to children justifies prohibition at the level of production should apply to women as well. The state should be as concerned to prevent harm to women as it is to children.

The antipornography movement and the codification and extension of its tenets in Dworkin and MacKinnon's antipornography ordinance have brought to light several aspects of pornography's effect on women that have hitherto been obscured by our conception of controls on pornography as a simple First Amendment issue. The most immediate and perhaps most powerful of these tenets is that the Minneapolis hearings on the proposed ordinance provided a forum and a respectful audience for the stories of those women who have been abused by pornography, whether directly or indirectly, whether by being coerced to produce it or to duplicate its images, or by being assaulted in imitation of it. Those hearings, along with similar hearings in Indianapolis and before the Meese Commission, have made it impossible for us to ignore the real harm that pornography has done to some women. The hearings have broken the silence that pornography itself sometimes imposes on women.

The antipornography movement has also provided us with an analysis of pornography not as a harmless (although sometimes distasteful) expression of free speech, but as an integral part of the patriarchal oppression and subordination of women through sex, which we also see in mainstream advertising and movies, in rape and other milder sexual threats and assaults, in sexual harassment on the job, and in nearly every other aspect of women's daily lives.

Anticensorship feminists, who contest antipornography feminists' analysis of pornography and its effect on women, do not at all dispute that pornography both mirrors and reinforces society's oppression of women through threats of sexual violence. Where anticensorship feminists differ from antipornography feminists is in their analysis of what pornography is, in their assumptions about what pornography means to women and how it affects us, in their characterization of men and of the likelihood that pornography will prompt men to erupt in real-world sexualized violence against women, and in their prescriptions for public policies to redress the harms caused by the oppression of women in the United States.

Anticensorship feminists assert that pornography is crucially a kind of speech, and not an action. While some violent pornography may be a record of real abuse, some of it is acted rather than enacted. Similarly, while there are real incidents of women being coerced into looking at pornography or imitating what it depicts, women can also choose to look at pornography, and to use it as an aid to fantasy and to the exploration of just the sex and power dynamic that antipornography feminists claim pornography reinforces. Pornography is not necessarily a record of real or even realistic sexual activity. In fact, its powerful appeal may stem from how little it has to do with reality: It is forbidden, transgressive, extreme, and unconstrained by the realities of human anatomy, of sexual function, or of tolerance for pain; it is, in short, impossible, and this is why its impact on real relations between men and women may not be as simple as antipornography feminists claim.[18]

As more women become producers of pornography—not only writing pornographic texts but producing pornographic photographs, videos, and movies—the sexually explicit images may become more oriented toward women's sexuality and so less alienating.[19] But Ellen Willis argues that women can learn to read even pornography written by men for other men as if it were written for us:

> [F]or women as for men [pornography] can also be a source of erotic pleasure. A woman who is raped is a victim; a woman who enjoys pornography (even if that means enjoying a rape fantasy) is in a sense a rebel, insisting on an aspect of her sexuality that has been defined as a male preserve. Insofar as pornography glorifies male supremacy and sexual alienation, it is deeply reactionary. But in rejecting sexual repression and hypocrisy—which have inflicted even more damage on women than on men—it expresses a radical impulse.[20]

In addition to claiming that there is a crucial difference between enjoying a fantasy and acting on that fantasy, Willis makes two other important points. First, pornography is not only about violence, as antipornography feminists assert, it is also about sex and about the intertwining, for women as well as men, of sex and power. Thus, it can be an aid to both exploring and exploding prevailing myths about women being politically and sexually passive and powerless. It might, in fact, be a realm in which women could experiment with power.[21]

Willis's second crucial point is that it is both possible and necessary for women to deconstruct pornography, to find in pornography a way to explore female sexuality and, by so doing, to upset the sexual and political hierarchy of which pornography is a mirror. When Willis says that women who enjoy pornography are expressing a radical impulse, she means that such women are reading against the grain of pornography and bringing to the fore the possibility that female sexual pleasure could be different from male sexual pleasure or that it could take varying forms and make varying demands. Using pornography against the usual intent of its creators would allow women to claim ownership of our own bodies and exercise our right to define and seek fulfillment of our own sexual desires.[22]

Anticensorship feminists point out that antipornography feminists have allied themselves with politically and morally conservative interests that have not traditionally been supportive of women's rights. They claim that this alliance is dangerous to women and to the goals of feminism, as well as the rights of all minorities, sexual or otherwise. In cities considering them, the antipornography ordinances have received a great deal of support from right-wing religious groups eager to use their provisions to outlaw "'sodomy' and 'disruption of the family unit' [and to] . . . 'restore ladies to what they used to be,'"[23] to "reinstate traditional sexual arrangements and the formerly inexorable link between reproduction and sexuality."[24] Even the 1986 Meese Commission appropriated the feminist notion that pornography degrades women, but changed the meaning of degradation to match its own conservative agenda.

Anticensorship feminists further claim that antipornography feminists base their opposition to pornography on two assumptions that lend themselves to appropriation by conservative antifeminist interests: that men are inherently violent and sexually uncontrolled and that women are only sexual victims. They assert that the Minneapolis ordinance's description of pornography "implies that heterosexual sex itself is sexist; that women do not engage in it of their own volition; and that behavior pleasurable to men is repugnant to women,"[25] and that the ordinance "resonates with the traditional concept that sex itself degrades women," and that "'good' women do not seek and enjoy sex."[26]

Anticensorship feminists dispute the claim that social-science research has shown a clear correlation between pornography and acts of violence against women. Often citing the same experiments, they come to very different conclusions. For example, the Meese Commission based its conviction that pornography causes violence against women on research by Edward Donnerstein. Others have used the same research as evidence that there is no causal link between violent pornography and sexual violence against women.[27] Donnerstein says that while "depictions of sexual violence . . . under some conditions, promote certain anti-social attitudes and behavior," mass media images containing little explicit sex may do the same thing. Overall, "existing research leaves too many questions unanswered."[28] Even questions about pornography that would seem to lend themselves to direct empirical investigation yield only slippery data. There is, for example, considerable disagreement about how much violence there is in pornography and whether pornography is more violent than it used to be.[29] (Everyone seems to agree that both violent and sexually suggestive images are more pervasive in mainstream media than they used to be.)

It is not by accident that pornography has provoked such an intense debate and such a confusing blurring of the boundaries between the sides of the debate, for pornography itself contains a fundamental contradiction. It is both violent and erotic, both frightening and seductive. Pornography affects our hopes and fears so powerfully precisely because of its dual nature. Thus, the problem is not that one side of the feminist debate over pornography is wrong, or even that the two sides are looking at different pornography. The problem is that the evidence—the pornography itself—supports both readings: It seems to offer a blueprint for the sexualized violence against women that is so pervasive in our society and it seems to offer a protected fantasy realm in which women as well as men can explore the erotic, the violent, the forbidden, and the desirable without committing to any real-world act. I have devoted most of this chapter to presenting strong cases for each of these feminist arguments precisely because each of them contains such important insights and each of them speaks to some part of every woman's experience, and I have wanted to do justice to both.

A PROPOSAL FOR A NEW FRAMEWORK

Proponents of the different sides of this debate would not agree with my assertion that both analyses are in many essentials correct and, moreover, that we can frame the issue of pornography in such a way that both analyses can exert influence on our responses to it. Rather, feminists on each side have attempted to discredit those on the other. Antipornography feminists assert that women who claim to enjoy pornography (whether as actors or consumers) are suffering from false consciousness and that women who resist additional controls on pornography in favor of the protections of the First Amendment are fooling themselves when they think the First Amendment ever protects women's speech. Anticensorship feminists assert that those who want to restrict pornography are afraid of sex and that they naively think that they can use the conservative interests with which they have allied themselves and the legal system to which they would refer civil suits for feminist ends, while, in truth, their own rhetoric is being used by those groups against feminist goals.

However, the contradiction between these analyses of pornography—that pornography represents both a violent and patriarchal depiction of the sexual subjugation of women and a fantasy realm in which women can learn about precisely the sexuality and the power that the patriarchy would deny us—also contains the pattern for a constructive way of thinking about feminism and pornography. If we can learn (and if we can teach others) to see both the threat and the promise of pornography, then we can use it as a different sort of practice—as a medium for radical reversals and disruptions of the normative patriarchal images of women.

This has been one of the most important lessons of feminism: that the symbols of our society and the mainstream images of ourselves that society offers to us can be read against their stated intent. It is, in fact, one of the tenets of feminism's most potent slogan, that the personal is political: We can examine the symbols and structures through which we understand our daily lives and, through that examination, we can change both the symbols and our lives. Pornography is the same as those more mainstream media images (advertising, movies, and television) that feminism has already taught us to critique and so to defuse; in that critiquing, it is liberating. Pornography is different only in that it involves sex, and our sexual drives and fantasies are often barely conscious, infantile, contradictory, mysteriously powerful, and not easily susceptible to rational discourse. This subtext that each of us brings to pornography gives it much of its power. It is important to note, however, that pornography has power over our fantasies, and only indirectly through us, the power to affect real-world relations between men and women. Pornography in itself has no more direct power to change reality than does any other image.[30]

What, then, should our public policy be? Because antipornography feminists have been so convincing about the dangers that pornography poses to some women and because they are so obviously right that the most violent pornographic images at least reinforce U.S. society's devaluation of women, it is tempting to try to craft some legal constraints on at least the most graphically violent pornography. For example, we could narrow the focus of the Minneapolis ordinance to constrain only the most violent and only photographic and film images instead of books. But even putting aside the difficulties of crafting such a law, I think it would be a misdirection of our resources. It would further split women along class lines and lines of sexual allegiance, and we don't need more legal policy. As critics of the Minneapolis ordinance have pointed out, we already have laws to protect us from most of the cited abuses; we just need to find better ways to enforce them.[31] The problems that the Minneapolis ordinance was designed to address are problems that have been with us for a long time: the violent abuse (sexual and otherwise) of women in the workplace and in the home, the socially sanctioned harassment and devaluation of women in small and large ways, the economic and political powerlessness of many women, and so forth. We have already gotten the laws and other institutional tools we need to combat the problems. What we need is a renewed commitment to using those tools; we need a renewed feminist policy.

For example, we don't need to claim that women, as an economically and sexually oppressed class, cannot ever give informed consent to posing for pornographic photographs or acting in pornographic movies. Asserting that we are no more capable of giving informed consent than a minor child does not seem like the best way to gain control over our lives or to increase our power in the patriarchy.[32] Neither does it seem necessarily true that the most common abuses to which pornographic models or sex workers are subjected are worse than those to which women in many (less well paid) jobs are subjected. Instead of trying to destroy the pornography industry, we need to bring pornography and the women who work in it into the mainstream of feminism. Instead of treating them wholly as victims or setting out to liberate them of their false consciousness, we can make room for these women's experiences within our model of acceptable behavior for feminists, and we can fight to improve job conditions and safety, pay, access to the power held by mostly male directors and producers, and so forth. We need to invade the realm of pornography and make it our own. In so doing, we not only create better working conditions for women, but we avail ourselves of yet another tool that we can use in the reconstruction of patriarchy's images of us and, hence, of patriarchy itself.

To accomplish this transformation, we have only to use more of the tried and true methods: educating ourselves and others, getting more women into government and law where public policy is made, joining with sex workers to make sure they are not being abused or coerced, and so forth. Specifically, I would like to see a reinvigoration of sex education in the schools (from grammar school to college) and I would like part of that sex education to be instruction in how to read both mainstream media and pornography to expose the myths they promulgate about women's sexuality. Ideally, such instruction would offer both sides of the pornography debate for students to consider. I would like to see women vote together consistently on women's issues and for women candidates so that we never again see the official blessing of sexual harassment that we saw in the confirmation hearings for Clarence Thomas, and so that the National Endowment for the Arts is never again held hostage to the beliefs of right-wing religious groups who believe that all depictions of sexuality in art are pornographic. We need more women in positions of legal and political power so that the people making and enforcing the laws have a personal sense of what those laws are designed to protect. If we had more women in police departments and district attorney's offices, those enforcing the laws would no longer assume that a woman's sexual history is useful in determining whether she's been raped, that a prostitute by definition cannot be raped, or that women secretly long for sexual violence.

Women working together can bring sex workers (prostitutes, topless dancers, nude models, and actors in pornographic films) into the mainstream of feminism. When we isolate these women as helpless victims of male violence, of childhood abuse, or of brainwashing and false consciousness, we silence them. But when we talk with them and learn about the variety of their experiences, we can begin to work together to protect all women. Pornography unveiled and taken out of the realm of the unmentionable and the illicit is pornography defused. Sex workers given a voice within mainstream feminism are able to call on more resources and are able to make more choices.

From the government, I would ask for a task force like those we have had in the past against drugs or organized crime. This task force would make a concerted effort to wipe out crimes against women and to enforce the existing laws against coercion and abuse, both sexual and otherwise. Many of the women who have testified that they were abused in the pornography industry have also testified that they did not know they had any recourse. A government task force could promulgate the information that every woman has legal recourse against abuse and could make sure all complaints are taken seriously and acted upon expeditiously.

From social-science researchers, I would ask for new experiments designed to measure the effect of education about images of sexualized violence against women. Preliminary results from the debriefing of subjects in more typical experiments indicate that those subjects gain a heightened sensitivity to violence against women. We must find out what kind of education works and spend our resources educating each other about how to behave in the world instead of fine-tuning inconclusive measurements in the lab.

From society, I ask for a renewed effort to create higher paying jobs for women so that women are not economically coerced into abusive jobs. I suggest we decriminalize prostitution and work to make sure that women's bodies are not our most valuable commodity. In every way possible, I would like women to learn to use the formerly terrifying power of the patriarchy against itself.[33]

Most important, we must not be silenced; rather, we must speak in all of the voices available to us. These voices include not only those of women who have felt victimized by pornography and those frightened or appalled by it but those interested in promulgating a feminist pornography, which explicitly explores female sexuality—heterosexual and homosexual, passive and concerned with power, and gentle and sado-masochistic.

ACKNOWLEDGMENTS

Thanks go to the friends and colleagues who read drafts of this chapter and helped me work through some of the issues: Elizabeth Heckendorn Cook, Tom Grey, Victoria Kahn, and Donna Kelley.

NOTES

1. Of course, every one of these positions on pornography that I will outline in reality occupies a broader part of the spectrum than I can convey in this chapter. Not every civil libertarian or anticensorship feminist subscribes to all of the beliefs I have attributed to their positions, or to only

those beliefs. I have tried to make clear, however, where the overlap and contradictions occur and why it is important that they do occur.

2. The *Miller v. California* ruling appeals to the "average person, applying community standards" and assumes that "serious literary, artistic, political, or scientific value" keeps a work from being obscene. These quotations are from the summary in P. Brest and A. Vandenberg, "Politics, Feminism, and the Constitution: The Anti-Pornography Movement in Minneapolis," *Stanford Law Review* 39 (1986): 607–666, 609–610.

3. I am using *pornography* and *obscenity* as interchangeable terms here because that is how most people tend to use them. The difference is legally important, however, because obscene speech is not protected by the First Amendment, and mere pornography is. For legal purposes, *obscene* means indecent or filthy, while *pornographic* material (from the Greek *pornographos*, the writing of whores) is that which is sexually explicit.

4. One of the basic texts for this conviction that fantasy and action are the same is from the Sermon on the Mount, Matthew 5:27–29: "You have learnt how it was said: You must not commit adultery. But I say this to you: if a man looks at a woman lustfully, he has already committed adultery with her in his heart. If your right eye should cause you to sin, tear it out and throw it away; for it will do you less harm to lose one part of you than to have your whole body thrown into hell" (Jerusalem Bible).

5. C. Jacobs, "Patterns of Violence: A Feminist Perspective on the Regulation of Pornography," *Harvard Women's Law Journal* 7(1) (Spring 1984): 5–55, 9.

6. R. Morgan, *Going Too Far* (New York: Random House, 1978), 169, cited in Jacobs, 1984, 13, and, with or without attribution, in almost every discussion of pornography.

7. A. Dworkin, "Against the Male Flood: Censorship, Pornography, and Equality," *Harvard Women's Law Journal* 8 (Spring 1985): 1–29, 9.

8. Ibid., 9, 16.

9. Robin West's analysis of pornography as the "legal text" of patriarchy also explores the simultaneous threat and promise of pornography. In her reading, the debate between antipornography and anticensorship feminists reflects this confusion or indeterminacy in pornography, which is just like the indeterminacy in any other legal text. R. West, "Pornography as a Legal Text: Comments from a Legal Perspective," *For Adult Users Only*, ed. S. Gubar and J. Hoff (Bloomington: Indiana University Press, 1989), 108–130.

10. For my version of events I have relied primarily on Brest and Vandenberg, but, in fact, none of the several accounts I read differed in any significant way. The Minneapolis City Council passed the amendment, but it was later vetoed by the mayor on the grounds that it was a violation of the

First Amendment. A similar version of the amendment was passed into law by the mayor of Indianapolis, and later was struck down by a federal judge. Attempts to pass a similar ordinance in Cambridge, Massachusetts; Los Angeles, California; and other cities have failed so far. On February 27, 1992, according to the *New York Times*, "The Supreme Court of Canada . . . upheld the obscenity provision of the criminal code, ruling that although the anti-pornography law infringes on the freedom of expression, it is legitimate to suppress materials that harm women." *New York Times*, February 28, 1992, A1, B10, 1.

11. Dworkin, 1985, 10.

12. My account of the contents of the proposed amendment to the Human Rights Ordinance of the City of Minneapolis is taken from several sources, primarily from Dworkin's (1985) account, from MacKinnon's accounts in "Pornography: Social Science, Legal, and Clinical Perspectives," by C. A. MacKinnon, E. Donnerstein, C. A. Champion, and C. R. Sunstein, in *Law and Inequality: A Journal of Theory and Practice*, 4, 1986, 17–49, and in the various essays in *Feminism Unmodified: Discourses on Life and Law* (Cambridge, Mass.: Harvard University Press, 1987), and from Brest and Vandenberg's (1986) detailed description of the hearings and their results.

13. Jacobs, 1984, 43. The analogy is often made to the idea of racism and the practice of segregation (that is, the idea of racism cannot be outlawed, but its practice in segregation can). See, for example, A. Dworkin as quoted in Brest and Vandenberg, 1986, 618: "Pornography is a practice of sexual exploitation. There is nothing illegal in trying to change the idea people have of women as a sexually subordinate people by attacking the practice of pornography, which is the actual practice of that idea."

14. Dworkin, 1985, 23.

15. Jacobs, 1984, 36.

16. Ibid., 37.

17. C. R. Sunstein, "Notes on Pornography and the First Amendment," part of the panel discussion in "Pornography: Social Science, Legal, and Clinical Perspectives," in *Law and Inequality: A Journal of Theory and Practice* 4 (1986): 17–49, 29.

18. M. Masud R. Kahn argues that pornography functions as a substitute for violence, that it dehumanizes both the self and the object of the fantasy, and that it ultimately negates imagination. He suggests that pornography "is therapeutic in so far as it transmutes the threat of total violence . . . into manageable distributed, dosed and eroticized language." M. M. R. Kahn, "Pornography and the Politics of Rage and Subversion," in *Alienation in Perversions*, ed. M. M. R. Kahn (Bloomington: Indiana University Press, 1979), 219–226, 223.

19. Candida Royalle's Femme Productions has been producing pornography from a woman's point of view since the early 1980s. For the viewpoints of women in the sex industry, see F. Delacoste and P. Alexander, eds., *Sex Work: Writings by Women in the Sex Industry* (Pittsburgh: Cleis Press, 1987); and L. Bell, ed., *Good Girls/Bad Girls: Feminists and Sex Trade Workers Face to Face* (Seattle: Seal Press, 1987).

20. E. Willis, "Feminism, Moralism, and Pornography" in *Powers of Desire: The Politics of Sexuality*, ed. A. Snitow, C. Stansell, and S. Thompson (New York: Monthly Review Press, 1983), 460–467, 464.

21. In response to claims that some women choose to act in pornographic movies or enjoy viewing pornography (even violent pornography), anti-pornography feminists claim that those women are themselves misogynist and that they are suffering from a false consciousness in which they have absorbed the views of the men who have power over them. "Accepting the 'joys of passivity' buys into the sexual culture of male supremacy—'a dynamic of control,' MacKinnon wrote, 'by which male dominance . . . eroticizes . . . that which maintains and defines male supremacy as a political system'" (Brest and Vandenberg, 1986), 637.

22. For an exploration of this concept within a Marxist/Freudian analysis of hard-core films, see L. Williams, "Fetishism and Hard Core: Marx, Freud, and the 'Money Shot,'" in Gubar and Hoff, 1989, 198–217, especially 215: "Thus, as the feature-length form of the genre develops, it tends to multiply the opportunities to investigate wider ranges of perverse sexual practices. Feminist and moral majoritists alike have tended to see only the increased violence of these forms of sexual representation. But it is important to realize as well that the very diversity of these practices contributes to the defeat of the phallic economy's original desire to fix the sexual identity of the woman as the mirror of its own desire."

23. L. Duggan, N. Hunter, and C. S. Vance, "False Promises: Feminist Anti-pornography Legislation in the U.S.," in *Women Against Censorship*, ed. V. Burstyn (Vancouver and Toronto: Douglas & MacIntyre, 1985), 130–151, 133.

24. N. D. Hunter and S. A. Law, "Brief Amici Curiae of Feminist Anti-Censorship Taskforce, et al., in *American Booksellers Association v. Hudnut*," *University of Michigan Journal of Law Reform* 21 (1, 2) 1985: 69–136, 71.

25. Duggan et al., 1985, 139.

26. Hunter and Law, 1985, 105, 129.

27. Almost every work cited in these notes refers to Donnerstein's studies. Those who are antipornography cite his studies to buttress their claim that men exposed to sexually violent images are more likely to say they would rape women. Those who are anti-antipornography cite the studies

to buttress their claim that studies on the effects of viewing pornography are inconclusive and that images of violence (which does not necessarily have anything to do with pornography) seem to have the most effect. I think this inconclusiveness means we are asking the wrong questions. Rather than asking, "How do men interpret pornography's images of women?" we should be asking, "How can we best educate men to interpret pornography's images of women?"

28. D. Linz and E. Donnerstein, "The Effects of Counter-Information on the Acceptance of Rape Myths," in *Pornography: Research Advances & Policy Considerations*, ed. D. Zillman and J. Bryant (Hillsdale, N.J.: Lawrence Erlbaum Associates, 1989), 259–288, 259. The authors recommend "educational interventions that would teach viewers to become more critical consumers of the mass media" (p. 259).

29. Here again sources on different sides of the debate have contradictory data. Among many other examples, Dworkin and MacKinnon cite examples purporting to show that violence in pornography has increased, as does the Meese Commission report. Hunter and Law, Vance, and others claim that violence has not increased. Donald Downs states that surveys conducted in the 1980s "suggest that the percentage of violence may have tapered off after the mid-1970s." He adds, however, that where violence is shown it "is likely to be much more graphic than in the past." D. A. Downs, *The New Politics of Pornography* (Chicago: The University of Chicago Press, 1989), 23. F. M. Christensen says, "Researchers have consistently found much less violence in sex movies than in others; and the most sexually explicit, the 'hard core' shows have the least violence of all. (It is Hollywood movies, not porno flicks, that most like combining sex with violence.)" F. M. Christensen, *Pornography: The Other Side* (New York: Praeger, 1990), 59.

30. I have deliberately not attempted to distinguish here between pornography and erotica because, in practice, that distinction comes down to, as Ellen Willis says, "What turns me on is erotic; what turns you on is pornographic." Antipornography feminists often try to make this distinction, but in fact the Minneapolis ordinance is so far reaching that it might well cover almost anyone's definition of erotica as well, since "the sexually explicit subordination of women [and] scenarios of degradation" might mean very different things to different people. These quotes are from Willis, 1983, 463, and the Minneapolis ordinance, as cited in Brest and Vandenberg, 1986, 619.

31. New laws will not force the patriarchy to care about violence against women. Existing laws already contain that promise of protection; we need to find ways to enforce them. For example, the Minneapolis ordinance provides for legal redress for assaults provoked by pornography, for coercion to imitate pornography, and for pornography's contribution to

an environment that subjugates women. But under existing tort law, if you are attacked (whether the attack is provoked by pornography or not) you can bring a legal action against your attacker. Rape, sexual assault, and kidnapping are already crimes. In many cases, if you are coerced into a pornographic performance and any record is made of that performance, you could sue for invasion of privacy. We already have obscenity laws for provision that pornography contributes to a violent and oppressive environment. For the specifics of this argument about which existing laws provide legal redress for those kinds of assaults covered by the Minneapolis ordinance, I have relied on L. Robel, "Pornography and Existing Law: What the Law Can Do," in Gubar and Hoff, 1985, 178–197. For one of many attacks on the Minneapolis ordinance on the grounds that it would be both difficult to enforce and too open to misuse against women's interests, see Hunter and Law, 1985.

32. Even when it is limited to child pornography, Ferber's criminalization of trafficking in child pornography may be dangerous. As the Jock Sturges case, which began in 1990, shows, this still leaves a great deal of interpretive power in the hands of the legal system, with very few checks on the system's definition of pornography or on its use of that power. In this case, an established San Francisco photographer's studio was shut down and his equipment and negatives confiscated because a lab technician reported that some of his images of children might be pornographic. While some of those images do explore the power relation of the (presumably clothed) adult male photographer to the nude child in front of the camera, none of them involves sexual activity of any sort. For one account of events, see A. O'Hehir, "Eye of the Beholder," *SF Weekly* (June 6, 1990), 10–12.

33. For a very persuasive analogy to the civil-rights movement's reinterpretation of the promises of the U.S. Constitution for blacks, see West, 1989.

GENDER EQUALITY AND EMPLOYMENT POLICY

❖ ❖ ❖

Deborah L. Rhode

Over the last quarter century, changes in ideological, economic, and demographic patterns have all contributed to major transformations in gender roles. Laws have both reflected and reinforced these changes. Since the early 1960s, the United States has developed a broad array of legislative, administrative, and judicial mandates against gender discrimination. The result has been unprecedented equality in formal treatment of the sexes, but a continued disparity in actual status. Legal initiatives have helped break barriers to entry for those seeking nontraditional employment, but most occupations remain highly segregated or stratified by sex. While men and women are now entitled to equal pay for the same work, relatively few males and females have, in fact, performed the same work. If domestic and paid labor are combined, the average woman works longer hours and receives substantially less income than the average man. Although women have entered elite professions in substantial numbers, they have tended to cluster at the lowest levels. Most female workers have remained in relatively low-status, low-paying, female-dominated occupations.

The following discussion explores the major institutional and ideological forces underlying these disparities. It begins with a brief overview of occupational inequality and the most commonly accepted strategies for coping with it: requirements of equal opportunity and

equal treatment. Although these strategies have been of vital importance in raising the cost of and consciousness about sex-based discrimination, they have not adequately addressed the full range of factors
that contribute to women's unequal work-force status.

Significant progress toward social justice will require alternative
frameworks. Equal opportunity is inadequate as a means and an end;
what is needed are fundamental changes in workplace practices,
premises, and priorities.

PATTERNS OF INEQUALITY

Despite an increase in antidiscrimination mandates, wide disparities
have persisted in the vocational status of men and women. In 1955,
the median annual wages of full-time female workers were approximately two-thirds of the annual wages of males. Over the next several
decades, that figure declined and then climbed back to roughly the
same percentage (70 percent of weekly wages).[1]

However, the above wage ratios do not capture the full extent of
gender differences in earnings, since only about half of all employed
women work full-time for the full year, and disproportionate numbers
lack employment-related benefits such as health and pension coverage.[2] Even among full-time workers, the average female college graduate still earns less than the average white male with a high school
diploma. The average black female college graduate in a full-time
position receives less than 90 percent of her white counterpart's salary
(which is equal to the earnings of a white male high school dropout).[3]
Women, particularly minority women, are also disproportionately represented among the unemployed and among involuntary part-time
workers.

These salary and unemployment disparities reflect broader patterns of occupational segregation and stratification. Most women employees are crowded into a small number of job categories, and about
half are in occupations that are at least 80 percent female.[4] Even in
gender-integrated occupations, women are likely to hold different jobs
and have different pay and promotion opportunities. Most jobs still
tend to be stratified by race and ethnicity as well as by sex, and women
of color remain at the bottom of the occupational hierarchy.[5]

Despite significant progress toward greater integration, some
projections suggest that at current rates of change, it would take
between 75 and 100 years to achieve complete occupational integration.[6] Some of the more dramatic improvements have been in formerly
male-dominated professions such as law, medicine, and management,

where women's representation ranged between 3 percent and 14 percent in the early 1960s and increased to levels of 20 percent to 40 percent by the early 1990s.[7] However, at the highest levels of power, status, and financial reward, significant disparities remain that cannot be explained solely by women's recent entry into those professions.

For example, in the early 1980s, female lawyers comprised 25 percent of all associates but only 6 percent of the partners in law firms; studies of lawyers with comparable education qualifications have also found that women are substantially less likely to reach partnership.[8] At all professional levels, underrepresentation of women of color is even greater than that of white women.

Gains in blue-collar employment have also been limited. For example, although the absolute number of women in the skilled trades increased fourfold between 1960 and 1980, women still hold only about 20 percent of those positions.[9] Nor has women's increasing interest in "men's work" been matched by a comparable increase in men's enthusiasm for "women's work." Within the most heavily female-dominated job sectors, such as clerical work, male representation has not significantly changed.[10]

Defenders of the conventional equal opportunity approach to employment discrimination typically dismiss these asymmetries as artifacts of cultural lag or employee choice and, in either case, as matters beyond the scope of legitimate legal concern. From their perspective, formal prohibitions on gender bias in educational and employment practices will, in time, prove sufficient to guarantee equal opportunity. Any remaining disparity in occupational status can be attributed to individual choice, capabilities, and commitment, and is not a ground for further legal intervention.

Yet most research suggests that the obstacles confronting women workers are more entrenched than the equal opportunity approach acknowledges. In identifying these obstacles, it is important to note at the outset certain complexities in the concept of occupational equality. It is not self-evident that proportional representation in all employment sectors is the ultimate ideal. To assume that, under conditions of full equality, women will make precisely the same occupational choices as men is to accept an assimilationist perspective that many feminists renounce. Yet one can remain agnostic about the precise degree of gender differentiation in the ideal society without losing sight of the disadvantages confronting women in this world.

In assessing those disadvantages, it is useful to distinguish two sorts of problems. Work-force inequalities reflect both the relatively low status and pay scales in female-dominated occupations and the factors discouraging women's entry and advancement in alternative employment contexts. These phenomena in turn depend on complex interrelationships among individual choices, social norms, discriminatory practices, and institutional structures.

INDIVIDUAL CHOICE AND SOCIALIZATION PATTERNS

Although individual choice plays an important role in virtually all theories of occupational inequality, the nature of that role is a matter of considerable dispute. According to human capital models of labor-force participation, gender differences in earnings and occupational status are largely attributable to differences in career investments. In essence, these models assume that women seek to balance work and family commitments by selecting female-dominated occupations that tend not to require extended training, long hours, inflexible schedules, or skills that deteriorate during absence from the work force.

Under this theory, the solution to women's workplace inequality lies with women themselves. In their crudest form, human capital approaches lead to a kind of Marie Antoinette response to occupational stratification. If women want positions with greater pay, prestige, and power, let them make different career investments; if female nurses want pay scales equivalent to male hotel clerks, let them become hotel clerks.[11]

This theory is questionable on several levels. Most studies have concluded that characteristics such as education and experience cannot account for more than half of current gender disparities in earnings.[12] On the whole, women who make comparable investments in time, preparation, and experience still advance less far and less quickly than men. Even in their most sophisticated forms, human capital approaches leave a vast range of questions unanswered. Why is it that females choose to be nurses rather than hotel clerks—or, for that matter, truck drivers, where job skills are even less likely to deteriorate with absence? Why don't male employees with family responsibilities disproportionately choose jobs requiring shorter hours? Answers to these questions require a more complex account of cultural norms and institutional constraints.

For many individuals, career decisions have been less the product of fully informed and independent preferences than the result of preconceptions about "women's work" that are shaped by cultural stereotypes, family and peer pressure, and the absence of alternative role models. Women who have deviated from traditional norms in job selection have generally received less social approval than those who have not. Many families also have discouraged career choices that would conflict with domestic duties, require geographic mobility, or entail greater prestige or income for wives than for husbands.[13] Such patterns can be especially pronounced among some minority groups, where males' education may carry greater priority than females'.[14] Job training, counseling, and recruitment networks have often channeled women toward conventional occupations, and socioeconomic barriers have limited employment aspirations.[15]

These constraints are reinforced by the mismatch between characteristics associated with femininity and characteristics associated with vocational achievement. The aggressiveness, competitiveness, dedication, and emotional detachment thought necessary for advancement in the most prestigious and well-paid occupations are seen as incompatible with the traits commonly viewed as attractive in women: cooperation, deference, sensitivity, and self-sacrifice. Despite substantial progress toward gender equality over the last several decades, these sexual stereotypes have been remarkably resilient.

Different socialization patterns have also led women to arrange their priorities in ways that mesh poorly with occupational structures. Although society's commitment to equal opportunity in vocational spheres has steadily increased, it has not extended to equal obligations in domestic spheres. Most contemporary studies have indicated that women still perform about 70 percent of the family tasks in an average household. Employed wives spend about twice as much time on homemaking tasks as employed husbands.[16]

As subsequent discussion in this chapter suggests, individual choices have also been constrained by unconscious discrimination and workplace structures. The result is a convergence of self-perpetuating social signals that reinforce occupational inequalities. Males' and females' different career investments have been heavily dependent on their perceptions of different opportunities.

Women have long faced relatively low wages in traditional vocations and substantial barriers to advancement in nontraditional pursuits. Under such circumstances, it has been economically rational for working couples to give priority to the husband's career, to relocate in accordance with his job prospects, and to assign wives a disproportionate share of domestic obligations. The gender division of labor in the home and workplace has been mutually reinforcing. Women's subordinate occupational status has encouraged them to make more modest career investments and to assume greater domestic responsibilities, both of which help perpetuate that subordination. To break this cycle will require treating individual choices not as fixed and independent phenomena, but as responses to cultural forces that are open to redirection.

DISCRIMINATORY PRACTICES AND OCCUPATIONAL DYNAMICS

Efforts to move beyond human capital explanations of occupational inequality have proceeded on several levels. One approach has focused on occupational segregation. Some commentators, drawing on dual labor market theories, have stressed men's concentration in the primary and women's in the secondary sector of the work force. Others have emphasized more general effects of occupational crowding (i.e., since women have remained clustered in a relatively small number of female-dominated occupations, the resulting oversupply of labor in those fields has depressed wage rates and increased unemployment).

Such approaches, while useful to a point, have left fundamental causal questions unaddressed. Why, for example, have women remained crowded in certain sectors of the labor market? Why have those sectors commanded relatively low status and economic reward, and why do males and females with comparable qualifications have different opportunities for advancement?

In seeking answers to such questions, researchers have accumulated increasing evidence on discrimination of various forms: deliberate, statistical, and unconscious. On the most overt level, economists have argued that competitive market forces do not necessarily discourage deliberate bias against women or minorities where employers have developed a "taste for discrimination."[17] Such tastes, founded on personal prejudice, customer or coworker preference, or favoritism toward male "breadwinners," have been identified in a wide range of contexts.[18] Litigation in the late 1980s revealed claims such as those advanced by owners of tuna fishing boats that excluded women. According to these owners, the presence of female employees would destroy morale and distract the crew: their boats would "catch fewer fish with women on board."[19]

The more insulated the labor market is from competitive forces, the more persistent these biases may prove. Even reasonably competitive markets will also permit what economists label "statistical discrimination," that is, discrimination premised on generalizations that are inaccurate in a large percentage of cases but that are nonetheless cheaper to indulge than refine. Long after statistical patterns erode, the effects of statistical discrimination often linger.[20] Once jobs become typed as male or female, socialization processes tend to per-petuate those labels.[21]

A final, and in contemporary society perhaps a most intransi-gent, form of discrimination operates at unconscious levels. Employer decision making has reflected the same stereotypes about male and female capabilities that have constrained employees' vocational choices. For example, surveys of a wide variety of decision makers have revealed that identical resumes or scholarly articles are rated significantly lower if the applicant or author is thought to be a woman rather than a man. Men's success is more likely to be attributed to ability and women's to luck.[22]

More overt, although often unintentional, forms of bias by col-leagues and coworkers have comparable consequences. Women in a wide range of employment settings remain outside the informal net-works of support, guidance, and information exchange that are critical to advancement.[23] All of these problems are especially acute for women of color, who face unconscious discrimination on two fronts, and whose small numbers make finding mentors and role models especially difficult.[24] Related problems involve sexual harassment, which not only impairs performance and restricts advancement but also discourages women from entering male-dominated environ-ments.[25]

The last decade has, to be sure, witnessed significant improve-ment in these areas. Court decisions banning sex-based discrimination by certain all-male clubs where key professional contacts are made, and decisions establishing legal liability for sexual harassment, have enabled more women to function effectively in the workplace.[26] Yet we have not solved these problems; we have only moved them to new levels. Women are still excluded from informal networks of support. As was apparent from the commentary following the Clarence Thomas confirmation hearings, a wide gap persists between legal prohibitions and workplace practices regarding sexual harassment.[27]

However, as long as women constitute small minorities in non-traditional employment contexts, substantial obstacles will remain. The presence of a few token females may do little to alter underlying stereotypes, and the pressures placed on such individuals make suc-cessful performance less likely.

Given these barriers and biases, women must work harder to succeed and when they do, they must deal with the envy and anxiety that success arouses. Those who do not advance under such circum-stances, or who become frustrated and opt for different employment, confirm the adverse stereotypes that worked against their advancement in the first place. The perception remains that women cannot make it by conventional standards, or are less committed to doing so. In either event, they do not seem to warrant the same investment in training, assistance, and promotion opportunities as their male counterparts.[28]

Again, the result is a subtle but self-perpetuating cycle in which individual choices are constrained by discriminatory practices. Not only has gender bias shaped employment opportunities and salary patterns, it has also affected the way workplace structures have adapted to women's participation.

INSTITUTIONAL CONSTRAINTS

In contemporary American society, any individual who seeks to balance significant work and family commitments confronts substantial barriers. Since, as noted earlier, women continue to assume the greater share of homemaking obligations, they also experience the greater share of workplace difficulties. The most obvious problems involve the length and rigidity of most working schedules, the absence of adequate parental leave provisions, and inadequacies in child-care services. Despite increasing innovation, the vast majority of workers lack opportunities for flexible schedules or meaningful part-time work.

By the early 1990s, the United States remained the only major Western industrialized nation that failed to guarantee maternity benefits or job-protected leaves. Federal legislation to ensure minimum family and medical leaves has repeatedly failed to survive presidential opposition. An equally chronic problem involves the inadequacies of child-care arrangements. Although by the late 1980s, over half of mothers with children under the age of 3 were in the work force, few employers were providing any child-care assistance.[29] Government support has been far too limited to fill the gap.[30]

For women, the lack of flexible scheduling options, temporary leave provisions, and child-care services carry significant occupational consequences. Short-term losses result when a female employee finds it necessary to forgo promotional and training opportunities, or leaves a particular job, together with its seniority and benefit provisions. Long-term costs result from a woman's discontinuous work history, which makes advancement within the best-paying job sectors more difficult. Those with substantial family commitments are rarely able to reach positions with greatest decision-making power in either the public or private sector. As a consequence, policies governing parental leave, working schedules, child care, and related issues are made by those individuals who are least likely to have experienced significant work-family conflicts. The solution is not "mommy tracks" that risk becoming mommy traps. If our concern is both promoting equality between the sexes and improving the quality of life for both of them, more fundamental gender-neutral initiatives are needed.

The details of more effective strategies for dependent care have been addressed elsewhere[31] and need not be reviewed here. Rather, what bears emphasis is the importance of both public- and private-sector initiatives in these areas. A useful first step would be federal legislation guaranteeing temporary leave for childbirth or dependent care, with wage replacement by employers or unemployment compensation packages. More incentives should be available for development of child-care programs, flexible scheduling alternatives, and meaningful part-time work.

THE LEGAL RESPONSE

As in other contexts, the law's primary approach to these occupational issues has focused on gender differences rather than gender disadvantages. The goal has been to prevent those with comparable abilities from experiencing different and unequal treatment because of sex. Under the equal protection guarantee of the Fourteenth Amendment, courts have prohibited various forms of intentional discrimination. Title VII of the Civil Rights Act bars both intentionally discriminatory actions and certain conduct that, while neutral on its face, has a disproportionate, adverse impact on women and is not justified by business necessity. Various legislative and administrative regulations have also required those receiving governmental contracts or assistance to implement affirmative action programs.[32] Taken together, these remedies have played a critical role in expanding women's employment opportunities. This approach has not, however, adequately confronted some of the deeper institutional and ideological forces that contribute to gender disadvantage.

Part of the problem stems from the law's frequent focus on individual intent and its reluctance to scrutinize conduct that does not seem specifically designed to discriminate against women. Given the unconscious level at which much gender bias operates, together with the costs—both financial and psychological—of initiating legal action, such a framework is highly limited. Similar limitations follow from the inadequacy of governmental and private employer support for strong forms of affirmative action or pay equity. Although the latter two issues have generated a vast literature that cannot be fully summarized here, a few general observations bear attention.

AFFIRMATIVE ACTION

Affirmative action strategies take a variety of forms, ranging from largely process-oriented requirements (such as special recruitment and training procedures) to preferential treatment for those individuals who are basically qualified for particular positions and who are members of underrepresented groups. The strongest requirements have typically grown out of court orders or litigation settlements; weaker forms have resulted from voluntary employer action or federal executive orders requiring government contractors and grantees to establish goals and timetables for employing underrepresented groups. Although such programs have been critical in securing progress for women and minorities, their implementation has been hampered by difficulties in evaluating compliance[33] and by opposition based on moral principles and practical consequences.

As a matter of principle, critics contend, gender- or race-based remedies subvert the premise they are seeking to establish; to assign preferences based on immutable and involuntary characteristics is to reinforce precisely the kind of criteria that society should seek to eliminate. Such preferences, opponents believe, also comprise fundamental concepts of individual merit and entitlement by penalizing white male job applicants who were not responsible for prior invidious treatment. To many observers, the case for preferential treatment for white women is particularly weak because they have not been subject to the same economic, educational, and cultural deprivations as racial and ethnic minorities.[34]

It is, of course, true that affirmative action disregards claims to be treated as an individual, not as a member of a particular racial or sexual group. But arguments that hold such claims preeminent come several generations early and several centuries late. Group treatment has been a pervasive feature of America's social, economic, and political landscape, and has exposed women as well as minorities to systematic deprivations. To equate a limited and temporary form of discrimination against a privileged group with pervasive and lasting discrimination against unprivileged groups is to obscure the most basic cultural meanings and consequences that flow from such treatment.

Differential treatment of white male employees neither reinforces cumulative disadvantages nor infringes on any right to treatment solely on the basis of individual merit. Most employment decision making already incorporates some factors that do not represent merit in any objectively measurable sense, such as personal connections and unconscious stereotypes. Particularly in upper-level positions, what job qualifications are most critical and which candidates possess them are often open to dispute. The increased representation of women and minorities, whose experience differs from their white male colleagues, may enrich the standards by which merit is measured. To take an obvious example, female academics may offer different perspectives on traditional intellectual paradigms than their male counterparts. The contributions of women's studies programs over the last two decades underscore the point.

Comparable difficulties surround critics' pragmatic objections to affirmative action. According to opponents, singling out women for special assistance can reinforce the very assumptions that society strives to dispel. From this perspective, de facto quotas will encourage selection of those who cannot succeed by conventional criteria and thus compromise organizational efficiency and entrench adverse stereotypes. Or, if women do perform effectively in a context of preferential treatment, their performance will be devalued. As long as the beneficiaries of affirmative action appear unable to advance without special favors, prejudices will remain unaffected.

Such claims are problematic on several levels. Since virtually all preferential treatment programs assist only those candidates who are basically qualified for the jobs at issue, the extent of efficiency losses is difficult to measure. Objective qualifications such as grades in school have notoriously poor predictive value. Nor has any systematic evidence demonstrated significant declines in job performance as the result of affirmative action programs.[35]

Although the stigma some individuals attach to affirmative action beneficiaries should not be discounted, neither should it be overvalued. The current underrepresentation of women and minorities in positions of influence is also stigmatizing. Former Assistant Attorney General Barbara Babcock put the point directly when asked how she felt about gaining her position because she was a woman. As she noted, "It feels better than being denied the position because you're a woman."[36]

To attain a social order in which wealth, power, and status are not distributed by gender, it is first necessary to dispel the stereotypes contributing to this distribution. Affirmative action advances that effort by placing a critical mass of women and minorities in nontraditional positions. More than a few isolated role models are necessary to counteract the latent prejudices and socialization processes that have perpetuated occupational inequalities.[37]

Such considerations argue for strengthening affirmative action at all levels. But neither should the limitations of this approach be overlooked. A fundamental concern is that preferential treatment will secure only entry- or token-level representation for the most upwardly mobile employees and thus help more to legitimatize than to challenge existing organizational values. In order to secure not just access to but alteration of existing workplace structures, other strategies are also essential.

PAY EQUITY

As a conceptual framework, comparable worth or pay equity has historical analogues in the medieval notions of a "just price." As a practical strategy, the concept gained support in the United States during the late 1970s and 1980s. Its primary objective has been to challenge pay disparities between male and female jobs that cannot be justified by factors relevant to employment performance and conditions. As pay equity advocates have noted, current wage scales reveal hosts of examples not readily squared with merit principles: public school teachers who earn less than state liquor store clerks, nurses who earn less than tree trimmers or sign painters, and librarians who earn less than crossing guards and water meter readers.[38]

Most alternative approaches rely on forms of job evaluation and are often lumped under the generic title of comparable worth. One type of job evaluation involves a *policy-capturing* technique. This approach focuses on the *relative* worth assigned to particular positions under existing wage rates, either the employer's own rates or those of similarly situated employers. Under this approach, employers identify factors relevant to compensation and score jobs in terms of those factors (such as skills, responsibility, and working conditions). Then, statistical regression techniques are used to assess the relative importance of such factors in predicting current wages and to establish a weight for each factor. Each job receives a rating based on its weighted characteristics.

This ranking can serve as the basis for adjusting pay scales or setting salaries for new jobs, although employers may make further modifications in response to market forces. To pay equity advocates, the policy-capturing approach is primarily useful in identifying racial or gender biases in application of the employer's own evaluation system. For example, statistical analysis can identify the importance an employer attaches to particular factors in male-dominated or gender-integrated jobs and then can determine whether the same factors command the same financial reward in female-dominated positions.

From a pay equity standpoint, the strength of this system is also the source of its limitation. By relying on the employer's own standards for establishing relative value, a policy-capturing technique avoids more subjective and divisive issues about the intrinsic value of particular jobs. It demands only that employers be consistent in application of their own weighting system across job categories, regardless of the gender, race, and ethnicity of employees and the pay at which they are willing to work. However, since a policy-capturing system uses existing wage rates to assess the relative importance of job characteristics, it will reflect gender and racial biases that have traditionally affected those rates.[39]

A more fundamental challenge to current salary-setting procedures is possible through techniques that focus on *intrinsic* worth. Under this approach, employers generally begin by defining the set of factors and factor weights that ought serve as the basis for pay differentials. Typically, this system will rank job characteristics such as skill, effort, responsibility, and working conditions, and then assign points to particular jobs based on their weighted characteristics. Compensation levels can then be adjusted to ensure parity between different jobs with similar ratings. By valuing job characteristics without explicit reference to employers' existing salaries or market rates, such techniques often expose underpayment of predominately female occupations. Although employers can adjust their compensation structures to reflect market pay rates as well as their own rankings, an a priori system has the advantage of making such adjustments visible.[40]

To varying degrees, both these relative and intrinsic worth approaches can call into question current wage structures. By the mid-1980s, one or both frameworks were influential in shaping comparable worth litigation, legislative lobbying, and collective bargaining strategies. For some, however, these approaches present a range of problems. The primary difficulty centers on how to define worth. In the United States, salaries are not based solely on relatively objective factors such as the skill, responsibility, and working conditions a job entails; the most cursory comparison of income levels for cabinet officials and fashion models makes the point directly. Pay structures also reflect the scarcity of labor supply and subjective judgments about merit.

Such subjectivity is especially visible in a priori intrinsic worth approaches. Gender biases can enter at any number of points: in the choice and weighting factors to be compensated, in their application to a given job, and in the standards for determining exemptions. How much weight should evaluators accord to particular skills and working conditions? By what criteria should skill be determined?

Some of the difficulties became obvious in one reevaluation study for salaried New York public employees. That study concluded that acquired (and hence compensable) abilities were necessary for zoo keepers in charge of baby animals, but that only innate (and hence noncompensable) abilities were necessary for day-care attendants responsible for human infants.[41] To critics, the fuzziness surrounding concepts of job value becomes particularly troubling if comparable worth becomes a major litigation tool in securing occupational equality. Experts using different evaluation systems often come up with quite different rankings for the same job. For courts to preside over battles among experts with no principled basis for choosing between them could impose substantial uncertainties, inconsistencies, and legal costs.

Moreover, to the extent that job reevaluation calls for major upward adjustments in women's salaries, opponents raise further objections. Business leaders typically argue that comparable worth will increase inefficiency and unemployment, decrease competitiveness with foreign manufacturers, encourage women to remain in predominately female-dominated occupations, and redistribute limited salary resources in favor of white middle-class women at the expense of lower-class minority men.[42]

However, both the magnitude and the distribution of such adverse consequences are open to question. Criticism of the "subjectivity" of comparable worth procedures tends to ignore the biases reflected in current wage structures, biases that already distort responses to labor supply and demand. Subjectivity is what we now have; the fact that it is embedded in existing market dynamics does not render it morally just or economically essential. Estimates of the aggregate price of pay equity have ranged between $2 billion and $150 billion, and projections of efficiency and GNP losses reflect similar variations.[43]

On the whole, available research suggests that the costs of pay equity have often been overestimated and the potential benefits underestimated. While comprehensive long-term data are lacking, it does not appear that the growing number of employers in the United States and abroad who have implemented comparable worth reforms have triggered the kinds of inflation, inefficiency, unemployment, or regressive distributional consequences that pay equity opponents generally claim. The typical costs of U.S. reforms, when phased in over a number of years, have been around 5 percent to 10 percent of employers' total wage rates.[44]

Moreover, the same job-evaluation procedures that have exposed evidence of gender bias often have revealed evidence of racial bias as well, and the resulting adjustments have benefited groups disadvantaged on both counts.[45] Although evidence concerning class is more mixed, some broad-scale comparable worth initiatives have suggested that job evaluation procedures are more likely to reveal overcompensation in male-dominated white-collar, not blue-collar, jobs.[46] Whatever short-term costs some workers sustain as a result of job reevaluations must also be measured against the potential long-term gains of making compensation criteria explicit and a subject for collective bargaining and organizing strategies.

Much of the objection to pay equity could be minimized if implementation occurred gradually, with some sensitivity to its costs and to the respective competencies of various decision makers: courts, legislatures, and participants in collective bargaining. It is well within judges' capabilities and statutory authority to enforce principles of relative worth and to hold employers accountable for salary discrimination that cannot be justified by their own evaluation criteria. Issues of intrinsic worth—that is, judgments about what criteria are most important and how those judgments should be made—can be addressed primarily through political and collective bargaining processes.

As with affirmative action, the most substantial risks of comparable worth are not those that conservatives invoke. The danger is less that it will prove too radical than that it will not prove radical enough. One disquieting possibility is that some narrow vision of pay equity will prevail, and that concerns about gender will overshadow concerns about race, class, and ethnicity. Narrow incremental reform strategies could result in a modified compensation hierarchy under which the haves still come out far ahead, but with more women among them. A related concern is that short-term political objectives could obscure broader normative issues. By cloaking job evaluation with a mantle of seemingly "scientific" objectivity, comparable worth adjustments could insulate wage hierarchies from more searching review.[47]

A more hopeful alternative is that pay equity initiatives will focus attention on fundamental questions not only of gender equality but of social priorities. How should various job and worker attributes be rewarded and how much differentiation across salary levels is appropriate? Are we comfortable with a society that pays more for jobs such as parking attendant than for those such as child-care attendant, whatever their male/female composition? Exploring the dynamics of comparable worth can enrich our understanding of class and gender inequalities and of the strategies best able to reduce them.[48]

Inspired by a social vision that emphasizes collective responsibility rather than individual competition, job reevaluation could become a strategy for narrowing economic inequality. It could also prompt a reassessment of paid and unpaid work traditionally done by women. From that vantage, comparable worth is potentially a radical concept, but not in the sense most critics claim. It need not invite the kind of centralized planning reflected in current state-run economies, which have scarcely dispensed with wage hierarchies or ensured gender equality. Rather, pay equity initiatives could help spark a rethinking of the scope of inequality and the ideologies that sustain it.

EMPLOYMENT POLICY AND STRUCTURAL CHANGE

If occupational equity is to become a serious national commitment, expressed in social policy as well as in political rhetoric, an array of strategies extending beyond antidiscrimination, affirmative action, or comparable worth mandates is needed. Women's subordinate labor-force status is a function of various factors, including sex-role socialization, workplace structures, and domestic constraints. Effective policy responses will require an equally varied set of public- and private-sector initiatives and a more systematic attempt to assess their relative success.

Although law has limited influence on socialization processes, it could play a more constructive role. Government-funded education, counseling, and vocational and job training programs often affect occupational choices. Yet despite formal mandates of gender equality, such programs have often served more to perpetuate than to counteract sex-role stereotypes.

Vocational education remains highly gender segregated, as do placements under government-sponsored job training programs.[49] Efforts to improve women's math and science skills and to interest men in traditionally female vocations have been at best sporadic. Too few financial incentives have been available to private employers for programs that challenge occupational segregation through recruitment, training, counseling, and restructured promotion ladders that bridge male- and female-dominated job sectors. All of these areas require greater governmental resources and more systematic study.[50]

Finally, and perhaps most fundamentally, employment-related issues must be conceived as part of a broader political agenda. Men's and women's positions in the labor market are affected by a wide array of public policies concerning education, housing, welfare, tax structure, and social services. Too many of these policies reflect outmoded assumptions about women's secondary labor-force status; too few address the structural problems that still confine many women to that role. For almost a century, some feminists have sought programs that were better designed to accommodate public and private life: cooperative residential housing, child care and homemaker services, and integrated urban planning sensitive to the needs of single parents and dual-career couples. Current demographic trends have invested such policies with new urgency, not only to promote gender equality in this generation but to provide decent environments for the next.

NOTES

1. National Committee on Pay Equity, *Briefing on the Wage Gap* (Washington, D.C.: National Committee on Pay Equity, 1989).

2. S. B. Kamerman and A. J. Kahn, *The Responsive Workplace* (New York: Columbia University Press, 1987).

3. D. L. Rhode, "The No-Problem Problem: Feminist Challenges and Cultural Change," *Yale Law Review* 100 (1991): 1731; and "Women at Work, Fact Sheet," Women's Work Force Network of Wider Opportunities for Women, National Commission on Working Women (Washington, D.C.: Winter 1990).

4. B. F. Reskin and H. I. Hartmann, *Women's Work, Men's Work: Sex Segregation on the Job* (Washington, D.C.: National Academy Press, 1986).

5. J. Malveaux, "Gender Difference and Beyond: An Economic Perspective on Diversity and Commonality Among Women," in *Theoretical Perspectives on Sexual Difference*, ed. D. L. Rhode (New Haven, Conn.: Yale University Press, 1990); and P. Rothenberg, *Racism and Sexism: An Integrated Study* (New York: St. Martin's Press, 1988).

6. A. H. Beller, "Occupational Segregation and the Earnings Gap," in *Comparable Worth: Issue for the 80's*, Volume I (Washington, D.C.: U.S. Commission on Civil Rights, 1984).

7. U.S. Bureau of the Census, *Census of Population, 1960, Volume One, Characteristics of the Population: U.S. Summary* (Washington, D.C.: U.S. Government Printing Office, 1964); U.S. Bureau of Labor Statistics, *Employment and Earnings* (Washington, D.C.: U.S. Government Printing Office, 1989); and Rhode, 1991.

8. Rhode, 1991; J. Abramson and B. Franklin, *Where Are They Now: The Women of Harvard Law* (Garden City, N.Y.: Doubleday, 1986); and American Bar Association, "Commission on Women in the Professions," *Report to the House of Delegates* (Chicago, Ill: American Bar Association, 1988).

9. C. Marano, "Prepared Statement for the Subcommittee on Employment Opportunities of the Committee on Education and Labor, U.S. House of Representatives, 2d Session," *Hearing on Women in the Workforce: Supreme Court Issues* (Washington, D.C.: U.S. Government Printing Office, 1986).

10. W. T. Bielby and J. N. Baron, "A Woman's Place Is with Other Women: Sex Segregation within Organizations," in *Sex Segregation in the Workplace: Trends, Explanations, Remedies,* ed. B. F. Reskin (Washington, D.C.: National Academy Press, 1984).

11. G. Becker, *Human Capital,* Second Edition (New York: Columbia University Press, 1975); and F. D. Blau, "Occupational Segregation and the Earnings Gap," in *Comparable Worth: Issue for the 80's,* 1984.

12. G. Duncan, *Years of Poverty, Years of Plenty* (Ann Arbor: University of Michigan, Survey Research Center, Institute for Social Research, 1984); H. I. Hartmann, P. A. Roos, and D. J. Treiman, "An Agenda for Basic Research on Comparable Worth," in *Comparable Worth: New Directions for Research,* ed. H. I. Hartmann (Washington, D.C.: National Academy Press, 1985); and H. J. Aaron and C. M. Lougy, *The Comparable Worth Controversy* (Washington, D.C.: Brookings, 1986).

13. D. R. Kaufman and B. L. Richardson, *Achievement and Women: Challenging the Assumptions* (New York: The Free Press, 1982); M. T. Mednick, "Women and the Psychology of Achievement: Implications for Personal and Social Change," in *Women in the Work Force,* ed. H. J. Bernadin (New York: Praeger, 1982); Reskin and Hartmann, 1986; and A. Hochschild and A. Machung, *The Second Shift: Working Parents and the Revolution at Home* (New York: Viking Press, 1989).

14. A. Mirande and E. Enriquez, *La Chicana* (Chicago: University of Chicago Press, 1979).

15. Reskin and Hartmann, 1986; P. A. Roos and B. Reskin, "Institutional Factors Contributing to Sex Segregation in the Workplace," in *Sex Segregation in the Workplace: Trends, Explanations, Remedies,* ed. B. F. Reskin, 1984; and D. L. Rhode, *Justice and Gender* (Cambridge, Mass.: Harvard University Press, 1989).

16. Rhode, 1991; and Hochschild and Machung, 1989.

17. G. Becker, *The Economics of Discrimination,* Second Edition (Chicago: University of Chicago Press, 1971).

18. J. Matthaei, *An Economic History of Women in America* (New York: Shocken, 1982).

19. *Caribbean Marine Services v. Baldridge,* 844 F2d 668 (9th Cir. 1988).

20. For example, recent data suggest that men and women with comparable qualifications holding comparable jobs do not have different turnover

rates in most job contexts (L. J. Waite and S. E. Berryman, *Women in Non-Traditional Occupations: Choice and Turnover* [Santa Monica, Calif.: Rand, 1985]; Reskin and Hartmann, 1986).

21. D. J. Treiman and H. I. Hartmann, *Women, Work, and Wages: Equal Pay for Jobs of Equal Value* (Washington, D.C.: National Academy Press, 1981).

22. B. Lott, "The Devaluation of Women's Competence," *Journal of Social Issues* 41 (Winter 1984): 51–58; Rhode, 1989; Rhode, 1991; and S. T. Shepela and A. T. Viviano, "Some Psychological Factors Affecting Sex Discrimination and Wages," in *Comparable Worth and Wage Discrimination*, ed. H. Remick (Philadelphia: Temple University Press, 1984).

23. N. Aisenberg and M. Harrington, *Women of Academe* (Amherst: University of Massachusetts Press, 1988); American Bar Association, 1988; R. M. Kanter, *Men and Women of the Corporation* (New York: Basic Books, 1977).

24. J. Fernandez, *Racism and Sexism in Corporate Life* (Lexington, Mass.: Lexington Books, 1981); C. R. Lawrence, "The Id, the Ego, and Equal Protection: Reckoning with Unconscious Racism," *Stanford Law Review* 39 (1987): 317–388; and Rothenberg, 1988.

25. C. MacKinnon, *Sexual Harassment of Working Women: A Case of Sex Discrimination* (New Haven, Conn.: Yale University Press, 1979); and S. Estrich, "Sex at Work," *Stanford Law Review* 43 (1991): 813.

26. *Meritor Savings Bank FSB v. Binson*, 477 U.S. 57 (1986); *Roberts v. United States Jaycees*, 468 U.S. 628 (1984); *New York State Club Association v. City of New York*, 108 S. Ct. 2225 (1988); and D. L. Rhode, "Association and Assimilation," *Northwestern Law Review* I (Fall 1986): 106–145.

27. D. L. Rhode, "Sexual Harassment," *Southern California Law Review* 65 (1992): 1459–1466.

28. C. F. Epstein, *Deceptive Distinction: Sex, Gender, and the Social Order* (New Haven, Conn.: Yale University Press, 1988); R. J. Menges and W. H. Exum, "Barriers to the Progress of Women and Minority Faculty," *Journal of Higher Education* 54 (March/April 1983): 123–144; Rhode, 1989; and Rhode, 1991.

29. Employee Benefit Research Institute (EBRI), *Issue Brief* 85 (December 1988): 15.

30. M. H. Strober and S. N. Dornbusch, "Public Policy Alternatives," in *Feminism, Children, and the New Families*, ed. S. N. Dornbusch and M. H. Strober (New York: Guilford Press, 1988).

31. N. Dowd, "Work and Family: Restructuring the Workplace," *Arizona Law Review* 32 (1990): 431; and Strober and Dornbush, 1988.

32. The most important regulations have been the Equal Pay Act of 1963, 29 U.S.C. Section 206 (banning sex discrimination in wages); Title VII of the

Civil Rights Act of 1964 (prohibiting sex discrimination in hiring, advancement, termination, and related terms of employment); and Executive Order 11375 (requiring federal contractors to establish affirmative action programs for women).

33. For example, disputes often arise about how to define the relevant applicant pool, which individuals best satisfy given job requirements, and what counts as sufficient good-faith efforts to meet goals and timetables (see E. Bartholet, "Application of Title VII to Jobs in High Places," *Harvard Law Review* 95 [March 1982]: 947–1027).

34. W. E. Block and M. A. Walker, *Discrimination, Affirmative Action, and Equal Opportunity: An Economic and Social Perspective* (Vancouver: The Fraser Institute, 1982); and A. H. Goldman, *Justice and Reverse Discrimination* (Princeton, N.J.: Princeton University Press, 1979).

35. Citizens' Commission on Civil Rights, *Affirmative Action: To Open the Doors of Job Opportunity, A Policy of Fairness and Compassion That Has Worked* (Washington, D.C.: Citizens' Commission on Civil Rights, 1984); and R. H. Fallon, "To Each According to His Ability; From None According to His Race; The Concept of Merit in the Law of Antidiscrimination," *Boston University Law Review* 60 (November 1980): 815–877.

36. Rhode, 1989.

37. B. Gutek, ed., *Sex Role Stereotyping and Affirmative Action Policy* (Los Angeles, Calif.: Institute of Industrial Relations, 1982); and M. M. Marini and M. C. Brinton, "Sex Typing in Occupational Socialization," in *Sex Segregation in the Workplace: Trends, Explanations, Remedies*, ed. B. F. Reskin, 1984.

38. D. L. Kirp, M. Strong, and M. G. Yudof, *Gender Justice* (Chicago: University of Chicago Press, 1985); and D. Savage, "San Jose's Equal Pay Plan Survives," *Los Angeles Times* (September 12, 1983).

39. C. A. Clauss, "Comparable Worth: The Theory, Its Legal Foundation, and the Feasibility of Implementation," *Journal of Law Reform* 20 (Fall 1986): 7–97; M. R. Killingsworth, "The Economics of Comparable Worth: Analytic, Empirical, and Policy Questions," in *Comparable Worth: New Directions for Research*; and R. J. Steinberg, "Identifying Wage Discrimination and Implementing Pay Equity Adjustments," in *Comparable Worth: Issue for the 80's*.

40. Clauss, 1986; and H. Remick and R. Steinberg, "Technical Possibilities and Political Realities: Concluding Remarks," in *Comparable Worth and Wage Discrimination*, ed. H. Remick (Philadelphia: Temple University Press, 1984).

41. D. Lauter, "How to Factor the Value of Workers' Skills," *National Law Journal* (January 2, 1984): 24.

42. M. E. Gold, *A Dialogue on Comparable Worth* (Ithaca, N.Y.: ILR Press, 1983); D. Fishel and E. P. Lazear, "Comparable Worth and Discrimination in Labor Markets," *University of Chicago Law Review* 53 (Summer 1986): 891–952; and P. Weiler, "The Wages of Sex: Limits of Comparable Worth," *Harvard Law Review* 99 (June 1986): 1718–1807.

43. Remick and Steinberg, 1984.

44. H. I. Hartmann, "Comparable Worth and Women's Economic Independence," in *Ingredients for Women's Employment Policy*, ed. C. Bose and G. Spitze (Albany: State University of New York Press, 1987).

45. National Committee on Pay Equity, *Pay Equity: An Issue of Race, Ethnicity, and Sex* (Washington, D.C.: National Committee on Pay Equity, 1987); and J. Scales-Trent, "Comparable Worth: Is This a Theory for Black Workers?" *Women's Rights Law Reporter* 8 (Winter 1984): 51–58.

46. Clauss, 1986.

47. J. Acker, *Doing Comparable Worth: Gender, Class, and Pay Equity* (Philadelphia: Temple University Press, 1989); and S. Evans and B. Nelson, *Wage Justice: Comparable Worth and the Paradox of Technocratic Reform* (Chicago: University of Chicago Press, 1989).

48. Rhode, 1989.

49. Reskin and Hartmann, 1986; and Roos and Reskin, 1984.

50. Reskin and Hartmann, 1986.

GIRLS, GENDER, AND SCHOOLS: EXCERPTS FROM *THE AAUW REPORT: HOW SCHOOLS SHORTCHANGE GIRLS*

*Susan McGee Bailey, Lynn Burbridge, Patricia Campbell,
Barbara Jackson, Fern Marx, and Peggy McIntosh*

In February 1990, President Bush and the National Governors' Association enunciated a series of ambitious education goals to be met by the year 2000.[1] The following year, *America 2000* was presented by the president and the Department of Education as a "plan to move every community in America toward these goals."[2] None of the strategies proposed in *America 2000* is gender-specific. Twenty years after the passage of Title IX of the Education Amendments of 1972 prohibiting discrimination on the basis of sex in educational programs receiving federal funding, girls are still absent from the national education agenda. Yet as the National Coalition for Women and Girls in Education has repeatedly noted, the National Education Goals cannot be met without specific attention to girls.[3]

The AAUW Report: How Schools Shortchange Girls, a comprehensive review of research on the participation, achievement, and treatment of girls in U.S. public schools, was funded by the American Association of University Women Educational Foundation and published by them in February 1992. The report was written by a team of researchers at the Wellesley College Center for Research on Women, headed by Center Director Susan McGee Bailey. Bailey was the principal author of the report which was coauthored by Lynn Burbridge, Patricia Campbell, Barbara Jackson, Fern Marx, and Peggy McIntosh. This chapter is excerpted from the report. A fuller discussion of the issues addressed here as well as further data and analysis on topics not included in this chapter, such as teen pregnancy, health and sex education, special education, vocational education, and extracurricular activities and sports, is contained in the original report.

OVERVIEW

The absence of attention to girls in the current education reform debate suggests that differences between and among girls and boys are irrelevant to education. But whether one looks at achievement scores, curricular design, self-esteem levels, or staffing patterns, it is clear that sex and gender make a difference in the nation's public elementary and secondary schools.*

Rather than acknowledging and exploring gender differences, the current debate ignores them. Report after report refers to "students" or "youth" or "eighth graders"—sex unspecified. This lack of specificity perpetuates the invisibility of girls and compromises the education of our nation's students. By ignoring the strengths and contributions as well as the educational needs of girls, the current debate is shortchanging not only our daughters but our sons as well.

Serious consideration of girls is not merely a matter of justice and accuracy; it is an issue of economic survival and basic common sense. Today's students are tomorrow's citizens, parents, and workers. It is they who will bear the responsibility for maintaining a vital and creative society. To ignore or overlook girls, to leave them on the sidelines in discussions of educational reform, is to deprive ourselves of the full potential of half of our work force, half of our citizenry, and at least half of the parents of the next generation.

Furthermore, when we ignore girls we lose sight of critical aspects of social development that our culture has traditionally assigned to women, but which are equally important for men. Girls *and* boys must be prepared for the relational worlds of family and community as well as for the more public worlds of employment and politics.

* The terms *sex* and *gender* are often used interchangeably. Throughout the report, we tried to use *sex* only when referring to individuals as biologically female or male and *gender* when referring also to different sets of expectations and limitations imposed by society on girls and boys simply because they are female or male. Despite our attempts to maintain these distinctions, the report reviewed research by many authors, and thus our usage usually conforms to that of the research we report.

YOUNG GIRLS: THE PRESCHOOL EXPERIENCE

By the time children of three or older enter a child-care or preschool setting, they already have experiences and skills that influence their perceptions and actions. In a discussion of sex equity in early child-hood education environments, Selma Greenberg of Hofstra University notes that young girls and boys have often acquired different skills and thus have different educational needs.[4]

There is a commonly held myth that early education environments meet the needs of girls better than boys.[5] But, rather than being better for girls, it would appear that many schools engage girls in activities in which they are already more proficient than are young boys. The traditional working assumption at the preschool level is that children need impulse control training, small muscle development, and language enhancement to be successful in their early years in school. Since many girls tend to achieve competency in these areas before they arrive in group settings, teachers turn their attention toward boys whose development in these areas lags behind that of girls.[6]

Many activities that young boys choose, such as large motor activities and investigatory and experimental activities, are considered "free play" and are not part of the regular, structured curriculum. If young girls are not specifically encouraged to participate in these "boy" activities, they will not receive a full and balanced set of educational experiences.

ISSUES OF ACHIEVEMENT

There is considerable evidence that girls get higher grades than boys throughout their school careers.[7] Test scores, however, because they measure all students on exactly the same material and are available nationally, are the measures most often used to discuss sex differences in achievement. The latest work on achievement differences presents a rather different picture from much of what has been reported and accepted in the past. The traditional wisdom that girls are better in verbal areas while boys excel in quantitative skills is less true today. Data indicate a narrowing of sex differences in tested achievement on a variety of measures. However, a narrowing of differences is not an absence of differences. Important insights can be gained by looking carefully at the continuing gender gaps in educational achievement and participation. Furthermore, research that looks at sex, race, ethnicity, and socioeconomic status (SES) reveals critical vulnerabilities among various groups of girls.

LANGUAGE ARTS AND READING

Research does not entirely support the still-common assumption that girls do better in verbal areas than do boys. Almost 20 years ago Eleanor Maccoby and Carol Jacklin challenged the prevailing view that girls performed better than boys on verbal measures in their early years.[8] However, researchers continued to document that girls outscored boys on tests of verbal ability starting at grade 5 or 6.[9] Recent work indicates that sex differences in verbal abilities have decreased markedly. Researchers completing a meta-analysis* comparing earlier studies of verbal abilities with more recent research conclude: "There are not gender differences in verbal ability at least at this time, in American culture, in the standard ways that verbal ability has been measured."[10]

A review of three representative surveys of reading skills indicates a mixed picture. In two major surveys—the National Assessment of Educational Progress (NAEP) and the National Education Longitudinal Survey (NELS)—girls perform better than boys on reading tests. In the High School and Beyond Survey (HSB) boys perform better than girls on reading and vocabulary tests. In all three surveys, the sex differences are very small.

One possible explanation for the differences in these surveys is that sex differences narrow as children grow older. This would be consistent with the very small difference found for 17-year-olds in the NAEP and the gains boys make relative to girls in the follow-up of the HSB cohort.[11]

Another explanation is that these differences may reflect differences in the tests given for each survey. The tests were shorter for HSB and much more comprehensive in the NAEP. If this is the explanation, it serves as another example of how apparent gender differences may actually reflect test differences, rather than differences in knowledge or ability.

Even within the NAEP reading test, the performance of boys relative to girls varied depending on the type of reading exercise. Boys did as well as girls on the expository passages and were most disad-

* Very simply put, meta-analysis is a statistical analysis of data from many different studies of the same topic that focuses on the relative size of the differences between groups or the "effects" of the study.

vantaged relative to girls in the literary passages. This is consistent with the finding that boys read more nonfiction than girls and girls read more fiction than boys.[12] This is also consistent with the finding that boys do slightly better than girls on other NAEP tests in subjects requiring good skills in expository reading and writing: civics, history, and geography.[13]

MATH AND SCIENCE

Goal four of the National Education Goals developed by the National Governors' Association in 1990 states, "By the year 2000, U.S. students will be the first in the world in science and mathematics achievement." If the United States is to remain competitive in world markets, the nation must have a technologically competent work force. Furthermore, American democracy cannot flourish in the twenty-first century without a scientifically literate citizenry. Thus, the achievement and participation of girls—and of boys from all racial and ethnic groups—in science and math is a topic of considerable importance to policymakers in business and industry as well as education.

MATH   Gender differences in mathematics achievement are small and declining. Recent meta-analyses find only very small differences in female and male performance in mathematics. Furthermore, meta-analyses comparing recent research with studies done in 1974 indicate a significant decline in gender differences.[14]

Gender differences in mathematics *do* exist, but are related to the age of the sample, how academically selective it is, and which cognitive level the test is tapping. Indeed, these three variables were found to account for 87 percent of the variance in one meta-analysis. For example, no gender differences were found in problem-solving ability in elementary and middle school girls and boys though moderate to small differences favoring males emerged in high school.[15] Large research studies support these results, finding no gender differences in math performance at age 9, minimal differences at age 13, and a larger difference favoring males at age 17. The most recent NAEP report finds few sex differences in grades 4 and 8 other than a higher average proficiency in measurement and estimation for boys. However, by grade 12, males showed a small advantage in every content area except algebra.

Larger differences are found at the higher academic and cognitive levels. For example, an earlier NAEP reported that 8.2 percent of the males but only 4.5 percent of the females were at the highest math levels, while 54 percent of the males and 48 percent of the females could do moderately complex procedures and reasoning.[16] The College Board reports that males in 1988 scored an average of 37 points higher than females on the Level I Math Achievement Test and 38 points higher on the Level II Math Achievement Test.[17]

Although less work has been done on the interaction of sex and ethnicity, that which has been done indicates that the patterns may differ for various groups. A study in Hawaii found nonwhite girls outperforming boys in math achievement and outnumbering boys in the highest achieving groups. Other studies have reported fewer gender differences in mathematics for minority students than for white students.[18]

SCIENCE   Gender differences in science achievement are not decreasing and may be increasing. While meta-analyses of studies of gender and science have not been done, the NAEP does track science performance. Its results indicate that for 9- and 13-year-olds, the combination of a lag in performance of females and significant increases in the performance of males has increased gender differences in science achievement for these students between 1978 and 1986. NAEP reported that the gender differences in science achievement are largest for 17-year-olds, and these differences have not changed since 1978. The areas of largest male advantage are physics, chemistry, earth science, and space sciences.[19]

In addition, differences exist in levels of achievement. NAEP found only 5 percent of 17-year-old girls as compared to 10 percent of 17-year-old boys scoring at or above NAEP's "highest cognitive level," defined as students' ability to integrate specialized knowledge.[20] Achievement test scores show a similar pattern. The Educational Testing Service (ETS) reports that in 1988, males scored on average 29 points higher than females on Advanced Placement (AP) biology tests, an 11 point improvement over the 40 point difference found in 1981; this is the only science area tested by ETS where gender differences have declined. Males continue to score about 56 points higher than females on the 1988 AP physics tests.[21]

COURSE TAKING PATTERNS: MATH AND SCIENCE

Gender differences in math course participation are small, occur only in higher level courses, and appear to be stable. The National Science Board found that approximately the same percentages of females and males took the same math courses up to calculus, which was taken by 7.6 percent of the boys but only 4.7 percent of the girls.[22] The 1991

NAEP reports that for the District of Columbia and the 37 states participating in the study, "Up to Algebra III/Pre-Calculus and Calculus, there were no gender differences in either course taking or average proficiency."[23]

Gender differences in the number of science courses students take are small. However, the pattern of course-taking differs, with girls being more apt to take advanced biology and boys being more apt to take physics and advanced chemistry. From 1982 to 1987, the National Science Board reported the average number of science courses a male high school student received increased from 2.25 to 2.69 while for female students the increase was from 2.13 to 2.57. A variety of studies have reported boys taking anywhere from 0.12 to 0.2 more science courses than girls.[24]

Approximately the same numbers of females and males take biology I and chemistry I, but more males take physics. In 1987, the National Science Board reported 25.3 percent of the males but only 15 percent of the females took physics. This is, however, an improvement. In 1982 18.2 percent of the males but only 10 percent of the females enrolled in physics.[25]

CAREER PLANS AND CONTINUATION IN SCIENCE

Gender differences show up in career plans as well. For example, a study of Rhode Island seniors found that 64 percent of the young men who had taken physics and calculus were planning to major in science or engineering in college compared to only 18.6 percent of the young women who had taken these courses.[26]

Girls who do go on in scientific fields after high school report that the encouragement provided by their teachers is very important.[27] One study reports that girls who went on to study engineering felt that teachers encouraged them; unfortunately, they also felt that counselors discouraged them.[28] Clearly differential treatment on the basis of sex contributes to the differences reported here, but there are other factors as well.

As they grow, girls and boys have different science experiences. Girls are more apt to have done biology-related activities and less apt to have done mechanical and electrical activities.[29] One study found that by third grade, 51 percent of boys and 37 percent of girls had used microscopes while by eleventh grade 49 percent of males and 17 percent of females had used an electricity meter. Gender differences in science-related activities may be reinforced within schools if children are allowed always to select science topics based on familiarity or interest.

Eighth grade boys have been found to use more science instruments in class, particularly physical science tools, such as power supplies. Although 9-year-old girls express interest in many science activities, they do not do as many as boys. This gender difference continued through ages 13 and 17 and was paralleled by an increasingly negative view of science, science classes, and science careers.[30]

Gender differences in confidence are strongly correlated with continuation in math and science classes. Math confidence is the surety a student has of her or his ability to learn and perform well in mathematics. Math confidence has been found to be more highly correlated with math performance than any other affective variable.

Females more than males have been found to doubt their confidence in math.[31] The ETS reported that gender differences in perceptions of being good at math increased with age. Third grade girls and boys thought they were good in math in about the same percentages (64 vs. 66); by seventh grade, a gender difference existed (57 percent vs. 64 percent); by eleventh grade the gap had widened (48 percent vs. 60 percent).[32] In a classic study, researchers Elizabeth Fennema and Julia Sherman found a strong correlation between math achievement and confidence and found a drop in both girls' math confidence and their achievement in the middle school years.[33] This drop in confidence *preceded* a decline in achievement.

One result of this decline in confidence is a lowering of the role that competence plays in girls' decisions about continuing in math and science. Researchers found that competence was a more important prerequisite for the attainment of male career ambitions than it was for females.[34] That is, females and males drop out of math and science for different reasons. Males who drop out of math and science tend to do so because of a lack of competence; that is, they cannot do the work; many females who drop out do so *even though* they can do the work.

Other researchers have also found that males are more apt than females to attribute their success to ability, but that females do tend to attribute failure to lack of ability.[35] As boys get older, those who do not like math come to believe that they don't like it because the subject itself is "not useful." Girls interpret their problems with math as personal failures. Boys are more likely to attribute the problems to the subject area itself.[36]

Concern about the difficulty or competitiveness of the field can also be an issue. One study found that the competitiveness of engineering was seen by girls as a major barrier to women entering engineering.[37] This finding is supported by research that finds girls who see themselves as highly competitive more interested in taking math and science courses than other girls.[38] For boys, degree of competitiveness is not related to interest in taking math and science.

While most students who dislike math do so because they consider it too hard, most students who dislike science say science is "not interesting." However, as girls grow older the pattern revealed in math is repeated in science. Adolescent girls are more likely than adolescent boys to find science uninteresting. Adolescent boys are more likely than girls to discount the importance of science itself.[39]

In addition, males are more apt than females to envision themselves using math as adults.[40] In assessing what factors they used to decide whether to continue in math, students listed usefulness of math followed by their confidence in doing math and their enjoyment of math.[41]

Gender stereotyping also appears to influence whether girls persist in mathematics. Data from the NAEP indicate that girls who reject traditional gender roles have higher math achievement than girls who hold more stereotyped expectations. Moreover, young women in advanced math classes tend not to see math as a "male" subject.[42]

Meta-analysis of affective variables associated with taking math courses indicate that gender differences are all small with the exception of the view of math as "something men do." Boys and young men see math as very "male."[43] A longitudinal study that tested students at sixth, eighth, tenth, and twelfth grades found that for girls a view of math as "male" was negatively correlated with math achievement at each grade level. This was the only affective variable on which consistent gender differences were found.[44]

RACE, SEX, SES, AND ACADEMIC ACHIEVEMENT

Some research indicates that sex differences favoring girls may be more pronounced among low-income students. This suggests that sex differences can cut either way, depending on social class. Thus, gender studies are as necessary for understanding the educational needs of boys as they are for understanding the needs of girls.

Unfortunately, little recent data have been published that permit an examination of student achievement by sex, race or ethnicity, and SES. In addition, little information is available on sex differences and gender issues in key programs funded by the U.S. Department of Education. A literature search produced almost no recent information on differences among girls and boys in compensatory, Native American, or bilingual education programs. This is particularly disheartening considering that these programs constitute over 20 percent of the Department of Education budget, with compensatory education alone representing two-thirds of the budget of the Office of Elementary and Secondary Education. These programs play a crucial role in addressing the educational needs of low-income and minority students, although at current funding levels less than half of those eligible for these services are receiving them.[45]

A special analysis was conducted using data from the NELS of eighth graders for 1988 and the HSB sophomore cohort for 1980. These data allow us to look at how students' sex, race or ethnicity, and SES affect their grades, test scores in reading and mathematics, and post-school plans.

Data were examined for blacks, whites, Native Americans, Asian Americans, and Hispanics. They were grouped by sex and SES (high SES or low SES).[46] In some parts of the analysis, sample sizes were too small to report, particularly in the case of Asian Americans and Native Americans. The results are summarized below.[47]

SES is the best predictor of both grades and test scores, but there are important sex and racial or ethnic differences. As expected, girls get better grades than boys in both data sets, even when controlling for SES. Asian-American girls consistently perform better than any other race/sex group. One exception is high-SES black girls whose grades are similar to, rather than better than, their male counterparts in the HSB data.

Although there were numerous racial differences, many disappeared when students from the same socioeconomic group were compared. Among eighth graders, low-SES whites are *more* likely than similar blacks and Hispanics to have low grades, although this is not the case in the high school data. The data confirm what has been known for many years: SES, more than any other variable, predicts educational outcomes.[48]

The limits that SES sets on achievement are most obvious from observing test scores in reading and mathematics. The data were most dramatic in the eighth grade sample. Very few low-SES students scored in the advanced reading or in the advanced math category; very few high-SES students read below basic or had below basic math skills. This is true regardless of race or gender. Contrary to popular myth, low-SES Asian-American students did not do significantly better than other low-SES students, when looking at eighth graders' test scores.

Among eighth graders, low-SES girls are less likely to test below basic in reading and math than low-SES boys. However, high-SES girls are *not* more likely to be in advanced reading than high-SES boys and they are less likely to be in advanced math when compared to high-SES boys. Thus, there is a marked bipolarity in the relative achievement of eighth grade girls: At low-SES levels they are more likely to do better than boys and at high-SES levels they are only as likely and often less likely to do as well as boys.

The reasons for these findings require further examination. Are more resources devoted to high-SES boys relative to high-SES girls than are provided to low-SES boys relative to their female counterparts? Do low-SES boys perceive limitations on their future job prospects more so than girls, therefore deciding to invest less in their education? Does low SES have a differential effect on the development of boys? In the light of the current policy attention to the particular education problems of poor black and Hispanic boys, it is interesting to note that most low-SES boys do less well than girls regardless of race and that—whatever differences exist—they do not persist at higher socioeconomic levels, at least in terms of test scores.[49] This suggests that closer attention should be focused on the interaction of gender and social class, as well as race, on education outcomes.

The HSB data do not show any sex differences favoring girls in test scores, even among low-SES students. In the senior year follow-up of the sophomore sample, sex differences generally favor males.

This does not discount the findings in NELS. The eighth graders are a later cohort, tested in 1988; the HSB sample was tested in 1980 and represents high school sophomores who were eighth graders in 1978—a full ten years' difference in the samples. More importantly, an analysis of the HSB sample indicates that some low-SES males dropped out before the HSB sample was drawn; thus, the greater similarity in scores between girls and boys may result from the diminished presence of low-performing boys in the sample.[50] Nevertheless, the data show that those boys who do stay in school make real gains in test scores relative to girls as they approach graduation.

High-SES boys clearly do better than high-SES girls in high school. The biggest sex differences are found among high-SES black students: Boys are well ahead of girls in reading and math scores. This is not the result of boys' dropping out since this is minimal among high-SES students. Studies of black students in desegregated schools indicate, however, that black girls do not do as well as black boys in this environment, often feeling excluded and socially isolated. Insofar as high-SES black youngsters are more likely to be in desegregated schools, this literature may provide an answer to the relatively lower performance of high-SES black girls.[51]

The NELS data also show that low-SES boys are more likely to have repeated at least one grade compared to low-SES girls. An extraordinary one-third of all low-SES boys are held back at least one grade. In spite of the media attention placed specifically on black boys, 29 percent of low-SES black girls were held back at least one grade. Taking into account data indicating that boys are more likely to be assigned to special education classes, however, a clear case can be made that in lower grades—before some boys drop out and other boys mature—male students of low SES face considerable difficulties.

Although SES is the main cause of differences in grades and test scores, racial differences persist in both data sets. High-SES Asian-American boys and girls and high-SES white girls were more likely to receive higher grades. A similar pattern was found in the high school data. Racial differences in grades among low-SES students tended to be small, but high-SES whites and Asian Americans did better than their counterparts.

As with grades, comparing students from the same SES groups diminishes some, but not all, racial differences in test scores. Asian Americans and whites generally have higher test scores than blacks and Hispanics.

Various reasons for these differences have been suggested. First, racial and ethnic minorities are more likely to attend poor schools with fewer resources. The persistence of racial segregation in housing means that nonpoor blacks are more likely to live in poverty neighborhoods (and, therefore, attend schools in low-income neighborhoods) than are nonpoor whites.[52] Thus SES is not a perfect proxy for access to good schools. Second, teacher expectations and their interaction patterns in relation to minority boys and girls will affect outcomes. These patterns are discussed in greater detail later in this chapter. Third, research by John Ogbu suggests that children who feel that they will be consigned to low-caste jobs because of their race or caste status, regardless of what they do, will have little motivation to persist in school.[53] Educational achievement must be examined within the overall social-cultural context and its influences on children's expectations about school and work.

Even though the HSB data show that boys' test scores are similar to or better than those of their female counterparts, girls are more likely to express an interest in going to college than boys in the HSB data. This is particularly true among high-SES students, except among blacks where girls are more likely than boys to express an interest in college regardless of SES. Male seniors express a greater interest in work or the military right after school. Black males in particular, and Hispanic males to a lesser extent, express an interest in the military to a much greater extent than do whites, even when controlling for SES or when controlling for test scores. This suggests that black males may view the military as an alternative to college that provides a better chance for upward mobility.

These sex differences in college plans are exemplified by data on those taking AP exams.[54] Among those taking AP exams in 1990, 52 percent were girls. Moreover, black and Latina girls are more likely to take AP exams than their male counterparts (64 percent and 56 percent to 60 percent, respectively).[55] Further, SES alone does not explain the greater interest girls have in college. Most students taking AP exams will be high-SES students.

DROPPING OUT OF SCHOOL

The dropout rate has become a key indicator of success for schools. But reliable, comparable data on dropouts are not readily available. In fact, there is no standard definition of a school dropout and a variety of measures are used to calculate dropout rates. There are two sources for dropout data: the data collected by state and local education agencies and the information that can be obtained from large, national surveys. Data collected by state and local agencies have been criticized because of poor record keeping. Often students who merely transfer to other schools are recorded as dropouts, and students who return to school or to general equivalency diploma (GED) programs—after dropping out for a short period—continue to be counted as dropouts. As a result, the high school dropout rates recorded by many cities may be overstated.[56]

Dropout statistics can also be derived from large surveys of the U.S. population such as the Current Population Survey or from education surveys such as HSB, sponsored by the Department of Education. These sources are sometimes criticized because they may undercount those most at risk of dropping out—such as young, minority males—and because they often do not permit detailed statistics on dropouts in specific locations. There are also disparities between what parents report for their children and what children report themselves. As with state and local data, national surveys may not identify those who return to school later in life.

One detailed study examining trends in dropout rates, using data from Current Population Surveys between 1968 and 1984, focused on those 34 years old or less (thus including those who may have returned to school in their twenties and early thirties). This study found that, since 1968, high school dropout rates for black males and females declined 40 percent, compared to a 32 percent decline for white females and a 27 percent decline for white males.[57] Overall declines for Hispanics have not been as dramatic. Nevertheless, among the 18- to 19-year-old Hispanic cohort, dropout rates declined 30 percent to 34 percent between 1978 and 1984.

Historically, girls—particularly black girls—have had lower dropout rates than boys, but recent data suggest a convergence in dropout rates. While the differences in dropout rates between black men and women have been dramatic, most recent data indicate a decided narrowing of differences between young black men and women.[58] Few gender differences have been found for Hispanics, and gender differences favoring girls are small for whites.

Among Hispanics, however, there are considerable differences by national origin; Puerto Rican and Cuban-American girls are more likely to drop out of school—both absolutely and in relation to their male counterparts—than Mexican-American and other Hispanic girls.[59]

Even when girls appear to be doing as well as or better than boys, many girls lose this advantage over time. While males are often more likely to drop out, there are indications that within two years of dropping out, black and Hispanic males are more likely to return to school to obtain a GED than black and Hispanic females.[60] This may explain why differences in high school attainment for black males and females appear to narrow among older black men and women. Finally, it should be noted that female dropouts have much higher poverty rates than male dropouts. Among blacks, the figures are 47 percent for black female dropouts compared to 29 percent for black male dropouts. Among Hispanic high school dropouts, 35 percent of the females are living in poverty compared to 24 percent of the males. For whites, the figures are 23 percent for white females, compared to only 15 percent of the males.[61] Comparable figures for Native Americans and Asian Americans are not available. It should be noted, however, that the economic status of Asian Americans is highly bipolar. In other words, while some groups do as well as whites, other groups, such as Vietnamese Americans and Cambodian Americans, have considerably higher poverty rates.[62]

The reasons for dropping out of school are often elusive and sometimes contradictory. The commonly held belief that female students drop out because they are pregnant reflects only part of the reality; 50 percent to 60 percent of female dropouts report leaving school for reasons other than pregnancy.[63] While some background characteristics associated with dropping out apply equally to boys and girls, female dropouts appear more likely to hold traditional gender-role stereotypes than girls who graduate.[64] Repeating one or more grades in school is a strong predictor of subsequent school dropout for both boys and girls, but girls who have been held back tend to leave school even earlier than boys.[65]

THE FORMAL CURRICULUM

The formal curriculum is the central message-giving instrument of the school. It creates images of self and the world for all students. The curriculum can strengthen or decrease student motivation for engagement, effort, growth, and development through the messages it delivers to students about themselves and the world.

Since the early 1970s, many studies have surveyed instructional materials for sex bias.[66] *Dick and Jane as Victims: Sex Stereotyping in Children's Readers* set a pattern for line-by-line examination of the messages about girls and boys delivered by texts, examples, illustrations, and thematic organization of material in everything from basal readers to science textbooks.[67] In 1971, a study of 13 popular U.S. history textbooks revealed that material on women comprised no more than 1 percent of any text, and that women's lives were trivialized and distorted when they were not omitted altogether.[68] Studies from the late 1980s reveal that although sexism has decreased in some school texts and basal readers, the problems persist, especially at the secondary school level in terms of what is considered important enough to study.[69]

A 1989 study of book-length works taught in high school English courses reports that in a national sample of public, independent, and Catholic schools, the ten books assigned most frequently included only one written by a woman and none by members of minority groups.[70] This research, which used as a baseline studies from 1963 and 1907, goes on to conclude that "the lists of most frequently required books and authors are dominated by white males, with little change in overall balance from similar lists 25 or 80 years ago."[71]

Virtually all textbook publishers now have guidelines for nonsexist language. Unfortunately, not all insist that authors follow them.[72] Change in textbooks is observable but not striking. Research on high school social studies texts reveals that while women are more often included, they are likely to be the usual "famous women," or women in protest movements. Rarely is there dual and balanced treatment of women and men, and seldom are women's perspectives and cultures presented on their own terms.[73] Researchers at a 1990 conference reported that even texts designed to fit within the current California guidelines on gender and race equity for textbook adoption showed subtle language bias, neglect of scholarship on women, omission of women as developers of history and initiators of events, and absence of women from accounts of technological developments.[74] An informal survey of 20 U.S. history textbooks compiled each year from 1984 to 1989 found a gradual but steady shift away from an overwhelming emphasis on laws, wars, and control over territory and public policy, toward an emphasis on daily lives of people in many kinds of circumstances.[75] The books, however, continued to maintain the abstract, disengaged tone that was characteristic of the earlier texts. The recommended assignments still relied heavily on debate techniques in which students were asked to develop an argument providing evidence to defend a single point of view. Few assignments offered an opportunity for students to reflect on a genuine variety of perspectives; few opportunities to consider feelings as well as actions were presented.[76]

GIRLS, SELF-ESTEEM, AND THE CURRICULUM

Researchers have puzzled over the drop in girls' self-esteem as they go through school, even though they do as well as boys on many standardized measures and get better grades. Teacher trainer Cathy Nelson attributes this drop in self-esteem to the negative messages delivered to girls by school curricula.[77] Students sit in classes that day in and day out deliver the message that women's lives count for less than men's. Historian Linda Kerber suggests a plausible connection between dropping self-esteem and curricular omission and bias: "Lowered self-esteem is a perfectly reasonable conclusion if one has been subtly instructed that what people like oneself have done in the world has not been important and is not worth studying."[78] There is no social science research to document cause and effect in this matter, but educators must take more responsibility for understanding that the curriculum is the central message-giving instrument of the school.

THE CLASSROOM AS CURRICULUM

Students can learn as much from what they experience in school as they can from the formal content of classroom assignments. Classroom interactions, both teacher with student and student with student, are critical components of education. These interactions shape a school. They determine in large measure whether a school becomes a community: a place where girls and boys can learn to value themselves and others, where both the rights and the responsibilities of citizens are fostered.

TEACHER-STUDENT INTERACTIONS

Whether one is looking at preschool classrooms or university lecture halls, at female teachers or male teachers, research spanning the past 20 years consistently reveals that males receive more teacher attention than do females.[79] In preschool classrooms boys receive more instructional time, more hugs, and more teacher attention.[80] The pattern persists through elementary school and high school. One reason is that boys demand more attention. Researchers David and Myra Sadker have studied these patterns for many years. They report that boys in one study of elementary and middle school students called out answers eight times more often than girls did. When boys called out, the typical teacher reaction was to listen to the comment. When girls called out, they were usually corrected with comments such as, "Please raise your hand if you want to speak."[81]

It is not only the attention demanded by male students that explains their greater involvement in teacher-student exchanges. Studies have found that even when boys do not volunteer, the teacher is more likely to solicit their responses.[82]

The issue is broader than the inequitable distribution of teacher contacts with male and female students; it also includes the inequitable *content* of teacher comments. Teacher remarks can be vague and superficial or precise and penetrating. Quality teacher comments provide students with insights into the strengths and weaknesses of their answers. Careful and comprehensive teacher reactions not only affect student learning but they can also influence student self-esteem.[83] The Sadkers conducted a large, three-year study of more than 100 fourth, sixth, and eighth grade classrooms. They identified four types of teacher comments: praise, acceptance, remediation, and criticism.

They found that while males received more of all four types of teacher comments, the difference favoring boys was greatest in the more useful teacher reactions of praise, criticism, and remediation. When teachers took the time and made the effort to specifically evaluate a student's performance, the student receiving the comment was more likely to be male.[84] These findings are echoed in other investigations, indicating that boys receive more precise teacher comments than girls in terms of both scholarship and conduct.[85] Research on teacher-student interaction patterns has rarely looked at the interaction of gender with race, ethnicity, or social class. The limited data available indicate that while males receive more teacher attention than females, white boys receive more attention than boys from various racial and ethnic minority groups.[86] Evidence also suggests that the attention minority students receive from teachers may be different in nature from that given to white children. In elementary school, black boys tend to have fewer interactions overall with teachers than do other students and yet they are the recipients of four to ten times the amount of qualified praise ("That's good, but . . .") as other students.[87] Black boys tend to be perceived less favorably and seen as less able by their teachers than other students.[88] The data are more complex for girls. Black girls have less interaction with teachers than white girls, but they attempt to initiate interaction much more often than white girls or than boys of either race. Research indicates that teachers may unconsciously rebuff these black girls and eventually they turn to peers for interaction, often becoming the class enforcer or go-between for other students.[89] Black females also receive less reinforcement from teachers than do other students, although their academic performance is often better than that of boys.[90]

In fact, when black girls do as well as white boys in school, teachers attribute their success to hard work, but assume that the white boys are not working up to their full potential.[91] This, coupled with the evidence that blacks are more often reinforced for their social behavior while whites are likely to be reinforced for their academic accomplishments, may contribute to low academic self-esteem in black girls.[92] Researchers have found that black females value their academic achievements less than black males in spite of their better performance.[93] Another student found that black boys have a higher science self-concept than black girls although there were no differences in achievement.[94]

SUCCESSFUL TEACHING STRATEGIES

A number of teaching strategies can promote more gender equitable learning environments. Research indicates that science teachers who were successful in encouraging girls shared several strategies.[95] These strategies included using more than one textbook, eliminating sexist language, and being fair in their treatment and expectations of both girls and boys.

Other research indicates that classrooms where there were no gender differences in math were "girl friendly" with less social comparison and competition and an atmosphere students thought was warmer and more fair.[96]

In their 1986 study, *Women's Ways of Knowing*, Belenky et al. point out that for many girls and women successful learning takes place in an atmosphere that enables students to empathetically enter into the subject they are studying, an approach to learning they term "connected knowing." The authors suggest that an acceptance of each individual's personal experiences and perspectives facilitates students' learning. They argue for classrooms that emphasize collaboration and provide space for diversity of opinion.[97]

Few classrooms foster connected learning, nor are the majority of classrooms designed to encourage cooperative behaviors and collaborative efforts. The need to evaluate, rank, and judge students can undermine collaborative approaches. One recent study that sampled third, fifth, and seventh grade students found that successful students reported fewer cooperative attitudes than did unsuccessful students. In this study, the effects of gender varied as a function of grade level. Third grade girls were more cooperative than their male peers, but by fifth grade the gender difference had disappeared.[98] Other studies have not reported this grade-level–gender interaction; rather, they indicate that girls tend to be more cooperative than boys, but that cooperative attitudes decline for all students as they mature.[99]

Some educators view the arrival of new classroom organizational structures as a harbinger of more effective and more equitable learning environments. "Cooperative learning" has been viewed as one of these potentially more successful educational strategies. Cooperative learning is designed to eliminate the negative effects of classroom competition while promoting a cooperative spirit and increasing heterogeneous and cross-race relationships. Smaller cooperative work groups are designed to promote group cohesion and interdependence and to mobilize these positive feelings to achieve academic objectives.[100] Progress and academic performance is evaluated on a group as well as an individual basis; the group must work together efficiently or all its members will pay a price.[101] A number of positive results have been attributed to cooperative learning groups, including increasing cross-race friendships, promoting academic achievement, mainstreaming students with disabilities, and developing mutual student concerns.[102]

However, positive cross-sex relationships may be more difficult to achieve than cross-race friendships or positive relationships among students with and without disabilities. First, as reported earlier in this chapter, there is a high degree of sex-segregation and same-sex friendships in the elementary and middle school years.[103] Researchers have found that the majority of elementary students preferred single-sex work groups.[104] Second, different communication patterns of males and females can be an obstacle to effective cross-gender relationships. Females are more indirect in speech, relying often on questioning, whereas more direct males are more likely to make declarative statements or even to interrupt.[105] Research indicates that boys in small groups are more likely to receive requested help from girls; girls' requests, on the other hand, are more likely to be ignored by the boys.[106] In fact, the male sex may be seen as a status position within the group. As a result, male students may choose to show their social dominance by not readily talking with females.[107]

Not only are the challenges to cross-gender cooperation significant, but cooperative learning as currently implemented may not be powerful enough to overcome these obstacles. Some research indicates that the infrequent use of small, unstructured work groups is not effective in reducing gender stereotypes, and, in fact, increases stereotyping. Groups often provided boys with leadership opportunities that increased their self-esteem. Females were seen as followers and were less likely to want to work in mixed-sex groups in the future.[108] Another study indicates a decrease in female achievement when females are placed in mixed-sex groups.[109] Other research on cooperative education programs have reported more positive results.[110] However, it is clear that merely providing a group learning experience now and then is not the answer to sex and gender differences in classrooms.

PROBLEMS IN STUDENT-STUDENT INTERACTIONS

The ways students treat each other during school hours is an aspect of the informal learning process with significant negative implications for girls. There is mounting evidence that boys do not treat girls well. Reports of peer-to-peer sexual harassment from junior high school and high school students are increasing. In the majority of cases a boy is harassing a girl.[111] Sex-biased peer interactions appear to be permitted, if not always approved.

Sexual harassment, unwelcome verbal or physical conduct of a sexual nature imposed by one individual on another, is prohibited under Title IX. However, sexual harassment is about power and authority as much as it is about sexuality; the person being harassed usually is less powerful than the person doing the harassing. Rather than being viewed as a serious incidence of misconduct, sexual harassment is often treated as a joke.

When boys line up to "rate" girls as they enter a room, when boys treat girls so badly that they are reluctant to enroll in courses where they may be the only female, when boys feel it is good fun to embarrass girls to the point of tears, it is no joke. Yet these types of behaviors are often viewed by school personnel as harmless instances of "boys being boys."

GENDER AND POWER

Data presented here reveal the extent to which girls and boys are treated differently in school classrooms and corridors. These data themselves should be a topic of discussion. They indicate power differentials that are perhaps the most evaded of all topics in our schools. Students are all too aware of "gender politics." In a recent survey, students in Michigan were asked, "Are there any policies, practices, including the behavior of teachers in classrooms, which have the effect of treating students differently based on their sex?" One hundred percent of the middle school and 82 percent of the high school students responding said "yes."[112]

Gender politics is a subject that many in our schools may prefer to ignore, but if we do not begin to discuss more openly the ways in which ascribed power, whether on the basis of race, sex, class, sexual orientation, or religion, affects individual lives, we will not be truly preparing our students for citizenship in a democracy.

NOTES

1. *National Educational Goals* (Washington, D.C.: National Governors' Association, 1990).

2. *America 2000: An Education Strategy* (Washington, D.C.: U.S. Department of Education, 1991), 1.

3. *Education for All: Women and Girls Speak Out on the National Education Goals* (Washington, D.C.: National Coalition for Women and Girls in Education, 1990); see also testimony submitted to the National Education Goals Panel by the National Coalition for Women and Girls in Education, May 1991.

4. S. Greenberg, "Educational Equity in Early Education Environments," in *Handbook for Achieving Sex Equity through Education*, ed. S. Klein (Baltimore, Md.: Johns Hopkins University Press, 1985), 457.

5. G. Ranck, "Are We Shortchanging Girls? A Response to 'Are We Shortchanging Boys?'" *Child Care Information Exchange* (July–August 1991): 20–22.

6. Greenberg, 1985, 460; A. Pellegrini and J. Perlmutter, "Classroom Contextual Effects on Children's Play," *Developmental Psychology* 25 (1989): 289–296.

7. See, for example, D. Rock and corporate authors, *Study of Excellence in High School: Longitudinal Study* (Princeton, N.J.: Educational Testing Service, 1985).

8. E. Maccoby and C. Jacklin, *The Psychology of Sex Differences* (Stanford, Calif.: Stanford University Press, 1974), 84.

9. Ibid.; D. Denno, "Sex Differences in Cognition: A Review and Critique of the Longitudinal Evidence," *Adolescence* 17 (Winter 1982): 779–788.

10. J. Hyde and M. Linn, "Gender Differences in Verbal Activity: A Meta-Analysis," *Psychological Bulletin* 104 (January 1988): 53–69.

11. L. Winfield and V. Lee, "Gender Differences in Reading Proficiency: Are They Constant Across Racial Groups?" (Paper presented at the Annual Meeting of the American Psychological Association, Washington, D.C., August 26, 1986).

12. National Assessment of Education Progress, *Reading Comprehension of American Youth: Do They Understand What They Read?* (Princeton, N.J.: Educational Testing Service, 1982).

13. I. Mullis, E. Owens, and G. Phillips, *Accelerating Academic Achievement: A Summary of Findings from 20 Years of NAEP* (Washington, D.C.: U.S. Department of Education, 1990).

14. L. Friedman, "Mathematics and the Gender Gap: A Meta-Analysis of Recent Studies on Sex Differences in Mathematical Tasks," *Review of Educational Research* 59 (1989): 185–213; J. Hyde, E. Fennema, and S. Lamon, "Gender Differences in Mathematics Performance: A Meta-Analysis," *Psychological Bulletin* 107 (1990): 139–155.

15. Hyde et al., 1990.

16. "The Gender Gap in Education: How Early and How Large," *Educational Testing Service Policy Notes* 2 (October 1989); J. Dossey, I. Mullis, M. Lindquist, and D. Chambers, *The Mathematics Report Card*, report no. 17-M-01 (Princeton, N.J.: Educational Testing Service, 1988), 54–55; *Women and Minorities in Science and Engineering* (Washington, D.C.: National Science Foundation, 1990), 14; I. Mullis, J. Dossey, E. Owen, and G. Phillips, *The State of Mathematics Achievement: NAEP's 1990 Assessment of the Nation and the Trial Assessment of the States* (Princeton, N.J.: Educational Testing Service, 1991), 15.

17. *1988 Profiles of SAT and Achievement Test Takers* (Princeton, N.J.: Educational Testing Service, 1988).

18. E. Moore and A. Smith, "Sex and Ethnic Group Differences in Mathematics Achievement: Results from the National Longitudinal Study," *Journal for Research in Mathematics Education* 18 (1987): 25–36; P. Brandon, B. Newton, and O. Hammond, "Children's Mathematics Achievement in

Hawaii: Sex Differences Favoring Girls," *American Educational Research Journal* 24 (1987): 25–36.

19. I. Mullis and L. Jenkins, *The Science Report Card*, report no. 17-S-01 (Princeton, N.J.: Educational Testing Service, 1988), 30–31; A. Lapointe, N. Mead, and G. Phillips, *World of Difference: An International Assessment of Mathematics and Science* (Princeton, N.J.: Educational Testing Service, 1989).

20. Mullis and Jenkins, 1988, 107–113.

21. Ibid.

22. National Science Board, *Science and Engineering Indicators—1989* (Washington, D.C.: National Science Foundation, 1990).

23. Mullis et al., 1991, 32.

24. National Science Board, *Indicators-1989*; A. Kolstad and J. Thorne, "Changes in High School Coursework from 1982–1987: Evidence from Two National Surveys" (Paper delivered at the Annual Meeting of the American Educational Research Association, San Francisco, March 1989); *Women and Minorities in Science and Engineering* (Washington, D.C.: National Science Foundation, 1990), 15.

25. National Science Board, 1990.

26. T. Dick and S. Rallis, "Factors and Influences on High School Students' Career Choices," *Journal of Research in Math Teaching* 22 (July 1991): 281–292.

27. N. Hewitt and E. Seymour, "Factors Contributing to High Attrition Rates Among Science and Engineering Undergraduate Majors" (Report to the Alfred P. Sloan Foundation, April 26, 1991), 100.

28. P. Campbell and S. Metz, "What Does It Take to Increase the Number of Women Majoring in Engineering?" (Conference proceedings of the American Society for Engineering Education, 1987), 882–887.

29. J. Kahle and M. Lakes, "The Myth of Equality in Science Classrooms," *Journal of Research in Science Teaching* 20 (1983): 131–140.

30. L. Zimmer and S. Bennett, "Gender Differences on the California Statewide Assessment of Attitudes and Achievement in Science" (Paper presented at the annual meeting of the American Educational Research Association, Washington, D.C., 1987); Mullis and Jenkins, 1988, 30–33.

31. L. Reyes and G. Stanic, "Race, Sex and Math," *Journal of Research in Math Education* 19 (1988): 26–43; E. Fennema and J. Sherman, "Sex Related Differences in Math Achievement, Spatial Visualization and Affective Factors," *American Educational Research Journal* 14 (1977): 51–71; L. Reyes, "Affective Variables and Mathematics Education," *The Elementary School Journal* 84 (1984): 558–581.

32. J. Dossey et al., *The Mathematics Report Card*, report no. 17-M-01 (Princeton, N.J.: Educational Testing Service, 1988).

33. Fennema and Sherman, 1977.

34. A. Kelly, "Does That Train Set Matter? Scientific Hobbies and Science Achievement and Choice" (Paper presented at the Girls and Technology Conference, Ann Arbor, July 1987); J. Eccles, "Bringing Young Women to Math and Science," in *Gender and Thought: Psychological Perspectives*, ed. M. Crawford and M. Gentry (New York: Springer-Verlag, 1989), 36–58.

35. C. Leder, "Teacher/Student Interactions in the Mathematics Classroom: A Different Perspective," in *Mathematics and Gender: Influences on Teachers and Students*, ed. E. Fennema and C. Leder (New York: Teachers College, 1990), 149–168.

36. American Association of University Women, *Shortchanging Girls, Shortchanging America* (Washington, D.C.: American Association of University Women, 1990), 13.

37. Campbell and Metz, 1987, 882–887.

38. P. MacCorquodale, "Self-Image Science and Math: Does the Image of 'Scientist' Keep Girls and Minorities from Pursuing Science and Math?" (Paper presented at the American Sociological Association Annual Meeting, San Antonio, 1984).

39. American Association of University Women, 1990, 14.

40. J. Armstrong, "A National Assessment of Participation and Achievement of Women in Mathematics," in *Women in Mathematics: Balancing the Equation*, ed. C. Chipman, L. Brush, and D. Wilson (Hillsdale, N.J.: Erlbaum, 1985), 56–94.

41. Ibid.

42. Ibid.

43. Hyde et al., 1990.

44. L. Tartre and E. Fennema, "Mathematics Achievement and Gender: A Longitudinal Study of Selected Cognitive and Affective Factors (Grades 6–12)" (Paper presented at the annual meeting of the American Educational Research Association, Chicago, April 1991).

45. B. Williams, P. Richmond, and B. Mason, *Designs for Compensatory Education: Conference Proceedings and Papers* (Washington, D.C.: Research and Evaluation Associates, Inc., 1987); and *School Success for Limited English Proficient Students* (Washington, D.C.: Council of Chief State School Officers, 1990). The proceedings from the compensatory-education conference cite the dearth of research by gender, economic status, and culture.

46. In the NELS, SES is a composite variable based on father's education, mother's education, father's occupation, mother's occupation, and family income. In HSB, SES is a composite of father's occupation, father's education, mother's education, family income, and material possessions in the household.

47. For copies of the tables and a more detailed discussion of these tables, see Lynn C. Burbridge, "The Interaction of Race, Gender, and Socioeconomic Status in Education Outcomes" (Paper presented at the American Sociological Association Annual Meeting, Cincinnati, August 24, 1991).

48. This finding has been recognized at least since the publication of J. Coleman's seminal report, *Equality of Educational Opportunity* (Washington, D.C.: U.S. Department of Health, Education, and Welfare, 1966). There is considerable debate on what this means for policy. Some suggest that there is little that schools can do to change the effects of SES, while others argue that more resources need to be targeted for poor youngsters.

49. As indicated earlier, girls consistently earn higher grades than boys and are less likely to be held back at year's end, regardless of SES. But grading and being held back may reflect perceptions of students' discipline and cooperativeness as well as their knowledge.

50. A recent analysis of the NELS confirms these findings: At the two-year follow-up, 6.8 percent of the students had dropped out of school before the tenth grade. Dropouts were disproportionately male and minority. See "First National Study of Young Dropouts Finds 6.8% Leave Before 10th Grade," *Education Week*, September 25, 1991.

51. E. Smith, "The Black Female Adolescent: A Review of the Educational, Career, and Psychological Literature," *Psychology of Women Quarterly* 6 (1982); N. St. John and R. Lewis, "Race and Social Structure of the Elementary School Classroom," *Sociology of Education* 48 (1975): 346–368; H. Sagar and J. Schofield, *Classroom Interaction Patterns Among Black and White Boys and Girls* (Washington, D.C.: National Institute of Education, 1980); B. Tatum, "Growing Up Black in White Communities: Racial Identity Development of Middle-Class African-American Adolescents," in *Adolescents, Schooling, and Social Policy*, ed. F. Miller (Albany: State University of New York Press, forthcoming).

52. K. Neckerman and W. Wilson, "Schools and Poor Communities," in *School Success for Students at Risk*, Council of Chief State School Officers (Orlando, Fla.: Harcourt Brace Jovanovich, Inc., 1988), 25–44.

53. J. Ogbu, *Minority Education and Caste* (New York: Academic Press, 1978).

54. Data on the AP exam for the years 1986 through 1990 were provided by the ETS in Princeton, New Jersey. (The tests are administered by the

College Board.) Data reported here are for 1990, but the same patterns are found since 1986, when data by race and gender first became available.

55. It must be kept in mind, however, that minorities represent a small proportion of all AP test takers: African Americans, Hispanics, and Native Americans represent 27 percent of all students in 1990, but only 10 percent of AP test takers. Asian Americans, on the other hand, represent less than 3 percent of all students, but 13 percent of AP test takers. Whites take the AP exam in proportion to their representation in the school population: 70 percent.

56. J. Mathews, "Faulty Figures Muddle Dropout Problem," *Washington Post,* June 2, 1991, A16.

57. R. Rumberger, "High School Dropouts: A Review of the Issues and Evidence," *Review of Educational Research* 57 (1987): 101–121.

58. Ibid.; V. Washington and J. Newman, "Setting Our Own Agenda: Exploring the Meaning of Gender Disparities among Blacks in Higher Education," *Journal of Negro Education* 60 (1991): 19–35; and P. Kaufman and M. McMillen, *Dropout Rates in the United States 1990* (Washington, D.C.: National Center for Education Statistics, 1991), 8.

59. T. McKenna and F. Ortiz, *The Broken Web, The Educational Experience of Hispanic American Women* (Berkeley, Calif.: Floricanto Press, 1988).

60. A. Kolstad and J. Owings, *High School Dropouts: What Changes Their Minds about School* (Washington, D.C.: Office of Educational Research and Improvement, U.S. Department of Education, 1986).

61. U.S. Department of Commerce, Bureau of the Census, *Poverty in the United States; 1988 and 1989* (Series P-60, No. 171) (Washington, D.C.: U.S. Government Printing Office, 1991), 83.

62. Commission on Civil Rights, *The Economic Status of Americans of Asian Descent: An Exploratory Investigation,* Clearinghouse Publication 95, October 1988.

63. W. Morgan, "The High School Dropout in an Overeducated Society" (Columbus: Ohio State University, Center for Human Resources Research, February 1984).

64. J. Earle, V. Roach, and K. Fraser for the Women's Equity Act Project, *Female Dropouts: A New Perspective* (Alexandria, Va.: National Association of State Boards of Education, 1987), 9; and R. Ekstrom, M. Goertz, J. Pollack, and D. Rock, "Who Drops Out of High School and Why? Findings from a National Study," *Teachers College Record* 87 (1986): 367. Data from the Hispanic Policy Development Project also report that tenth-grade girls who expected to be married and/or mothers before age 20 had higher dropout rates.

65. M. Fine and N. Zane, "Bein' Wrapped Too Tight: When Low Income Women Drop Out of High School," *Women's Studies Quarterly* 19 (Spring/Summer 1991): 77–99, 81.

66. For general reviews of curriculum research, see P. Arlow and C. Froschl, "Textbook Analysis," in *High School Feminist Studies*, ed. F. Howe (Old Westbury, N.Y.: The Feminist Press, 1976), xi–xxviii; K. Scott and C. Schau, "Sex Equity and Sex Bias in Instructional Materials," and P. Blackwell and L. Russo, "Sex Equity Strategies in the Content Areas," in *Handbook for Achieving Sex Equity Through Education*, ed. S. Klein (Baltimore, Md.: Johns Hopkins University Press, 1985), 218–260; and M. Hulme, "Mirror, Mirror on the Wall: Biased Reflections in Textbooks and Instructional Materials," in *Sex Equity in Education: Readings and Strategies*, ed. A. Carelli (Springfield, Ill.: Charles C. Thomas, 1988), 187–208.

67. Women on Words and Images, *Dick and Jane as Victims: Sex Stereotyping in Children's Readers* (Princeton, N.J.: Women on Words and Images, 1975); Women on Words and Images, *Help Wanted: Sexism in Career Education Materials* (Princeton, N.J.: Women on Words and Images, 1976); and Women on Words and Images, *Sexism on Foreign Language Texts* (Princeton, N.J.: Women on Words and Images, 1976). See also L. Weitzman and D. Rizzo, *Biased Textbooks* and *Images of Males and Females in Elementary School Textbooks* (Washington, D.C.: Resource Center on Sex Roles in Education, 1976); and G. Britton and M. Lumpkin, *A Consumer's Guide to Sex, Race, and Career Bias in Public School Textbooks* (Corvallis, Oreg.: Britton Associates, 1977).

68. J. Trecker, "Women in U.S. History High School Textbooks," *Social Education* 35 (3) (1971): 249–260, 338.

69. O. Davis, G. Ponder, L. Burlbaw, M. Garza-Lubeck, and A. Moss, "A Review of U.S. History Textbooks," *The Education Digest* 52(3) (November 1986): 50–53; M. Hitchcock and G. Tompkins, "Basal Readers: Are They Still Sexist?" *The Reading Teacher* 41 (3) (December 1987): 288–292; M. Tetreault, "Integrating Women's History: The Case of United States History High School Textbooks," *The History Teacher* 19 (February 1986): 211–262; M. Tetreault, "The Journey from Male-Defined to Gender-Balanced Education," *Theory into Practice* 25(4) (Autumn 1986): 227–234; A. Nilsen, "Three Decades of Sexism in School Science Materials," *School Library Journal* 34(1) (September 1987): 117–122; E. Hall, "One Week for Women? The Structure of Inclusion of Gender Issues in Introductory Textbooks," *Teaching Sociology* 16(4) (October 1988): 431–442; and P. Purcell and L. Stewart, "Dick and Jane in 1989," *Sex Roles* 22(2,4) (February 1990): 177–185.

70. A. Applebee, *A Study of Book-Length Works Taught in High School English Courses* (Albany: Center for the Learning and Teaching of Literature, State University of New York School of Education, 1989).

71. Ibid., 18.

72. Scott and Schau, 1985, 226. See also the discussion by B. Wright in "The Feminist Transformation of Foreign Language Teaching," in *Women in German Yearbook 1*, ed. M. Burkhard and E. Waldstein (Lanham, Md.: University Press of America, 1985), 95–97. Wright lists 13 publishing houses that issued guidelines between 1972 and 1981 on avoiding or eliminating sex stereotypes. She discusses problems of noncompliance, as well as the limits of strategies for elimination of simple sex stereotyping in the face of larger problems such as overwhelmingly masculine and/or elite perspectives in texts as a whole.

73. Tetreault (1986): 211–262; "Women in the Curriculum," *Comment on Conferences and Research on Women* (February 1986): 1–2; and "Rethinking Women, Gender, and the Social Studies," *Social Education* 51 (March 1987): 171–178.

74. Newsletter of the Special Interest Group on Gender and Social Justice, National Council for Social Studies, December 1990.

75. Surveys were taken in the Andrew W. Mellon, Geraldine Rockefeller Dodge, Kentucky and National SEED Project Seminars for College and School Teachers, sponsored by the Wellesley College Center for Research on Women. Twenty U.S. history textbooks were analyzed each year with regard to the representation of women as authors/editors and subjects in text and illustrations and the representation of domains of life outside of war, law, policy, government, and management of public affairs.

76. Homework assignments and study questions given in textbooks most frequently depend on the type of knowing that the authors of *Women's Ways of Knowing* identify as "separated," in which the mode is detached or distant from the subject. Girls and women, in a study of students in six schools and colleges, preferred a mode of knowing that the investigators named "connected," which involves empathetic identification with the subject. The investigators call for more "connected teaching," in which the capacity for identification is seen as an aspect of knowing and of learning about course content. M. Belenky, D. Clinchy, N. Goldberger, and J. Tarule, *Women's Ways of Knowing: Development of Self, Voice and Mind* (New York: Basic Books, 1986), 100–130, 214–229.

77. C. Nelson, "Gender and the Social Studies: Training Preservice Secondary Social Studies Teachers," Ph.D. diss. (Minneapolis: University of Minnesota, 1990), 8, 38–39.

78. L. Kerber, "'Opinionative Assurance': The Challenge of Women's History" (Address to the Organization of History Teachers, American Historical Association, New York, N.Y., December 28, 1990), 11.

79. See, for example, J. Brophy and T. Good, *Teacher-Student Relationships:*

Causes and Consequences (New York: Holt, Rinehart, and Winston, 1974); M. Jones, "Gender Bias in Classroom Interactions," *Contemporary Education* 60 (Summer 1989): 216–222; M. Lockheed, *Final Report: A Study of Sex Equity in Classroom Interaction* (Washington, D.C.: National Institute of Education, 1984); M. Lockheed and A. Harris, *Classroom Interaction and Opportunities for Cross-Sex Peer Learning in Science* (Paper presented at the Annual Meeting of the American Educational Research Association, New York, April 1989); M. Sadker and D. Sadker, "Sexism in the Classroom: From Grade School to Graduate School," *Phi Delta Kappan* 68 (1986): 512; and R. Spaulding, *Achievement, Creativity and Self-Concept Correlates of Teacher-Pupil Transactions in Elementary School* (Cooperative Research Project No. 1352) (Washington, D.C.: U.S. Department of Health, Education and Welfare, 1963).

80. L. Serbin, K. O'Leary, R. Kent, and I. Tonick, "A Comparison of Teacher Responses to the Pre-Academic and Problem Behavior of Boys and Girls," *Child Development* 44 (1973): 796–804; and M. Ebbeck, "Equity for Boys and Girls: Some Important Issues," *Early Child Development and Care* 18 (1984): 119–131.

81. D. Sadker, M. Sadker, and D. Thomas, "Sex Equity and Special Education," *The Pointer* 26 (1981): 33–38.

82. D. Sadker and M. Sadker, "Is the OK Classroom OK?," *Phi Delta Kappan* 55 (1985): 358–367.

83. J. Brophy, "Teacher Praise: A Functional Analysis," *Review of Educational Research* 51 (1981): 5–32; and A. Gardner, C. Mason, and M. Matyas, "Equity, Excellence and 'Just Plain Good Teaching!'" *The American Biology Teacher* 51 (1989): 72–77.

84. M. Sadker and D. Sadker, *Year 3: Final Report, Promoting Effectiveness in Classroom Instruction* (Washington, D.C.: National Institute of Education, 1984).

85. D. Baker, "Sex Differences in Classroom Interactions in Secondary Science," *Journal of Classroom Interaction* 22 (1986): 212–218; J. Becker, "Differential Treatment of Females and Males in Mathematics Classes," *Journal for Research in Mathematics Education* 12 (1981): 40–53; L. Berk and N. Lewis, "Sex Role and Social Behavior in Four School Environments," *Elementary School Journal* 3 (1977): 205–221; and L. Morse and H. Handley, "Listening to Adolescents: Gender Differences in Science Classroom Interaction," in *Gender Influences in Classroom Interaction*, ed. L. Wilkerson and C. Marrett (Orlando, Fla.: Academic Press, 1985), 37–56.

86. Sadker and Sadker, 1984; and L. Grant, "Race-Gender Status, Classroom Interaction and Children's Socialization in Elementary School," in *Gender Influences in Classroom Interaction*, ed. L. Wilkinson and C. Marrett, 57–75.

87. Grant, 1985, 66.

88. C. Cornbleth and W. Korth, "Teacher Perceptions and Teacher-Student Interaction in Integrated Classrooms," *Journal of Experimental Education* 48 (Summer 1980): 259–263; and B. Hare, *Black Girls: A Comparative Analysis of Self-Perception and Achievement by Race, Sex and Socioeconomic Background*, report no. 271 (Baltimore, Md.: Johns Hopkins University, Center for Social Organization of Schools, 1979).

89. S. Damico and E. Scott, "Behavior Differences Between Black and White Females in Desegregated Schools," *Equity and Excellence* 23 (1987): 63–66; and Grant, 1985. See also J. Irvine, "Teacher-Student Interactions: Effects of Student Race, Sex, and Grade Level," *Journal of Educational Psychology* 78 (1986): 14–21.

90. Damico and Scott, 1987; and Hare, 1979.

91. Damico and Scott, 1987; and L. Grant, "Black Females' 'Place' in Integrated Classrooms," *Sociology of Education* 57 (1984): 98–111.

92. Damico and Scott, 1987.

93. D. Scott-Jones and M. Clark, "The School Experience of Black Girls: The Interaction of Gender, Race and Socioeconomic Status," *Phi Delta Kappan* 67 (March 1986): 520–526.

94. Washington and Newman, 1991.

95. J. Kahle, *Factors Affecting the Retention of Girls in Science Courses and Careers: Case Studies of Selected Secondary Schools* (Reston, Va.: The National Association of Biology Teachers, October 1983).

96. J. Eccles, "Bringing Young Women to Math and Science," in *Gender and Thought: Psychological Perspectives*, ed. M. Crawford and M. Gentry (New York: Springer-Verlag, 1989).

97. Belenky et al., 1986.

98. G. Engelhard and J. Monsaas, "Academic Performance, Gender and the Cooperative Attitudes of Third, Fifth and Seventh Graders," *Journal of Research and Development in Education* 22 (1989): 13–17.

99. A. Ahlgren and D. Johnson, "Sex Differences in Cooperative and Competitive Attitudes from 2nd Through the 12th Grades," *Developmental Psychology* 15 (1979): 45–49; B. Herndon and M. Carpenter, "Sex Differences in Cooperative and Competitive Attitudes in a Northeastern School," *Psychological Reports* 50 (1982): 768–770; and L. Owens and R. Straton, "The Development of Cooperative, Competitive and Individualized Learning Preference Scale for Students," *Journal of Educational Psychology* 50 (1980): 147–161.

100. S. Sharan, P. Hare, C. Webb, and R. Hertz-Lazarowitz, eds., *Cooperation*

in Education (Provo, Utah: Brigham Young University Press, 1980); S. Bossert, *Task Structure and Social Relationships* (Cambridge, Mass.: Harvard University Press, 1979); and W. Shrum, N. Cheek, and S. Hunter, "Friendship in the School: Gender and Racial Homophily," *Sociology of Education* 61 (1988): 227–239.

101. E. Aronson, *The Jigsaw Classroom* (Beverly Hills, Calif.: Sage, 1978); D. DeVries and K. Edwards, "Student Teams and Learning Games: Their Effects on Cross-Race and Cross-Sex Interaction," *Journal of Educational Psychology* 66 (1974): 741–749; P. Okebukola, "Cooperative Learning and Students' Attitude to Laboratory Work," *Social Science and Mathematics* 86 (1986): 582–590; and R. Slavin, "How Student Learning Teams Can Integrate the Desegregated Classroom," *Integrated Education* 15 (1977): 56–58.

102. N. Blaney, C. Stephan, D. Rosenfield, E. Aronson, and J. Sikes, "Interdependence in the Classroom: A Field Study," *Journal of Educational Psychology* 69 (1977): 121–128; DeVries and Edwards, 1974; Sharan et al., 1980; R. Slavin, "Cooperative Learning," *Review of Educational Research* 50 (1980): 315–342; R. Slavin, "Cooperative Learning and Desegregation," in *Effective School Desegregation*, ed. W. Hawley (Berkeley, Calif.: Sage, 1981); R. Weigle, P. Wiser, and S. Cook, "The Impact of Cooperative Learning Experiences on Cross-Ethnic Relations and Attitude," *Journal of Social Issues* 3 (1975): 219–244.

103. M. Hallinan, *The Evolution of Children's Friendship Cliques* (ERIC Document Reproduction Service no. ED 161556, 1977); R. Best, *We've All Got Scars: What Boys and Girls Learn in Elementary School* (Bloomington: Indiana University Press, 1983); J. Eccles-Parsons, "Sex Differences in Mathematics Participation," in *Women in Science*, ed. M. Steinkamp and M. Maehr (Greenwich, Conn.: JAI Press, 1984); and M. Hallinan and N. Tumma, "Classroom Effects on Change in Children," *Sociology of Education* 51 (1978): 170–282.

104. M. Lockheed, K. Finklestein, and A. Harris, *Curriculum and Research for Equity: Model Data Package* (Princeton, N.J.: Educational Testing Service, 1979).

105. B. Eakins and R. Eakins, "Sex Roles, Interruptions, and Silences in Conversation," in *Sex Differences in Human Communication*, ed. B. Thorne and N. Henley (Boston: Houghton Mifflin, 1978); N. Henley and B. Thorne, "Women Speak and Men Speak: Sex Differences and Sexism in Communications, Verbal and Nonverbal," in *Beyond Sex Roles*, ed. A. Sargent (St. Paul, Minn.: West Publishing Company, 1977); R. Lakoff, *Language and Women's Place* (New York: Harper Colophon Books, 1976); and D. Tannen, *You Just Don't Understand: Women and Men in Conversation* (New York: William Morrow, 1990).

106. L. Wilkinson, J. Lindow, and C. Chiang, "Sex Differences and Sex Segregation in Students' Small-Group Communication," in *Gender Influences in Classroom Interaction*, ed. L. Wilkinson and C. Marret (Orlando, Fla.: Academic Press, 1985), 185–207.

107. J. Berger, T. Conner, and M. Fisek, eds., *Expectation States Theory: A Theoretical Research Program* (Cambridge, Mass.: Winthrop, 1974); and M. Lockheed and A. Harris, "Cross-Sex Collaborative Learning in Elementary Classrooms," *American Educational Research Journal* 21 (1984): 275–294.

108. Lockheed and Harris, 1984.

109. C. Weisfeld, G. Weisfeld, R. Warren, and D. Freedman, "The Spelling Bee: A Naturalistic Study of Female Inhibitions in Mixed-Sex Competitions," *Adolescence* 18 (1983): 695–708.

110. For example, M. Lockheed and A. Harris, "Classroom Interaction and Opportunity for Cross-Sex Peer Learning in Science," *Journal of Early Adolescence* 2(2) (1982): 135–143.

111. S. Strauss, "Sexual Harassment in the School: Legal Implications for Principals," *National Association of Secondary School Principals Bulletin* 72 (1988): 93–97; and N. Stein, "Survey on Sexual Harassment," *Vocational Options in Creating Equity, VI* (Boston: Department of Education, 1990), 1.

112. State of Michigan, Department of Education, Office of Sex Equity in Education, "The Influence of Gender Role Socialization on Student Perceptions," June 1990.

CONTRIBUTORS

Nancy E. Adler is professor of medical psychology, Departments of Psychiatry and Pediatrics, at the University of California, San Francisco, and director of the Health Psychology Program. She received her Ph.D. from Harvard University. Her research has focused mainly on social-psychological factors in the creation and resolution of unwanted pregnancy, including adolescent motivation for pregnancy and decision making regarding contraceptive use, and psychological responses following abortion.

Carolyn AlRoy is project coordinator for an inner-city AIDS prevention project at Rutgers University. She received her B.A. from Rutgers University and completed her master's work in psychology at Kean College in 1990. She has been involved in AIDS prevention research since 1990.

Susan McGee Bailey is director of the Wellesley College Center for Research on Women. She has directed the Resource Center on Educational Equity at the Council of Chief State School Officers in Washington, D.C., and the Policy Research Office on Women's Education at Harvard and Radcliffe. A former elementary and junior high school teacher, she has a Ph.D. in social science research from the University of Michigan, has conducted postdoctoral research in public health in Latin America, and has lectured and written extensively on issues of gender equity.

Lynn Burbridge is an associate director and research associate at the Wellesley College Center for Research on Women. She has a Ph.D. in economics from Stanford University. Her research has focused on the impact of public policies on minorities, women, and youth. Her previous experience includes research at the Urban Institute and the Joint Center for Political and Economic Studies in Washington, D.C.

Patricia Campbell is director of Campbell-Kibler Associates, a research and evaluation consulting firm. Formerly associate professor of research, measurement, and statistics at Georgia State University, she has degrees in mathematics and instructional technology and a Ph.D. in teacher education from Syracuse University. She has written extensively; her books, book chapters, and articles include "Redefining the 'Girl Problem' in Mathematics" and *What Will Happen If . . . Young Children and the Scientific Method.*

Laura L. Carstensen is an assistant professor at Stanford University in the Department of Psychology. She obtained her B.S. at the University of Rochester in 1978 and her Ph.D. in clinical psychology from West Virginia University in 1983. Professor Carstensen is interested in life-span development, particularly in old age.

Sanford M. (Sandy) Dornbusch has been a professor at Stanford University since 1959. Educated at Syracuse and the University of Chicago, he previously taught at Harvard and the University of Washington. He is currently Reed Hodgson Professor of Human Biology and professor of sociology and education. Formerly director of the Stanford Center for the Study of Families, Children and Youth, he is now chair of its advisory board. He is the first sociologist to be chairman of three different sections of the American Sociological Association (Methodology, Social Psychology, and Sociology of Education). He has been elected president of the Society for Research on Adolescence for 1992–94, the first nonpsychologist to receive that honor.

Diana B. Dutton is an associate adjunct professor in the Department of Social and Behavioral Sciences, University of California at San Francisco, and a senior research associate at the Stanford University School of Medicine, where she is the associate director of the Robert Wood Johnson Clinical Scholar Program, a postgraduate training program in the social sciences for physicians. She holds a Ph.D. in social policy analysis from the Massachusetts Institute of Technology, and has taught health policy and medical sociology at Stanford and at the University of California at Berkeley School of Public Health. She is the author of *Worse Than the Disease: Pitfalls of Medical Progress* (Cambridge University Press, 1988), as well as numerous articles on social class and health, medical care in different practice settings, and public participation in science policy.

M. Isa Fernandez is a member of the AIDS Program staff of the National Institute of Mental Health. She received her B.A. from Florida International University and her Ph.D. in psychology from Michigan State University in 1986. She worked for the Centers for Disease Control at the National AIDS Information and Education Program and was special assistant to the deputy director for HIV, Center for Prevention Services, in the area of Evaluation and Behavioral Sciences.

Barbara Jackson is professor at the Graduate School of Education at Fordham University. She has an Ed.D. from the Graduate School of Education at Harvard University. Formerly, she served as professor and dean of the School of Education at Morgan State University and as associate professor at Atlanta University. Among her many articles is "Parent Choice and Empowerment: New Roles for Parents," written with Bruce Cooper.

Loretta Sweet Jemmott is an assistant professor of nursing at Rutgers University. She received her B.S. from Hampton Institute and her Ph.D. in human sex education from the University of Pennsylvania in 1987, and is a member of Sigma Theta Tau International Nursing Society. She has published numerous articles in the area of African-American adolescent sexuality and AIDS prevention, and has been appointed to the New Jersey governor's AIDS Advisory Board, where she co-chairs the Education and Prevention Committee.

Kathleen B. Jones is professor and chair of the Department of Women's Studies at San Diego State University. She is the author of *Compassionate Authority: Democracy and the Representation of Women* (Routledge, 1992) and coeditor, with Anna Jonasdottir, of *The Political Interests of Gender* (Sage, 1988).

Madeleine Kahn is an assistant professor of English at Mills College, and the author of *Narrative Transvestism: Rhetoric and Gender in the Eighteenth-Century English Novel* (Cornell University Press, 1991). She received her B.A. from Swarthmore College and her Ph.D. from Stanford University.

Iris F. Litt is currently professor of pediatrics and director of the Division of Adolescent Medicine at Stanford University School of Medicine and director of the Institute for Research on Women and Gender at Stanford University. She is editor of *The Journal of Adolescent Health*. Her particular research interests are eating disorders, substance abuse, and pregnancy prevention among adolescent women. She is the author of more than 100 scholarly publications and is currently writing a book on women's health.

Ruth B. Mandel is professor at the Eagleton Institute of Politics at Rutgers University and director of Eagleton's Center for the American Woman and Politics (CAWP). She writes and speaks widely about women and leadership with particular emphasis on women as political candidates, women in office, women's political networks, and the "gender gap." She is the author of *In the Running: The New Woman Candidate* (Ticknor & Fields, 1981). In 1984, she was executive producer of *Not One of the Boys*, a 60-minute film produced by CAWP to document the progress women are making and the obstacles they encounter as they enter political life.

Fern Marx is a research associate at the Wellesley College Center for Research on Women, where she directs the Center's Teen Parent Project. She is a mid-career fellow at the Yale University Bush Center in Child Development and Social Policy. She has written widely on child care, early childhood education, and teen pregnancy, and is a post-doctoral candidate at the Florence Heller School, Brandeis University.

Sherri Matteo is deputy director of the Institute for Research on Women and Gender at Stanford University and a lecturer for Stanford's Programs in Human Biology and Feminist Studies. She received her Ph.D. from Cornell University in social/personality psychology and has published widely in the areas of sex-role stereotyping and women's health. She is coeditor of the *Proceedings of the 1989 Conference of the Society for Menstrual Cycle Research* and *Androgyny Revisited*.

Peggy McIntosh is an associate director at the Wellesley College Center for Research on Women and founder and co-director of the K–12 National SEED (Seeking Educational Equity and Diversity) Project on Inclusive Curriculum. She has taught at the elementary and secondary school levels and has held several university positions. Her Ph.D. in English is from Harvard University. She writes and lectures on women's studies, curriculum change, and systems of unearned privilege.

Ann O'Leary is an assistant professor at Rutgers University. She received her B.A. from the University of Pennsylvania and completed her doctorate in psychology at Stanford University in 1986. She has published numerous articles on health and behavior, psychoneuroimmunology, and AIDS prevention. She is a member of the Technical Advisory Group for the International Center for Research on Women's "Women and AIDS" program and a collaborator in the National Institute of Mental Health's "Multisite Trial of Behavioral Strategies to Prevent HIV."

Monisha Pasupathi is a psychology graduate student at Stanford University. She received her B.A. in 1991 from Case Western Reserve University. She is interested in social development across the life-span, with an emphasis on adulthood and aging.

Diana M. Pearce is director of the Women and Poverty Project at Wider Opportunities for Women in Washington, D.C. In 1991–92, she was a Visiting Scholar at the Institute for Research on Women and Gender at Stanford University. She received her Ph.D. in sociology and social work from the University of Michigan. She is writing a book on women's poverty entitled *No Bread, No Roses*. She has written widely on racial discrimination in housing and schools, women's economic inequality, and poverty and coined the phrase "the feminization of poverty." She also has served as an expert witness in school desegregation cases, testified before Congress, and helped found and lead several coalitions, such as the Women and Housing Task Force, and the Women, Work, and Welfare Coalition.

Deborah L. Rhode is professor of law and former director of the Institute for Research on Women and Gender at Stanford University. She received her undergraduate and legal education from Yale University and clerked for Supreme Court Justice Thurgood Marshall. Her work on gender discrimination includes *Justice and Gender* (Harvard University Press, 1989), *Theoretical Perspectives on Sexual Difference* (Yale University Press, 1989), and *The Politics of Pregnancy: Adolescent Sexuality and Public Policy* (with Annette Lawson; Yale University Press, forthcoming).

Stephanie Riger is professor of psychology and women's studies and director of the Women's Studies Program at the University of Illinois at Chicago. In 1990–91, she was a Visiting Scholar at Stanford University's Institute for Research on Women and Gender. She is the coauthor of *The Female Fear: The Social Cost of Rape* (with Margaret T. Gordon; University of Illinois Press, 1991). She teaches and writes on women in organizations, and the impact of urban settings on women. Her paper "Women in Management: An Exploration of Competing Paradigms," which appeared in *American Psychologist*, received the Association for Women in Psychology's Distinguished Publication Award.

Mariana Suarez-Al-Adam is a graduate student in social psychology at Rutgers University. She is conducting research in the area of Latin culture and AIDS.

Jeanne M. Tschann is assistant research psychologist in the Departments of Psychiatry and Pediatrics, University of California, San Francisco. She obtained her Ph.D. at the University of California, Santa Cruz. Her research interests include interpersonal relationships, particularly family process, and adolescent health-risk behavior.

INDEX